Patterns in Poetry

Harry M. Brown

Midwestern University

John Milstead

Oklahoma State University

Scott, Foresman and Company

————Franklin P. Adams "Those Two Boys," from *Tobogganing on Parnassus*, by Franklin P. Adams. Copyright 1911 by Doubleday & Company, Inc. Reprinted by permission of the publisher. ————Conrad Aiken "Morning Song of Senlin," from *Collected Poems* by Conrad Aiken. Copyright 1953 by Conrad Aiken. Reprinted by permission of Oxford University Press, Inc.   ————W. H. Auden, "Paysage Moralisé," copyright 1945 by W. H. Auden. Reprinted from *The Collected Poetry of W. H. Auden*, by permission of Random House, Inc. and Faber and Faber Ltd.; "Something Is Bound to Happen," copyright 1934 and renewed 1961 by W. H. Auden. Reprinted from *The Collected Poetry of W. H. Auden*, by permission of Random House, Inc. and Faber and Faber Ltd.; "The Unknown Citizen," copyright 1940 by W. H. Auden. Reprinted from *The Collected Poetry of W. H. Auden*, by permission of Random House, Inc. and Faber and Faber Ltd   ————Elizabeth Bishop "The Imaginary Iceberg," from *North and South* by Elizabeth Bishop. Copyright 1946 by Houghton Mifflin Company. Reprinted by permission of the publisher.   ————Louise Bogan "The Dream" and "Women," reprinted with permission of Farrar, Straus & Giroux, Inc. from *Collected Poems* by Louise Bogan. Copyright 1954 by Louise Bogan.   ————Brother Antoninus "The Stranger," from William Everson (Brother Antoninus), *The Residual Years*. Copyright 1948 by New Directions. Reprinted by permission of New Directions Publishing Corporation; "The Making of a Cross," from *The Crooked Lines of God* by Brother Antoninus. Reprinted by permission of the University of Detroit Press.   ————Hart Crane "To Brooklyn Bridge," from *Complete Poems & Selected Letters & Prose of Hart Crane* by Hart Crane. Permission by Liveright, Copyright 1933, 1958, 1966 by Liveright Publishing Corp. Publishers, New York.   ————E. E. Cummings "Poem, or Beauty Hurts Mr. Vinal," copyright 1926, by Horace Liveright; renewed, 1954, by E. E. Cummings. Reprinted from his volume, *Poems 1923–1954*, by permission of Harcourt, Brace & World, Inc.; "a wind has blown the rain away and blown" and "in Just-," copyright, 1923, 1951 by E. E. Cummings. Reprinted from his volume, *Poems 1923–1954*, by permission of Harcourt, Brace & World, Inc.; "somewhere i have never travelled," copyright, 1931, 1959, by E. E. Cummings, Reprinted from his volume, *Poems 1923–1954*, by permission of Harcourt, Brace & World, Inc.; "anyone lived in a pretty how town," copyright, 1940, by E. E. Cummings. Reprinted from his volume, *Poems 1923–1954*, by permission of Harcourt, Brace & World, Inc.; "when god decided to invent" and "pity this busy monster, manunkind," copyright 1944, by E. E. Cummings. Reprinted from his volume, *Poems 1923–1954* by permission of Harcourt, Brace & World, Inc.   ————Emily Dickinson Poems by Emily Dickinson from *The Poems of Emily Dickinson*, copyright 1890, 1891, 1896 by Roberts Brothers, 1914. . .1930 by Martha Dickinson Bianchi.   ————Richard Eberhart Poems by Richard Eberhart from *Collected Poems 1930–1960* by Richard Eberhart. Copyright © 1960 by Richard Eberhart. Reprinted by permission of Oxford University Press, Inc. and Chatto & Windus Ltd.   ————T. S. Eliot "Morning at the Window," "Gerontion," "The Love Song of J. Alfred Prufrock," and "Preludes," from *Collected Poems 1909–1962* by T. S. Eliot, copyright 1936, by Harcourt, Brace & World, Inc.; copyright, © 1963, 1964, by T. S. Eliot. Reprinted by permission of Harcourt, Brace & World, Inc. and Faber and Faber, London.   ————Kenneth Fearing "Homage," from *New and Selected Poems* by Kenneth Fearing. Reprinted by permission of Indiana University Press.   ————John Gould Fletcher "The Skaters," from *Preludes and Symphonies* by John Gould Fletcher. Reprinted by permission of Houghton Mifflin Company.   ————Robert Frost "Design," from *Complete Poems of Robert Frost*. Copyright 1936 by Robert Frost. Copyright © 1964 by Lesley Frost Ballantine. Reprinted by permission of Holt, Rinehart and Winston, Inc.; other poems by Frost from *Complete Poems of Robert Frost*. Copyright 1916, 1923, 1928, by Holt, Rinehart and Winston, Inc. Copyright 1942, 1944, 1951, © 1956 by Robert Frost. Copyright © 1964 by Lesley Frost Ballantine. Reprinted by permission of Holt, Rinehart and Winston, Inc.   ————Robert Graves "Richard Roe and John Doe," reprinted by permission of Collins-Knowlton-Wing, Inc. Copyright © 1955 by Robert Graves.   ————Thomas Hardy "In Time of 'The Breaking of Nations,'" reprinted with permission of The Macmillan Company from *Collected Poems* by Thomas Hardy. Copyright 1925, 1953 by The Macmillan Company. Used by permission of the Trustees of the Hardy Estate, The Macmillan Co. of Canada Ltd., and Macmillan & Co. Ltd.; "The Man He Killed," "In Tenebris," "The Darkling Thrush," and "Ah, Are You Digging on My Grave?" reprinted with permission of The Macmillan Company from *Collected Poems* by Thomas Hardy. Copyright 1925 by The Macmillan Company. Used by permission of the Trustees of the Hardy Estate, The Macmillan Co. of Canada Ltd., and Macmillan & Co. Ltd.   ————H. D. (Hilda Doolittle) "Heat," reprinted by permission of Grove Press, Inc. Copyright © 1957, by Norman Holmes Pearson.   ————Ralph Hodgson "Stupidity Street," reprinted with permission of The Macmillan Company from *Poems* by Ralph Hodgson. Copyright 1917 by The Macmillan Company, renewed 1945 by Ralph Hodgson. Used by permission of Macmillan & Co. Ltd. and The Macmillan Company of Canada Limited.   ————Gerard Manley

Part I   Guides To Meaning   1

Introduction
>A SLUMBER DID MY SPIRIT SEAL   *William Wordsworth*   **2**

>**The Form of Poetry   3**

>**Imagery   4**

>**Metaphorical Language   5**

Chapter 1   **Structural Patterns   6**

>**Idea Pattern   6**

>TO BE, OR NOT TO BE   *William Shakespeare*   **6**

>**Guides to Idea Pattern   8**

>DO NOT GO GENTLE INTO THAT GOOD NIGHT   *Dylan Thomas*   **10**
>'TIS BETTER TO HAVE LOVED AND LOST
>>*Alfred, Lord Tennyson*   **12**

>WHEN I HAVE FEARS THAT I MAY CEASE TO BE   *John Keats*   **13**

>**Study Poems with Aids to Analysis   14**

>ACQUAINTED WITH THE NIGHT   *Robert Frost*   **14**
>THE DIVINE IMAGE   *William Blake*   **14**
>ON REFUSAL OF AID BETWEEN NATIONS
>>*Dante Gabriel Rossetti*   **15**

>**Image Pattern   16**

>THE WIND HAS SUCH A RAINY SOUND   *Christina Rossetti*   **17**
>I TASTE A LIQUOR NEVER BREWED   *Emily Dickinson*   **17**
>SONNET 73   *William Shakespeare*   **18**

>**Guides to Image Pattern   19**

>SONNET 130   *William Shakespeare*   **20**

>**Study Poems with Aids to Analysis   20**

>CARGOES   *John Masefield*   **20**
>ANTHEM FOR DOOMED YOUTH   *Wilfred Owen*   **21**
>THE NIGHT IS DARKENING   *Emily Brontë*   **21**

>**Narrative Pattern   22**

>BONNY BARBARA ALLAN   *Anonymous*   **22**

>**Guides to Narrative Pattern   24**

>WHEN I HEARD THE LEARN'D ASTRONOMER   *Walt Whitman*   **25**
>AH, ARE YOU DIGGING ON MY GRAVE?   *Thomas Hardy*   **26**
>IS MY TEAM PLOUGHING?   *A. E. Housman*   **28**

>**Study Poems with Aids to Analysis   29**

>OH, SEE HOW THICK THE GOLDCUP FLOWERS
>>*A. E. Housman*   **29**

>JANET WAKING   *John Crowe Ransom*   **30**

Chapter 2   **Syntax and Situation   32**
>ONE'S-SELF I SING   *Walt Whitman*   **34**

SONG OF THE SIRENS   *William Browne*   **34**
THE MAGI   *William Butler Yeats*   **36**

Study Poems with Aids to Analysis   **37**

JEALOUSY   *Mary Elizabeth Coleridge*   **37**
VALE, AMOR!   *William Sharp*   **38**
HOW ANNANDALE WENT OUT   *E. A. Robinson*   **39**
SPECULATIVE   *Robert Browning*   **39**
A VALEDICTION: FORBIDDING MOURNING   *John Donne*   **40**

Chapter 3   **First-Level Meaning**   **43**
DESIGN   *Robert Frost*   **43**
IN TIME OF "THE BREAKING OF NATIONS"   *Thomas Hardy*   **45**

Study Poems with Aids to Analysis   **46**

SONG (HOW MANY TIMES)   *Thomas Lovell Beddoes*   **46**
THE THREE FISHERS   *Charles Kingsley*   **46**
HOMAGE   *Kenneth Fearing*   **47**
WESTERN WIND   *Anonymous*   **48**
SUSPENSE   *D. H. Lawrence*   **48**
EDWARD   *Anonymous*   **49**
THE PASSIONATE SHEPHERD TO HIS LOVE
    Christopher Marlowe   **51**
THE NYMPH'S REPLY   *Sir Walter Ralegh*   **52**
THE CLOD AND THE PEBBLE   *William Blake*   **53**
TO–(ONE WORD IS TOO OFTEN PROFANED)
    Percy Bysshe Shelley   **53**
THOU ART INDEED JUST, LORD   *Gerard Manley Hopkins*   **54**
DULCE ET DECORUM EST   *Wilfred Owen*   **55**
AN ELEMENTARY SCHOOL CLASSROOM IN A SLUM
    Stephen Spender   **56**

Part II   **The Poetic Idiom**   **59**

Chapter 4   **The Image**   **60**
THAW   *Edward Thomas*   **61**
WHEN ICICLES HANG   *William Shakespeare*   **61**
THE BRAIN IS WIDER THAN THE SKY   *Emily Dickinson*   **63**
BREAK, BREAK, BREAK   *Alfred, Lord Tennyson*   **64**

EXERCISE: IDENTIFYING IMAGES   **65**

Study Poems with Aids to Analysis   **66**

HEAT   *H. D. (Hilda Doolittle)*   **66**
SONG   *W. J. Turner*   **66**
A DESCRIPTION OF THE MORNING   *Jonathan Swift*   **67**
THE SKATERS   *John Gould Fletcher*   **67**
THE SHELL   *James Stephens*   **68**
THE ENAMEL GIRL   *Genevieve Taggard*   **69**
SONNET 116   *William Shakespeare*   **70**
TO AUTUMN   *John Keats*   **71**
KUBLA KHAN   *Samuel Taylor Coleridge*   **72**

Chapter **5** **Metaphor and Related Figures of Similarity** **74**

EXERCISE: DISTINGUISHING LITERAL AND FIGURATIVE STATEMENTS **74**

Metaphor **75**

WHEN LOVELY WOMAN STOOPS TO FOLLY *Oliver Goldsmith* **76**

EXERCISE: IDENTIFYING METAPHORS **77**

AN ARAB LOVE SONG *Francis Thompson* **77**
HOPE IS THE THING WITH FEATHERS *Emily Dickinson* **78**
THE LAST WORD *Matthew Arnold* **78**
RECESSIONAL *Rudyard Kipling* **79**

Study Poems with Aids to Analysis **81**

TO LUCASTA, GOING TO THE WARS *Richard Lovelace* **81**
A SOLDIER *Robert Frost* **81**
SONNET 65 *William Shakespeare* **82**

Other Figures of Similarity **83**

A BIRTHDAY *Christina Rossetti* **83**
SONNET ON CHILLON *George Gordon, Lord Byron* **84**
AMPLE MAKE THIS BED *Emily Dickinson* **85**

EXERCISE: IDENTIFYING FIGURES OF SIMILARITY **85**

Study Poems with Aids to Analysis **86**

TO A. D. *William Ernest Henley* **86**
LONDON, 1802 *William Wordsworth* **87**
SONG: TO CELIA *Ben Jonson* **87**
MY GALLEY, CHARGED WITH FORGETFULNESS
    Sir Thomas Wyatt **88**
DAYS *Ralph Waldo Emerson* **89**
THE PULLEY *George Herbert* **90**
CARELESS LOVE *Stanley Kunitz* **90**
BECAUSE I COULD NOT STOP FOR DEATH *Emily Dickinson* **91**
TOMORROW, AND TOMORROW, AND TOMORROW
    William Shakespeare **92**
TO HIS COY MISTRESS *Andrew Marvell* **93**
LOVE'S DIET *John Donne* **94**

Chapter **6** **Irony and Related Figures of Incongruity** **96**

Irony **96**
ONCE IN A SAINTLY PASSION *James Thomson* **96**
THOSE TWO BOYS *Franklin P. Adams* **97**
SOLILOQUY OF THE SPANISH CLOISTER *Robert Browning* **98**
THE UNKNOWN CITIZEN *W. H. Auden* **101**

Other Figures of Incongruity **102**
SHE DWELT AMONG THE UNTRODDEN WAYS
    William Wordsworth **102**
THE BUSTLE IN A HOUSE *Emily Dickinson* **103**
THE COMPUTATION *John Donne* **103**
BATTER MY HEART, THREE PERSON'D GOD *John Donne* **104**

EXERCISE: IDENTIFYING FIGURES OF INCONGRUITY **105**

Study Poems with Aids to Analysis 106

WAR IS KIND *Stephen Crane* **106**
THE MAN HE KILLED *Thomas Hardy* **107**
STUPIDITY STREET *Ralph Hodgson* **108**
A CASE *Anonymous* **108**
A SONNET UPON A STOLEN KISS *George Wither* **108**
PROUD MAISIE *Sir Walter Scott* **109**
THE LATEST DECALOGUE *Arthur Hugh Clough* **110**
THE KINGDOM OF GOD *Francis Thompson* **110**
OZYMANDIAS *Percy Bysshe Shelley* **111**
SONG (GO AND CATCH A FALLING STAR) *John Donne* **112**
WHEN GOD DECIDED TO INVENT *E. E. Cummings* **113**
THE GLORY, JEST, AND RIDDLE *Alexander Pope* **114**
MORNING SONG OF SENLIN *Conrad Aiken* **114**

Chapter **7** **Symbol 117**

ELDORADO *Edgar Allan Poe* **117**
CLIFF KLINGENHAGEN *E. A. Robinson* **118**
THE TIGER *William Blake* **119**
THE LAMB *William Blake* **120**
THE SECOND COMING *William Butler Yeats* **122**
THE DARKLING THRUSH *Thomas Hardy* **123**

EXERCISE: KINDS AND MEANINGS OF SYMBOLS 124

Study Poems with Aids to Analysis 125

TO HELEN *Edgar Allan Poe* **125**
GIFTS *Mary Elizabeth Coleridge* **125**
RICHARD ROE AND JOHN DOE *Robert Graves* **126**
PHILOMELA *Matthew Arnold* **126**
STOPPING BY WOODS ON A SNOWY EVENING *Robert Frost* **127**
THE CASTLE *Edwin Muir* **128**
THE SICK ROSE *William Blake* **129**
TO A LOCOMOTIVE IN WINTER *Walt Whitman* **130**
THE DREAM *Louise Bogan* **131**
SEALS, TERNS, TIME *Richard Eberhart* **132**
LA BELLE DAME SANS MERCI *John Keats* **133**
THE YACHTS *William Carlos Williams* **134**

Chapter **8** **Denotation, Connotation, Allusion 136**

Denotation 136

Connotation 137
IN A STATION OF THE METRO *Ezra Pound* **137**
HUSWIFERY *Edward Taylor* **138**
GOD'S GRANDEUR *Gerard Manley Hopkins* **139**
PARTING, WITHOUT A SEQUEL *John Crowe Ransom* **140**
PITY THIS BUSY MONSTER, MANUNKIND *E. E. Cummings* **141**

Allusion 142
KARMA *E. A. Robinson* **142**

Study Poems with Aids to Analysis 144

SONNET—TO SCIENCE *Edgar Allan Poe* **144**
THREES *Carl Sandburg* **144**

JABBERWOCKY *Lewis Carroll* **145**
THE HARLOT'S HOUSE *Oscar Wilde* **146**
SPRING AND FALL *Gerard Manley Hopkins* **147**
SOMEWHERE I HAVE NEVER TRAVELLED *E. E. Cummings* **148**
METAMORPHOSIS *Wallace Stevens* **149**
NOW SLEEPS THE CRIMSON PETAL *Alfred, Lord Tennyson* **150**

Chapter **9** **Sound and Rhythm** **151**

Patterns of Sound **152**
THE SPLENDOR FALLS *Alfred, Lord Tennyson* **152**

Rhyme **153**

Other Kinds of Sound Repetition **154**

Vowel and Consonant Sounds **155**

EXERCISE: VOWEL AND CONSONANT SOUNDS **156**

Study Poems with Aids to Analysis **157**
REQUIESCAT *Matthew Arnold* **157**
TO NIGHT *Percy Bysshe Shelley* **158**

Patterns of Rhythm **159**

The Metrical Foot **159**

The Metrical Line **161**

EXERCISE: BASIC METER **162**

Study Poems with Aids to Analysis **162**

ON SEEING A HAIR OF LUCRETIA BORGIA
        Walter Savage Landor **162**
SLOW, SLOW, FRESH FOUNT *Ben Jonson* **163**

Variations in Rhythm **163**
THE WORLD IS TOO MUCH WITH US *William Wordsworth* **163**

Specialized Rhythm Forms **167**

EXERCISE: VARIATIONS IN RHYTHM **168**

Patterns in Stanza **169**
HAPPY THOUGHT *Robert Louis Stevenson* **169**

EXERCISE: THE SONNET **171**

WHOSO LIST TO HUNT *Thomas Wyatt* **171**
SINCE THERE'S NO HELP *Michael Drayton* **171**

Study Poems with Aids to Analysis **173**

SONG (OLD ADAM) *Thomas Lovell Beddoes* **173**
FULL FATHOM FIVE *William Shakespeare* **174**
BOOT AND SADDLE *Robert Browning* **174**
SWEET AND LOW *Alfred, Lord Tennyson* **175**
SCYTHE SONG *Andrew Lang* **175**
A WIND HAS BLOWN *E. E. Cummings* **176**
WEEP YOU NO MORE, SAD FOUNTAINS *Anonymous* **176**

LINES (WHEN THE LAMP IS SHATTERED)
  Percy Bysshe Shelley **177**
WHAN THAT APRILLE WITH HIS SHOURES SOOTE
  Geoffrey Chaucer **178**
WHEN THE HOUNDS OF SPRING *Algernon Charles Swinburne* **178**

Part III   **Cultural Contexts** **181**

Introduction **182**

Chapter **10**   **The Renaissance (1500–1660)** **184**
  ULYSSES' SPEECH ON DEGREE *William Shakespeare* **185**
  IT WAS A LOVER *William Shakespeare* **188**

  Study Poems **189**

  ONE DAY I WROTE HER NAME UPON THE STRAND
    Edmund Spenser **189**
  THE GOOD-MORROW *John Donne* **189**
  MAN *George Herbert* **190**
  TO THE VIRGINS, TO MAKE MUCH OF TIME
    Robert Herrick **191**
  HERO AND LEANDER *John Donne* **192**
  ON TIME *John Milton* **192**

Chapter **11**   **The Restoration and Eighteen Century (1660–1800)** **193**
  INTENDED FOR SIR ISAAC NEWTON *Alexander Pope* **193**
  BE HOMER'S WORKS YOUR STUDY AND DELIGHT
    Alexander Pope **194**
  HERE LIES OUR MASTER, CHARLES THE KING
    John Wilmot **195**

  Study Poems **197**

  A SONG FOR ST. CECILIA'S DAY *John Dryden* **197**
  A HINTED WISH *Samuel Johnson* **199**
  EPIGRAM ENGRAVED ON THE COLLAR OF A DOG
    Alexander Pope **199**
  THE SPACIOUS FIRMAMENT ON HIGH *Joseph Addison* **199**
  ODE TO EVENING *William Collins* **200**
  FROM AN ESSAY ON MAN *Alexander Pope* **201**
  A MAN'S A MAN FOR A' THAT *Robert Burns* **202**
  ON THE UNIFORMITY AND PERFECTION OF NATURE
    Philip Freneau **203**

Chapter **12**   **The Nineteenth Century** **205**
  THE TABLES TURNED *William Wordsworth* **205**
  THE GARDEN OF LOVE *William Blake* **207**
  FROM THE PRELUDE *William Wordsworth* **208**
  FROM ENDYMION *John Keats* **208**
  THE WISH, THAT OF THE LIVING WHOLE
    Alfred, Lord Tennyson **209**
  WAITING *William Ernest Henley* **210**
  A LAST WORD *Ernest Dowson* **211**
  A MAN SAID TO THE UNIVERSE *Stephen Crane* **212**

Study Poems 212

LINES WRITTEN IN EARLY SPRING *William Wordsworth* **212**
PROMETHEUS *George Gordon, Lord Byron* **213**
ISRAFEL *Edgar Allan Poe* **214**
WEST LONDON *Matthew Arnold* **216**
IN TENEBRIS, I *Thomas Hardy* **216**
NON SUM QUALIS ERAM BONAE SUB REGNO CYNARAE
    Ernest Dowson **217**
IMPRESSION DU MATIN *Oscar Wilde* **218**
GOD FASHIONED THE SHIP OF THE WORLD CAREFULLY
    Stephen Crane **218**

Chapter 13 **The Twentieth Century 219**

MORNING AT THE WINDOW *T. S. Eliot* **219**
THE EAGLE AND THE MOLE *Elinor Wylie* **220**
WHEN ALL MY FIVE AND COUNTRY SENSES SEE
    Dylan Thomas **221**

Study Poems 222

AN IRISH AIRMAN FORESEES HIS DEATH
    William Butler Yeats **222**
SHINE, PERISHING REPUBLIC *Robinson Jeffers* **222**
ANYONE LIVED IN A PRETTY HOW TOWN
    E. E. Cummings **223**
THE END OF THE WORLD *Archibald MacLeish* **224**
EFFORT AT SPEECH BETWEEN TWO PEOPLE
    Muriel Rukeyser **224**
IDENTITY *Hyam Plutzik* **226**

Part IV **The Critical View** **227**

Introduction 228

Chapter 14 **Readings in Criticism 229**

THE NATURE OF POETRY *Donald Stauffer* **229**
INSPIRATION (*from ION*) *Plato* **238**
STYLE (*from POETICS*) *Aristotle* **239**
IMITATION (*from POETICS*) *Aristotle* **240**
HOW TO CRITICIZE POETRY (*from AN ESSAY ON CRITICISM*)
    Alexander Pope **241**
THE GENERAL AND THE PARTICULAR (*from RASSELAS*)
    Samuel Johnson **243**
POETIC IMAGINATION (*from BIOGRAPHIA LITERARIA*)
    Samuel Taylor Coleridge **243**
POETRY AND EMOTIONAL NEED (*from "ON POETRY IN
    GENERAL"*) *William Hazlitt* **245**
POETS AS LEGISLATORS OF THE WORLD (*from A DEFENSE OF
    POETRY*) *Percy Bysshe Shelley* **246**
POETRY AND ACTION (*from PREFACE TO POEMS, 1853*)
    Matthew Arnold **246**
PRELIMINARY PROBLEMS *Yvor Winters* **250**

Part V   Poems for Study   261

Chapter 15   Review Analysis and Evaluation   262

TO A WATERFOWL *William Cullen Byrant* 263
SONG OF THE NIGHT AT DAYBREAK *Alice Meynell* 265
ON FIRST LOOKING INTO CHAPMAN'S HOMER *John Keats* 265
HYMN TO THE NIGHT *Henry Wadsworth Longfellow* 266
THE ARSENAL AT SPRINGFIELD *Henry Wadsworth Longfellow* 267
INVICTUS *William Ernest Henley* 269
ULYSSES *Alfred, Lord Tennyson* 270

Chapter 16   The Continuing Tradition   274

William Shakespeare
Sonnets

56 SWEET LOVE, RENEW THY FORCE 274,
60 LIKE AS THE WAVES 274
64 WHEN I HAVE SEEN BY TIME'S FELL HAND
    DEFACED 275
71 NO LONGER MOURN FOR ME 275
138 WHEN MY LOVE SWEARS THAT SHE IS MADE OF
    TRUTH 275

From the plays
LET's TALK OF GRAVES (*RICHARD II*) 276
ALL THE WORLD'S A STAGE (*AS YOU LIKE IT*) 276
HAD IT PLEASED HEAVEN (*OTHELLO*) 277
OUR REVELS NOW ARE ENDED (*THE TEMPEST*) 278

John Donne
THE SUN RISING 278
THE CANONIZATION 279
THE ECSTASY 280
LOVE'S DEITY 282
From Holy Sonnets
I AM A LITTLE WORLD MADE CUNNINGLY 282
AT THE ROUND EARTH'S IMAGINED CORNERS 283

George Herbert
VIRTUE 283
THE COLLAR 284
TEMPTATION 284

John Milton
HOW SOON HATH TIME 285
WHEN I CONSIDER HOW MY LIGHT IS SPENT 286
METHOUGHT I SAW 286
BETTER TO REIGN IN HELL (*PARADISE LOST*) 286
ADAM'S FALL (*PARADISE LOST*) 287
SAMSON'S BLINDNESS (*SAMSON AGONISTES*) 288

Thomas Gray
ELEGY WRITTEN IN A COUNTRY CHURCHYARD 290

William Blake

> **From Songs of Innocence**
> INTRODUCTION 293
> NURSE'S SONG 294
> HOLY THURSDAY 294
> THE CHIMNEY SWEEPER 295
> THE LITTLE BLACK BOY 295
>
> **From Songs of Experience**
> NURSE'S SONG 296
> HOLY THURSDAY 296
> THE CHIMNEY SWEEPER 297
> LONDON 297
> THE HUMAN ABSTRACT 298
> A POISON TREE 298
> TO SEE A WORLD 299
> AND DID THOSE FEET IN ANCIENT TIME 299

Robert Burns

> GREEN GROW THE RASHES 299
> WILLIE BREW'D A PECK O' MAUT 300
> A RED, RED ROSE 301
> O, WERT THOU IN A CAULD BLAST 301

William Wordsworth

> MY HEART LEAPS UP WHEN I BEHOLD 302
> I WANDERED LONELY AS A CLOUD 302
> COMPOSED UPON WESTMINISTER BRIDGE,
>   SEPTEMBER 3, 1802 303
> IT IS A BEAUTEOUS EVENING, CALM AND FREE 303
> LINES COMPOSED A FEW MILES ABOVE TINTERN
>   ABBEY 304

Samuel Taylor Coleridge

> THE RIME OF THE ANCIENT MARINER 307

Percy Bysshe Shelley

> ENGLAND in 1819 324
> THE INDIAN SERENADE 324
> LOVE'S PHILOSOPHY 325
> TO–(MUSIC, WHEN SOFT VOICES DIE) 325
> MUTABILITY 325
> ODE TO THE WEST WIND 326
> THIS IS THE DAY (*PROMETHEUS UNBOUND*) 328

John Keats

> ON THE GRASSHOPPER AND THE CRICKET 329
> THE DEVON MAID 329
> BRIGHT STAR 329
> ODE ON A GRECIAN URN 330
> ODE TO A NIGHTINGALE 331
> ODE ON MELANCHOLY 333

Edgar Allan Poe

> THE CITY IN THE SEA 334
> TO ONE IN PARADISE 336
> THE HAUNTED PALACE 336
> ANNABEL LEE 338

Alfred, Lord Tennyson

  From In Memoriam
    PROLOGUE   **339**
      7   DARK HOUSE, BY WHICH ONCE MORE I
         STAND   **340**
     28   THE TIME DRAWS NEAR THE BIRTH OF
         CHRIST   **340**
     54   OH YET WE TRUST   **341**
     96   YOU SAY, BUT WITH NO TOUCH OF SCORN   **341**
   114   WHO LOVES NOT KNOWLEDGE?   **342**
   131   O LIVING WILL THAT SHALT ENDURE   **343**

Robert Browning
  MY LAST DUCHESS   **343**
  "CHILDE ROLAND TO THE DARK TOWER CAME"   **345**

Walt Whitman
  TO THE MAN-OF-WAR BIRD   **351**
  WHEN LILACS LAST IN THE DOORYARD BLOOM'D   **351**

Matthew Arnold
  TO MARGUERITE — CONTINUED   **358**
  DOVER BEACH   **359**
  THE FORSAKEN MERMAN   **360**

Emily Dickinson
  I LIKE A LOOK OF AGONY   **363**
  A NARROW FELLOW IN THE GRASS   **363**
  A DEATH-BLOW IS A LIFE-BLOW   **364**
  THE BRAIN WITHIN ITS GROOVE   **364**
  I KNOW THAT HE EXISTS   **364**
  THERE CAME A WIND LIKE A BUGLE   **365**
  PAIN HAS AN ELEMENT OF BLANK   **365**
  I STEPPED FROM PLANK TO PLANK   **366**
  APPARENTLY WITH NO SURPRISE   **366**
  THE SOUL SELECTS HER OWN SOCIETY   **366**
  A FACE DEVOID OF LOVE OR GRACE   **366**

  Gerard Manley Hopkins
  THE WINDHOVER   **367**
  FELIX RANDAL   **367**
  I WAKE AND FEEL THE FELL OF DARK   **368**
  THE CAGED SKYLARK   **368**

A. E. Housman
  REVEILLE   **369**
  ON WENLOCK EDGE   **369**
  FROM FAR, FROM EVE AND MORNING   **370**
  WITH RUE MY HEART IS LADEN   **370**
  ALONG THE FIELD AS WE CAME BY   **370**
  COULD MAN BE DRUNK FOREVER   **371**
  TERENCE, THIS IS STUPID STUFF   **371**
  THE CHESTNUT CASTS HIS FLAMBEAUX   **373**

William Butler Yeats
  THE SONG OF WANDERING AENGUS   **374**

NO SECOND TROY **374**
SAILING TO BYZANTIUM **375**
LEDA AND THE SWAN **376**
AMONG SCHOOL CHILDREN **376**
THE CIRCUS ANIMALS' DESERTION **378**

Chapter *17* **The Range of Modern Poetry 380**

THE ROAD NOT TAKEN *Robert Frost* **380**
THE ONSET *Robert Frost* **381**
THE MOST OF IT *Robert Frost* **381**
DISILLUSIONMENT OF TEN O'CLOCK *Wallace Stevens* **382**
PETER QUINCE AT THE CLAVIER *Wallace Stevens* **382**
THE IDEA OF ORDER AT KEY WEST *Wallace Stevens* **384**
HORAE BEATAE INSCRIPTIO *Ezra Pound* **385**
THE PLUNGE *Ezra Pound* **386**
GALE IN APRIL *Robinson Jeffers* **386**
THE BLOODY SIRE *Robinson Jeffers* **387**
THE MIND IS AN ENCHANTING THING *Marianne Moore* **387**
PRELUDES *T. S. Eliot* **388**
THE LOVE SONG OF J. ALFRED PRUFROCK *T. S. Eliot* **390**
GERONTION *T. S. Eliot* **393**
EPISTLE TO BE LEFT IN THE EARTH *Archibald MacLeish* **395**
IN JUST *E. E. Cummings* **397**
POEM, OR BEAUTY HURTS MR. VINAL *E. E. Cummings* **397**
WOMEN *Louise Bogan* **399**
PROEM: TO BROOKLYN BRIDGE *Hart Crane* **400**
GO TO THE SHINE THAT'S ON A TREE *Richard Eberhart* **401**
THE HORSE CHESTNUT TREE *Richart Eberhart* **401**
SOMETHING IS BOUND TO HAPPEN *W. H. Auden* **402**
PAYSAGE MORALISÉ *W. H. Auden* **403**
ELEGY FOR JANE *Theodore Roethke* **404**
THE IMAGINARY ICEBERG *Elizabeth Bishop* **405**
THE STRANGER *Brother Antoninus* **406**
THE MAKING OF THE CROSS *Brother Antoninus* **406**
SHE WAS THE GIRL WITHIN THE PICTURE FRAME
    Delmore Schwartz **407**
THE SELF UNSATISFIED RUNS EVERYWHERE
    Delmore Schwartz **408**
THE MINUTE *Karl Shapiro* **408**
THE FORCE THAT THROUGH THE GREEN FUSE DRIVES THE
    FLOWER *Dylan Thomas* **409**
FERN HILL *Dylan Thomas* **410**
CHILDREN OF LIGHT *Robert Lowell* **411**
THE BEAUTIFUL CHANGES *Richard Wilbur* **412**
JUGGLER *Richard Wilbur* **412**
GREENWICH OBSERVATORY *Sidney Keyes* **413**
PLOWMAN *Sidney Keyes* **414**
TO THE WESTERN WORLD *Louis Simpson* **414**
RINGING THE BELLS *Anne Sexton* **415**

Index of First Lines and Titles 416

Index of Authors with Titles 426

Part I

Guides to Meaning

Introduction

Poetry is the most disciplined and the most exacting of the verbal arts. It requires sensitivity to ideas, to emotions, and to all kinds of sensory images, and it requires intellectual flexibility to be able to respond to these stimuli simultaneously. For example, consider this poem:

A SLUMBER DID MY SPIRIT SEAL

A slumber did my spirit seal;
    I had no human fears:
She seemed a thing that could not feel
    The touch of earthly years.

No motion has she now, no force;   5
    She neither hears nor sees;
Rolled round in earth's diurnal course,
    With rocks, and stones, and trees.

                —William Wordsworth

The first stanza contains two opposing ideas: the poet's soul sealed in slumber and the implied vitality and charm of the girl. We note at once something odd about the relationship: the joy of love somehow implies spiritual slumber, and the slumber of the first stanza is parallel to the death in the second stanza. The girl who had seemed above fate is now one with the inanimate rocks and stones and trees. For the poet, the girl's death has meant an awakening from the slumber of illusion—but an awakening not to joy but to despair.

We realize at once that the poet's experience is not commonplace, nor is his reaction to it. The usual implication of the death of a loved one is gloom, perhaps withdrawal, but Wordsworth's poem states the shock of recognition that comes with truth, that is, with the soul's awakening from slumber. With the girl's death, he now has "human fears" and a sense of mortality. Structurally, the description of life is carried over into the second stanza: "motion," "force," and "sees" give added poignancy to the loss because the vivid memory of life in the poet's mind is contrasted to the too-solid objects he cites in the last line.

The poem's rhythm fits its mood. All the lines end in a mark of punctuation except line 3, and this line goes on more smoothly than the others, without a stop, in order to emphasize the movement and life of the girl. The other rhythmic variations occur in lines 5 and 8, where the commas accentuate the lifelessness, the quality of life brought to a stop.

This analysis of Wordsworth's poem, although it is comparatively brief, is still considerably longer than the poem itself. Much more could be said about the poem, but we can single out three of the basic characteristics of poetry which we want to consider here: (1) the distinctive form of poetry, (2) the use of imagery, and (3) metaphorical language.

The Form of Poetry

First, we are going to make an obvious and oversimplified distinction, because it is essential to clarify the subject of poetic form at an elementary level. Let us distinguish the terms poetry *and* poem. *Poetry is the more general term. For example, Joseph Conrad and D. H. Lawrence are prose writers who have extended passages in their novels that could justly be called poetry because of the concentrated expression of images, emotions, and ideas in them, and the use of metaphorical language. But we do not ordinarily call such passages poems.*

A poem has its characteristic imagery and metaphorical language within some kind of verse pattern. It has a definite form. Anyone can tell that a poem is a poem by looking at it. It looks *different from prose. A poem has certain external signs that identify it. It may have a rhyme scheme and a regular stanzaic pattern. It will certainly have lines of varying length.*

The form of a poem imposes a close relationship between words and mean-ing, between the way the words are used, their sound and rhythm as well as their denotation, and the effect that the poet is striving for. This close rela-tionship between form and content is perhaps the chief reason poetry is the most lasting form of verbal expression.

The form of a poem is important also because it causes us to read it with a different attitude from that which we bring to a short story or to an essay. We expect a poem to have a distinctive quality of expression. We remember memorable phrases from poetry, "To be, or not to be," "'Tis better to have loved and lost." When we remember phrases from prose, it is likely to be because such poetic devices as accentuated rhythm and repetition are used in them: "of the people, by the people, for the people."

Imagery

A second important element in poetry is the image. An image is anything physical, a "thing." Anything that we can see, hear, touch, taste, or smell is an image. In "A Slumber Did My Spirit Seal," rocks, stones, and trees are images. A rose, a girl, a sword, a bridge, a stream, the sea, the sun—these are things that the poet uses in his poems. It does not matter whether he takes his images from the present or the past, from the city or the country; Insofar as they are a part of physical experience, they are a part of poetry. Coleridge in The Rime of the Ancient Mariner *wrote a religious poem in which many of the images are taken from a sea voyage: water, ship, albatross, and so on. T. S. Eliot in* The Waste Land *uses many images from modern city life: a bridge, a hotel, a public house, false teeth, and so on.*

Although not all poetry relies heavily on the use of images, it is safe to say that most poetry does. Much of the enjoyment of poetry comes from responding to the visual and aural suggestions in a poem, and to the imagery that appeals to other senses. Further, much of the vividness of poetic communication comes from the images. In the following passage from The Rime of the Ancient Mariner, *Coleridge makes the mariner's situation immediate and intense to us largely through the images he uses.*

> And now there came both mist and snow,
> And it grew wondrous cold:
> And ice, mast-high, came floating by,
> As green as emerald.
>
> And through the drifts the snowy clifts   5
> Did send a dismal sheen:
> Nor shapes of men nor beasts we ken—
> The ice was all between.
>
> The ice was here, the ice was there,
> The ice was all around: 10
> It cracked and growled, and roared and howled,
> Like noises in a swound!

This passage contains more imagery than does "A Slumber Did My Spirit Seal," but Coleridge uses his ice imagery almost solely for narrative description, whereas the Wordsworth poem illustrates both of the important characteristics of imagery. First, the poet uses a thing, usually a thing that is part of our lives as well as his: rocks, stones, trees (we have something in common with objects we all know about), and second, these images imply something—and what they imply is likely to be similar for all of us. Rocks, stones, and trees are all nonhuman and inanimate. Thus the effect of the poet's loss in "A Slumber . . ." is intensified for the reader by the contrast between the living girl in the first stanza and the lifeless things the poet cites at the end of the poem.

Metaphorical Language

It is through metaphor that language gives thought and feeling their most powerful and beautiful expression.

What is metaphor? A common definition is that "metaphor is the implied comparison of two unlike things." This comparison expresses, describes, or defines one thing as though it were the other thing. "My heart is full of love" defines the heart as a vessel (cup or bowl) which is filled with a substance (love). In Wordworth's poem, the word slumber is a metaphor for a state of suspension in which the soul is sealed (another metaphor) from reality. And the use of the words feel and touch implies a tactile communication between the girl and time.

For the moment, let us be content with these three characteristics of poetry: (1) distinctive form, (2) imagery, and (3) metaphor. Because these are the most important elements to consider in a poem, they will help you to begin analyzing poetry. . . . But as you analyze, and as you use this book, do not forget the single most important characteristic of poetry—it is poetry. You can take a poem and make an analysis of it, but the odds are astronomical against your taking that analysis and from it making the poem, or an equally effective poem. The theme of the Wordsworth poem with which we began might be stated as follows: "The poet feels despair over the death of a girl who had been full of life." But this graceless statement omits all of the overtones that make up the total effect of the poem. (Stating the theme is not the same thing as reproducing the experience of reading, of course, a fact not only true of poetry but of other types of writing as well. The theme of Dostoievski's Crime and Punishment is stated in the title, but it takes a very, very long novel to give the full psychological and religious effects the author intended.)

That the analysis of "A Slumber Did My Spirit Seal" is longer than the poem itself reminds us that the poem is poetry. A poem is a very compressed form of expression. It concentrates ideas, emotions, and sensory impressions in a brief space. It is the work of a poet, not an analyst. The language of poetry is exact and it is metaphorical. The effect of the form and concentration of poetry is to make the language memorable. The great passages of poetry are usually the best expression of their idea, and the great poets often seem—in retrospect—to have had the best ideas of their time.

Chapter 1

Structural Patterns

Compression of form can make a poem hard to understand. With many ideas, images, and metaphors packed into a very few words, the reader can be overwhelmed if he tries to grasp a poem all at once. He must first break the poem down to its smallest parts, or minimum sense units; these he can manage. Once the reader has defined the parts, he can begin to see the structural pattern of the whole poem, and so have a definite framework for working further into the poem.

The structure of a poem is usually built on one or more of three patterns—the *idea pattern*, the *image pattern*, or the *narrative pattern*. The *idea pattern* is a progression of ideas moving to some kind of resolution. The *image pattern* makes use of a dominant image or series of images to form a total impression. The *narrative pattern* is a series of incidents moving to a denouement.

Idea Pattern

To illustrate an idea pattern, we can look at the soliloquy in Shakespeare's *Hamlet*, beginning "To be, or not to be." At first reading, as Hamlet puzzles over the alternatives of whether to live or die, the passage may appear difficult. It will seem less so, however, if we break the passage into its parts and thus identify its pattern of ideas.

> To be, or not to be—that is the question:
> Whether 'tis nobler in the mind to suffer
> The slings and arrows of outrageous fortune
> Or to take arms against a sea of troubles,

And by opposing end them. To die—to sleep—   *5*
No more; and by a sleep to say we end
The heartache, and the thousand natural shocks
That flesh is heir to. 'Tis a consummation
Devoutly to be wish'd. To die—to sleep.
To sleep—perchance to dream: ay, there's the rub!   *10*
For in that sleep of death what dreams may come
When we have shuffled off this mortal coil,
Must give us pause. There's the respect
That makes calamity of so long life.
For who would bear the whips and scorns of time,   *15*
Th' oppressor's wrong, the proud man's contumely,
The pangs of despis'd love, the law's delay,
The insolence of office, and the spurns
That patient merit of th' unworthy takes,
When he himself might his quietus make   *20*
With a bare bodkin? Who would fardels bear,
To grunt and sweat under a weary life,
But that the dread of something after death—
The undiscover'd country, from whose bourn
No traveller returns—puzzles the will,   *25*
And makes us rather bear those ills we have
Than fly to others that we know not of?
Thus conscience does make cowards of us all,
And thus the native hue of resolution
Is sicklied o'er with the pale cast of thought,   *30*
And enterprises of great pitch and moment
With this regard their currents turn awry
And lose the name of action.

Hamlet (Act III, sc. i)

The passage has a four-part structure. The first part, sentence 1, (lines 1–5) is the introduction. It poses a question of alternatives —whether to live or to die. The second part, sentences 2, 3, and 4 (lines 5–9), considers one alternative—the desirability of dying. The third part, sentences 5 through 9 (lines 9–27), considers the other alternative—the undesirability of dying. The fourth part, the last sentence (lines 28–33) gives the conclusion as an impasse between the two alternatives, and we end with the dilemma with which the soliloquy began.

In the first part, Hamlet states his proposition in line 1 as bare alternatives—"To be, or not to be." He then makes a restatement amplifying the alternatives to tell us that "not to be" means suicide and "to be" means "to suffer . . . outrageous fortune." With the "to be" side of the question defined as suffering and trouble, Hamlet moves to consider the one alternative, "not to be," the desirability of dying. Synonyms provide transition. The phrase "end them" in line 5 leads to "die," and "die" to "sleep," with its pleasant connotations. Such a pleasant end to the heartache and the shocks is "Devoutly to be wish'd."

But the repetition of "to die" and "to sleep" in line 9 carries Hamlet's thoughts to another characteristic of sleep, and he shifts to consider the third main idea of the soliloquy, the undesirability of "not to be." The one deterrent to dying is "dreams." If death as a sleep can mean an end to the shocks of living, it can also mean dreams. And because we do not know what dreams may come in the sleep of death, we pause. We cannot act in favor of suicide, and it is this not knowing which deters us. Hamlet suggests that nobody would bear the calamities of life (he enumerates a series of six calamities in apposition to the "whips and scorns of time") when he could so easily kill himself, except for that one deterrent, the dread of dreams, the dread of something after death. The "rather" in line 26 (the close of part 3) contradicts the "wish'd" of line 9 (the close of part 2).

Thus Hamlet reaches a conclusion after questioning the alternatives. The very thought ("conscience") leaves us without "resolution" to make a choice ("lose the name of action"). Although the ills of life make "not to be" devoutly wished, thinking shows us the other side of the question. By the end of the soliloquy, Hamlet has taken us back to the impasse of the beginning. "To be or not to be" is still the question.

Guides to Idea Pattern

The foregoing analysis of Shakespeare's "To be, or not to be" illustrates a method for handling the structure of ideas in a poem. There are four important guides to finding the idea pattern:

1. *Identify the sentences and sense units.*

The sentence is the usual sense unit, but expect variations. Look for compounds, qualifying clauses, groups of sentences as units, and the stanza as a unit. Use a pencil in your book if necessary to mark off the shifts in ideas within a poem. Punctuation marks indicate shifts. Colons, semicolons, commas, and dashes are helpful signs of different degrees of shift or interruption in movement of ideas.

For instance, the first sentence of Hamlet's soliloquy contains one main idea—the posing of the problem which the whole passage traces out; the dash, the colon, and the comma show that the idea is broken into parts, three slightly different statements of the same idea.

2. *Identify connecting words.*

Words like *if, but,* and *thus* are tangible signs of an idea pattern. They are not only signs of separate ideas, but also signs of a special kind of meaning relationship between the ideas. As you read a poem, underline such connecting words, identify the ideas they connect, and study the relationship. For instance, the use of "or" and "not to be" and the use of "Whether . . . or" in the first sense unit of Hamlet's soliloquy tell us the passage is organized by alternatives.

The nine connectives and their meanings in the same soliloquy can give an idea of just how important connectives are in the idea pattern of a poem:

Connective	*Functional Meaning*
or	alternative
whether . . . or	alternative
and (nine times)	series, additive
for	causal
when (we have shuffled)	temporal
when (he himself)	conditional
but that	eliminative
rather, than	comparative
thus	result

There are many other common connectives besides those used in Hamlet's soliloquy, of course. Some of the more common are *if* (conditional), *although* (concessional), *but* (contrasting), *by* (instrumental), *in order* (purpose). Learn to identify these as guides to meaning.

3. *Identify special patterns of words and phrases.*

Hamlet's soliloquy makes use of a number of standard verbal patterns that give definite signs of structure.

to be, or not to be whether to suffer . . . or . . . end them	restatement
thus conscience and thus the native hue of resolution	compound
for who would bear. . . ? who would fardels bear. . . ?	repetition
to die — to sleep to die — to sleep	repetition
who would bear?	rhetorical question
wrong, contumely, pangs, delay, insolence, and spurns	series

Who would fardels bear . . . but that the dread of something after death . . . puzzles the will?	interruptions
death undiscovered country	appositive
question, pause, puzzles the will, lose the name of action	synonyms

slings and arrows of outrageous fortune,
    sea of troubles, heartache,
    shocks, calamity, whips and scorns
    of time, fardels, weary life, ills
	synonyms

4. *Identify the overall idea pattern.*

Sometimes it helps to make a paraphrase of the idea content of the poem. Start with the close of the poem; the final sense unit often tells what the whole poem is about. See how the poem ends, and then look back to see by what stages the poet arrived at his conclusion. The sentences, the connectives, and the special patterns will serve as guides. If the poem is a finished art form, it will have a resolution of the thought process as well as an artistic resolution. A poem is not a whodunit—you are allowed to look at the ending first. The conclusion of the Hamlet soliloquy gives us the very impasse between thought and action that the first line poses and the body of the soliloquy puzzles over.

In a modern poem with a style and tone quite different from Hamlet's soliloquy, Dylan Thomas asserts a "to be" attitude toward life.

DO NOT GO GENTLE INTO THAT GOOD NIGHT

Do not go gentle into that good night,
Old age should burn and rave at close of day;
Rage, rage against the dying of the light.

Though wise men at their end know dark is right,
Because their words had forked no lightning they   5
Do not go gentle into that good night.

Good men, the last wave by, crying how bright
Their frail deeds might have danced in a green bay,
Rage, rage against the dying of the light.

Wild men who caught and sang the sun in flight,   *10*
And learn, too late, they grieved it on its way,
Do not go gentle into that good night.

Grave men, near death, who see with blinding sight
Blind eyes could blaze like meteors and be gay,
Rage, rage against the dying of the light.   *15*

And you, my father, there on the sad height,
Curse, bless, me now with your fierce tears, I pray.
Do not go gentle into that good night.
Rage, rage against the dying of the light.

The basic principles of analyzing idea structure dictate first a quick check of ordinary sentence structure and punctuation. This shows us that each stanza makes a statement in itself, with stanzas 1 and 6 also using two imperatives to express the idea. Each stanza has a different subject ("old age," "wise men," "good men," etc.) and stanzas 2–5 are alike in being more specific in subject, with stanza 6 most specific of all ("my father"). Further checking shows us that the "And" in the last stanza is not just a coordinator, but also has a summarizing, concluding, and climactic effect. The poet's father should rage as the others have raged.

This resolution gets us close to the overall idea of the poem, and we are now ready to analyze it carefully from its beginning to see how it arrives at this concluding effect.

We can identify three main sense units. The first sense unit (stanza 1) states the theme and urges resistance to dying. The second sense unit (stanzas 2–5) gives four instances of men who do resist dying. The third sense unit (stanza 6) makes a personal appeal to the poet's father.

The first sense unit is made up of a generalization (line 2) and two imperatives (lines 1 and 3) urging an attitude toward dying. The generalization is reinforced by the imperative "Do not go gentle . . . " and its synonym "Rage, rage against . . . ." A pattern of repetition follows from the opening generalization as stanzas 2–5 give four instances of men who all resist dying as they approach death and find the achievements of their lives unsatisfactory.

The idea of the approach of death is worked into each stanza and sense unit by a pattern of synonyms for death used at the end of each line in stanza 1 and once in every other stanza ("good night," "close of day," "the dying of the light," "at their end . . . dark," "last wave," "too late," the word "death" itself, and "sad height"). The key phrases "good night" and "dying of the light" are also repeated throughout.

Thus the repetition of synonyms and of sentence patterns set up in stanza 1 carries the idea structure throughout the poem.

In the final stanza, both repeated phrases are brought together with a specific and personal application. The poet calls upon his dying father to be like the four kinds of men just described and not "go gentle" but to "Rage, rage against the dying of the light."

The following poem by Tennyson affirms human love over emotional and moral emptiness, even though the loss of that love may cause sorrow.

'TIS BETTER TO HAVE LOVED AND LOST

I envy not in any moods
  The captive void of noble rage,
  The linnet born within the cage,
That never knew the summer woods;

I envy not the beast that takes   5
  His license in the field of time,
  Unfettered by the sense of crime,
To whom a conscience never wakes;

Nor, what may count itself as blest,
  The heart that never plighted troth   10
  But stagnates in the weeds of sloth;
Nor any want-begotten rest.

I hold it true, whate'er befall;
  I feel it, when I sorrow most—
  'Tis better to have loved and lost   15
Than never to have loved at all.

Repetitions of negative phrase patterns ("I envy not," "Nor") and punctuation (especially the two periods, the three semicolons, and the dash) give clearly the signs of structure.

The poem divides into two main sense units—the negation (stanzas 1–3) and the affirmation (stanza 4). Each sense unit is composed of a single sentence, that is, stanzas 1–3, and stanza 4. The first sense unit has three subdivisions and a summary, as indicated by the semicolons. We can outline the three kinds of life the poet negates by following the repetition of "I envy not _____; I envy not _____; Nor _____." The second "Nor" in stanza 3 introduces the basic principle of what the poet is rejecting: Not in "any" case does he envy a condition of "rest" if it is begotten by some "want" or deficiency in man.

He rejects three conditions of rest in an ascending scale through stanzas 1–3: deficiency in emotion (stanza 1), in conscience (stanza 2), and in human love (stanza 3). The captive has rest from the torments of emotion ("moods," "noble rage"); the beast is free of the torments of conscience; and the "heart" that has not joined to another in love is free of the sorrow that comes through loss. But the poet envies not these nor any other such conditions of "rest."

He affirms human love. Even though one who loves another has made himself vulnerable to the torments of sorrow — for circumstances ("whate'er befall") may bring the loss of the loved one — yet the poet asserts

> 'Tis better to have loved and lost
> Than never to have loved at all.

Now look at Keats's "When I have Fears . . . " marked as it might be for sense units. Then — with the help of the Aids to Analysis — study the three poems that follow.

Sample Markup of Idea Pattern

Sense Units

WHEN I HAVE FEARS THAT I MAY CEASE TO BE

1. when
   (fame)

2. when
   (fame)

3. when
   (love)

4. then

When I have fears that I may cease to be
Before my pen has glean'd my teeming brain,
Before high-piled books, in charact'ry,
Hold like rich garners the full-ripen'd grain; //
When I behold, upon the night's starr'd face,
Huge cloudy symbols of a high romance,
And think that I may never live to trace
Their shadows, with the magic hand of chance; //
And when I feel, fair creature of an hour!
That I shall never look upon thee more,
Never have relish in the faery power
Of unreflecting love! Then on the shore
Of the wide world I stand alone, and think
Till Love and Fame to nothingness do sink.

—John Keats

vocab: writing

vocab: imaginative story

vocab: instinctual

Resolution: Love and fame become valueless when one fears he shall die before he achieves them.

summary words

Study Poems

ACQUAINTED WITH THE NIGHT

I have been one acquainted with the night.
I have walked out in rain — and back in rain.
I have outwalked the furthest city light.

I have looked down the saddest city lane.
I have passed by the watchman on his beat   5
And dropped my eyes, unwilling to explain.

I have stood still and stopped the sound of feet
When far away an interrupted cry
Came over houses from another street,

But not to call me back or say good-bye;   10
And further still at an unearthly height,
One luminary clock against the sky

Proclaimed the time was neither wrong nor right.
I have been one acquainted with the night.

— Robert Frost

Aids to Analysis:

The idea structure is a pattern of generalization, specific instances, and restatement.

1. *Mark off the specific instances in support of the opening generalization. What patterns of repetition connect these instances?*

2. *What detail or details in each instance suggest that being "acquainted with the night" is an unhappy condition?*

3. *Paraphrase each of the instances. In interpreting the meaning, give special attention to the connectives* When *(line 8),* But *(line 10), and* And *(line 11).*

THE DIVINE IMAGE

To Mercy, Pity, Peace, and Love
All pray in their distress;
And to these virtues of delight
Return their thankfulness.

For Mercy, Pity, Peace, and Love   5
Is God, our Father dear,
And Mercy, Pity, Peace, and Love
Is man, His child and care.

For Mercy has a human heart,
Pity a human face,   10
And Love, the human form divine,
And Peace, the human dress.

Then every man, of every clime,
That prays in his distress,
Prays to the human form divine,   15
Love, Mercy, Pity, Peace.

And all must love the human form,
In heathen, Turk, or Jew;
Where Mercy, Love, and Pity dwell
There God is dwelling too.   20

—William Blake

Aids to Analysis

The idea structure moves in logical stages from the fact of man in his distress praying to "Mercy, Pity, Peace, and Love" to the conclusion that man there-fore must love the human form whether "heathen, Turk, or Jew."

The major stages of thought are marked by the connectives For *(line 5),* For *(line 9),* Then *(line 13), and* And *(line 17). What ideas are connected by these words? Note the contrasts, parallels, and causal relationships between* distress *and* delight, God *and* man, human *and* human form divine.

ON REFUSAL OF AID BETWEEN NATIONS

Not that the earth is changing, O my God!
  Nor that the seasons totter in their walk,—
  Not that the virulent ill of act and talk
Seethes ever as a winepress ever trod,—
Not therefore are we certain that the rod   5
  Weighs in thine hand to smite thy world; though now
  Beneath thine hand so many nations bow,
So many kings:—not therefore, O my God!—

But because Man is parcelled out in men
  Today; because, for any wrongful blow,   10
    No man not stricken asks, "I would be told

> Why thou dost strike"; but his heart whispers then,
>   "He is he, I am I." By this we know
>   That our earth falls asunder, being old.

—Dante Gabriel Rossetti

Aids to Analysis

The idea structure of this poem can be outlined by studying connectives and patterns of repetition. After the first reading, go back and mark all such tangible signs of structure.

1. *Mark the two parts of the cause-and-effect pattern indicated by "therefore." It will help you to list the items in the negative series beginning "Not that . . . ." What is the important effect that these signs do "not therefore" indicate?*

2. *What contrasting turn of thought is introduced by "But because"?*

3. *The words "because" and "but" are repeated (lines 10, 12). Connect the material linked by these repetitions to the meaning of "Man" and "men" in line 9.*

4. *The final sentence provides a summarizing statement. Show how it relates to the whole poem. What is the antecedent of "this"? What is "we know" a synonym for? What is "earth falls asunder" a restatement of?*

Image Pattern

A second pattern of organization is the image pattern. Identifying the image pattern may serve as an additional dimension to analyzing a poem, or the image pattern may serve as the most immediate way into first-level meaning.

The additional dimension of image pattern, for example, expands our understanding of the "To be, or not to be" soliloquy. We find images of action ("Take arms against a sea of troubles") opposed to images suggesting passivity ("suffer the slings and arrows of outrageous fortune"). Thus the pattern of images reinforces our understanding of Hamlet's central problem.

A fuller treatment of imagery will be taken up in Chapter 4, "The Image," in Part II. Here we are concerned with studying image pattern as one of the three types of structure in a poem.

One way in which a poet may use an image pattern for primary structure is illustrated in the following poems by Christina Rossetti and Emily Dickinson, both of whom take a single general image (Rossetti, a storm; Dickinson, a drunken person) and use it to tie together specific images to develop their themes. A second way is illustrated by Shakespeare's sonnet beginning "That time of year . . . ." This poem approaches a single theme from the standpoint of three different image patterns. Note in each of the poems that the theme is brought out by patterns of images rather than by explicit statement.

THE WIND HAS SUCH A RAINY SOUND

The wind has such a rainy sound
　Moaning through the town,
The sea has such a windy sound—
　Will the ships go down?

The apples in the orchard　　　　　　　　　　　5
　Tumble from their tree.
Oh, will the ships go down, go down,
　In the windy sea?

—Christina Rossetti

In this poem the theme of impending danger is suggested by the image pattern of a violent storm. The main images are wind, sea, ships, and apples; from these Christina Rossetti creates a pattern of storm. A sinister and forlorn tone is suggested by the images of sound (*rainy, moaning, windy*), and violence is suggested by the images of action (ships going down and apples tumbling from the tree). The repeated question "Will the ships go down?" combines both danger and violence. We feel the impending danger almost entirely through the images.

In the next poem, observe how Emily Dickinson makes use of an image of a drunken person to express her theme of a happy spiritual experience of nature. Only an image pattern is used; there is no direct statement of the theme.

I TASTE A LIQUOR NEVER BREWED

I taste a liquor never brewed,
From tankards scooped in pearl;
Not all the vats upon the Rhine
Yield such an alcohol!

Inebriate of air am I,   5
And debauchee of dew,
Reeling, through endless summer days,
From inns of molten blue.

When landlords turn the drunken bee
Out of the foxglove's door,   10
When butterflies renounce their drams,
I shall but drink the more!

Till seraphs swing their snowy hats,
And saints to windows run,
To see the little tippler   15
Leaning against the sun!

This poem, an excellent example of the poet communicating a vivid experience by using images, increases in emotional intensity from the description of the "liquor never brewed" to the heavenly excitement in the last stanza. The beginning and the end are thus joined by the idea of a transcendental spiritual experience, the intensity increasing with each successive stanza. Each stanza uses a specific aspect of the larger idea of drunkenness. Stanza 1 describes the "drink"; stanza 2, the "drunken" actions; stanza 3, the inordinate consumption of this liquor; and stanza 4, the excitement in heaven over the "little tippler." Nature is kept before the reader by specific references throughout: "air," "dew," "bee," etc.

Shakespeare's Sonnet 73 has three sets of images, each distinct but joined by the single idea that love is intensified by the awareness of approaching death. The relationship between the sets of images is also strengthened by the progressive emphasis upon death, each quatrain making a more specific allusion to it than the preceding four lines.

SONNET 73

That time of year thou mayst in me behold
When yellow leaves, or none, or few, do hang
Upon those boughs which shake against the cold,
Bare ruin'd choirs, where late the sweet birds sang;
In me thou see'st the twilight of such day   5
As after sunset fadeth in the west,
Which by and by black night doth take away,
Death's second self, that seals up all in rest.
In me thou see'st the glowing of such fire
That on the ashes of his youth doth lie,   10

As the death-bed whereon it must expire,
Consumed with that which it was nourish'd by.
> This thou perceiv'st, which makes thy love more strong,
> To love that well which thou must leave ere long.

The image of bare boughs dominates the first quatrain; twilight, followed by night, dominates lines 5–8. Self-consuming fire in lines 9–12 intensifies the idea of death. Characteristically, Shakespeare ends his sonnet with a generalization. The ending generalization (lines 13–14), with its summary word *This*, states in idea form what the three previous sense units have suggested through images.

The three images in this poem form a pattern based upon three cycles of nature, each more limited in time and space and therefore more intense than the one before. The cycle of the seasons is followed by the cycle of day and night, which in turn is followed by the cycle of fire to ashes. The imminence of death having been established by his pattern of images, Shakespeare is ready for the couplet, which contains the poem's most direct guide to the theme.

Guides to Image Pattern

1. *Identify the images.*
2. *Identify the image pattern.*
   a. Are the images parts of a single larger image (as they are in "The Wind Has Such a Rainy Sound" and "I Taste a Liquor Never Brewed")?
   b. Are the images separate images joined by a single theme (as they are in Sonnet 73)?
3. *In what way do the images support the structural pattern?*
   a. Is the structural pattern entirely one of images?
   b. Is the image pattern joined with another pattern, such as idea pattern?
4. *What theme, idea, or emotion do the images suggest?*

Now look at Shakespeare's Sonnet 130, "My Mistress' Eyes . . .," marked as it might be for images and image pattern. Note the profusion of images, taken by Shakespeare from standard Elizabethan conceits and then, invariably, denied or turned on themselves. (Having done this, the poet then resolves the contrasts in his couplet.) Next—with the help of the Aids to Analysis—study the three poems that follow.

Sample Markup of Image Pattern

SONNET 130

Sense Units

Contrast

Image 1:
My mistress' eyes are nothing like the sun;
Coral is far more red than her lips' red; //

Image 2: If snow be white, why then her breasts are dun; //

Image 3: If hairs be wires, black wires grow on her head. //

Image 4:
I have seen roses damasked red and white,
But no such roses see I in her cheeks; //

Image 5:
And in some perfumes is there more delight
Than in the breath that from my mistress reeks. //

Image 6:
I love to hear her speak, yet well I know
That music hath a far more pleasing sound; //

Image 7:
I grant I never saw a goddess go;
My mistress, when she walks, treads on the ground. //

Yet:
And yet, by heaven, I think my love as rare
As any she belied with false compare.

—*William Shakespeare*

Resolution :

eyes :
breasts :
hair :
cheeks :
breath :
voice :
walks :

parts of larger image

Study Poems

CARGOES

Quinquireme of Nineveh from distant Ophir,
Rowing home to haven in sunny Palestine,
With a cargo of ivory,
And apes and peacocks,
Sandalwood, cedarwood, and sweet white wine.   5

Stately Spanish galleon coming from the Isthmus,
Dipping through the Tropics by the palm-green shores,
With a cargo of diamonds,
Emeralds, amethysts,
Topazes, and cinnamon, and gold moidores.   10

Dirty British coaster with a salt-cake smoke stack,
Butting through the Channel in the mad March days,
With a cargo of Tyne coal,
Road-rails, pig-lead,
Firewood, iron-ware, and cheap tin trays.   15

—*John Masefield*

Aids to Analysis

1. *In what ways does the dominant image of cargoes vary from stanza to stanza?*
2. *What are the most significant differences between the different kinds of cargoes?*
3. *Does Masefield indicate by the image pattern any idea or implication beyond the descriptions? If he does, explain what it is.*

ANTHEM FOR DOOMED YOUTH

What passing-bells for these who die as cattle?
Only the monstrous anger of the guns.
Only the stuttering rifles' rapid rattle
Can patter out their hasty orisons.
No mockeries for them; no prayers nor bells,   5
Nor any voice of mourning save the choirs,—
The shrill, demented choirs of wailing shells;
And bugles calling for them from sad shires.

What candles may be held to speed them all?
Not in the hands of boys, but in their eyes   10
Shall shine the holy glimmers of good-byes.
The pallor of girls' brows shall be their pall;
Their flowers the tenderness of patient minds,
And each slow dusk a drawing-down of blinds.

—Wilfred Owen

Aids to Analysis

The idea pattern of the poem may be seen as a two-part structure—two questions and their ironic answers.

1. *What separate images support the dominant image of "passing bells" in stanza 1? What images of sound contrast with the normal sounds of an anthem?*

2. *What separate images support the event that the candles allude to in stanza 2?*

THE NIGHT IS DARKENING

The night is darkening round me,
   The wild winds coldly blow;
But a tyrant spell has bound me,
   And I cannot, cannot go.

The giant trees are bending   5
　Their bare boughs weighed with snow;
The storm is fast descending,
　And yet I cannot go.

Clouds beyond clouds above me,
　Wastes beyond wastes below;   10
But nothing drear can move me:
　I will not, cannot go.

                    —*Emily Brontë*

Aids to Analysis

1.　*What do the words* But *and* And yet *tell about the structural pattern?*

2.　*What is the dominant image in each stanza? What is the total "picture"?*

3.　*What do we know about the speaker's emotions in relation to the scene?*

4.　*Each stanza has the same structure: description in the first two lines and the expression of a mood in the last two. Describe this mood as you understand it by the end of the poem. It might be helpful to try to define the "tyrant spell."*

Narrative Pattern

A narrative pattern is built on a series of incidents moving to a denouement, an outcome or resolution. With varying emphasis, a narrative pattern presents characters, settings, and movements in time. In the basic narrative pattern, the incidents are central, as in the following ballad.

BONNY BARBARA ALLAN

It was in and about the Martinmas time,
　When the green leaves were a falling,
That Sir John Graeme, in the West Country,
　Fell in love with Barbara Allan.

He sent his man down through the town,   5
　To the place where she was dwelling:
"O haste and come to my master dear,
　Gin ye be Barbara Allan."

O hooly, hooly rose she up,
 To the place where he was lying,   *10*
And when she drew the curtain by,
 "Young man, I think you're dying."

"O it's I'm sick, and very, very sick,
 And 'tis a' for Barbara Allan";
"O the better for me ye's never be,   *15*
 Tho your heart's blood were a spilling.

"O dinna ye mind, young man," said she,
 "When ye was in the tavern a drinking,
That ye made the healths gae round and
   round,
 And slighted Barbara Allan?"   *20*

He turned his face unto the wall,
 And death was with him dealing:
"Adieu, adieu, my dear friends all,
 And be kind to Barbara Allan."

And slowly, slowly raise she up,   *25*
 And slowly, slowly left him,
And sighing said, she could not stay,
 Since death of life had reft him.

She had not gane a mile but twa,
 When she heard the dead-bell ringing,   *30*
And every jow that the dead-bell geid,
 It cry'd "Woe to Barbara Allan!"

"O mother, mother, make my bed!
 O make it soft and narrow!
My love has died for me today,   *35*
 I'll die for him tomorrow."

        —Anonymous

  The story of Bonny Barbara may be marked off into five incidents: Sir John Graeme's falling in love with her (stanza 1), his sending for her in urgency (stanza 2), the dialogue between the lovers at the dying man's bedside (stanzas 3 – 7), her returning home (stanza 8), and her preparing to die (stanza 9).

  The first incident initiates the love story. The second shows a time gap and creates suspense. The third incident, the deathbed scene, is the crucial scene, first, because of the startling discovery of death, and then because we learn of causes, motives, attitudes, and relationships between characters. John Graeme is dying because of grief over Barbara's spurning him ("'tis a' for Barbara Allan"). She has spurned him because he "slighted" her in giving the health at the taverns. She is hard-hearted in her lack of sympathy ("Tho your heart's blood were a spilling"). But Graeme, in spite of his being so cruelly rejected, still loves her ("be kind to"). Apparently her resentment is based on a misunderstanding—he did not intentionally slight her; she had his heart all the time. The fourth incident, her returning home, prepares for her change of attitude ("woe to"). The fifth incident, the request to the mother, gives the reason for the woe in the fourth incident. Barbara, in contradiction to her hard-heartedness before Graeme's death, realizes too late that she loves him—enough to die for him.

From these simple incidents we get the barest essentials of a tragedy of love: the death of Sir John is provoked by a slighted woman's desire for revenge, and she in turn resolves on her own death out of love for him and grief over his death. Other interpretations are possible, for here, as with most ballads, much is left unsaid. The foregoing analysis of "Bonny Barbara Allan" illustrates a method of handling the narrative structure of a poem.

Guides to Narrative Pattern

1. *Identify the incidents or episodes.* A change of time, a change of setting, or a turn of events is a guide.

2. *Identify the narrative pattern.* Three aspects of narrative structure are important:

   a. Denouement. The denouement is the product or outcome of the events that precede. When Barbara Allan says "I'll die for him tomorrow," we can look back and see what steps led her to that grim resolution.

   b. Exposition. Clear up expository details. The time gap between stanzas 1 and 2 is the only vagueness of exposition in "Barbara Allan." Otherwise, the ballad includes definite time and place, identities of speakers, and quotation marks to set off different speakers. Some poems may leave such details to be inferred from the context. In any case, identify settings and changes of settings, different speakers and characters, and time and time-movements.

   c. Incident and character. Understand the cause-and-effect relationship between incidents. Barbara Allan's concluding "I'll die for him" is tied causally ("My love has died for me") to the "woe" of stanza 8, and that, in turn, is tied to the incident at the bedside of her lover. Look for sequences, climaxes, and crucial incidents, which show changes, reverses, realizations. The bell crying "woe" in the fourth incident in "Barbara Allan" shows a change from hard-heartedness. Note the progression of the events to the end of the poem.

In "Barbara Allan" the narrative pattern is central. It presents a series of events or episodes moving to a denouement. In other poems, the narrative structure may be contributory to another purpose. It may be used to dramatize and reveal character — as in many of Browning's poems, such as "My Last Duchess," and in many of Robinson's poems, such as "Miniver Cheevy." Narrative structure may further be used to express ideas, generalizations about life, attitudes, and emotions. On a large scale, it can reflect a philosophical or cultural system as in Milton's *Paradise Lost*. On a smaller scale, it may show the meaning and emotion of a personal experience, as in many of Frost's poems, such as "Stopping by Woods on a Snowy Evening" and "Two Tramps in Mud-Time."

The following poem by Whitman uses a sequence of scenes or incidents to make a point of comparison and to suggest an attitude. No direct statement of the viewpoint is made. The materials are presented as three stages of a personal experience happening in a time pattern. By distinguishing and relating the separate movements in the narrative structure, we can begin to grasp the viewpoint.

WHEN I HEARD THE LEARN'D ASTRONOMER

When I heard the learn'd astronomer,
When the proofs, the figures, were ranged in columns before me,
When I was shown the charts and diagrams, to add, divide, and
    measure them,
When I sitting heard the astronomer where he lectured with much
    applause in the lecture-room,
How soon unaccountable I became tired and sick,   5
Till rising and gliding out I wander'd off by myself,
In the mystical moist night air, and from time to time,
Look'd up in perfect silence at the stars.

                                — Walt Whitman

We can mark off three incidents or turns of events within a very brief time span, each signaled by a time word. First ("When") he hears the astronomer lecture, second ("How soon") he becomes tired and sick, and third ("Till") he wanders off to look up at the stars. We are now ready to ask significant questions. What is the nature of each event? What turns in events are there? What is the relationship of one event to the other?

We see that it was *because* of the statistical, pedantic nature of the lecture about stars that the poet became tired and sick. In turn, his wandering off alone to look up in perfect silence at the stars is his refutation of such lectures. The last event contrasts with the first—"by myself" instead of with a crowd; "perfect silence" instead of "applause"; "mystical" instead of "learn'd" and "proofs"; and the looking up at instead of hearing about. We arrive at a sense of the poet's attitude: that one's experiences with nature should be immediate, personal, and vital. (Note that besides narrative pattern, image pattern and idea pattern were also used in analysis of the poem.)

The following poem uses a narrative pattern composed entirely of dialogue. Here the narrative or dramatic situation is used to suggest a generalization about life and the emotion growing out of that generalization.

AH, ARE YOU DIGGING ON MY GRAVE?

"Ah, are you digging on my grave
   My loved one?—planting rue?"
—"No; yesterday he went to wed
One of the brightest wealth has bred.
'It cannot hurt her now,' he said,   *5*
   'That I should not be true.'"

"Then who is digging on my grave?
   My nearest dearest kin?"
—"Ah, no; they sit and think, 'What use!
What good will planting flowers produce?   *10*
No tendance of her mound can loose
   Her spirit from Death's gin.'"

"But some one digs upon my grave?
   My enemy?—prodding sly?"
—"Nay; when she heard you had passed the Gate   *15*
That shuts on all flesh soon or late,
She thought you no more worth her hate,
   And cares not where you lie."

"Then, who is digging on my grave?
   Say—since I have not guessed!"   *20*
—"O it is I, my mistress dear,
Your little dog, who still lives near,
And much I hope my movements here
   Have not disturbed your rest?"

"Ah, yes! *You* dig upon my grave . . .   *25*
  Why flashed it not on me
That one true heart was left behind!
What feeling do we ever find
To equal among human kind
  A dog's fidelity!"   *30*

"Mistress, I dug upon your grave
  To bury a bone, in case
I should be hungry near this spot
When passing on my daily trot.
I am sorry, but I quite forgot   *35*
  It was your resting-place."

—Thomas Hardy

Since this poem is developed entirely by dialogue, it is necessary to identify speakers and settings, as well as to clarify and to relate the parts of the dramatic situation.

The speakers and setting are easily identified as the dead girl questioning the dog at her graveside. Their dialogue breaks into five episodes. Stanzas 1–4 each contain a question by the girl and an answer by the dog. Stanza 5 presents the girl's comment when she learns that the speaker is the dog; stanza 6, the dog's correction of the girl's comment.

The first three episodes of question and answer are similar. As the girl hopefully asks who is at her grave, the dog answers to the effect that nobody cares for her enough to come to her grave. The difference between the incidents is the person named. They descend in order of importance or closeness to the girl—lover, relative, enemy. Each answer leads to the next person and question. As the dog announces his presence in the fourth answer, the girl's hopes rise momentarily, leading to the fifth episode. As she tries to build her hopes on the "dog's fidelity," we see how far she has moved from her "loved one" of stanza 1. The dog's final statement is simply an ironic reflection of the responses by lover, relative, and enemy—"I quite forgot/It was your resting-place." We should be able to arrive at the generalization: A person is little remembered after he has died.

Now look at Housman's "Is My Team Ploughing" marked as it might be for narrative pattern. Then—with the help of Aids to Analysis —study the two poems that follow.

Sample Markup of Narrative Pattern

Sense Units

"IS MY TEAM PLOUGHING?"

punct.

1. *Question :*
Life as usual?
— *by dead man*

"Is my team ploughing,
  That I was used to drive
And hear the harness jingle
  When I was man alive?"— — *punct.*

work : "ploughing"

Answer : Yes,
life as usual
— *by ?*

Ay, the horses trample,
  The harness jingles now;
No change though you lie under
  The land you used to plough.

2. *Q —*

"Is football playing
  Along the river shore,
With lads to chase the leather,
  Now I stand up no more?"

play : "playing"

A —

Ay, the ball is flying,
  The lads play heart and soul;
The goal stands up, the keeper
  Stands up to keep the goal.

3. *Q —*

"Is my girl happy,
  That I thought hard to leave,
And has she tired of weeping
  As she lies down at eve?"

love : "my girl"

A —

Ay, she lies down lightly,
  She lies not down to weep:
Your girl is well contented.
  Be still, my lad, and sleep.

4. *Q —*

"Is my friend hearty,
  Now that I am thin and pine,
And has he found to sleep in
  A better bed than mine?"

*friendship :
"my friend"*

A —

Yes, lad, I lie easy,
  I lie as lads would choose;
I cheer a dead man's sweetheart,
  Never ask me whose.

— *by friend*

—*A. E. Housman*

*Resolution : Note scenes building up to this
ironic disclosure.*

Study Poems

OH SEE HOW THICK THE GOLDCUP FLOWERS

Oh see how thick the goldcup flowers
  Are lying in field and lane,
With dandelions to tell the hours
  That never are told again.
Oh may I squire you round the meads   *5*
  And pick you posies gay?
— 'T will do no harm to take my arm.
  'You may, young man, you may.'

Ah, spring was sent for lass and lad,
  'Tis now the blood runs gold,   *10*
And man and maid had best be glad
  Before the world is old.
What flowers to-day may flower to-morrow,
  But never as good as new.
—Suppose I wound my arm right round—   *15*
  ' 'Tis true, young man, 'tis true.'

Some lads there are, 'tis shame to say,
  That only court to thieve,
And once they bear the bloom away
  'Tis little enough they leave.   *20*
Then keep your heart for men like me
  And safe from trustless chaps.
My love is true and all for you.
  'Perhaps, young man, perhaps.'

Oh, look in my eyes then, can you doubt?   *25*
  —Why, 'tis a mile from town.
How green the grass is all about!
  We might as well sit down.
—Ah, life, what is it but a flower?
  Why must true lovers sigh?   *30*
Be kind, have pity, my own, my pretty,—
  'Good-bye, young man, good-bye.'

—A. E. Housman

Aids to Analysis

1. *Mark off the speeches made by the young man and those made by the young woman.*

2. *What indications are there of setting and change of setting?*

3. *What actions take place?*

4. *What is the central idea in each speech of the young man?*

5. *In what way is each speech of the young woman a specific response to what the young man has just said?*

6. *What are the four stages leading to the final action of the young woman's saying, "Good-bye"?*

JANET WAKING

Beautifully Janet slept
Till it was deeply morning. She woke then
And thought about her dainty-feathered hen,
To see how it had kept.

One kiss she gave her mother.   5
Only a small one gave she to her daddy
Who would have kissed each curl of his shining baby;
No kiss at all for her brother.

"Old Chucky, old Chucky!" she cried,
Running on little pink feet upon the grass   10
To Chucky's house, and listening. But alas,
Her Chucky had died.

It was a transmogrifying bee
Came droning down on Chucky's old bald head
And sat and put the poison. It scarcely bled,   15
But how exceedingly

And purply did the knot
Swell with the venom and communicate
Its rigor! Now the poor comb stood up straight
But Chucky did not.   20

So there was Janet
Kneeling on the wet grass, crying her brown hen
(Translated far beyond the daughters of men)
To rise and walk upon it.

And weeping fast as she had breath   25
Janet implored us, "Wake her from her sleep!"
And would not be instructed in how deep
Was the forgetful kingdom of death.

—*John Crowe Ransom*

Aids to Analysis

1. *Mark off the six episodes. Guides are changes in time, changes in setting, or turns of events (as "So" in stanza 6 and "And" in stanza 7 show turns of events).*

2. *What changes take place in Janet's mood or attitude through the various scenes? Look for key terms to suggest dominant moods in the different episodes: (1) "Beautifully"; "how it had kept"; (2) "kiss"; (3) "transmogrifying"; "old bald head"; (4) "Kneeling" and "crying"; (5) "implored"; (6) "would not be instructed."*

3. *Relate parts of the poem to see what change or realization has come to Janet.*
   a.   Compare the attitude in scene 3 ("transmogrifying"; "alas") with that in scene 4 ("kneeling" and "crying").
   b.   Compare the serious tone of the final line with the light tone of "Chucky did not."
   c.   Note that words in the final stanza echo words in the first stanza and then consider the changed situation (deep, sleep, Wake).
   d.   What meanings does "waking" have in the poem?
   e.   What discovery has Janet made about the death of her hen?
   f.   What is her response to that discovery?

Chapter 2

Syntax and Situation

The problems a student—or any reader of poetry—meets in understanding a poem are often more apparent than real. A reader may come away from a poem feeling he only half understands it simply because he has not put his knowledge of sentence structure to use or has not checked the meanings of some of the poem's words in the dictionary. If the student clears away some of these first-level, often mechanical, obstructions to meaning, the whole poem may suddenly become meaningful.

Five areas that may provide help in first-level guides to meaning are the poem's *title*, its *vocabulary*, *syntax*, the *situation*, and the *speaker*.

Title. The title is the first lead into most poems. Directly or indirectly, it may give you an important suggestion about the subject or tone. "Cargoes" tells us the subject of Masefield's poem, drawing our special attention to what the ships are carrying. In "Anthem for Doomed Youth," Owen introduces his ironic tone with the title, which contrasts the religious implications of *anthem* (a hymn of praise) with the fact that the soldiers are "doomed." The reader is thus prepared for the ironic bitterness of the poem as a whole.

Vocabulary. The reader needs to be sure of unfamiliar, unknown, and ambiguous words. In "Cargoes" the main vocabulary problem is the first word, *quinquireme*—a vessel of antiquity with five banks of oars. *Transmogrifying* in John Crowe Ransom's "Janet Waking" means transforming, especially in a grotesque or strange manner. Ransom's use of this word, for its tone, helps him establish Janet's unawareness of the seriousness of death.

Syntax. Some problems in comprehension may be solved simply by putting a statement into a recognizable prose order. Your initial difficulties in understanding a poem may stem from nothing more than the inversion of normal word order by the poet, his use of an ellipsis, or an extended interruption of some kind, such as between a subject and verb, or some oddity in punctuation. "Janet Waking" has some distinctive syntactical patterns. In lines 19–20, "Now the poor comb stood up straight/But Chucky did not," we see a shift in meaning of the phrase *stood up straight*. The verb is, of course, understood in line 20. The syntax of line 22, "crying her brown hen," becomes clear if we add *to* after *crying*, though once we have reached first-level meaning we should forget about the insertion, to appreciate the effect Ransom is aiming at.

Shakespeare's sonnet beginning "That time of year thou may'st in me behold" opens with the syntactical variant of the direct object coming before the verb. ("Thou may'st in me behold that time of year . . .") Line 4 uses "Bare ruin'd choirs" as an appositive for "boughs" in line 3.

Situation. In a narrative or dramatic situation the reader needs to know the time, the setting, the connection between characters, and the order of incidents. We need to understand immediately that the first speaker in "Ah, Are You Digging on My Grave?" is a dead person. Whoever is digging replies to the question in each stanza, though we do not know the digger's identity until the fourth stanza. "Janet Waking" begins in the morning with the peace and freshness of a child's world. The fact that it is morning, and the fact that Janet is just waking, contrast ironically with the death she is about to discover.

Speaker. It is important to distinguish the poet from the rhetorical stance he takes in a poem. It is a first-level error to think that an "I" point of view necessarily means a poem is autobiographical. There are three common identities of "I" that the poet may make use of.

1. **"I" as fictitious character.** Sometimes the situation clearly indicates that a fictitious character is speaking. "Ah, Are You Digging on My Grave?" and "Bonny Barbara Allan" are dialogues with fictitious characters.

2. **"I" as poet.** Frequently a poet writes a lyric poem on a subject of personal concern. Milton's sonnet "On His Blindness" and Dylan Thomas' "Do Not Go Gentle Into That Good Night" are such personal expressions. Milton is wondering what he—John Milton—will do to serve God now that he is blind. Thomas asks his father to defy death, not accept it with passive resignation.

3. **"I" as persona.** The persona is a mask, a device or voice that the poet uses to speak through. The "I" used as persona is the poet speaking as Man rather than as a man. He is the voice of a universalized humanity, an ideal, sometimes almost a prophet uttering words that call upon the reader to expand his vision and become something larger than his usual private self. Poets are sometimes accused of

egotism and bombast, but such a charge fails to distinguish between
the poet as an individual and the poet as the voice of representative
Man. Whitman's "One's-Self I Sing" is a clear example of the "I" used
as persona.

ONE'S-SELF I SING

One's-Self I sing, a simple separate person,
Yet utter the word Democratic, the word En-Masse.

Of physiology from top to toe I sing,
Not physiognomy alone nor brain alone is worthy for the
Muse, I say the Form complete is worthier far,
The Female equally with the Male I sing.   5

Of Life immense in passion, pulse, and power,
Cheerful, for freest action form'd under the laws divine,
The Modern Man I sing.

Note that there is a broad middle ground between the "I" as poet
and the "I" as persona. In this middle area the poet often begins with
a personal experience and then changes tone to a profound or ecstatic
burst of poetry that impresses the reader as a representative rather
than an individual voice. It is as though the power of the poet's words
combine with a special insight to form an independent object (the
poem); this is quite a different thing from one person communicating
with another person in verse. Emily Dickinson's "I Taste a Liquor
Never Brewed" and Whitman's "When I Heard the Learn'd Astronomer" are examples of a poet's starting from personal experience and
then expanding into a universalized statement, the "I" thereby seeming
to change from a personal or private "I" to the persona.

Not all poems present problems of understanding in the five areas
of *title*, *vocabulary*, *syntax*, *situation*, and *speaker*. Except for long
poems ("The Love Song of J. Alfred Prufrock," say, or "'Childe Roland to the Dark Tower Came'") few present problems in all of these
areas. But if such problems are present, they must be cleared up before
you can go on to the larger implications of the poem. The importance of
clearing up such problems can be seen in the following poem:

SONG OF THE SIRENS

Steer hither, steer, your wingèd pines,
   All beaten mariners,

Here lie Love's undiscovered mines,
   A prey to passengers;
Perfumes far sweeter than the best   *5*
Which make the phoenix' urn and nest.
   Fear not your ships,
Nor any to oppose you, save our lips;
   But come on shore,
Where no joy dies till Love hath gotten more.   *10*
For swelling waves, our panting breasts
   Where never storms arise,
Exchange; and be awhile our guests:
   For stars gaze on our eyes.
The compass Love shall hourly sing,   *15*
And as he goes about the ring,
   We will not miss
To tell each point he nameth with a kiss.

           —William Browne

The *title* is especially important here because we can hardly establish the meaning of the poem without it. By connecting the title to the poem, we learn that the poem is sung not by just any women, but by sirens. And in the title converge the other problems of *vocabulary*, *situation*, and *speaker*. Sirens are seductresses, archetypes of the feminine figure at its most alluring and most destructive. The *speakers* of the poem are the sirens, speaking to the mariners; and the *situation* (of siren singers luring mariners) can be identified with the original sirens of Greek mythology. So we know the call of the sirens is a call of temptation and a call to destruction. The theme is not just a woman-sailor scene, but the recurring theme of man's being tempted to his destruction by the allurements of women.

To see just what the sirens are singing, we have to examine the *syntax* used in the poem. We have to do such things as straighten out inversions, expand ellipses, modernize archaic idioms, and connect basic words in sentence structure as distinct from interrupters. When we have dealt with these problems, we have a close paraphrase which preserves the trend of thought but reserves the more significant and subtle aspects of poetic idiom for later consideration:

Ellipsis, line 5	—(*Here lie*) perfumes far sweeter than the best
Idiom, lines 7–8	—*Do* not fear *for* your ships, Nor any to oppose you, *except* our lips.

Ellipsis, line 10	— Where no joy dies till Love has more *joy*.
Inversion, lines 11–13	— Exchange our panting breasts, where storms never arise, For swelling waves; And be our guests awhile.
Inversion, Idiom, line 14	— Gaze on our eyes, *instead of* stars.
Inversion, Ellipsis, line 15	— Love shall hourly sing the points of the compass.
Idiom, line 17	— We will not *fail*
Inversion, Idiom, line 18	— To *count off* with a kiss each point he names.

After dealing with *title, vocabulary, speaker, situation,* and *syntax,* we have solved most of the problems of understanding this poem and the groundwork is laid for considering its aesthetic and thematic problems.

In the following, more complex poem, the problems of title, situation, speaker, and vocabulary are still more closely related to the overall theme.

THE MAGI

Now as at all times I can see in the mind's eye,
In their stiff, painted clothes, the pale unsatisfied ones
Appear and disappear in the blue depth of the sky
With all their ancient faces like rain-beaten stones,
And all their helms of silver hovering side by side,   5
And all their eyes still fixed, hoping to find once more,
Being by Calvary's turbulence unsatisfied,
The uncontrollable mystery on the bestial floor.

— William Butler Yeats

The first and simplest step is to deal with title and vocabulary. Without the title we could not be sure that the "pale unsatisfied ones" are Magi. We may need to look up "Magi" in the dictionary to understand the significance of associating them with Calvary instead of only with the birth of Christ as in Biblical tradition. The situation will then be seen to be quite different from that of the traditional visit of the wise men. These Magi return to the birthplace of Christ at some indefinite time after the crucifixion. Once this unusual situation is established, we can begin the significant study of the poem.

The identity of the speaker, the "I," becomes an important problem as we analyze the poem more fully. In this instance the "I" is the *persona* (or mask) assumed by the poet for presenting his vision or point of view. Through the persona the poet expresses his vision of the Magi returning to Christ's birthplace because they are disturbed by the "turbulence" of Calvary. The persona sees the sculptured, stylized imagery of clothes and faces depicting the unsatisfied Magi ("stiff," "painted," "pale," "ancient faces," "rain-beaten stones"), and the intensity and humble uncertainty of the Magi's hope ("hovering," "eyes still fixed, hoping").

Through the persona we can consider the "turbulence" that disturbs them. What "mystery" do they want to control? What is there about the "mystery on the bestial floor" that makes it uncontrollable?

Study Poems

JEALOUSY

"The myrtle bush grew shady
  Down by the ford."—
"Is it even so?" said my lady.
  "Even so!" said my lord.
"The leaves are set too thick together   5
  For the point of a sword."

"The arras in your room hangs close,
  No light between!
You wedded one of those
  That see unseen."—   10
"Is it even so?" said the King's Majesty.
  "Even so!" said the Queen.

—Mary Elizabeth Coleridge

Aids to Analysis:

There are problems in title, situation, speaker, and vocabulary. The basic structure is a narrative-dramatic pattern.

1.   *What help does the title give in understanding the two incidents?*

2.   *In the first stanza, what are the lord and the lady discussing? The fact that the myrtle in ancient times was sacred to Venus will give a lead.*

3.   *How is the situation in the second stanza similar to that in the first stanza? How is it different?*

4.   *What images indicate that the jealousy is based upon suspicion rather than direct evidence?*

5.   *Explain the uses of "even so."*

VALE, AMOR!

We do not know this thing
  By the spoken word;
It is as though in a dim wood
  One heard a bird
  Suddenly sing—   5
Then in the twinkling of an eye
A shadow glooms the earth and sky,
And we stand silent, startled, in a changed mood.

It is but a little thing
  The leaping sword,   10
When in the startled silence of changed mood
  It comes as when a bird
  Doth suddenly sing.
But thrust of sword or agony of soul
Are alike swift and terrible and strong,   15
And no foot stirs the dead leaves of that silent wood.

—William Sharp

Aids to Analysis

The main problem is the Latin of the title. The basic structure of the poem is an image pattern.

1.   *Look up the two words of the title in the dictionary. Vale is defined in desk dictionaries. The meaning of Amor is available by inference from "amorous."*

2.   *Relate the three dominant images of "singing bird," "sword," and "wood" to the title.*

HOW ANNANDALE WENT OUT

"They called it Annandale — and I was there
To flourish, to find words, and to attend:
Liar, physician, hypocrite, and friend,
I watched him; and the sight was not so fair
As one or two that I have seen elsewhere: 5
An apparatus not for me to mend —
A wreck, with hell between him and the end,
Remained of Annandale; and I was there.
I knew the ruin as I knew the man;
So put the two together, if you can,   10
Remembering the worst you know of me.
Now view yourself as I was, on the spot —
With a slight kind of engine. Do you see?
Like this . . . You wouldn't hang me? I thought not."

— Edwin Arlington Robinson

Aids to Analysis

The main problems are situation, speaker, and vocabulary. The basic structure is a narrative-dramatic pattern.

1. *What is the significance of the quotation marks?*

2. *Who is the speaker?*

3. *To whom is he speaking?*

4. *What is the speaker's profession?*

5. *List the pronouns and nouns that identify Annandale after "it" in line 1.*

6. *Look up the meanings of "engine" in the dictionary. What is the significance of the speaker's using "engine" instead of "instrument"?*

7. *What happens in the last line between the question mark and "I thought not"?*

SPECULATIVE

Others may need new life in Heaven —
    Man, Nature, Art — made new, assume!
Man with new mind old sense to leaven,
    Nature — new light to clear old gloom,
Art that breaks bounds, gets soaring-room.   5

I shall pray: "Fugitive as precious—
    Minutes which passed—return, remain!
Let earth's old life once more enmesh us,
    You with old pleasure, me—old pain,
So we but meet nor part again!"   *10*

—Robert Browning

Aids to Analysis

The main problem is syntax. The basic structure is an idea pattern.

1. *What is the grammatical function of "Man, Nature, Art"? What word in line 1 are the three words connected to?*

2. *The terms "made new" and "assume" are elliptical constructions. What has been "made new"? What is the reader asked to "assume"?*

3. *What things are as "fugitive" as they are "precious"?*

4. *What is the subject of "return"?*

5. *What ellipsis does the dash in line 9 indicate?*

6. *Examining the idea structure of the poem shows that the first stanza and the second stanza express opposing views. What are these views?*

A VALEDICTION: FORBIDDING MOURNING

As virtuous men pass mildly away,
    And whisper to their souls, to go,
Whilst some of their sad friends do say,
    The breath goes now, and some say, No;

So let us melt, and make no noise,   *5*
    No tear-floods, nor sigh-tempests move,
'Twere profanation of our joys
    To tell the laity our love.

Moving of th' earth brings harms and fears,
    Men reckon what it did and meant,   *10*
But trepidation of the spheres,
    Though greater far, is innocent.

Dull sublunary lovers' love
    (Whose soul is sense) cannot admit
Absence, because it doth remove   *15*
    Those things which elemented it.

But we by a love, so much refined,
   That our selves know not what it is,
Inter-assuréd of the mind,
   Care less, eyes, lips, and hands to miss.   *20*

Our two souls therefore, which are one,
   Though I must go, endure not yet
A breach, but an expansion,
   Like gold to airy thinness beat.

If they be two, they are two so   *25*
   As stiff twin compasses are two;
Thy soul the fixed foot makes no show
   To move, but doth, if the other do.

And though it in the center sit,
   Yet when the other far doth roam,   *30*
It leans, and hearkens after it,
   And grows erect, as that comes home.

Such wilt thou be to me, who must
   Like th' other foot, obliquely run;
Thy firmness makes my circle just,   *35*
   And makes me end, where I begun.

                —*John Donne*

Aids to Analysis

Many problems in syntax and situations are represented in Donne's poem. The basic structure is idea pattern, which makes use of image pattern and narrative-dramatic pattern.

1.   *Examine the title as a guide to the situation and subject of the poem. Check the meaning of* valediction. *Determine what reason the speaker has for "forbidding mourning."*

2.   *It will help you to be* very *sure of the meanings of the following words:* profanation, laity, trepidation, sublunary, obliquely, innocent, element-ed, refined, *and* just.

3.   *Examine the syntax carefully to clarify basic subject—verb—complement patterns, ellipses, inversions, and interruptions. The following illustrate points of difficulty:*
    a.   What is the connection between So *in stanza 2 and* As *in stanza 1? Note the semicolon ending stanza 1.*
    b.   What is the subject of the verb move *in stanza 2? Note that* tear-floods *and* sigh-tempests *are direct objects.*

    c.   *In stanza 3 complete the elliptical comparison — greater "far" than what?*

    d.   *In stanza 5 what is the subject of the verb* care? *What comparison is implied in* less, *that is, less than* who? *What are the direct objects of* to miss?

4.   *The poem has a clearly defined idea pattern. Outline this pattern, noting Donne's careful use of transitional and connective words. Note especially the turning point of the poem marked by* therefore *in stanza 6.*

5.   *Note the dominant images in stanzas 1–2, 3, 4–6, and 7–9. What idea do they express in common? What relationship do you find between the idea pattern and the image pattern?*

Chapter 3

First-Level Meaning

To summarize the techniques introduced so far, we will mark "Design" by Robert Frost according to the principles treated under Structural Patterns and Syntax and Situation. Then we will itemize and discuss the elements in this preliminary markup.

Following this analysis we will mark another poem but leave it to the student to explain the details as an exercise in coming to the first-level meaning of a poem.

Sample Markup of Sense Units

title:

speaker

vocab:

DESIGN

Sense Units

vocab:

Common theme:
white; design

I found a dimpled spider, fat and white,
On a white heal-all, holding up a moth
Like a white piece of rigid satin cloth—
Assorted characters of death and blight
Mixed ready to begin the morning right,
Like the ingredients of a witches' broth—
A snow-drop spider, a flower like a froth,
And dead wings carried like a paper kite.

Image { *1. spider*
2. flower
3. moth }

Image:
Repetition

Question 1:
flower
Question 2: spider
Question 3: moth

What had that flower to do with being white,
The wayside blue and innocent heal-all?
What brought the kindred spider to that height,
Then steered the white moth thither in the night?

Image:
Repetition

answer and
Qualifier

What but design of darkness to appall?—
If design govern in a thing so small.

—*Robert Frost*

Resolution :   *Repetition of title word*

Aids to Analysis

Syntax and Situation

1. **Title.** Design *has the general meaning of "purpose" or "plan." We note also that the word occurs in each of the last two lines.*

2. **Vocabulary.** Design *has two general meanings that may apply here: (1) plan in the sense of purpose — a relatively abstract meaning; (2) plan in the sense of a sketch or outline or perhaps the actual arrangement of parts — a relatively sensuous, perhaps artistic implication.*
   Frost describes the heal-all *flower for us.*

3. **Syntax.** *There are no difficult problems of syntax. The dashes at the end of lines 3 and 6 set off a descriptive appositive of the three images.*

4. **Situation.** *The first two lines tell us all we need to know of the situation. The speaker at some time in the past found the spider, the heal-all, and the moth in the "design" he describes.*

5. **Speaker.** *From the poem itself there is no reason to think that this is a fictitious character speaking. We can assume the "I" is Frost. In the last six lines, however, the poem develops such broad implications that we may suspect that the "I" of the poet is verging into the "I" of the persona. The poem seems to start out as autobiographical incident and to conclude as a representative philosophical comment.*

Structural Patterns

1. **Narrative pattern.** *Such narrative as the poem has is clear and simple. The speaker found the spider, the heal-all, and the moth.*

2. **Image pattern.** *The spider, the heal-all, and the moth are the central images. Frost keeps them before us throughout the poem. Their whiteness is the dominant color impression. Night and darkness in lines 12 and 13 contrast sharply with the white. Also, in lines 4–6 Frost introduces a darker implication of the white design of the original picture. A pattern emerges: white — darkness; life — death. There is some connection — but what?*

3. **Idea pattern.** *From the simplest of narrative situations and the three images Frost proceeds to a complex abstraction. His idea pattern is composed of a three-part question, an answer, and a qualifier. What power had brought the three things together to form the design? Lines 4–6, following the introductory description, introduce dark implications. The morning begins "right" with ingredients of death. Having asked the questions about purpose, the poet returns even more starkly to*

his answer in line 13: "design of darkness to appall." But Frost is not through with the subject yet. He has a qualifying statement that makes the whole possibility even darker: perhaps there is no design or purpose at all in such a small event with such small objects. The white design with its intermixture of life and death may have no meaning whatsoever because the "design of darkness" governs only larger things. At this point we wonder, perhaps, what kinds of things are governed by the force of design.

Our analysis of the idea structure shows us also that the image pattern is an integral part of the poem. The patterns of images pose the question, and in doing so lead us to the terrifying speculation that brings us back to the image of design we started with.

Sample Markup of Sense Units

IN TIME OF "THE BREAKING OF NATIONS"

Sense Units

Common theme: simple, basic, human activity

Image 1: Only a (man) harrowing clods
    In a slow silent walk
    With an old (horse) that stumbles and nods
    Half asleep as they stalk. //

Image 2: Only thin (smoke) without flame
    From the heaps of couch-grass; //
Idea 1: Yet this will go onward the same
contrast Though (Dynasties) pass. //

Image 3: Yonder a (maid and her wight)
    Come whispering by: //
Idea 2: (War's annals will fade into night)
restatement Ere their story die.

—*Thomas Hardy*

Title: Check
Jeremiah 51:20
Situation:

Speaker: observer
vocab:

vocab:

vocab:

Resolution

Near synonyms:
nations
dynasties
annals

Study Poems

SONG

How many times do I love thee, dear?
  Tell me how many thoughts there be
      In the atmosphere
      Of a new-fall'n year,
Whose white and sable hours appear   *5*
  The latest flake of Eternity: —
So many times do I love thee, dear.

How many times do I love again?
  Tell me how many beads there are
      In a silver chain   *10*
      Of evening rain,
Unravelled from the tumbling main,
  And threading the eye of a yellow star: —
So many times do I love again.

      — Thomas Lovell Beddoes

Aids to Analysis

1. *Both stanzas follow an idea pattern of question, answer, and restatement. Identify the repeated word and phrases and the punctuation that indicate the three main sense units in each stanza.*

2. *How does the dominant image in each stanza appropriately, though figuratively, answer the question "How many times"?*

THE THREE FISHERS

Three fishers went sailing away to the West,
  Away to the West as the sun went down;
Each thought on the woman who loved him the best;
  And the children stood watching them out of the town;
For men must work, and women must weep,   *5*
And there's little to earn, and many to keep,
  Though the harbor bar be moaning.

Three wives sat up in the lighthouse tower,
And they trimmed the lamps as the sun went down;
They looked at the squall, and they looked at the shower, *10*
  And the night-rack came rolling up ragged and brown.

But men must work, and women must weep,
Though storms be sudden, and waters deep,
   And the harbor bar be moaning.

Three corpses lay out on the shining sands   *15*
  In the morning gleam as the tide went down,
And the women are weeping and wringing their hands
  For those who will never come home to the town;
For men must work, and women must weep,
And the sooner it's over, the sooner to sleep;   *20*
   And good-by to the bar and its moaning.

          —*Charles Kingsley*

Aids to Analysis

1. *Mark off the separate incidents or situations.*

2. *What is the dominant unifying image in each incident?*

3. *What patterns of repetition relate one stanza to another?*

4. *What basic experiences are expressed through the incidents of the poem?*

HOMAGE

They said to him, "It is a very good thing that you have done, yes,
  both good and great, proving this other passage to the Indies.
  Marvelous," they said. "Very. But where, Señor, is the gold?"

They said: "We like it, we admire it very much, don't misunder-
  stand us, in fact we think it's almost great. But isn't there,   *5*
  well, a little too much of this Prince of Denmark? After all,
  there is no one quite like you in your lighter vein."
"Astonishing," they said. "Who would have thought you had it in
  you, Orville?" They said, "Wilbur, this machine of yours is
  amazing, if it works, and perhaps some day we can use it to   *10*
  distribute eggs, or to advertise."

And they were good people, too. Decent people.
They did not beat their wives. They went to church. And they kept
  the law.

          —*Kenneth Fearing*

Aids to Analysis

1. *Mark off the main incidents or sense units.*

2. *Identify the speakers ("they") in each incident. To whom are they speaking in each case?*

3. *Identify the two sides of the contrast or contradiction ("but") in each situation.*

4. *What implications do the three incidents have in common that make the ironic conclusion appropriate?*

WESTERN WIND

Western wind, when wilt thou blow?
The small rain down can rain,—
Christ, if my love were in my arms
And I in my bed again!

—Anonymous

Aids to Analysis

1. *What is the situation? What do we know about the person speaking?*
2. *What mood do the images suggest?*

SUSPENSE

The wind comes from the north
Blowing little flocks of birds
Like spray across the town,
And a train roaring forth
Rushes stampeding down   5
South, with flying curds
Of steam, from the darkening north.

Whither I turn and set
Like a needle steadfastly,
Waiting ever to get   10
The news that she is free;
But ever fixed, as yet,
To the lode of her agony.

—D. H. Lawrence

Aids to Analysis

1. *What are the separate parts of the dominant image of* north *in stanza 1? What impression do the images give?*

2. *How is the image of* north *related to the imagery of stanza 2?*

3. *What is the meaning of* set *and* lode?

4. *What is the "Suspense" of the title about?*

EDWARD

"Why does your brand sae drap wi' bluid,
    Edward, Edward?
Why does your brand sae drap wi' bluid,
  And why sae sad gang ye, O?"
"O I ha'e killed my hawk sae guid,   5
    Mither, mither,
O I ha'e killed my hawk sae guid,
  And I had nae mair but he, O."

"Your hawkes bluid was never sae reid,
    Edward, Edward.   10
Your hawkes bluid was never sae reid,
  My dear son I tell thee, O."
"O I ha'e killed my reid-roan steed,
    Mither, mither,
O I ha'e killed my reid-roan steed,   15
  That erst was sae fair and free, O."

"Your steed was auld and ye ha'e gat mair,
    Edward, Edward.
Your steed was auld and ye ha'e gat mair:
  Som other dule ye dree, O."   20
"O I ha'e killed my fader dear,
    Mither, mither,
O I ha'e killed my fader dear,
  Alas and wae is me, O!"

"And whatten penance wul ye dree for that,   25
    Edward, Edward?
And whatten penance wul ye dree for that,
  My dear son, now tell me, O?"

    "I'll set my feet in yonder boat,
        Mither, mither,   *30*
    I'll set my feet in yonder boat,
        And I'll fare over the sea, O."

    "And what wul ye do wi' your towers and your ha',
        Edward, Edward?
    And what wul ye do wi' your towers and your ha',   *35*
        That were sae fair to see, O?"
    "I'll let thame stand til they down fa',
        Mither, mither,
    I'll let thame stand til they down fa',
        For here never mair maun I be, O."   *40*

    "And what wul ye leave to your bairns and your wife,
        Edward, Edward,
    And what wul ye leave to your bairns and your wife,
        When ye gang over the sea, O?"
    "The warldes room: late them beg thrae life,   *45*
        Mither, mither,
    The warldes room: late them beg thrae life,
        For thame never mair wul I see, O."

    "And what wul ye leave to your ain mither dear,
        Edward, Edward?   *50*
    And what wul ye leave to your ain mither dear,
        My dear son, now tell me, O?"
    "The curse of hell frae me sal ye bear,
        Mither, mither,
    The curse of hell frae me sal ye bear,   *55*
        Sic counseils ye gave to me, O."

                          —*Anonymous*

Aids to Analysis

1.   *Mark off the incidents of the poem. Guides are quotation marks, changes of speaker, and repetitions of phrase patterns.*

2.   *Identify the two climaxes of the poem.*

3.   *What has Edward's mother done to him that he should curse her at the end?*

THE PASSIONATE SHEPHERD TO HIS LOVE

Come live with me and be my love,
And we will all the pleasures prove
That hills and valleys, dales and fields,
And all the craggy mountains yields.

There will we sit upon the rocks   5
And see the shepherds feed their flocks,
By shallow rivers, to whose falls
Melodious birds sing madrigals.

There will I make thee beds of roses
And a thousand fragrant posies,   10
A cap of flowers, and a kirtle
Embroider'd all with leaves of myrtle.

A gown made of the finest wool,
Which from our pretty lambs we pull,
Fair linèd slippers for the cold,   15
With buckles of the purest gold.

A belt of straw and ivy buds
With coral clasps and amber studs:
And if these pleasures may thee move,
Come live with me and be my love.   20

The shepherd swains shall dance and sing
For thy delight each May-morning:
If these delights thy mind may move,
Then live with me and be my love.

—Christopher Marlowe

Aids to Analysis

1. *Study the title to establish situation—the occasion and the characters.*

2. *Check in the dictionary for the meaning of* kirtle *and* swain.

3. *List the specific "pleasures" the man offers the girl if she will "live with me and be my love."*

4. *Does the poem tell the effect the shepherd's "line" has on the girl?*

5. *How persuasive would you judge his line to be?*

THE NYMPH'S REPLY

If all the world and love were young,
And truth in every shepherd's tongue,
These pretty pleasures might me move
To live with thee and be thy Love.

Time drives the flocks from field to fold,   5
When rivers rage and rocks grow cold;
And Philomel becometh dumb;
The rest complains of cares to come.

The flowers do fade, and wanton fields
To wayward winter reckoning yields: 10
A honey tongue, a heart of gall,
Is fancy's spring, but sorrow's fall.

Thy gowns, thy shoes, thy beds of roses,
Thy cap, thy kirtle, and thy posies
Soon break, soon wither, soon forgotten,   15
In folly ripe, in reason rotten.

Thy belt of straw and ivy buds,
Thy coral clasps and amber studs,
All these in me no means can move
To come to thee and be thy Love.   20

But could youth last, and love still breed,
Had joys no date, nor age no need,
Then these delights my mind might move
To live with thee and be thy Love.

—Sir Walter Ralegh

Aids to Analysis

1. *The title is the first indication that the poem is a companion piece to the preceding poem by Marlowe. Find other details which relate Ralegh's poem to Marlowe's.*

2. *Check in the dictionary for the meaning of* Philomel. *What are the possible meanings of* spring *and* fall *in their context in stanza 3?*

3. *What does the girl find wrong with the specific "pleasures" and "delights" offered by the man?*

4. *List the specific conditions under which these "delights" might move the girl to "live with thee and be thy Love."*

5.   *Study the final stanza to see how it summarizes the sense units of the rest of the poem and how it forms a resolution to the situation and to the poem.*

THE CLOD AND THE PEBBLE

"Love seeketh not Itself to please,
Nor for itself hath any care,
But for another gives its ease,
And builds a Heaven in Hell's despair."

So sung a little Clod of Clay   5
Trodden with the cattle's feet,
But a Pebble of the brook
Warbled out these metres meet:

"Love seeketh only Self to please,
To bind another to Its delight,   10
Joys in another's loss of ease,
And builds a Hell in Heaven's despite."

                                        — *William Blake*

Aids to Analysis

1.   *Identify the separate sense units, images, and characters (with their speeches and situations).*

2.   *Paraphrase the philosophy of the Clod and the philosophy of the Pebble.*

3.   *Define* Heaven *and* Hell *as used here.*

4.   *Define* Love *as used in stanza 1 and as used in stanza 3. How does the difference in their situations in life help to explain the difference in the Clod's and the Pebble's view of Love?*

TO—

One word is too often profaned
    For me to profane it,
One feeling too falsely disdained
    For thee to disdain it;
One hope is too like despair   5
    For prudence to smother,
And pity from thee more dear
    Than that from another.

I can give not what men call love,
  But wilt thou accept not 10
The worship the heart lifts above
  And the Heavens reject not—
The desire of the moth for the star,
  Of the night for the morrow,
The devotion to something afar 15
  From the sphere of our sorrow?

      —Percy Bysshe Shelley

Aids to Analysis

1. *Fill out the elliptical syntax of lines 7–8 according to the pattern of the first six lines.*

2. *Following the repetitions of phrase pattern, mark off the sense units of stanza 1.*

3. *Using the connective* But *as a guide, mark off the two main sense units of stanza 2.*

4. *How are the four key terms in stanza 1* (word, feeling, hope, pity) *related to* love *and* worship *in stanza 2?*

5. *Find three synonyms for* worship.

THOU ART INDEED JUST, LORD

Thou art indeed just, Lord, if I contend
With thee; but, sir, so what I plead is just.
Why do sinners' ways prosper? and why must
Disappointment all I endeavor end?
  Wert thou my enemy, O thou my friend, 5
How wouldst thou worse, I wonder, than thou dost
Defeat, thwart me? Oh, the sots and thralls of lust
Do in spare hours more thrive than I that spend,
Sir, life upon thy cause. See, banks and brakes
Now, leavèd how thick! lacèd they are again 10
With fretty chervil, look, and fresh wind shakes
Them; birds build—but not I build; no, but strain,
Time's eunuch, and not breed one work that wakes.
Mine, O thou lord of life, send my roots rain.

      —Gerard Manley Hopkins

Aids to Analysis

1. *Inversions, interruptions, and ellipses make the reading of this poem tortuous (as the praying man's conflict is tortuous). Read the poem carefully, picking out subjects, connecting them with their verbs, and putting complements and modifiers in normal order. For instance, line 4 contains inversion, ellipsis, and interruption. In more conventional order it reads: "And why must disappointment end all that I endeavor?"*

    Some guides:
    a. *What is the verb or verbs for the subject* thou *in line 6 (*wouldst *is a helper verb). What does the adverb phrase "worse . . . than thou dost" modify?*
    b. *In lines 9–12, what are thickly* leavèd *and* lacèd?
    c. *In lines 12–13, observe the usual function of the coordinate conjunctions* but *and* and *in order to identify the subject of* strain *and* breed.

2. *Check in the dictionary to find which meaning or meanings apply to the following words:* if, so, sots, thralls, brakes, fretty, chervil, eunuch, wakes.

3. *Mark off the sense units. You could begin with the six separate sentences. Then note the compounds and comparisons.*

4. *Point out the contrasts and contradictions in the poem. Some signs of contrast are* but *(used three times), the comparisons* worse . . . than *and* more . . . than, *the implications of the rhetorical questions, and the images in contrast.*

5. *What specific natural process is dominant in the natural images of the last six lines? How does this process contrast with the poet's condition?*

6. *Look at the last line to see just what the poet is praying for.*

DULCE ET DECORUM EST

Bent double, like old beggars under sacks,
Knock-kneed, coughing like hags, we cursed through sludge,
Till on the haunting flares we turned our backs,
And towards our distant rest began to trudge.
Men marched asleep. Many had lost their boots,   5
But limped on, blood-shod. All went lame, all blind;
Drunk with fatigue; deaf even to the hoots
Of gas-shells dropping softly behind.

Gas! Gas! Quick, boys! — An ecstasy of fumbling,
Fitting the clumsy helmets just in time,   *10*
But someone still was yelling out and stumbling
And flound'ring like a man in fire or lime.
Dim through the misty panes and thick green light,
As under a green sea, I saw him drowning.

In all my dreams before my helpless sight   *15*
He plunges at me, guttering, choking, drowning.

If in some smothering dreams, you too could pace
Behind the wagon that we flung him in,
And watch the white eyes writhing in his face,
His hanging face, like a devil's sick of sin,   *20*
If you could hear, at every jolt, the blood
Come gargling from the froth-corrupted lungs
Bitter as the cud
Of vile, incurable sores on innocent tongues, —
My friend, you would not tell with such high zest   *25*
To children ardent for some desperate glory,
The old lie: *Dulce et decorum est*
Pro patria mori.

                                        — *Wilfred Owen*

Aids to Analysis

1. *The Latin quotation at the end may be translated, "Sweet and fitting it is to die for (one's) country."*

2. *What is the central incident in each stanza?*

3. *What is the dominant image in each stanza?*

4. *Trace the idea pattern of stanza 4 by following the two uses of the conditional "if" to the consequence and its appositive.*

5. *How do the patterns of narrative, image, and idea prepare the reader to accept the resolution of the poem: "The old lie"?*

AN ELEMENTARY SCHOOL CLASSROOM IN A SLUM

Far far from gusty waves these children's faces.
Like rootless weeds, the hair torn round their pallor.
The tall girl with her weighed-down head. The paper-
seeming boy, with rat's eyes. The stunted, unlucky heir
Of twisted bones, reciting a father's gnarled disease,   *5*

His lesson from his desk. At back of the dim class
One unnoted, sweet and young. His eyes live in a dream
Of squirrel's game, in tree room, other than this.

On sour cream walls, donations. Shakespeare's head,
Cloudless at dawn, civilized dome riding all cities.   *10*
Belled, flowery, Tyrolese valley. Open-handed map
Awarding the world its world. And yet, for these
Children, these windows, not this world, are world,
Where all their future's painted with a fog,
A narrow street sealed in with a lead sky,   *15*
Far far from rivers, capes, and stars of words.

Surely, Shakespeare is wicked, the map a bad example
With ships and sun and love tempting them to steal—
For lives that slyly turn in their cramped holes
From fog to endless night? On their slag heap, these children   *20*
Wear skins peeped through by bones and spectacles of steel
With mended glass, like bottle bits on stones.
All of their time and space are foggy slum.
So blot their maps with slums as big as doom.

Unless, governor, teacher, inspector, visitor,   *25*
This map becomes their window and these windows
That shut upon their lives like catacombs,
Break O break open till they break the town
And show the children to green fields, and make their world
Run azure on gold sands, and let their tongues   *30*
Run naked into books, the white and green leaves open
History theirs whose language is the sun.

                                                      —Stephen Spender

Aids to Analysis

1. *Outline the four stages of development suggested by each stanza.*

2. *Study the title to understand the setting and to prepare for the indictment in stanza 3 and the challenge in stanza 4.*

3. *Mark off the two sense units connected by* unless *in stanza 4 to see the resolution of the poem and the point of the poem.*

4. *What condition common to the children is suggested by the images in stanza 1?*

5. *Explain the pun* reciting *in its relationship to the "gnarled disease" of the father.*

6. *Distinguish the different worlds in stanza 2. Distinguish the different windows in stanza 4. How do the two main images of Shakespeare and the Tyrolese map in stanzas 2–3 connect to the different worlds?*

7. *Find contrasting images of health and deterioration. What pattern is there in the imagery?*

8. *Explain the relationship between nature, books, and children in stanza 4.*

Part II

The Poetic Idiom

Chapter 4

The Image

An image is anything that we can see, hear, smell, touch, or taste. That is, an image is anything that we can experience through the senses. An image may be a whole object (apple), or it may be a set of images appealing to more than one sense (hot, crackling fire). It may include an action (falling apple).

Note that in the above examples the image is the object referred to rather than the word itself. For the sake of convenience the word *apple* is called an image though we realize of course that it is literally a word that represents the physical object that grows on apple trees.

We *see* people and trees and the sun. We *hear* cars and lawnmowers. Food, flowers, and perfume—not to mention less pleasant odors—stimulate our sense of *smell*. We *touch* clothes, water, flesh. We *taste* food and drink. A girl is sensitive to the slightest change in clothing fashion. A boy can tell the make and model of most cars. We are aware of people. We can tell what mood they are in by their gestures, their facial expressions, the tone of their voices, how they are reaching toward us, and so on.

Poetry demands that we intensify our response to images. The reader must do his part in making an image real. Yew, axe, rose, ship, night, wolf, tomb, cataract, tears—these are words chosen at random from poems. They remain merely words until we apply our own experience and imagination to make them vivid.

Find the images in the following poem and identify the sense that each appeals to. Remember that an image may be more than a single word.

THAW

Over the land freckled with snow half-thawed
The speculating rooks at their nests cawed,
And saw from elm-tops, delicate as flower of grass,
What we below could not see, Winter pass.

—Edward Thomas

Images are important in poetry for one basic reason: they are concrete. And because they are concrete, they communicate immediately and intensely to the reader. Concreteness is one of the surest means of communication. Abstractions like "discomfort" and "comfort" are vague. Their implications vary from person to person. An image, on the other hand, arouses similar reactions in almost every reader. Shakespeare, for example, in his description of winter, uses vivid, common images to make the reader feel the discomfort and comfort of winter.

WHEN ICICLES HANG

When icicles hang by the wall,
    And Dick the shepherd blows his nail,
And Tom bears logs into the hall,
    And milk comes frozen home in pail,
When blood is nipped and ways be foul,   5
    Then nightly sings the staring owl:
        "Tu-whit, tu-who!"
        A merry note,
While greasy Joan doth keel the pot.

When all aloud the wind doth blow,   10
    And coughing drowns the parson's saw,
And birds sit brooding in the snow,
    And Marian's nose looks red and raw,
When roasted crabs hiss in the bowl,
    Then nightly sings the staring owl: 15
        "Tu-whit, tu-who!"
        A merry note,
While greasy Joan doth keel the pot.

—William Shakespeare

This song, from *Love's Labour's Lost*, consists almost entirely of simple images. All five senses are drawn upon. The weather is cold.

There are icicles, the milk is frozen, the wind blows, people react. The shepherd blows on his fingers to warm them, birds sit in the snow, the woman's nose is red. It is the time of coughs that drown out the parson.

Opposed to these images of cold and discomfort are images of warmth and genial anticipation. Each stanza has the same structure: images of discomfort are balanced by images of genial relief. Tom brings the logs for a fire, crab apples are being cooked, the maidservant cools the pot, and the owl sings "a merry note." This is the special joy of winter, the comfort and geniality that man creates for himself to escape the cold. The images enable us to feel this mood, even to the anticipation of tasting the food in preparation. This is "winter" described and made immediate by images.

Instead of explaining what he means abstractly and at length, the poet uses an image which the reader actualizes in his imagination. From this image the reader himself has a reaction, a feeling by which the poet communicates with him. The poet does not have to tell us in abstractions that Marian's nose is cold and sore. The image of "red and raw" makes us see and feel the discomfort.

Suppose the subject is love and gratitude and peace and the beauty of ordinary life. Whitman expresses these emotions through images in the following passage from *When Lilacs Last in the Door-yard Bloom'd*, his poem on the death of Lincoln.

> O what shall I hang on the chamber walls?
> And what shall the pictures be that I hang on the walls,
> To adorn the burial-house of him I love?
>
> Pictures of growing spring and farms and homes,
> With the Fourth-month eve at sundown, and the gray smoke lucid
>   and bright,   5
> With floods of the yellow gold of the gorgeous, indolent, sinking
>   sun, burning, expanding the air,
> With the fresh sweet herbage under foot, and the pale green leaves
>   of the trees prolific,
> In the distance the flowing glaze, the breast of the river, with a
>   wind-dapple here and there,
> With ranging hills on the banks, with many a line against the sky,
>   and shadows,
> And the city at hand with dwellings so dense, and stacks of chim-
>   neys,   10
> And all the scenes of life and the workshops, and the workmen
>   homeward returning.

In the background are death and mourning. There are certain conventions associated with death. Death is part of the natural cycle. The death of nature in the winter is followed by new life in the spring. The death of man is followed by his spiritual rebirth. So Whitman sets his picture in the spring ("Fourth-month eve").

The grief of Lincoln's death overshadows the nation. At the same time, like all deaths, it implies rebirth. Since Lincoln is identified as the symbol of the nation, the rebirth of his spirit is best conveyed in the picture of spring over America that Whitman sketches in generalized images. This picture is Lincoln's legacy. It is the rebirth of his spirit in growth and peace and beauty and broad landscape.

There are images of life: "growing spring," "homes," "gray smoke," "fresh sweet herbage," "all the scenes of life." There are images of light: the smoke is "lucid and bright," "the gorgeous, indolent, sinking sun," the "flowing glaze" of the river. Everything is growing, expansive: "growing spring," and "the sun, burning, expanding the air." There is the fluid beauty of the river, suggesting life and movement, and there is the freedom and expanse of the "ranging hills." There is the life of masses of people ("dwellings so dense") and a feeling of activity and completeness in the scene of the workmen returning home at evening. After the introductory lines, the passage begins with the images of growing spring and concludes on a note of fulfillment and peace. This is the spirit of Lincoln and his bequest to the nation. The effect is accomplished entirely through images.

Let us take an example of images used to express an abstraction—the power and scope of the brain.

THE BRAIN IS WIDER THAN THE SKY

The brain is wider than the sky,
   For, put them side by side,
The one the other will include
   With ease, and you beside.

The brain is deeper than the sea,   5
   For, hold them, blue to blue,
The one the other will absorb,
   As sponges, buckets do.

The brain is just the weight of God,
   For, lift them, pound for pound,   *10*
And they will differ, if they do,
   As syllable from sound.

—Emily Dickinson

The poem gives a feeling of the power and scope of the brain. The first two stanzas use the images of the sky and the sea to suggest that man dominates his environment. The phrasing implies man's ability to grasp effortlessly the widest sky and the deepest sea within his comprehension. From this sense of power, the poet proceeds in the third stanza to introduce man's affinity with God. Man's greatness and his strength are in his spirit ("The brain is just the weight of God").

To make her point vivid and immediate, the poet has used homely images (sponges, buckets, syllable) and images of action ("put them side by side," "hold them," "lift them"). It is by these images that we feel the power and scope of the brain. We understand that the power of comprehension is the divine power ("weight") in man.

Tennyson's "Break, Break, Break" is more indirect in its image pattern. The sea and its related images carry almost the whole burden of the meanings, functioning as emotional equivalents for the thoughts the poet cannot express.

BREAK, BREAK, BREAK

Break, break, break,
    On thy cold gray stones, O Sea!
And I would that my tongue could utter
    The thoughts that arise in me.

O well for the fisherman's boy,   5
    That he shouts with his sister at play!
O well for the sailor lad,
    That he sings in his boat on the bay!

And the stately ships go on
    To their haven under the hill;   10
But O for the touch of a vanished hand,
    And the sound of a voice that is still!

Break, break, break
    At the foot of thy crags, O Sea!
But the tender grace of a day that is dead   15
    Will never come back to me.

—*Alfred, Lord Tennyson*

The dominant image of the sea ties together the other images. The boy and his sister, the sailor, and the ship are harmoniously related to the sea. The people are happy, and the stately ship has a haven it is going to. The speaker, however, has a more complex relationship to the images. A similarity between the gloom of the speaker and the scene is implied in the word *And*. There is also a significant contrast. He cannot "utter the thoughts that arise" in him, but the other people can give vent to their emotions. They shout and sing, perhaps because they are meaningfully related to others and to their activities. The speaker's silence is a prelude to and a reflection of the loss of what he once meaningfully related to ("the sound of a voice that is still," which is now gone with the "vanished hand"). These images explain the speaker's isolation and the contrast between the sea and its happy world on the one hand and his own internal emptiness on the other.

Finally, in the last stanza, the speaker contrasts the insistent beat of the sea — now implying the steady round of the life connected with it — to his own loss. Perhaps the sea here becomes a symbol of fate. The loss is irrevocable. In other words, the image of the sea suggests both life and death, happiness and sorrow, as it is associated with one set of images or the other. This poem is an excellent example of the function of imagery: the images are concrete, and because they are concrete, they communicate immediately and intensely.

EXERCISE: Identifying Images

1. Tell which of the senses each of the following images appeals to.
    a.   a patient etherized upon a table. (Eliot)
    b.   Go and catch a falling star. (Donne)
    c.   Where ignorant armies clash by night. (Arnold)
    d.   The sedge has wither'd from the lake
         And no birds sing. (Keats)
    e.   And soon I saw a roaring wind. (Coleridge)
    f.   Drink deep, or taste not the Pierian spring. (Pope)
    g.   and taste
         Good thick stupefying incense smoke! (Browning)
    h.   My love is like a red, red rose. (Burns)
    i.   I heard the trailing garments of the Night. (Longfellow)
    j.   The winds that will be howling at all hours,
         And are up-gathered now like sleeping flowers. (Wordsworth)

2. Find twenty images from the poems in the anthology, Part V, at the back of the book. Choose at least two from each of the five senses.

Study Poems

HEAT

O wind, rend open the heat,
cut apart the heat,
rend it to tatters.

Fruit cannot drop
through this thick air—   5
fruit cannot fall into heat
that presses up and blunts
the points of pears
and rounds the grapes.

Cut through the heat—   10
plow through it,
turning it on either side
of your path.

       —H. D. *(Hilda Doolittle)*

Aids to Analysis

1. *What senses do the images appeal to?*

2. *To what extent are the images appropriate for the subject?*

SONG

Lovely hill-torrents are
    At cold winterfall;
Among the earth's silence, they
    Stonily call.

Gone Autumn's pageantry;   5
    Through woods all bare
With strange, locked voices
    Shining they stare!

       —W. J. *Turner*

Aids to Analysis

Much of the effect of this poem is achieved by images involving contrast (life, movement, sound, movement against the opposite). Pick out the images and note the contrasts—as, "silence" vs. "call"; "stonily" vs. "call."

A DESCRIPTION OF THE MORNING

Now hardly here and there an hackney-coach
Appearing, showed the ruddy morn's approach.
Now Betty from her master's bed had flown,
And softly stole to discompose her own;
The slip-shod 'prentice from his master's door   5
Had pared the dirt, and sprinkled round the floor.
Now Moll had whirled her mop with dextrous airs,
Prepared to scrub the entry and the stairs.
The youth with broomy stumps began to trace
The kennel-edge, where wheels had worn the place.   10
The small-coal man was heard with cadence deep,
Till drowned in shriller notes of chimney-sweep:
Duns at his lordship's gate began to meet;
And brickdust Moll had screamed through half the street.
The turnkey now his flock returning sees,   15
Duly let out a-nights to steal for fees:
The watchful bailiffs take their silent stands,
And schoolboys lag with satchels in their hands.

—Jonathan Swift

Aids to Analysis

The overall tone of the poem is realistic. List images that contribute to this tone.

THE SKATERS

Black swallows swooping or gliding
In a flurry of entangled loops and curves;
The skaters skim over the frozen river.
And the grinding click of their skates as they
    impinge upon the surface,
Is like the brushing together of thin wing-tips
    of silver.

—John Gould Fletcher

Aids to Analysis

1. *Analyze the imagery in the poem for coherence. Define the sound of a "grinding click." What are the respective meanings of "skim over" and "impinge upon"?*

2. *The two main images are the swallows and the skaters. How would you describe their relationship?*

THE SHELL

I

And then I pressed the shell
Close to my ear,
And listened well.

And straightway, like a bell,
Came low and clear   5
The slow, sad murmur of far distant seas

Whipped by an icy breeze
Upon a shore
Wind-swept and desolate.

It was a sunless strand that never bore   10
The footprint of a man,
Nor felt the weight

Since time began
Of any human quality or stir,
Save what the dreary winds and wave incur.   15

II

And in the hush of waters was the sound
Of pebbles, rolling round;
For ever rolling, with a hollow sound:

And bubbling sea-weeds, as the waters go,
Swish to and fro   20
Their long cold tentacles of slimy grey;

There was no day;
Nor ever came a night
Setting the stars alight

To wonder at the moon: 25
Was twilight only, and the frightened croon,
Smitten to whimpers, of the dreary wind

And waves that journeyed blind . . .
And then I loosed my ear. — Oh, it was sweet
To hear a cart go jolting down the street!

—James Stephens

Aids to Analysis

1. *What images bring out the inhuman qualities of the scene?*

2. *What indications are there that the images may (or may not) be recalled from actual experience?*

3. *What is the essential difference between the images of the last two lines and the preceding ones?*

THE ENAMEL GIRL

Fearful of beauty, I always went
Timidly indifferent:

Dainty, hesitant, taking in
Just what was tiniest and thin;

Careful not to care   5
For burning beauty in blue air;

Wanting what my hand could touch—
That not too much;

Looking not to left or right
On a honey-silent night;   10

Fond of arts and trinkets, if
Imperishable and stiff.

They never played me false, nor fell
Into fine dust. They lasted well.

They lasted till you came, and then   15
When you went, sufficed again.

But for you, they had been quite
All I needed for my sight.

You faded. I never knew
How to unfold as flowers do,   20

Or how to nourish anything
To make it grow. I wound a wing

With one caress; with one kiss
Break most fragile ecstasies . . .

Now terror touches me when I   25
Dream I am touching a butterfly.

—Genevieve Taggard

Aids to Analysis

Be sure of the meaning of enamel.

1.   *How is the image of enamel related to the idea of fear and hesitancy of the first 14 lines?*

2.   *What two general kinds or qualities of experience are contrasted in lines 1–14?*

3.   *What kind of experiences "never played one false"?*

4.   *What effect did the speaker's lover have on her? What effect did she have on her lover?*

SONNET 116

Let me not to the marriage of true minds
Admit impediments. Love is not love
Which alters when it alteration finds,
Or bends with the remover to remove.
O, no! it is an ever-fixèd mark   5
That looks on tempests and is never shaken;
It is the star to every wand'ring bark,
Whose worth's unknown, although his height be taken.
Love's not Time's fool, though rosy lips and cheeks
Within his bending sickle's compass come;   10
Love alters not with his brief hours and weeks,
But bears it out even to the edge of doom.
    If this be error, and upon me proved,
    I never writ, nor no man ever loved.

—*William Shakespeare*

Aids to Analysis

1.   *Explain the meaning of lines 1–4.*

2.   *Define the following words:* mark, bark, compass.

3.   *What theme in lines 1–4 is illustrated by the images in lines 5–8? What theme in lines 1–4 is illustrated by the images in lines 9–12?*

TO AUTUMN

I

Season of mists and mellow fruitfulness,
　Close bosom-friend of the maturing sun;
Conspiring with him how to load and bless
　With fruit the vines that round the thatch-eves run;
To bend with apples the mossed cottage-trees,　　　　　*5*
　And fill all fruit with ripeness to the core;
　　To swell the gourd, and plump the hazel shells
With a sweet kernel; to set budding more,
　And still more, later flowers for the bees,
　Until they think warm days will never cease,　　　　*10*
　　For Summer has o'er-brimmed their clammy cells.

II

Who hath not seen thee oft amid thy store?
　Sometimes whoever seeks abroad may find
Thee sitting careless on a granary floor,
　Thy hair soft-lifted by the winnowing wind;　　　　*15*
Or on a half-reaped furrow sound asleep,
　Drowsed with the fume of poppies, while thy hook
　　Spares the next swath and all its twinèd flowers:
And sometimes like a gleaner thou dost keep
　Steady thy laden head across a brook;　　　　　　*20*
　Or by a cider-press, with patient look,
　　Thou watchest the last oozings hours by hours.

III

Where are the songs of Spring? Ay, where are they?
　Think not of them, thou hast thy music too,—
While barrèd clouds bloom the soft-dying day,　　　　*25*
　And touch the stubble-plains with rosy hue;
Then in a wailful choir the small gnats mourn
　Among the river sallows, borne aloft
　　Or sinking as the light wind lives or dies;
And full-grown lambs loud bleat from hilly bourn;　　*30*
　Hedge-crickets sing; and now with treble soft
　The red-breast whistles from a garden-croft;
　　And gathering swallows twitter in the skies.

—John Keats

Aids to Analysis

1. *"To Autumn" has images appealing to each of the five senses. Find an example of each.*

2. *Keats uses specific images to create a dominant impression in each stanza. Identify the common quality that connects the images in each stanza.*

3. *State the theme of the poem in terms of the image pattern.*

KUBLA KHAN

In Xanadu did Kubla Khan
A stately pleasure-dome decree:
Where Alph, the sacred river, ran
Through caverns measureless to man
   Down to a sunless sea.   5
So twice five miles of fertile ground
With walls and towers were girdled round:
And there were gardens bright with sinuous rills,
Where blossomed many an incense-bearing tree;
And here were forests ancient as the hills,   10
Enfolding sunny spots of greenery.

But oh! that deep romantic chasm which slanted
Down the green hill athwart a cedarn cover!
A savage place! as holy and enchanted
As e'er beneath a waning moon was haunted   15
By woman wailing for her demon-lover!
And from this chasm, with ceaseless turmoil seething,
As if this earth in fast thick pants were breathing,
A mighty fountain momently was forced:
Amid whose swift half-intermitted burst   20
Huge fragments vaulted like rebounding hail,
Or chaffy grain beneath the thresher's flail:
And 'mid these dancing rocks at once and ever
It flung up momently the sacred river.

Five miles meandering with a mazy motion   25
Through wood and dale the sacred river ran,
Then reached the caverns measureless to man,
And sank in tumult to a lifeless ocean:
And 'mid this tumult Kubla heard from far
Ancestral voices prophesying war!   30
   The shadow of the dome of pleasure
   Floated midway on the waves;

Where was heard the mingled measure
From the fountain and the caves.
It was a miracle of rare device,   35
A sunny pleasure-dome with caves of ice!

A damsel with a dulcimer
In a vision once I saw:
It was an Abyssinian maid,
And on her dulcimer she played,   40
Singing of Mount Abora.
Could I revive within me
Her symphony and song,
To such a deep delight 'twould win me,
That with music loud and long,   45
I would build that dome in air,
That sunny dome! those caves of ice!
And all who heard should see them there,
And all should cry, Beware! Beware!
His flashing eyes, his floating hair!   50
Weave a circle round him thrice,
And close your eyes with holy dread,
For he on honey-dew hath fed,
And drunk the milk of Paradise.

—*Samuel Taylor Coleridge*

Aids to Analysis

1. *Stanza 1: What specifically do we know about the pleasure dome in this stanza?*

2. *Stanza 2: What does this stanza tell us about the origin and the course of the sacred river?*

3. *From your reading of stanzas 1 and 2, explain the difference in effect between the imagery describing the pleasure dome and the imagery describing the rest of the area.*

4. *Stanza 3: What is meant by "the mingled measure"? How is the pleasure dome "a miracle of rare device"?*

5. *Stanza 4: What is the relationship between music and the pleasure dome? Why would the sight of the speaker produce "holy dread"?*

6. *Trace the images of sound in the poem. What patterns do you find? For example, do you find a possible connection between such images as "ancestral voices," the tumult of the river, and the song of the damsel?*

Chapter 5

Metaphor
and Related Figures of Similarity

Figurative language is a way of saying one thing but actually meaning another. There are two basic figures of speech: metaphor and irony. This chapter will discuss metaphor and the next chapter will deal with irony.

Metaphor and its related figures are forms of comparison or similarity. Irony and its related figures deal in contrasts or incongruities. In each case, the literal image, phrase, or statement is in some way different from the intended or "real" meaning. In "The bird is flying" the bird is literal and nothing more than a bird, such as a sparrow or a robin. But the following statement is not made about a bird at all:

> The Bird of Time has but a little way
> To flutter, and the Bird is on the Wing.

The statement is about time, and the bird is figurative. Time is described as a bird in order to give a characteristic of the bird to time—its swiftness. In this way abstractions can be made immediate and concrete, by comparing them to images common to us.

Figurative language is not always so easy to identify as is the "Bird of Time." Because figurative language is used so much in poetry, the student must learn to distinguish the literal and the figurative.

EXERCISE: Distinguish between literal and figurative statements. If the statement is figurative, identify the word or words that make it so.

1.   My mistress' eyes are nothing like the sun. (Shakespeare)

2.   No where lives a woman true and fair. (Donne)

3. Beauty is truth, truth beauty. (Keats)

4. And ice, mast high, came floating by
    As green as emerald. (Coleridge)

5. Full fathom five thy father lies;
    Of his bones are coral made. (Shakespeare)

6. The snow had begun in the gloaming,
    And busily all the night
    Had been heaping field and highway
    With a silence deep and white. (James Russell Lowell)

7. But a bold peasantry, their country's pride,
    When once destroyed, can never be supplied. (Goldsmith)

8. I was angry with my friend,
    I told my wrath, my wrath did end;
    I was angry with my foe,
    I told it not, my wrath did grow. (Blake)

9. I arise from dreams of thee
    In the first sweet sleep of night,
    When the winds are breathing low,
    And the stars are shining bright. (Shelley)

10. Flower in the crannied wall,
    I pluck you out of the crannies,
    I hold you here, root and all, in my hand,
    Little flower—but *if* I could understand
    What you are, root and all, and all in all,
    I should know what God and man is. (Tennyson)

Metaphor

A metaphor is a word or phrase that expresses, describes, or defines one thing as though it were another thing. The comparison applies certain characteristics of the one thing to the other. For example, the phrase "sunny disposition" brings together two different things, the sun and the disposition, in order to describe the disposition in terms of some of the pleasant characteristics we associate with the sun.

Because metaphors are so important in poetry, you should learn to identify them readily.

WHEN LOVELY WOMAN STOOPS TO FOLLY

When lovely woman stoops to folly,
  And finds too late that men betray,
What charm can soothe her melancholy,
  What art can wash her guilt away?

The only art her guilt to cover,   5
  To hide her shame from every eye,
To give repentance to her lover,
  And wring his bosom — is to die.

— Oliver Goldsmith

The main use of metaphor here is in the verbs — *stoops*, *soothe*, *wash*, *cover*, *hide*, and *wring*. Literally they would indicate physical actions, but here they describe emotional or mental conditions. "Wash her guilt away" is a metaphor because *guilt* is an abstraction, but the word *wash* implies that it is physical, like dirt, and also like dirt something to be removed as undesirable. Another, "To hide her shame from every eye" makes shame (an abstraction) seem physical by implying that it can be hidden from sight, and also something unworthy that should be hidden. A third example is "wring his bosom." Both *wring* and *bosom* are physical in their implications, but we know that one does not literally *wring* a bosom. *Bosom*, then, refers by association to feelings or emotions. Any "wringing" is to be done figuratively to the emotions, and therefore wring means *afflict*. The phrase thus gives the idea of making the lover feel the emotion of remorse.

It should not be too difficult to recognize metaphors and to realize their importance if we understand that our language is full of metaphor. Although we as individuals do not often create metaphors, we use them more frequently than we may think. We have a "flash" of insight, and so we "jump" at a chance. We "drive" a bargain, we "smooth over" "ruffled" feelings, and we "cut" a class.

The language is full of dead metaphors that also attest to the metaphorical quality of ordinary language. Although these dead metaphors have lost their power as figurative language, we can easily see their origin in metaphorical relationships. A bed has a "head," a "foot," and "legs"; a book has "leaves" and a "spine."

Slang is another instance of metaphor, for slang is basically metaphor. "Cool," "chick," "square," "hit the road," "hit the sack," and so on, enliven our language as long as they stay fresh. Such words reflect man's effort to make abstractions immediate and concrete and to express his experience imaginatively.

Thus, although the poet's language is more disciplined and more original than ordinary speech, its metaphors may not be so far removed from our own ways of thinking as we may at first believe.

EXERCISE: Identifying Metaphors

1.   List fifteen metaphors in common use. For instance, from schoolwork: "he never cracks a book"; from sports: "gridiron"; from cars: "hot rod"; from business: "in the red." Distinguish between dead metaphors and those that still have figurative effect.

2.   Identify the metaphors in the following poems and be prepared to explain their literal meaning.

AN ARAB LOVE SONG

The hunchèd camels of the night
Trouble the bright
And silver waters of the moon.
The Maiden of the Morn will soon
Through Heaven stray and sing,   5
Star gathering.

Now while the dark about our loves is strewn,
Light of my dark, blood of my heart, O come!
And night will catch her breath up, and be dumb.

Leave thy father, leave thy mother   10
And thy brother;
Leave the black tents of thy tribe apart!
Am I not thy father and thy brother,
And thy mother?
And thou—what needest with thy tribe's black tents   15
Who hast the red pavilion of my heart?

—*Francis Thompson*

Aids to Analysis

1.   *What lead does the title give us in identifying the speaker in the poem and the person to whom the poem is addressed?*

2.   *What request is the speaker making?*

3.   *Explain the meaning of the following metaphors: "hunchèd camels of the night"; "silver waters of the moon"; "Maiden of the Morn"; "star gathering"; "red pavilion of my heart."*

4.   *Identify the other metaphors in the poem.*

HOPE IS THE THING WITH FEATHERS

Hope is the thing with feathers
That perches in the soul,
And sings the tune without the words,
And never stops at all,

And sweetest in the gale is heard;   *5*
And sore must be the storm
That could abash the little bird
That kept so many warm.

I've heard it in the chillest land,
And on the strangest sea;   *10*
Yet, never, in extremity,
It asked a crumb of me.

— Emily Dickinson

Aids to Analysis

1. *What particular images develop the dominant bird metaphor in the poem?*

2. *Explain the meaning of the following metaphors: "the tune without the words"; "That kept so many warm"; "never, in extremity,/It asked a crumb of me."*

THE LAST WORD

Creep into thy narrow bed,
Creep, and let no more be said!
Vain thy onset! all stands fast.
Thou thyself must break at last.

Let the long contention cease!   *5*
Geese are swans, and swans are geese.
Let them have it how they will!
Thou art tired; best be still.

They out-talked thee, hissed thee, tore thee?
Better men fared thus before thee;   *10*
Fired their ringing shot and passed,
Hotly charged — and sank at last.

Charge once more, then, and be dumb!
Let the victors, when they come,
When the forts of folly fall,   15
Find thy body by the wall!

—Matthew Arnold

Aids to Analysis

1.   *What is the dominant image pattern in the poem?*

2.   *What does the title tell us about the metaphorical implications of this image pattern?*

3.   *What does the question mark in line 9 imply?*

4.   *What is the literal meaning of line 6?*

5.   *What are the "forts of folly"?*

6.   *What does the last line mean?*

Metaphors are not merely decorative. They are functional, and perhaps essential, in developing a theme and conveying the emotional force necessary to the experience of a poem. Let us look at Kipling's "Recessional" to see how metaphor may operate in a poem:

RECESSIONAL

God of our fathers, known of old,
   Lord of our far-flung battle line,
Beneath whose awful hand we hold
   Dominion over palm and pine—
Lord God of Hosts, be with us yet,   5
Lest we forget—lest we forget!

The tumult and the shouting dies;
   The Captains and the Kings depart:
Still stands Thine ancient sacrifice,
   An humble and a contrite heart.   10
Lord God of Hosts, be with us yet,
Lest we forget—lest we forget!

Far-called, our navies melt away;

On dune and headland sinks the fire:
Lo, all our pomp of yesterday   *15*
   Is one with Nineveh and Tyre!
Judge of the Nations, spare us yet,
Lest we forget—lest we forget!

If, drunk with sight of power, we loose
   Wild tongues that have not Thee in awe,   *20*
Such boasting as the Gentiles use,
   Or lesser breeds without the Law—
Lord God of Hosts, be with us yet,
Lest we forget—lest we forget!

For heathen heart that puts her trust   *25*
   In reeking tube and iron shard,
All valiant dust that builds on dust,
   And guarding, calls not Thee to guard.
For frantic boast and foolish word—
Thy Mercy on Thy People, Lord!   *30*

The metaphors relate consistently to two main points of reference, war and religion. The images relating to war are contrasted to images relating to religion, by which device Kipling contrasts pride in military power with spiritual humility. He suggests through a series of metaphors the vanity of military power (*dies, melt away, sinks, drunk,* etc.) and develops the central theme that physical force is empty (*dust*) without the true power of humility (*Thine ancient sacrifice, contrite heart*). All the while the meaning behind the metaphor is seen in the biblical allusions. We need to refer to the Old Testament to understand allusions such as "Lord God of Hosts." We also need to have an idea of the biblical meaning of *dust* if line 27 is to make any sense.

By means of metaphor Kipling conveys the relationship between pride in military power and spiritual humility. That is, he is exploring war and religion in metaphorical terms. His conclusion is more complex than it appears to be at first. He is not saying that war is bad in itself, only that the "frantic boast" that puts its reliance only on military force is evil. He does not have to argue this point. His allusions to the Old Testament give him all the argument he needs. Kipling is warning his contemporaries that they must be humble before God and do His will or (stanza 3), like the heathen cities of old, their pomp and power will disappear. Humility leads us to do God's will, in which case we are assured of virtuous action. His people should speak and act within God's law.

Study Poems

TO LUCASTA, GOING TO THE WARS

Tell me not, sweet, I am unkind,
   That from the nunnery
Of thy chaste breast and quiet mind,
   To war and arms I fly.

True, a new mistress now I chase: 5
   The first foe in the field;
And with a stronger faith embrace
   A sword, a horse, a shield.

Yet this inconstancy is such
   As thou, too, shall adore;   10
I could not love thee, dear, so much,
   Loved I not honor more.

          —*Richard Lovelace*

Aids to Analysis

1. *Explain the argument or conflict in stanza 1.*

2. *What is the "new mistress"?*

3. *What is the meaning of "inconstancy" in this context?*

4. *What three patterns of imagery and metaphor are represented by* mistress, foe, *and* faith *in stanza 2? What other words in the poem are connected to each of these three words?*

A SOLDIER

He is that fallen lance that lies as hurled,
That lies uplifted now, come dew, come rust,
But still lies pointed as it plowed the dust.
If we who sight along it round the world,
See nothing worthy to have been its mark,   5
It is because like men we look too near,
Forgetting that as fitted to the sphere,
Our missiles always make too short an arc.
They fall, they rip the grass, they intersect
The curve of earth, and striking, break their own;   10

They make us cringe for metal-point on stone.
But this we know, the obstacle that checked
And tripped the body, shot the spirit on
Further than target ever showed or shone.

—*Robert Frost*

Aids to Analysis

In the first reading, pay careful attention to the meaning of uplifted, *and identify the antecedent of "their own" in line 10.*

1. *Identify and explain the various ways in which the "He" is like a lance.*

2. *What does* obstacle *in line 12 mean?*

3. *What do* body *and* spirit *in line 13 have to do with the theme of the poem?*

4. *What other images in the poem are related to body and spirit respectively? What is the meaning of these metaphors?*

SONNET 65

Since brass, nor stone, nor earth, nor boundless sea,
But sad mortality o'er-sways their power,
How with this rage shall beauty hold a plea,
Whose action is no stronger than a flower?
O, how shall summer's honey breath hold out   5
Against the wrackful siege of battering days,
When rocks impregnable are not so stout,
Nor gates of steel so strong, but Time decays?
O fearful meditation! where, alack,
Shall Time's best jewel from Time's chest lie hid?   10
Or what strong hand can hold his swift foot back?
Or who his spoil of beauty can forbid?
        O, none, unless this miracle have might,
        That in black ink my love may still shine bright.

—*William Shakespeare*

Aids to Analysis

1. *Find the metaphors that state the power of time, and those relating to beauty.*

2. *What words relate these two subjects of time and beauty?*

3. *Having now identified the main subjects and the metaphors that relate them, state the theme of the poem down to line 12.*

4. *Do you think that the metaphors in the last two lines are clearly related to the metaphors in the preceding twelve lines? Explain your judgment.*

Other Figures of Similarity

Simile. A simile is a comparison between two unlike things using *as, like,* or *than.* "My love is like a red, red rose" is a simile. So is "his nose was as sharp as a pen." "Mary is prettier than a spring morning" is a simile, but "Mary is prettier than Susan" is not, because the comparison is literal.

The first stanza in this poem by Christina Rossetti is developed mainly by similes.

A BIRTHDAY

My heart is like a singing bird
  Whose nest is in a watered shoot;
My heart is like an apple-tree
  Whose boughs are bent with thickset fruit;
My heart is like a rainbow shell   5
  That paddles in a halcyon sea;
My heart is gladder than all these
  Because my love is come to me.

Raise me a dais of silk and down;
  Hang it with vair and purple dyes;   *10*
Carve it in doves and pomegranates,
  And peacocks with a hundred eyes;
Work it in gold and silver grapes,
  In leaves and silver fleurs-de-lys;
Because the birthday of my life   *15*
  Is come, my love is come to me.

Personification. Personification gives human qualities to an abstract idea, an inanimate object, or an animal. The use may be brief, as in the first line of Blake's "Mad Song": "The wild winds weep" and later in the poem "makes mad the roaring winds."

A more sustained use of personification is seen in Byron's "Sonnet on Chillon." The use of *thou* and *thy* in reference to Liberty and later the use of *thy* referring to Chillon demonstrate the personification of both an abstraction and a physical object. Capitalizing the initial letter of an abstraction, such as Liberty, is also a common means of personifying. Compare Milton's "Laughter, holding both his sides" and Keats' "Joy, whose hand is ever at his lips." But like Byron's *Liberty*, the personification does not depend merely upon capitalization but upon the image with human characteristics ("hand . . . lips"). Note that "thy sons" in line 5 gives the personification an additional dimension, that of motherhood.

SONNET ON CHILLON

Eternal Spirit of the chainless Mind!
Brightest in dungeons, Liberty! thou art:
For there thy habitation is the heart—
The heart which love of thee alone can bind;
And when thy sons to fetters are consigned—   5
To fetters, and the damp vault's dayless gloom,
Their country conquers with their martyrdom,
And Freedom's fame finds wings on every wind.
Chillon! thy prison is a holy place,
And thy sad floor an altar—for 'twas trod,   10
Until his very steps have left a trace
Worn, as if thy cold pavement were a sod,
By Bonnivard!—May none those marks efface!
For they appeal from tyranny to God.

—George Gordon, Lord Byron

Apostrophe. Apostrophe is a type of personification which addresses an inanimate thing as if it were living or an absent person as if he were present. In "Sonnet on Chillon," apostrophe is used in *Liberty* (line 2) and *Chillon* (line 9).

Synecdoche. Synecdoche substitutes a significant part for the whole, as factory *hands* (but not *teeth*) for worker; *wheels* (but not *trunk*) as slang for *car*. The Ancient Mariner cries "A sail! A sail!" which is synecdoche for "A ship! A ship!"

Metonymy. Metonymy is the use of one image for another that it is so closely related to that when we mention the one we think of the other: *crown* for *king*. "The Moving Finger writes. . . ."

Synaesthesia. Synaesthesia is the mixing of images that appeal to more than one sense: "cool blues," "warm reds," "a touching sight," "bell-shaped tones." "And the press'd watch return'd a silver sound" from Pope's *The Rape of the Lock*. In the following poem, line 7 uses synaesthesia:

AMPLE MAKE THIS BED

Ample make this bed.
Make this bed with awe;
In it wait till judgment break
Excellent and fair.

Be its mattress straight,   5
Be its pillow round;
Let no sunrise' yellow noise
Interrupt this ground.

— *Emily Dickinson*

The conceit. A conceit is a farfetched or elaborate figure of speech. Romeo's exclamation on seeing Juliet at the balcony is a conceit.

But, soft! what light through yonder window breaks?
It is the east, and Juliet is the sun.
Arise, fair sun, and kill the envious moon,
Who is already pale and sick with grief
That thou, her maid, art far more fair than she.

Juliet is metaphorically transformed into the sun. The sun is then personified and apostrophized. The moon also is personified, and then compared ironically to Juliet, who has suddenly returned to her human status as maid to the moon.

The conceit is more popular in some periods than in others. Elizabethan love poetry and the poetry of the seventeenth-century metaphysical poets abound in conceits.

EXERCISE: Identify the figures of similarity in the following statements.

1. For my poor heart is run astray
   After the eyes that passed this way. (Pope)

2. Your hands must come
   To the cold tomb. (Shirley)

3. When I have seen by Time's fell hand defaced. (Shakespeare)

4. We have given our hearts away, a sordid boon! (Wordsworth)

5. King Arthur's table, man by man
   Had fallen in Lyonesse about their Lord. (Tennyson)

6. I hid my heart in a nest of roses. (Swinburne)

7.   But most by numbers judge a poet's song. (Pope)

8.   Her long loose yellow locks lyke golden wyre. (Spenser)

9.   To see a world in a grain of sand. (Blake)

10.   When Faith is kneeling by his bed of death,
      And innocence is closing up his eyes. (Drayton)

11.   Ride ten thousand days and nights
      Till age snow white hairs on thee. (Donne)

12.   To follow knowledge like a sinking star. (Tennyson)

13.   Brightest in dungeons, Liberty, thou art. (Byron)

14.   The ice about thy heart melts as the snow. (Longfellow)

15.   The grave's a fine and private place,
      But none, I think, do there embrace. (Marvell)

Study Poems

TO A. D.

The nightingale has a lyre of gold,
    The lark's is a clarion call;
And the blackbird plays but a boxwood flute,
    But I love him best of all.

For his song is all of the joy of life,   5
    And we in the mad, spring weather,
We two have listened till he sang
    Our hearts and lips together.

—William Ernest Henley

Aids to Analysis

1.   Identify and label the figures of speech in stanza 1. What impressions do they give of the songs of the three birds?

2.   What kind of figure is "mad, spring weather"? What kind is "he sang/Our hearts and lips together"?

LONDON, 1802

Milton! thou shouldst be living at this hour:
England hath need of thee: she is a fen
Of stagnant waters: altar, sword, and pen,
Fireside, the heroic wealth of hall and bower,
Have forfeited their ancient English dower   5
Of inward happiness. We are selfish men;
Oh! raise us up, return to us again;
And give us manners, virtue, freedom, power.
Thy soul was like a Star, and dwelt apart;
Thou hadst a voice whose sound was like the sea: 10
Pure as the naked heavens, majestic, free,
So didst thou travel on life's common way,
In cheerful godliness; and yet thy heart
The lowliest duties on herself did lay.

—William Wordsworth

Aids to Analysis

1. *Identify and label the first figure of speech in the sonnet.*

2. *What kind of figures are* altar, sword, *and* pen?

3. *What is the subject of "Have forfeited"? In view of the word "their" in line 5, what figure of speech is the subject of "Have forfeited"? Compare this answer to question 2 above.*

4. *Identify the similes in the poem.*

5. *What figure of speech is* heart *in line 13?*

SONG: TO CELIA

Drink to me only with thine eyes,
  And I will pledge with mine;
Or leave a kiss but in the cup,
  And I'll not look for wine.
The thirst that from the soul doth rise   5
  Doth ask a drink divine;
But might I of Jove's nectar sup,
  I would not change for thine.

I sent thee late a rosy wreath,
  Not so much honouring thee   10

> As giving it a hope, that there
>   It could not withered be.
> But thou thereon didst only breathe,
>   And sent'st it back to me;
> Since when it grows, and smells, I swear,   15
>   Not of itself but thee.

—*Ben Jonson*

Aids to Analysis

1. *What kinds of figures of speech are in lines 1 and 2? What do these lines mean?*

2. *Is the "cup" in line 3 literal or metaphorical? In answering, determine its relationship to "Drink" in line 1.*

3. *State the theme as it is developed in stanza 1.*

4. *What is the meaning of the action of sending the rosy wreath and having it returned? What relationship does this action show between the man and the woman in the poem?*

5. *Determine whether or not stanza 2 develops the theme of stanza 1. Be ready to explain your analysis.*

MY GALLEY, CHARGED WITH FORGETFULNESS

> My galley, charged with forgetfulness,
> Thorough sharp seas in winter nights doth pass
> 'Tween rock and rock; and eke my foe, alas,
> That is my lord, steereth with cruelness;
> And every hour, a thought in readiness,   5
> As though that death were light in such a case;
> An endless wind doth tear the sail apace
> Of forced sighs, and trusty fearfulness;
> A rain of tears, a cloud of dark disdain,
> Hath done the wearied cords great hinderance;   10
> Wreathed with error and eke with ignorance,
> The stars be hid that led me to this pain.
> Drowned is reason that should me comfort,
> And I remain, despairing of the port.

—*Sir Thomas Wyatt*

Aids to Analysis

1. *State the theme as it is developed in the octave. Does the same development continue into the quatrain? Into the couplet? ("Thorough" in line 2 is our* through, *and "eke" in lines 3 and 11 is our* also.*)*

2. *The printer who first published this sonnet called it "The Lover Compareth His State to a Ship in Perilous Storm Tossed on the Sea." Does this supplied title help in determining the poem's theme? ("Charged with forgetfulness" in line 1 means that the poet's ship is freighted with neglect.)*

3. *Do you think the poem would have profited by a less metaphorical statement of its theme? Do you think that Wyatt (or Petrarch, from whose Italian Wyatt translated this poem) could have written 14 lines of poetry if he had more directly stated his theme?*

DAYS

Daughters of Time, the hypocritic Days,
Muffled and dumb like barefoot dervishes,
And marching single in an endless file,
Bring diadems and fagots in their hands.
To each they offer gifts after his will,   *5*
Bread, kingdoms, stars, and sky that holds them all.
I, in my pleachèd garden, watched the pomp,
Forgot my morning wishes, hastily
Took a few herbs and apples, and the Day
Turned and departed silent. I, too late,   *10*
Under her solemn fillet saw the scorn.

        — Ralph Waldo Emerson

Aids to Analysis

1. *The initial capital of "Days" in line 1 suggests that Emerson intended to personify the word. What other indications in the poem point to personification?*

2. *What figure of speech is "gifts"? What does "gifts" mean?*

3. *What are the more specific meanings of the various synonyms for "gifts" in the poem?*

4. *What reason is there for having the plural "Days" in line 1 but the singular "Day" in line 9?*

THE PULLEY

When God at first made man,
Having a glass of blessings standing by,
   "Let us," said He, "pour on him all we can.
Let the world's riches, which dispersèd lie,
   Contract into a span."   5

   So strength first made a way;
Then beauty flowed, then wisdom, honour, pleasure.
   When almost all was out, God made a stay,
Perceiving that, alone of all His treasure,
   Rest in the bottom lay.   10

   "For if I should," said He,
"Bestow this jewel also on my creature,
   He would adore my gifts instead of me
And rest in nature, not the God of nature;
   So both should losers be.   15

   "Yet let him keep the rest,
But keep them with repining restlessness.
   Let him be rich and weary, that at last,
If goodness lead him not, yet weariness
   May toss him to my breast."   20

            —*George Herbert*

Aids to Analysis

1. *In what sense can the situation in the poem be described as a "pulley"?*

2. *Would you consider this metaphor of the pulley to be a conceit? Explain.*

CARELESS LOVE

Who have been lonely once
Are comforted by their guns.
Affectionately they speak
To the dark beauty, whose cheek
Beside their own cheek glows.   5
They are calmed by such repose,
Such power held in hand;
Their young bones understand
The shudder in that frame.

Without nation, without name,   10
They give the load of love,
And it's returned, to prove
How much the husband heart
Can hold of it: for what
This nymphomaniac enjoys   15
Inexhaustibly is boys.

—*Stanley Kunitz*

Aids to Analysis

1.   *What words suggest that "guns" is personified?*

2.   *What is the literal and the metaphorical meaning of "nymphomaniac"?*

3.   *How would you describe the relationship between the soldier and his gun as described in this poem?*

4.   *What does the phrase "the husband heart" tell us of the relationship between the soldier and his gun?*

5.   *What does the dominant "love" metaphor tell us about the poet's idea of the character of the soldier?*

BECAUSE I COULD NOT STOP FOR DEATH

Because I could not stop for Death,
He kindly stopped for me;
The carriage held but just ourselves
And Immortality.

We slowly drove, he knew no haste,   5
And I had put away
My labor, and my leisure too,
For his civility.

We passed the school where children played
At wrestling in a ring;   10
We passed the fields of gazing grain,
We passed the setting sun.

We paused before a house that seemed
A swelling of the ground;
The roof was scarcely visible,   15
The cornice but a mound.

Since then 'tis centuries; but each
Feels shorter than the day
I first surmised the horses' heads
Were toward eternity.   *20*

— *Emily Dickinson*

Aids to Analysis

1.   *You will notice that Emily Dickinson capitalizes* Death *and* Immortality.
     How do you tell whether one or both of these words is a personification?

2.   *What figure of speech is* "put away" *in stanza 2?*

3.   *What are the metaphorical implications of* "school," "fields of gazing
     grain," *and* "setting sun" *in stanza 3?*

4.   *What is the* house *in stanza 4?*

5.   *What figure of speech is* carriage *in stanza 1? What does it mean?*

TOMORROW, AND TOMORROW, AND TOMORROW

Tomorrow, and tomorrow, and tomorrow,
Creeps in this petty pace from day to day
To the last syllable of recorded time,
And all our yesterdays have lighted fools
The way to dusty death. Out, out, brief candle!   *5*
Life's but a walking shadow, a poor player
That struts and frets his hour upon the stage
And then is heard no more: it is a tale
Told by an idiot, full of sound and fury,
Signifying nothing.   *10*

— *William Shakespeare*

Aids to Analysis

1.   *This passage from* Macbeth *(Act V, sc. v) contains images of movement,
     images of sound, and images of light. Identify them, decide what figures
     of speech they are, and explain their meaning.*

2.   *What relationship do you find between the images of light? The images
     of sound? The images of movement?*

3.   *What metaphors suggest brevity and signify* "nothing"?

TO HIS COY MISTRESS

Had we but world enough, and time,
This coyness, lady, were no crime.
We would sit down, and think which way
To walk, and pass our long love's day.
Thou by the Indian Ganges' side   5
Shouldst rubies find; I by the tide
Of Humber would complain. I would
Love you ten years before the flood,
And you should, if you please, refuse
Till the conversion of the Jews.   10
My vegetable love should grow
Vaster than empires and more slow;
An hundred years should go to praise
Thine eyes, and on thy forehead gaze;
Two hundred to adore each breast,   15
But thirty thousand to the rest;
An age at least to every part,
And the last age should show your heart.
For, lady, you deserve this state,
Nor would I love at lower rate.   20
   But at my back I always hear
Time's wingèd chariot hurrying near;
And yonder all before us lie
Deserts of vast eternity.
Thy beauty shall no more be found,   25
Nor, in thy marble vault, shall sound
My echoing song; then worms shall try
That long-preserved virginity,
And your quaint honour turn to dust,
And into ashes all my lust: 30
The grave's a fine and private place,
But none, I think, do there embrace.
   Now therefore, while the youthful hue
Sits on thy skin like morning dew,
And while thy willing soul transpires   35
At every pore with instant fires,
Now let us sport us while we may,
And now, like amorous birds of prey,
Rather at once our time devour
Than languish in his slow-chapped power.   40
Let us roll all our strength and all
Our sweetness up into one ball,
And tear our pleasures with rough strife
Thorough the iron gates of life;
Thus, though we cannot make our sun   45
Stand still, yet we will make him run.

                   — *Andrew Marvell*

Aids to Analysis

Identify all figures of speech and explain their meaning in the poem.

LOVE'S DIET

To what a cumbersome unwieldiness
And burdenous corpulence my love had grown,
    But that I did, to make it less,
    And keep it in proportion,
Give it a diet, made it feed upon   5
That which love worst endures, discretion.

Above one sigh a day I allowed him not,
Of which my fortune, and my faults had part;
    And if sometimes by stealth he got
    A she sigh from my mistress' heart,   10
And thought to feast on that, I let him see
'Twas neither very sound, nor meant to me.

If he wrung from me a tear, I brined it so
With scorn or shame, that him it nourished not;
    If he sucked hers, I let him know   15
    'Twas not a tear, which he had got;
His drink was counterfeit, as was his meat;
For, eyes which roll towards all, weep not, but sweat.

Whatever he would dictate, I writ that,
But burnt my letters; when she writ to me,   20
    And that that favour made him fat,
    I said, if any title be
Conveyed by this, Ah, what doth it avail,
To be the fortieth name in an entail?

Thus I reclaimed my buzzard love, to fly   25
At what, and when, and how, and where I choose;
    Now negligent of sport I lie,
    And now as other falconers use,
I spring a mistress, swear, write, sigh and weep;
And the game killed, or lost, go talk, and sleep.   30

—John Donne

Aids to Analysis

1.   *Outline the idea structure of the poem.*

2. *Identify the figures of speech illustrated in the following words to determine their meaning in the poem:* love; diet; by stealth; to feast; wrung; nourished; title; entail; to fly; game killed.

3. *In stanza 5 Donne uses "buzzard love" as the central image. What is the effect of changing this metaphor from the preceding stanzas?*

4. *What are the most obvious conceits in the poem?*

Chapter 6

Irony
and Related Figures of Incongruity

Irony is the expression of a discrepancy between the apparent and the real. There are three common types of irony: *verbal irony* (discrepancy between the real and the apparent meaning of words); *irony of situation* (discrepancy between the expected and the actual outcome); *dramatic irony* (discrepancy between what words mean to the speaker and what they mean to the reader or audience). **Verbal irony.** The following poem is an example of verbal irony:

ONCE IN A SAINTLY PASSION

Once in a saintly passion,
    I cried with desperate grief,
"O Lord, my heart is black with guile,
    Of sinners I am chief."
Then stooped my guardian angel   5
    And whispered from behind,
"Vanity, my little man,
    You're nothing of the kind."

           —*James Thomson*

The most notable incongruity in this humorous poem is that between the Christian teaching of humility and the supposed repentance of the speaker. With a sure sense of climax, Thomson does not reveal the irony until line 7 with the word *Vanity*. Vanity is a pride in false and showy things. Once we think of pride and vanity, the religious admonition to humility should occur to us. Now we have the incongruity that is the basis for irony. The speaker says that he is a repentant sinner, but in reality a good deal of sin in the form of vanity is lurking behind the pious words.

Other words now take on ironic overtones. "Saintly" is ironic because we know that he is really not "saintly," just proud to think he is so. "Passion," which in the Christian context implies the noble agony of a martyr, becomes a trivial emotion, as does the grief that he proclaims as "desperate." "Chief" becomes the epitome of self-righteousness, which is deflated by the patronizing "my little man." He is "nothing of the kind" — neither important enough nor honest enough to be chief of sinners and by implication nowhere near to being chief of repenters.

Irony of situation brings out the incongruity between what is expected and what actually happens or between what seems to be and what actually is. This use of irony is necessarily much more common in narrative than in lyric poetry. It is especially effective in drama and prose fiction. Poe's "The Masque of the Red Death" ends ironically when the revellers meet the Red Death in the castle-like abbey where they went to escape it. King Lear discovers that, contrary to his original belief, Cordelia is the true and loving daughter; the others are evil. The following poem illustrates irony of situation in light verse.

THOSE TWO BOYS

When Bill was a lad he was terribly bad,
   He worried his parents a lot;
He'd lie and he'd swear and pull little girls' hair;
   His boyhood was naught but a blot.

At play and in school he would fracture each rule —   5
   In mischief from autumn to spring;
And the villagers knew when to manhood he grew
   He would never amount to a thing.

When Jim was a child he was not very wild;
   He was known as a good little boy;   10
He was honest and bright and the teacher's delight —
   To his mother and father a joy.

All the neighbors were sure that his virtue'd endure,
   That his life would be free of a spot;
They were certain that Jim had a great head on him   15
   And that Jim would amount to a lot.

And Jim grew to manhood and honor and fame
   And bears a good name;
While Bill is shut up in a dark prison cell —
   You never can tell.   20

          —Franklin P. Adams

Dramatic irony describes a situation in which the audience or reader knows more than the characters do, and therefore the statements and the incidents have a different implication for the observer than they have for the characters themselves. Dramatic irony, like irony of situation, is common in drama and prose fiction. Probably the most famous example of dramatic irony is the *Oedipus Rex* of Sophocles, in which Oedipus spends most of the play looking for the culprit responsible for the city's plague when the audience knows all along that the person responsible is Oedipus himself.

Farce relies heavily on dramatic irony. We all know of plots in which one character is trying to live two or three different lives at the same time. The audience is in on the joke, but the other characters are not.

In poetry we look for possible dramatic irony in a narrative or a monologue which reveals that the character's opinion of himself and the author's opinion of him are at odds. This kind of irony is illustrated in Browning's "Soliloquy of the Spanish Cloister."

SOLILOQUY OF THE SPANISH CLOISTER

Gr-r-r—there go, my heart's abhorrence!
  Water your damned flower-pots, do!
If hate killed men, Brother Lawrence,
  God's blood, would not mine kill you!
What? your myrtle-bush wants trimming?   5
  Oh, that rose has prior claims—
Needs its leaden vase filled brimming?
  Hell dry you up with its flames!

At the meal we sit together;
  Salve tibi! I must hear   10
Wise talk of the kind of weather,
  Sort of season, time of year:
Not a plenteous cork-crop: scarcely
  Dare we hope oak-galls, I doubt;
What's the Latin name for "parsley"?   15
  What's the Greek name for Swine's Snout?

Whew! We'll have our platter burnished,
  Laid with care on our own shelf!
With a fire-new spoon we're furnished,
  And a goblet for ourself,   20
Rinsed like something sacrificial
  Ere 'tis fit to touch our chaps—
Marked with L. for our initial!
  (He-he! There his lily snaps!)

Saint, forsooth! While brown Dolores   *25*
   Squats outside the Convent bank
With Sanchicha, telling stories,
   Steeping tresses in the tank,
Blue-black, lustrous, thick like horsehairs,
   — Can't I see his dead eye glow,   *30*
Bright as 'twere a Barbary corsair's?
   (That is, if he'd let it show!)

When he finishes refection,
   Knife and fork he never lays
Cross-wise, to my recollection,   *35*
   As do I, in Jesu's praise.
I the Trinity illustrate,
   Drinking watered orange-pulp —
In three sips the Arian frustrate;
   While he drains his at one gulp.   *40*

Oh, those melons! if he's able
   We're to have a feast! so nice!
One goes to the Abbot's table,
   All of us get each a slice.
How go on your flowers? None double?   *45*
   Not one fruit-sort can you spy?
Strange! — And I, too, at such trouble,
   Keep them close-nipped on the sly!

There's a great text in Galatians,
   Once you trip on it, entails   *50*
Twenty-nine distinct damnations,
   One sure, if another fails;
If I trip him just a-dying,
   Sure of heaven as sure can be,
Spin him round and send him flying   *55*
   Off to hell, a Manichee?

Or, my scrofulous French novel
   On grey paper with blunt type!
Simply glance at it, you grovel
   Hand and foot in Belial's gripe;   *60*
If I double down its pages
   At the woeful sixteenth print,
When he gathers his greengages,
   Ope a sieve and slip it in't?

Or, there's Satan! — one might venture   *65*
   Pledge one's soul to him, yet leave

Such a flaw in the indenture
  As he'd miss till, past retrieve,
Blasted lay that rose-acacia
  We're so proud of! *Hy, Zy, Hine.* . . .   *70*
'St, there's Vespers! *Plena gratiâ*
  Ave, Virgo! Gr-r-r — you swine!

The monk's intense hatred for Brother Lawrence is itself ironic, since within the supposedly Christian context we expect love instead of hate. The dramatic irony reaches its climax in stanza 5, when we see that his own standards of piety are completely spurious. The irony is heightened by the fact that the speaker gives these actions as examples of his own piety.

It is easy to see why the ironic tone is especially important in twentieth-century writing. The contradictions of our century lend themselves to irony. Our world seems to be one of surface glitter and inner turmoil. We have an abundance of cars, houses, clothes, planes, schools, roads, and above all, money that we look to for happiness and satisfaction, and at the same time we have persistent and articulate complaints. There are more consistent attempts at world peace and yet more devastating wars than ever before.

We have more churches, but fewer literate people have an extensive knowledge of the Bible or live pious lives. Farmers are more expert at producing food than ever before, but the specter of starvation stalks the world.

A writer therefore can readily treat the world in terms of verbal irony, irony of situation, and dramatic irony. When he thinks of a single human being, more than likely he thinks of a sociological statistic, for as members of our various institutions we have a statistical rather than an individual significance. The word *individual* under these conditions becomes almost automatically an instance of verbal irony.

Irony of situation is illustrated in the division of the world into the rich and the poor. Although we have greater wealth and more effective means of production than ever before, the vast majority of the world's people live in poverty. Perhaps an even greater irony that we live with today is the fact that in the twentieth century the Western World has achieved or is well on the way to achieving almost all the goals which mankind had formerly set for themselves: control of disease, production of enough food, creating enough wealth for all to have a share, extension of life expectancy, making knowledge and culture available to all, and so on. Yet we do not find our writers characterizing the twentieth century as a time of happiness but rather as a time of despair, violence, and bitter dissatisfaction.

The detached observer in today's world looks upon the victim of modern life and creates dramatic irony. The writer, scholar, historian, psychologist, or philosopher may see modern man as driven by an inward despair and disillusionment that makes his pursuit of success and happiness doomed to failure. The subject, being the victim of his environment and therefore under the illusion that he will attain his goals, is unaware of his condition. The detached observer, however, has—or thinks he has—the perspective and insight to foresee the inevitable frustration and failure.

W. H. Auden describes this cultural dilemma in the following poem. If you look at the end of the poem first, you will immediately see the irony, though the poem is ironic from the beginning.

THE UNKNOWN CITIZEN

(To JS/07/M/378 This Marble Monument Is Erected
by the State)

He was found by the Bureau of Statistics to be
One against whom there was no official complaint,
And all the reports on his conduct agree
That, in the modern sense of an old-fashioned word, he was a
  saint,
For in everything he did he served the Greater Community.   5
Except for the War till the day he retired
He worked in a factory and never got fired,
But satisfied his employers, Fudge Motors Inc.
Yet he wasn't a scab or odd in his views,
For his Union reports that he paid his dues,   10
(Our report on his Union shows it was sound)
And our Social Psychology workers found
That he was popular with his mates and liked a drink.
The Press are convinced that he bought a paper every day
And that his reactions to advertisements were normal in every
  way.   15
Policies taken out in his name prove that he was fully insured,
And his Health-card shows he was once in hospital but left it
  cured.
Both Producers Research and High-Grade Living declare
He was fully sensible to the advantages of the Installment Plan
And had everything necessary to the Modern Man,   20
A phonograph, a radio, a car and a frigidaire.
Our researchers into Public Opinion are content
That he held the proper opinions for the time of year;
When there was peace, he was for peace; when there was war,
  he went.

He was married and added five children to the population, 25
Which our Eugenist says was the right number for a parent of
    his generation,
And our teachers report that he never interfered with their
    education.
Was he free? Was he happy? The question is absurd:
Had anything been wrong, we should certainly have heard.

                                  —W. H. Auden

Aids to Analysis

*In the first line "He," which implies identity, is incongruous, linked as it is
with "the Bureau of Statistics," which treats human beings as numbers, with
no concern for individuality in any particular number. "Official" and
"reports" in the next two lines also have an impersonal tone. The word
"saint" in line 4 brings the cultural incongruity into sharp focus. Auden
invites us to consider the contrast between "saint" in the "old-fashioned"
sense of spiritual virtue, and "saint" in the modern sense of conformity and
mediocrity, that is, the loss of identity in culturally determined thought
and action.*

1.   Check the definition of saint *in the dictionary. Which definitions contribute to the irony in the poem? Look up* normal, satisfied, sound, necessary, *and* right.

2.   What is the effect of Auden's capitalizing such words as "Greater
Community" and "War"?

3.   Explain the meaning of the last two lines.

Other Figures of Incongruity

Understatement. As its name implies, understatement is a form of
irony in which the surface meaning of a statement is less emphatic
than the actual intended meaning. Wordsworth's "She Dwelt Among
the Untrodden Ways" ends with understatement.

SHE DWELT AMONG THE UNTRODDEN WAYS

She dwelt among the untrodden ways
   Beside the springs of Dove,
A Maid whom there were none to praise
   And very few to love:

A violet by a mossy stone   5
  Half hidden from the eye!
— Fair as a star, when only one
  Is shining in the sky.

She lived unknown, and few could know
  When Lucy ceased to be;   10
But she is in her grave, and, oh,
  The difference to me!

                    — *William Wordsworth*

Emily Dickinson's "The Bustle in a House" demonstrates a more complex use of understatement. Grief is described in the metaphor of housework, as though sorrow is controlled by careful attention to workaday detail. The effect of grief is intensified by the controlled understatement.

THE BUSTLE IN A HOUSE

The bustle in a house
The morning after death
Is solemnest of industries
Enacted upon earth, —

The sweeping up of heart,   5
And putting love away
We shall not want to use again
Until eternity.

                    — *Emily Dickinson*

Hyperbole (overstatement). Hyperbole is an intentionally exaggerated statement. "My heart stopped" means "I was shocked" or "I was afraid." "Age cannot wither her, nor custom stale/Her infinite variety. . ." is part of a famous description of Cleopatra in Shakespeare's *Antony and Cleopatra*. "My heart is crushed," says Manfred (in Byron's *Manfred*). Sometimes hyperbole is used at some length. Pope's *The Rape of the Lock* exaggerates the importance of the activities of polite society to such a degree that the reader cannot help seeing that the whole situation is supremely ridiculous. In other instances hyperbole is used to show intensity of feeling.

THE COMPUTATION

For the first twenty years since yesterday
I scarce believed thou couldst be gone away;

For forty more I fed on favors past,
And forty on hopes that thou wouldst they might last.
Tears drowned one hundred, and sighs blew out two;   *5*
A thousand, I did neither think nor do,
Or not divide, all being one thought of you;
Or in a thousand more forgot that too.
Yet call not this long life, but think that I
Am, by being dead, immortal. Can ghosts die?   *10*

              —John Donne

Paradox. A paradox is a statement which contradicts or seems to contradict itself. In irony, as in understatement and hyperbole, the incongruities are unresolved. That is, we are always aware of the contrast between the actual and the ideal or between the literal meaning and the implied meaning. Paradox may resolve the incongruity. The contradiction may be only at the surface level. It has been said that "nature imitates art." Since Nature is not conscious of art at all, the statement is flagrantly self-contradictory. We might resolve the paradox, however, in this way: Our way of looking at nature is influenced by the style of art we are used to. If we read too much Poe at an impressionable age, we may see life as pervaded by death, and if we are influenced by Wilde we may look on life very flippantly. In stimulating our emotions, art influences our attitudes, and therefore art has its effect upon nature (life, reality), which resolves the paradox.

    Many paradoxes are quite serious. Christianity has many famous paradoxes. The conception of the Trinity is a paradox. "The first shall be last and the last shall be first" is a paradox. Pope describes man as "The glory, jest, and riddle of the world." This paradox compresses many truths and mysteries about complex man into a brief space.

    Donne is famous for his paradoxes. The following poem is a network of paradoxes leading to a religious resolution—salvation.

BATTER MY HEART, THREE PERSON'D GOD

Batter my heart, three person'd God; for, you
As yet but knock, breathe, shine, and seek to mend;
That I may rise, and stand, o'erthrow me, and bend
Your force, to break, blow, burn and make me new.
I, like an usurp'd town, to'another due,   *5*
Labor to'admit you, but Oh, to no end,
Reason your viceroy in me, me should defend,
But is captiv'd, and proves weak or untrue.
Yet dearly I love you, and would be loved fain,
But am betroth'd unto your enemy: *10*

Divorce me, untie, or break that knot again,
Take me to you, imprison me, for I
Except you'enthral me, never shall be free,
Nor ever chaste, except you ravish me.

—*John Donne*

The general structure of the poem is based on a paradox. The octave deals with violence and the sestet deals with love. Donne's conception becomes increasingly complex as the poem progresses until, by the end, it seems as though the ideas can be expressed only in paradox.

In lines 1–4 God is seen as a force opposing the person speaking, itself a paradoxical conception of God. Then, in lines 5–8 Donne internalizes the conflict. Man struggles against himself: "I . . . Labor to' admit you," but "Reason . . . is captiv'd." The word *Yet* in line 9 marks the turn from violence to love as the theme. In the sestet Donne proceeds to draw upon the sexual as well as the religious implications of love to develop the idea of God's love. Since the physical and the spiritual are opposed in the ascetic aspect of Christianity, paradoxes are inevitable when the two ideas are joined. *Chaste* is opposed to *ravish.*

Throughout the poem the religious idea of freedom through submission to the will of God underlies the general conflict. At first glance, the conflict seems incongruous with love. Actually, the paradox is resolved. The metaphor of conflict reflects the psychological reality of religious doubt and struggle, which is the overall theme of the poem.

EXERCISE: Identify the figures of incongruity in the following lines.

1. Stone walls do not a prison make nor iron bars a cage. (Lovelace)

2. If the fool would persist in his folly he would become wise. (Blake)

3. Last week I saw a woman flayed, and you will hardly believe how much it altered her person for the worse. (Swift)

4. The child is father of the man. (Wordsworth)

5. My vegetable love should grow
   Vaster than empires, and more slow. (Marvell)

6. And sleepless lovers, just at twelve awake. (Pope)

7. The dead shall live, the living die,
   And music shall untune the sky. (Dryden)

8. A little learning is a dangerous thing;
   Drink deep, or taste not the Pierian spring;
   There shallow draughts intoxicate the brain,
   And drinking largely sobers us again. (Pope)

9. A little black thing among the snow,
   Crying "weep, weep!" in notes of woe!
   "Where are thy father and mother, say?"
   "They are both gone up to the church to pray." (Blake)

10. Music hath charms to soothe the savage breast,
    To soften rocks, or bend a knotted oak. (Congreve)

Study Poems

WAR IS KIND

Do not weep, maiden, for war is kind.
Because your lover threw wild hands toward the sky
And the affrighted steed ran on alone,
Do not weep.
War is kind.   5

    Hoarse, booming drums of the regiment,
    Little souls who thirst for fight,
    These men were born to drill and die.
    The unexplained glory flies above them,
    Great is the battle-god, great, and his kingdom —   10
    A field where a thousand corpses lie.

Do not weep, babe, for war is kind.
Because your father tumbled in the yellow trenches,
Raged at his breast, gulped and died,
Do not weep.   15
War is kind.

    Swift blazing flag of the regiment,
    Eagle with crest of red and gold,
    These men were born to drill and die.
    Point for them the virtue of slaughter,   20
    Make plain to them the excellence of killing
    And a field where a thousand corpses lie.

Mother whose heart hung humble as a button
On the bright splendid shroud of your son,
Do not weep.   *25*
War is kind.

                              — *Stephen Crane*

Aids to Analysis

1.   *Outline the idea structure of the poem.*

2.   *What contradiction in the poem makes the title ironic?*

3.   *In stanza 2 explain the irony in "Little souls," "were born to drill and die," "unexplained glory," and "Great." In stanza 4 explain the irony of "virtue" and "excellence."*

4.   *What human values does Crane use for his ironic comment on man?*

THE MAN HE KILLED

            "Had he and I but met
                By some old ancient inn,
        We should have sat us down to wet
                Right many a nipperkin!

            "But ranged as infantry,   *5*
                And staring face to face,
        I shot at him as he at me,
                And killed him in his place.

            "I shot him dead because —
                Because he was my foe,   *10*
        Just so: my foe of course he was;
                That's clear enough; although

            "He thought he'd 'list, perhaps,
                Off-hand like — just as I —
        Was out of work — had sold his traps —   *15*
                No other reason why.

            "Yes; quaint and curious war is!
                You shoot a fellow down
        You'd treat if met where any bar is,
                Or help to half-a-crown."   *20*

                              — *Thomas Hardy*

Aids to Analysis

1. *How is the poem an example of irony of situation?*

2. *Find three or four examples of verbal irony.*

STUPIDITY STREET

I saw with open eyes
Singing birds sweet
Sold in the shops
For the people to eat,
Sold in the shops of   5
Stupidity Street.

I saw in a vision
The worm in the wheat,
And in the shops nothing
For people to eat: 10
Nothing for sale in
Stupidity Street.

—*Ralph Hodgson*

Aids to Analysis

1. *Explain the parallel and the contrast between line 1 and line 7.*

2. *What words give the poem its ironic tone?*

A CASE

As I was going up the stair
I met a man who wasn't there.
He wasn't there again today—
I wish to God he'd go away.

—*Anonymous*

A SONNET UPON A STOLEN KISS

Now gentle sleep hath closèd up those eyes
Which waking kept my boldest thoughts in awe,
And free access unto that sweet lip lies,
From whence I long the rosy breath to draw;
Methinks no wrong it were if I should steal   5

From those two melting rubies one poor kiss;
None sees the theft that would the thief reveal,
Nor rob I her of aught that she can miss;
Nay, should I twenty kisses take away,
There would be little sign I had done so;   *10*
Why then should I this robbery delay?
Oh! she may wake and therewith angry grow.
   Well, if she do, I'll back restore that one,
   And twenty hundred thousand more for loan.

                        —George Wither

Aids to Analysis

Find examples of paradox, overstatement, and verbal irony in the poem.

PROUD MAISIE

Proud Maisie is in the wood,
   Walking so early;
Sweet Robin sits on the bush,
   Singing so rarely.

"Tell me, thou bonny bird,   *5*
   When shall I marry me?"
"When six braw gentlemen
   Kirkward shall carry ye."

"Who makes the bridal bed,
   Birdie, say truly?"   *10*
"The gray-headed sexton
   That delves the grave duly.

"The glowworm o'er grave and stone
   Shall light thee steady;
The owl from the steeple sing,   *15*
   'Welcome, proud lady.'"

                —Sir Walter Scott

Aids to Analysis

1.   *How does this poem illustrate irony of situation?*

2.   *What examples of dramatic irony do you find?*

THE LATEST DECALOGUE

Thou shalt have one God only; who
Would be at the expense of two?
No graven images may be
Worshipped, except the currency;
Swear not at all; for, for thy curse   5
Thine enemy is none the worse:
At church on Sunday to attend
Will serve to keep the world thy friend:
Honour thy parents; that is, all
From whom advancement may befall: 10
Thou shalt not kill; but need'st not strive
Officiously to keep alive:
Do not adultery commit;
Advantage rarely comes of it:
Thou shalt not steal; an empty feat,   15
When it's so lucrative to cheat:
Bear not false witness; let the lie
Have time on its own wings to fly:
Thou shalt not covet, but tradition
Approves all forms of competition.   20

—Arthur Hugh Clough

Aids to Analysis

Clough bases his irony on the contrast between the teachings of the Ten Commandments and the values men actually live by.

1.   *What words in the first eight lines establish the ironic tone?*

2.   *Summarize the contemporary values that Clough says men live by.*

THE KINGDOM OF GOD

"IN NO STRANGE LAND"

O world invisible, we view thee,
O world intangible, we touch thee,
O world unknowable, we know thee,
Inapprehensible, we clutch thee!

Does the fish soar to find the ocean,   5
The eagle plunge to find the air—
That we ask of the stars in motion
If they have rumor of thee there?

Not where the wheeling systems darken,
And our benumbed conceiving soars!—   *10*
The drift of pinions, would we hearken,
Beats at our own clay-shuttered doors.

The angels keep their ancient places—
Turn but a stone and start a wing!
'Tis ye, 'tis your estrangéd faces,   *15*
That miss the many-splendored thing.

But (when so sad thou canst not sadder)
Cry—and upon thy so sore loss
Shall shine the traffic of Jacob's ladder
Pitched betwixt Heaven and Charing Cross.   *20*

Yea, in the night, my Soul, my daughter,
Cry—clinging Heaven by the hems;
And lo, Christ walking on the water,
Not of Genesareth, but Thames!

                    —*Francis Thompson*

Aids to Analysis

1. *What words establish the paradox in stanza 1?*

2. *What criticism of man's religion is made in stanza 2?*

3. *What are the paradoxes in lines 9 and 10?*

4. *What images carry over from stanza 3 to stanza 4?*

5. *What are the syntactical problems of lines 5–6?*

6. *What is the paradox of lines 19–20?*

7. *Help in explaining the quotation in the title may be found in Exodus 2:22 and Psalm 137:4.*

OZYMANDIAS

I met a traveller from an antique land
Who said: Two vast and trunkless legs of stone
Stand in the desert. Near them, on the sand,
Half sunk, a shattered visage lies, whose frown,
And wrinkled lip, and sneer of cold command,   *5*
Tell that its sculptor well those passions read

Which yet survive, stamped on these lifeless things,
The hand that mocked them and the heart that fed:
And on the pedestal these words appear:
"My name is Ozymandias, king of kings: *10*
Look on my works, ye Mighty, and despair!"
Nothing beside remains. Round the decay
Of that colossal wreck, boundless and bare
The lone and level sands stretch far away.

— Percy Bysshe Shelley

Aids to Analysis

1. *How is the contrast between the first three lines and the rest of the poem ironic?*

2. *What is the irony involving the sculptor?*

SONG

Go and catch a falling star,
  Get with child a mandrake root,
Tell me where all past years are,
  Or who cleft the devil's foot;
Teach me to hear mermaids singing,   *5*
Or to keep off envy's stinging,
        And find
        What wind
Serves to advance an honest mind.

If thou be'st born to strange sights,   *10*
  Things invisible to see,
Ride ten thousand days and nights
  Till age snow white hairs on thee;
Thou, when thou return'st, wilt tell me
All strange wonders that befell thee,   *15*
        And swear
        No where
Lives a woman true, and fair.

If thou find'st one, let me know;
  Such a pilgrimage were sweet.   *20*
Yet do not; I would not go,
  Though at next door we might meet.
Though she were true when you met her,

And last, till you write your letter,
    Yet she   25
    Will be
False, ere I come, to two, or three.

            —*John Donne*

Aids to Analysis

1. *Find two examples of paradox in stanzas 1 and 2.*

2. *Find two examples of hyperbole.*

3. *Find the serious theme in stanzas 1 and 2.*

4. *In your own words explain the paradox in stanza 3.*

WHEN GOD DECIDED TO INVENT

when god decided to invent
everything he took one
breath bigger than a circustent
and everything began

when man determined to destroy   5
himself he picked the was
of shall and finding only why
smashed it into because

            —*E. E. Cummings*

Aids to Analysis

1. *What is the dominant impression of stanza 1?*

2. *What words in stanza 2 suggest that man is being ironically contrasted to God.*

3. *State the difference between the process of creation and the process of destruction as suggested by Cummings.*

4. *After a first reading, define the relationship between "was" and "shall." Then determine why man finds "only why." What is the relationship between "why" and "because"?*

THE GLORY, JEST, AND RIDDLE

Know then thyself, presume not God to scan,
The proper study of Mankind is Man.
Placed on this isthmus of a middle state,
A Being darkly wise, and rudely great:
With too much knowledge for the Sceptic side,   5
With too much weakness for the Stoic's pride,
He hangs between; in doubt to act, or rest;
In doubt to deem himself a God, or Beast;
In doubt his Mind or Body to prefer;
Born but to die, and reas'ning but to err;   10
Alike in ignorance, his reason such,
Whether he thinks too little, or too much:
Chaos of Thought and Passion, all confused;
Still by himself abused, or disabused;
Created half to rise, and half to fall;   15
Great lord of all things, yet a prey to all;
Sole judge of Truth, in endless Error hurled:
The glory, jest, and riddle of the world!

—Alexander Pope

Aids to Analysis

1.   *The last line of this passage is a paradox. Point out any other instances of paradox you can find in the passage.*

2.   *Define the relationship between the first two lines and the rest of the passage. What will we find out about man when we study him?*

3.   *Do you find any irony in the relationship between the first two lines and the rest? Explain.*

MORNING SONG OF SENLIN

It is morning, Senlin says, and in the morning
When the light drips through the shutters like the dew,
I arise, I face the sunrise,
And do the things my fathers learned to do.
Stars in the purple dusk above the rooftops   5
Pale in a saffron mist and seem to die,
And I myself on a swiftly tilting planet
Stand before a glass and tie my tie.
Vine leaves tap my window,

Dew-drops sing to the garden stones,   *10*
The robin chirps in the chinaberry tree
Repeating three clear tones.

It is morning. I stand by the mirror
And tie my tie once more.
While waves far off in a pale rose twilight   *15*
Crash on a white sand shore.
I stand by a mirror and comb my hair:
How small and white my face! —
The green earth tilts through a sphere of air
And bathes in a flame of space.   *20*
There are houses hanging above the stars
And stars hung under a sea . . .
And a sun far off in a shell of silence
Dapples my walls for me . . .

It is morning, Senlin says, and in the morning   *25*
Should I not pause in the light to remember god?
Upright and firm I stand on a star unstable,
He is immense and lonely as a cloud.
I will dedicate this moment before my mirror
To him alone, for him I will comb my hair.   *30*
Accept these humble offerings, cloud of silence!
I will think of you as I descend the stair.

Vine leaves tap my window,
The snail-track shines on the stones,
Dew-drops flash from the chinaberry tree   *35*
Repeating two clear tones.

It is morning, I awake from a bed of silence,
Shining I rise from the starless waters of sleep.
The walls are about me still as in the evening,
I am the same, and the same name still I keep.   *40*

The earth revolves with me, yet makes no motion,
The stars pale silently in a coral sky.
In a whistling void I stand before my mirror,
Unconcerned, and tie my tie.

There are horses neighing on far-off hills   *45*
Tossing their long white manes,
And mountains flash in the rose-white dusk,
Their shoulders black with rains . . .

It is morning. I stand by the mirror
And surprise my soul once more;   *50*

The blue air rushes above my ceiling,
There are suns beneath my floor . . .

. . . It is morning, Senlin says, I ascend from darkness
And depart on the winds of space for I know not where,
My watch is wound, a key is in my pocket,   55
And the sky is darkened as I descend the stair.
There are shadows across the windows, clouds in heaven,
And a god among the stars; and I will go
Thinking of him as I might think of daybreak
And humming a tune I know . . .   60

Vine-leaves tap at the window,
Dew-drops sing to the garden stones,
The robin chirps in the chinaberry tree
Repeating three clear tones.

—Conrad Aiken

Aids to Analysis

The poem is organized in terms of a series of contrasts between Senlin's activities and the larger world around him.

1. *What do we learn about his actions and the reason for them in lines 1–8?*

2. *What contrast do you see between Senlin and the repeated images of vine leaves, dew drops, and the rain?*

3. *Define the irony in his religious musings in stanza 4.*

4. *Stanzas 4 and 6 contain images of motion. How are these in contrast to Senlin?*

5. *Describe the emotional and spiritual condition of Senlin. Why do you think that Aiken presents this personality ironically rather than sympathetically?*

6. *In what respects is Senlin a representative figure?*

Chapter 7

Symbol

A symbol is an image that stands for or brings to mind something else, usually an abstract quality or relationship of some sort. The Cross (Christianity), a rose (love), and a sunrise (hope) are well-known symbols.

Since a symbol is based on an image and since a symbol is like a metaphor in that it relates a physical object to something else, you should learn to distinguish between an image, a metaphor, and a symbol.

An *image* is a physical object or experience of some kind (rocks, stones, trees).

A *metaphor* uses an image to define or describe something else on a single occasion by bringing out one or more points of comparison ("A slumber did my spirit seal").

A *symbol* is an image that has absorbed meaningful and permanent associations beyond itself as a physical object. Some common symbols are The Stars and Stripes (The United States), the sea (life), and a river (time).

We may note the distinctions between image, metaphor, and symbol in the following poem: "Eldorado" by Poe. The word *shadow* is used in three different ways. In stanza 1 it is an image, in stanzas 2 and 3 it is a metaphor, and in stanza 4 it is a symbol.

ELDORADO

Gayly bedight,
A gallant knight,
In sunshine and in shadow,
Had journeyed long,
Singing a song,
In search of Eldorado.

5

But he grew old,
　This knight so bold,
And o'er his heart a shadow
　　Fell as he found　　　　　　　　　　　　*10*
　No spot of ground
That looked like Eldorado.

And, as his strength
　Failed him at length,
He met a pilgrim shadow —　　　　　　　　　*15*
　"Shadow," said he,
　"Where can it be,
This land of Eldorado?"

"Over the Mountains
　Of the Moon,　　　　　　　　　　　　　　*20*
Down the Valley of the Shadow,
　Ride, boldly ride,"
　The shade replied,
"If you seek for Eldorado!"

Aids to Analysis

1.　*Relate the successive uses of* shadow *to the definition of image, metaphor, and symbol.*

2.　*Is* Eldorado *an image, a metaphor, or a symbol? What does it mean?*

Let us now consider what to look for in identifying a symbol in a poem. Edward Arlington Robinson uses wormwood as a symbol in "Cliff Klingenhagen."

CLIFF KLINGENHAGEN

Cliff Klingenhagen had me in to dine
With him one day; and after soup and meat,
And all the other things there were to eat,
Cliff took two glasses and filled one with wine
And one with wormwood. Then, without a sign　　*5*
For me to choose at all, he took the draught
Of bitterness himself, and lightly quaffed
It off, and said the other one was mine.
And when I asked him what the deuce he meant
By doing that, he only looked at me　　　　　　*10*
And grinned, and said it was a way of his.
And though I know the fellow, I have spent
Long time a-wondering when I shall be
As happy as Cliff Klingenhagen is.

How do we know that Robinson intended wormwood to be a symbol? For one thing, he repeats it often enough that it acquires certain implications and associations through this repetition. It is mentioned three times in the fourteen lines: "wormwood," line 5; "draught of bitterness," lines 6–7; and the pronoun "it" in line 8. Secondly, the last six lines tell us that the image stands for something besides itself. Robinson raises a question ("what the deuce he meant/By doing that"), and gives a direction for the answer by "happy" in line 14, which implies a connection between happiness and drinking wormwood. These indicators point to a significance far beyond the mere physical drink itself.

Blake's "The Tiger" is another example of a symbol identified in the poem.

As a help in laying the groundwork for analyzing the tiger as a symbol, it may be useful to know three of the possible, commonly accepted interpretations: (1) the Tiger is created by the same force that created the Lamb and is therefore in the last analysis good; (2) the Tiger symbolizes evil or the force for evil; (3) the creator of the Tiger is unknown and unknowable, and therefore the question that Blake asks is not intended to have an answer.

THE TIGER

Tiger! Tiger! burning bright
In the forests of the night,
What immortal hand or eye
Could frame thy fearful symmetry?

In what distant deeps or skies   5
Burnt the fire of thine eyes?
On what wings dare he aspire?
What the hand dare seize the fire?

And what shoulder, and what art,
Could twist the sinews of thy heart?   10
And when thy heart began to beat,
What dread hand? and what dread feet?

What the hammer? what the chain?
In what furnace was thy brain?
What the anvil? what dread grasp   15
Dare its deadly terrors clasp?

When the stars threw down their spears,
And watered heaven with their tears,
Did he smile his work to see?
Did he who made the Lamb make thee?   20

Tiger! Tiger! burning bright
In the forests of the night,
What immortal hand or eye,
Dare frame thy fearful symmetry?

The whole poem is devoted to the image of the Tiger, and so we
suspect on that score alone that this is a very significant animal. Further, we see that Blake is also interested in the force that created the
Tiger, perhaps more interested in that than the Tiger itself. Each
sentence is actually a rhetorical question that poses the same problem:
What is the force that created the Tiger? This pattern of questions
points to a symbolic function for the Tiger and also gives us an idea of
what the Tiger symbolizes. We remember that a symbol is a physical
object—an image—that *stands for* something else, usually (though not
necessarily) an abstraction or a relationship of some sort. Here, Blake
creates a symbol of the powerful and mysterious force that formed the
Tiger. We are not forced outside the poem for the general significance
of the symbol. Some mysterious power is symbolized in the Tiger. This
much, the poem makes clear. (A study of Blake's mythology is helpful
in understanding the poem as fully as possible, but the point here is
simply that Blake established the Tiger as a symbol and gave us a clue
to its general meaning within the context of the poem itself.)

The symbols in Blake's "The Lamb" are readily identified when
the reader knows that it is a companion poem to "The Tiger."

THE LAMB

Little Lamb, who made thee?
Dost thou know who made thee?
Gave thee life, and bid thee feed,
By the stream and o'er the mead;
Gave thee clothing of delight,   5
Softest clothing, woolly, bright;
Gave thee such a tender voice,
Making all the vales rejoice?
Little Lamb, who made thee?
Dost thou know who made thee?   10

Little Lamb, I'll tell thee,
Little Lamb, I'll tell thee:
He is called by thy name,
For He calls Himself a Lamb,
He is meek, and He is mild;   15
He became a little child.

I a child, and thou a lamb,
We are callèd by His name.
   Little Lamb, God bless thee!
   Little Lamb, God bless thee!   *20*

   Symbols acquire their meaning from three main sources: (1) from common, universal human experiences at both the conscious and the unconscious levels (*archetypal symbols*); (2) from a body of thought and beliefs within a culture, such as its myths, religion, social traditions (*cultural symbols*); (3) from within the art work itself, wherein the writer repeatedly uses an image or a metaphor until it takes on an increasingly definable and stable set of suggestions (*contextual symbol*).

   The *archetypal symbol* is independent of time and place. The sun and the earth are often used as archetypal symbols. Unlike styles in clothing, they do not depend upon a particular society for their acceptance and meaning. The sea is an especially important symbol, implying both life and death or death and (spiritual) rebirth, as in the story of Jonah. The journey in Poe's "Eldorado" is an archetypal symbol of man's search for meaning in life.

   Cultural symbols, as the name implies, are closely related to a particular culture. The lamb in Blake's poem is a cultural symbol of innocence. This type of symbol is as broad or narrow as the meaning of *culture* itself. It is also related to historical events. The book as a symbol of scholarship would apply only since the time that knowledge has been communicated primarily through the printed word. Likewise, the scientist's laboratory, the businessman's dollar sign, and the painter's brush and palette, though symbols of long standing, do not apply before certain dates in history.

   Each generation, and many subgroups within a generation, have many symbols that pass away as one generation gives way to the next. We attach symbolic significance to the kind of car we drive, the neighborhood we live in, the clubs and organizations we belong to, and even the labels in the clothes we wear. The next generation will value different labels and different clubs.

   Contextual symbols take their implications from the poem or other literary work in which they appear, or from a special background that the author has developed (as for example, Blake's "tiger"). Contextual symbols are also called private symbols or personal symbols. The contextual symbol takes its meaning from the poem itself. For example, Walt Whitman in *When Lilacs Last in the Dooryard Bloom'd* created three symbols which strengthened the structure and emotional impact of the poem: the star, symbolizing Lincoln; the thrush, symbolizing the poet mourning the death of

Lincoln; and the lilac, symbolizing the poet's love and the love of the
nation for the dead President.

The following poem makes use of archetypal, cultural, and contextual symbols. Try to identify them.

THE SECOND COMING

Turning and turning in the widening gyre
The falcon cannot hear the falconer;
Things fall apart; the centre cannot hold;
Mere anarchy is loosed upon the world,
The blood-dimmed tide is loosed, and everywhere   5
The ceremony of innocence is drowned;
The best lack all conviction, while the worst
Are full of passionate intensity.

Surely some revelation is at hand;
Surely the Second Coming is at hand.   10
The Second Coming! Hardly are those words out
When a vast image out of *Spiritus Mundi*
Troubles my sight: somewhere in sands of the desert
A shape with lion body and the head of a man,
A gaze blank and pitiless as the sun,   15
Is moving its slow thighs, while all about it
Reel shadows of the indignant desert birds.
The darkness drops again; but now I know
That twenty centuries of stony sleep
Were vexed to nightmare by a rocking cradle,   20
And what rough beast, its hour come round at last,
Slouches towards Bethlehem to be born?

—*William Butler Yeats*

Aids to Analysis

*A gyre (a cone, a spiral) is a symbol relating to Yeats' theory of historical
cycles. According to this theory, history tends to move toward a period of
coherence, and then away from coherence into disintegration in a never-
ending, spiraling process.*

Probably the most extensive and the most powerful source of
symbols is nature itself. Being less subject to change than man-made
objects, natural symbols give a feeling of permanence in the face of
subjective change and insecurity. While the steam locomotive, once

the modern symbol of power, gives way to the diesel (which has not replaced it as a symbol), winter remains the symbol of death, and spring remains the symbol of rebirth and renewed vitality. Modern man cannot match the vitality of nature. The druggist's pills suggest disease rather than health. The battleship gives way to the rocket, but we cannot imagine Hardy's thrush giving way to any mechanical invention.

THE DARKLING THRUSH

I leant upon a coppice gate
    When Frost was specter-gray,
And Winter's dregs made desolate
    The weakening eye of day.
The tangled bine-stems scored the sky   5
    Like strings of broken lyres,
And all mankind that haunted nigh
    Had sought their household fires.

The land's sharp features seemed to be
    The Century's corpse outleant,   10
His crypt the cloudy canopy,
    The wind his death-lament.
The ancient pulse of germ and birth
    Was shrunken hard and dry,
And every spirit upon earth   15
    Seemed fervorless as I.

At once a voice arose among
    The bleak twigs overhead
In a full-hearted evensong
    Of joy illimited;   20
An aged thrush, frail, gaunt, and small,
    In blast-beruffled plume,
Had chosen thus to fling his soul
    Upon the growing gloom.

So little cause for carolings   25
    Of such ecstatic sound
Was written on terrestrial things
    Afar or nigh around,
That I could think there trembled through
    His happy good-night air   30
Some blessed Hope, whereof he knew
    And I was unaware.

Aids to Analysis

Hardy's thrush as a natural symbol has a nearly universal application. To emphasize this universality, Hardy uses such phrases as "all mankind." What other phrases does he use to relate the symbolic thrush to a broad and recurrent human predicament?

A particularly important type of natural symbol is the fertility symbol. Sometimes the fertility symbol is specifically sexual. It may suggest the male organ—phallic symbol—a spear, a lance, a snake. It may represent the womb—a cup, a bowl, a cave, a mountain. Fertility symbols may also be broadly generative (plants, trees). The earth is commonly a generative symbol, with sexual overtones since it is usually referred to in the feminine (Mother Earth). In any case, the fertility symbol implies life, growth, and the reproductive principle.

By extension, the fertility symbol also symbolizes intellectual, emotional, and spiritual vitality. Anything that grows is healthy, and anything that fails to grow or decays and is unable to reproduce itself is unhealthy and dying. The desert, being relatively sterile, is a common symbol of death, both physical and spiritual. A fountain, on the other hand, is an obvious symbol of the source of life. The generative principle creates life and sustains the spirit. From antiquity man has spoken of the waters of life, and the biblical "dust unto dust" acknowledges our origin in the earth.

EXERCISE: Kinds and Meanings of Symbols

You will find it useful to systematize your knowledge of symbols at a first-level meaning. Determine the general symbolic meaning in each instance.

Archetypal symbols:
    Usually nature symbols. Spring, summer, autumn, winter; day-night; dawn-noon-sunset; the earth; the sea; mountain; mountain peak; the sun; the moon; blood; desert; water; snake; dust; egg; fire; fountain.

Cultural symbols:
    Related to the traditions and institutions in Western culture or among a particular people or in a particular area. The Cross; a Christmas tree; a wedding ring; a mortarboard; scales; a flag; peace pipe; lamb; rose; Santa Claus; turkey; shepherd; torch; valentine; a car; clothes.

Study Poems

TO HELEN

Helen, thy beauty is to me
    Like those Nicean barks of yore,
That gently, o'er a perfumed sea,
    The weary, way-worn wanderer bore
    To his own native shore.   *5*

On desperate seas long wont to roam,
    Thy hyacinth hair, thy classic face,
Thy Naiad airs have brought me home
    To the glory that was Greece,
    And the grandeur that was Rome.   *10*

Lo! in yon brilliant window-niche
    How statue-like I see thee stand,
Thy agate lamp within thy hand!
    Ah, Psyche, from the regions which
    Are Holy-land.   *15*

            —*Edgar Allan Poe*

Aids to Analysis

1.   *What details suggest that Helen is a symbol?*

2.   *What particular effect of Helen is brought out in each stanza?*

3.   *What is the total symbolic meaning of Helen?*

GIFTS

I tossed my friend a wreath of roses, wet
    With early dew, the garland of the morn.
He lifted it—and on his brow he set
    A crackling crown of thorn.

Against my foe I hurled a murderous dart.   *5*
    He caught it in his hand—I heard him laugh—
I saw the thing that should have pierced his heart
    Turn to a golden staff.

          —*Mary Elizabeth Coleridge*

Aids to Analysis

Which of the images are used as metaphors? Which as symbols?

RICHARD ROE AND JOHN DOE

Richard Roe wished himself Solomon,
Made cuckold, you should know, by one John Doe:
Solomon's neck was firm enough to bear
Some score of antlers more than Roe could wear,

Richard Roe wished himself Alexander,   5
Being robbed of house and land by the same hand:
Ten thousand acres or a principal town
Would have cost Alexander scarce a frown.

Richard Roe wished himself Job the prophet,
Sunk past reclaim in stinking rags and shame —   10
However ill Job's plight, his own was worse:
He knew no God to call on or to curse.

He wished himself Job, Solomon, Alexander,
For patience, wisdom, power to overthrow
Misfortune; but with spirit so unmanned   15
That most of all he wished himself John Doe.

— Robert Graves

Aids to Analysis

Identify the cultural symbols and explain their meaning in the poem.

PHILOMELA

Hark! ah, the nightingale —
The tawny-throated!
Hark, from that moonlit cedar what a burst!
What triumph! hark! — what pain!
O wanderer from a Grecian shore,   5
Still, after many years, in distant lands,
Still nourishing in thy bewildered brain
That wild, unquenched, deep-sunken, old-world pain —
Say, will it never heal?
And can this fragrant lawn   10

With its cool trees, and night,
And the sweet, tranquil Thames,
And moonshine, and the dew,
To thy racked heart and brain
Afford no balm?   *15*

Dost thou tonight behold,
Here, through the moonlight on this English grass,
The unfriendly palace in the Thracian wild?
Dost thou again peruse
With hot cheeks and seared eyes   *20*
The too clear web, and thy dumb sister's shame?
Dost thou once more assay
Thy flight, and feel come over thee,
Poor fugitive, the feathery change
Once more, and once more seem to make resound   *25*
With love and hate, triumph and agony,
Lone Daulis, and the high Cephissian vale?
Listen, Eugenia—
How thick the bursts come crowding through the leaves!
Again—thou hearest?   *30*
Eternal passion!
Eternal pain!

—Matthew Arnold

Aids to Analysis

1. *Look in the dictionary for the origin of the story of Philomela.*

2. *Read the poem carefully for the poet's own explanation of the symbolic meaning.*

STOPPING BY WOODS ON A SNOWY EVENING

Whose woods these are I think I know.
His house is in the village though;
He will not see me stopping here
To watch his woods fill up with snow.

My little horse must think it queer   *5*
To stop without a farmhouse near
Between the woods and frozen lake
The darkest evening of the year.

He gives his harness bells a shake
To ask if there is some mistake.   *10*
The only other sound's the sweep
Of easy wind and downy flake.

The woods are lovely, dark and deep.
But I have promises to keep,
And miles to go before I sleep,   *15*
And miles to go before I sleep.

                                        —*Robert Frost*

Aids to Analysis

1. *Explain the conflict in stanzas 1–3.*

2. *Explain the conflict in stanza 4.*

3. *How are the conflicts related?*

4. *What do the woods symbolize?*

THE CASTLE

All through that summer at ease we lay,
And daily from the turret wall
We watched the mowers in the hay
And the enemy half a mile away.
They seemed no threat to us at all.   *5*

For what, we thought, had we to fear
With our arms and provender, load on load,
Our towering battlements, tier on tier,
And friendly allies drawing near
On every leafy summer road.   *10*

Our gates were strong, our walls were thick,
So smooth and high, no man could win
A foothold there, no clever trick
Could take us, have us dead or quick.
Only a bird could have got in.   *15*

What could they offer us for bait?
Our captain was brave and we were true. . . .
There was a little private gate,

A little wicked wicket gate.
The wizened warder let them through.   *20*

Oh then our maze of tunnelled stone
Grew thin and treacherous as air.
The cause was lost without a groan,
The famous citadel overthrown,
And all its secret galleries bare.   *25*

How can this shameful tale be told?
I will maintain until my death
We could do nothing, being sold;
Our only enemy was gold,
And we had no arms to fight it with.   *30*

—*Edwin Muir*

Aids to Analysis

There may be a problem in determining what the castle symbolizes. Perhaps it symbolizes nothing at all, but is simply a story in verse. The following questions are designed to help you understand significant parts of the poem before you arrive at your interpretation.

1. *Is there anything to indicate that such words as* enemy *and* allies *have meaning beyond a military context?*

2. *Do the parts of the castle suggest a broader meaning? For example, the "maze of tunnelled stone" and the "wicked wicket gate."*

3. *The last two lines say that the gold could not be fought. What kind of arms would one use to fight gold?*

THE SICK ROSE

O Rose, thou art sick!
The invisible worm
That flies in the night,
In the howling storm,

Has found out thy bed   *5*
Of crimson joy,
And his dark secret love
Does thy life destroy.

—*William Blake*

Aids to Analysis

1. *What ideas and associations are connected with the rose? With the worm?*

2. *What indications are there that the rose and the worm are not natural companions?*

3. *What do the rose and the worm seem to symbolize? Are they archetypal, cultural, or contextual symbols or are they some combinations of these?*

4. *State the theme of the poem.*

TO A LOCOMOTIVE IN WINTER

Thee for my recitative,
Thee in the driving storm even as now, the snow, the
    winter-day declining,
Thee in thy panoply, thy measur'd dual throbbing and
    thy beat convulsive,
Thy black cylindric body, golden brass and silvery steel,
Thy ponderous side-bars, parallel and connecting rods,
    gyrating, shuttling at thy sides,   5
Thy metrical, now swelling pant and roar, now tapering
    in the distance,
Thy great protruding head-light fix'd in front,
Thy long, pale, floating vapor-pennants, tinged with deli-
    cate purple,
The dense and murky clouds out-belching from thy
    smokestack,
Thy knitted frame, thy springs and valves, the tremulous
    twinkle of thy wheels,   10
Thy train of cars behind, obedient, merrily following,
Through gale or calm, now swift, now slack, yet steadily
    careening;
Type of the modern — emblem of motion and power —
    pulse of the continent,
For once come serve the Muse and merge in verse, even
    as here I see thee,
With storm and buffeting gusts of wind and falling snow, 15
By day thy warning ringing bell to sound its notes,
By night thy silent signal lamps to swing.

Fierce-throated beauty!
Roll through my chant with all thy lawless music, thy
    swinging lamps at night,
Thy madly-whistled laughter, echoing, rumbling like an
    earthquake, rousing all,   20
Law of thyself complete, thine own track firmly holding,

> (No sweetness debonair of tearful harp or glib piano
>   thine,)
> Thy trills of shrieks by rocks and hills return'd,
> Launch'd o'er the prairies wide, across the lakes,
> To the free skies unpent and glad and strong.   25

> — *Walt Whitman*

Aids to Analysis

1. *What characteristics of the locomotive does Whitman establish in lines 1–18?*

2. *What additional meaning does he give to the locomotive in lines 18–25?*

3. *Describe the relationship between man and nature that Whitman develops through the symbol of the locomotive.*

THE DREAM

> O God, in the dream the terrible horse began
> To paw at the air, and make for me with his blows.
> Fear kept for thirty-five years poured through his mane,
> And retribution equally old, or nearly, breathed through his nose.

> Coward complete, I lay and wept on the ground   5
> When some strong creature appeared, and leapt for the rein.
> Another woman, as I lay half in a swound
> Leapt in the air, and clutched at the leather and chain.

> Give him, she said, something of yours as a charm.
> Throw him, she said, some poor thing you alone claim.   10
> No, no, I cried, he hates me; he's out for harm,
> And whether I yield or not, it is all the same.

> But, like a lion in a legend, when I flung the glove
> Pulled from my sweating, my cold right hand,
> The terrible beast, that no one may understand,   15
> Came to my side, and put down his head in love.

> — *Louise Bogan*

Aids to Analysis

1. *The dominant images of the dream are the terrible horse, the other woman, and the action of giving "something of yours." Discuss these as contextual, cultural, and archetypal symbols.*

2. *What is the significance of the age of the woman?*

3. *What is the significance of the poem's ending in love?*

SEALS, TERNS, TIME

The seals at play off Western Isle
In the loose flowing of the summer tide
And burden of our strange estate —

Resting on the oar and lolling on the sea,
I saw their curious images,   5
Hypnotic, sympathetic eyes

As the deep elapses of the soul.
O ancient blood, O blurred kind forms
That rise and peer from elemental water:

I loll upon the oar, I think upon the day,   10
Drawn by strong, by the animal soft bonds
Back to a dim pre-history;

While off the point of Jagged Light
In hundreds, gracefully, the fork-tailed terns
Draw swift esprits across the sky.   15

Their aspirations dip in mine,
The quick order of their changing spirit,
More freedom than the eye can see.

Resting lightly on the oarlocks,
Pondering, and balanced on the sea,   20
A gauze and spindrift of the world,

I am in compulsion hid and thwarted,
Pulled back in the mammal water,
Enticed to the release of the sky.

— *Richard Eberhart*

Aids to Analysis

1. *What do the seals symbolize? What do the terns symbolize?*

2. *How is the meaning of the two symbols related in the speaker?*

LA BELLE DAME SANS MERCI

O, what can ail thee, knight-at-arms!
  Alone and palely loitering!
The sedge is withered from the lake,
  And no birds sing.

O, what can ail thee, knight-at-arms!   5
  So haggard and so woe-begone?
The squirrel's granary is full,
  And the harvest's done.

I see a lily on thy brow
  With anguish moist and fever dew,   10
And on thy cheek a fading rose
  Fast withereth too.

"I met a lady in the meads,
  Full beautiful—a faery's child:
Her hair was long, her foot was light,   15
  And her eyes were wild.

"I made a garland for her head,
  And bracelets too, and fragrant zone;
She looked at me as she did love,
  And made sweet moan.   20

"I set her on my pacing steed,
  And nothing else saw all day long;
For sideways would she bend, and sing
  A faery's song.

"She found me roots of relish sweet,   25
  And honey wild, and manna dew,
And sure in language strange she said,
  'I love thee true.'

"She took me to her elfin grot,
  And there she wept and sighed fùll sore   30
And there I shut her wild wild eyes
  With kisses four.

"And there she lullèd me asleep,
  And there I dreamed—ah! woe betide!—
The latest dream I ever dreamed   35
  On the cold hill's side.

"I saw pale kings, and princes too,
   Pale warriors, death-pale were they all;
They cried—'La belle Dame sans Merci
   Hath thee in thrall!'   *40*

"I saw their starved lips in the gloom,
   With horrid warning gapèd wide,
And I awoke, and found me here
   On the cold hill's side.

"And this is why I sojourn here,   *45*
   Alone and palely loitering,
Though the sedge is withered from the lake,
   And no birds sing."

                                        —John Keats

Aids to Analysis

1.   *What images suggest death?*

2.   *What images suggest dream or illusion?*

3.   *Determine the relationship between these two sets of images.*

4.   *What does the "beautiful lady" symbolize?*

THE YACHTS

contend in a sea which the land partly encloses
shielding them from the too heavy blows
of an ungoverned ocean which when it chooses

tortures the biggest hulls, the best man knows
to pit against its beating and sinks them pitilessly.   *5*
Mothlike in mists, scintillant in the minute

brilliance of cloudless days, with broad bellying sails
they glide to the wind tossing green water
from their sharp prows while over them the crew crawls

ant-like, solicitously grooming them, releasing,   *10*
making fast as they turn, lean far over and having
caught the wind again, side by side, head for the mark.

In a well guarded arena of open water surrounded by
lesser and greater craft which, sycophant, lumbering
and flittering follow them, they appear youthful, rare   *15*

as the light of a happy eye, live with the grace
of all that in the mind is feckless, free and
naturally to be desired. Now the sea which holds them

is moody, lapping their glossy sides, as if feeling
for some slightest flaw but fails completely.   *20*
Today no race. Then the wind comes again. The yachts

move, jockeying for a start, the signal is set and they
are off. Now the waves strike at them but they are too
well made, they slip through, though they take in canvas.

Arms with hands grasping seek to clutch at the prows.   *25*
Bodies thrown recklessly in the way are cut aside.
It is a sea of faces about them in agony, in despair

until the horror of the race dawns staggering the mind,
the whole sea become an entanglement of watery bodies
lost to the world bearing what they cannot hold. Broken,   *30*

beaten, desolate, reaching from the dead to be taken up
they cry out, failing, failing! their cries rising
in waves still as the skillful yachts pass over.

—William Carlos Williams

Aids to Analysis

1. *What is the difference between the "ungoverned ocean" (line 3) and the
    sea where the yachts race?*

2. *What characteristics of the yachts are established in stanzas 1–6?*

3. *Describe the relationship between the yachts and the sea in which they
    are sailing in stanzas 1–6.*

4. *Describe the relationship between the yachts and the sea in lines 18–33.
    Explain how this relationship differs from that in stanzas 1–6.*

5. *What is the symbolic meaning of yachts, sea, ocean, and land?*

Chapter 8

Words:
Denotation, Connotation, Allusion

In this chapter we will consider three ways in which a word may have meaning in a poem. It has a restricted definition or core meaning, known as its *denotation*. It may have implied associations, known as its *connotation*. Finally, it may function as an *allusion*, which is an indirect reference to another word or idea of greater meaning.

Example: Sunday

Denotation: The first day of the week
Connotation: A day of worship
Allusion: Hypocritical (as in "a Sunday Christian")

Denotation

The first step in understanding a word is to be sure of its denotation, often called its dictionary definition. This may be just a matter of clearing up your understanding of an unfamiliar word by checking the dictionary. But since most words can have several definitions, you may have to check the context carefully to see which meaning or meanings are intended. For example, in the phrase "She was frightened by the bay," any of several things could be responsible for her fright. It could be a horse, a window, a body of water, a piece of land, a dog, a sick room, etc. Only further context can tell us — such as "She was frightened by the bay as the dog came closer."

Connotation

Words are also used for their connotations or emotional meanings beyond the usual dictionary definition. In the sentence about the baying of the dog, our attitude toward the denotative dog is influenced by whether it is called dog, cur, hound, mongrel, or mutt. Mark Antony's famed "Cry, 'Havoc,' and let slip the *dogs* of war," would have stirred no pulse if he had used a word for dog with different connotations:

> Cry, *"Havoc," and let slip the* puppies *of war.*
> Cry, *"Havoc," and let slip the* mutts *of war.*

One denotation of *mother* is a woman who has borne a child. The word has connotations of security, warmth, love, selflessness. The term "female parent" has the same denotation as "mother" but the connotation is quite different. Female Parent Day is not likely to become an important event in our culture. Notice that both denotation and connotation are important in this brief poem:

IN A STATION OF THE METRO

The apparition of these faces in the crowd;
Petals on a wet, black bough.

—Ezra Pound

We must understand the denotation of "Metro" and "apparition" before we can see the image the poem is developing. "Metro" is an underground railway or subway. An "apparition" is anything which appears, especially suddenly. These words identify the situation and the scene: apparently the viewer sees the faces in the train coming into the station, or, perhaps, on the platform. These faces remind him of "Petals on a wet, black bough." They are related to the dark mass; yet they seem somehow detached.

Multiple meanings as well as single denotations are important in the poem. Checking the dictionary meanings against the context, we find that "apparition" is used here in both of its common definitions: "anything that appears, especially suddenly" and "ghost or phantom." These connotations add an unworldly tone that the word "appearance" would not give us. Likewise, "petal" gives us a denotation and a connotation that "flower" or "blossom" would not give. A blossom on a black bough is whole and growing, promising life to come. A petal on a black bough is severed, already dead.

With such careful study of denotations and connotations of words in their context, the image acquires meaning and emotion.

The denotations are of first concern in Edward Taylor's "Huswifery," if we are to understand the dominant metaphor of producing cloth. We need some knowledge of how a spinning wheel operates and what its various parts are (flyer, spool, etc.). Often the meaning of a strange word can be found by careful use of the dictionary. In stanza 2, you will find help by looking up the verb *full*.

HUSWIFERY

Make me, O Lord, thy Spinning Wheele compleat.
  Thy Holy Worde my Distaff make for mee.
Make mine Affections thy Swift Flyers neate
  And make my Soule thy holy Spoole to bee.
  My Conversation make to be thy Reele   5
  And reele the yarn thereon Spun of thy Wheele.

Make me thy Loome then, knit therein this Twine:
  And make thy Holy Spirit, Lord, winde quills:
Then weave the Web thyselfe. The yarn is fine.
  Thine Ordinances make my Fulling Mills.   *10*
  Then dy the Same in Heavenly Colours Choice,
  All pinkt with Varnisht Flowers of Paradise.

Then cloath therewith mine Understanding, Will,
  Affections, Judgment, Conscience, Memory;
My Words, and Actions, that their shine may fill   *15*
  My wayes with glory and thee glorify.
  Then mine apparell shall display before yee
  That I am Cloathd in Holy robes for glory.

              —Edward Taylor

Aids to Analysis

1. *List the words that need to be defined and consult your dictionary.*

2. *What is the central image in each stanza?*

3. *Note the dates of the author in the Index to learn the approximate time when the poem was written and check on the meanings of words that may have changed with the cultural context: Look in your dictionary for earlier definitions of these words:* varnish'd, affections, pinked.

Since a poem is a condensed form of expression, you must frequently look beyond a single precise denotation of a word to multiple meanings. See how many dictionary definitions of the words are pertinent to the context in the following poem:

GOD'S GRANDEUR

The world is charged with the grandeur of God.
    It will flame out, like shining from shook foil;
    It gathers to a greatness, like the ooze of oil
Crushed. Why do men then now not reck his rod?
Generations have trod, have trod, have trod;   *5*
    And all is seared with trade; bleared, smeared with toil;
    And wears man's smudge and shares man's smell: the soil
Is bare now, nor can foot feel, being shod.

And for all this, nature is never spent;
    There lives the dearest freshness deep down things;   *10*
And though the last lights off the black West went
    Oh, morning, at the brown brink eastward, springs—
Because the Holy Ghost over the bent
    World broods with warm breast and with ah! bright wings.

                       —*Gerard Manley Hopkins*

Notice the precise denotation of the words expressing the idea of God's potential or hidden, rather than open and fulfilled, action. The words "charged," "flame out," "shining from shook foil," "gathers," and "ooze . . . crushed" support the idea that man must do something if he is to perceive the grandeur of God.

Important multiple meanings are contained in "spent," "bent," and "broods." "Nature is never spent" has the meaning of being inexhaustible or never used up, and also never taken advantage of or used by man, who by contrast does spend in the "trade" of line 6. The "bent" world gives a geographical image of the curvature of earth and a religious sense of the moral twist in the nature of man who does not heed God's counsel and does need the help of the Holy Ghost. The word "broods" in context with "breast" and "wings" carries at least three of the common dictionary definitions of the verb: to think deeply and anxiously about something, to hover over or protect, and to sit on to hatch (as eggs). These denotations help give a sense of an everpresent potential and operative grandeur of God which is there with "bright wings" for man even though man does not grasp it.

Connotations are especially important in the following poem:

PARTING, WITHOUT A SEQUEL

She has finished and sealed the letter
At last, which he so richly has deserved,
With characters venomous and hatefully curved,
And nothing could be better.

But even as she gave it,   5
Saying to the blue-capped functioner of doom,
"Into his hands," she hoped the leering groom
Might somewhere lose and leave it.

Then all the blood
Forsook the face. She was too pale for tears,   10
Observing the ruin of her younger years.
She went and stood

Under her father's vaunting oak
Who kept his peace in wind and sun, and glistened
Stoical in the rain; to whom she listened   15
If he spoke.

And now the agitation of the rain
Rasped his sere leaves, and he talked low and gentle,
Reproaching the wan daughter by the lintel;
Ceasing and beginning again.   20

Away went the messenger's bicycle,
His serpent's track went up the hill forever,
And all the time she stood there hot as fever
And cold as any icicle.

—*John Crowe Ransom*

We see the tragic-comic aspects of a young girl ending an attachment, perhaps her first love affair. The situation is tragic to her, and we feel for her as she seeks solace from her father. But the theatrical and melodramatic connotations of words and phrases describing the girl's emotions do not convince us of tragedy. She will get over it.

Among the theatrical and melodramatic effects are the title with the storybook "Parting" and "Sequel." There is also melodrama in "so richly has deserved," "hatefully curved," "serpent's track" (implying the evil of a Satan), and "too pale for tears" (tears do not depend upon blood in the face). "Into his hands" and "functioner of doom" are pretentious. Special exaggerations are used in "ruin of her younger years" and "forever." Childish responses show up in her vengeful and smug "nothing could be better" and her hoping the messenger will lose the letter.

We feel for the girl by the last stanza. Her torn emotions of hot and cold are believable. But the lightness is sustained by the image and tone of the triple *bicycle — icicle* rhyme and the final effect is not that of deep tragedy.

Coinages. Poets may coin words for purely nonsensical fun, as Lewis Carroll did in "Jabberwocky." Or they may use coined words seriously for special meanings and effects. With this purpose, both denotation and connotation are involved. The best way to understand coined words is to use a little free imagination to associate the coined word with the standard words it was built from. A "thinkathon" would be a long, grueling thinking contest. A "squiggle" is a combination of "squirm" and "wiggle." E. E. Cummings illustrates the serious use of coined words.

PITY THIS BUSY MONSTER, MANUNKIND

pity this busy monster,manunkind,

not. Progress is a comfortable disease:
your victim (death and life safely beyond)

plays with the bigness of his littleness
— electrons deify one razorblade   5
into a mountainrange;lenses extend

unwish through curving wherewhen till unwish
returns on its unself.
                           A world of made
is not a world of born — pity poor flesh   10

and trees,poor stars and stones,but never this
fine specimen of hypermagical

ultraomnipotence. We doctors know

a hopeless case if — listen:there's a hell
of a good universe next door;let's go   15

                        — *E. E. Cummings*

The first coinage, *manunkind*, combines two words, *mankind* and *unkind,* with a pun on the word *kind*, both a biological species and having a sympathetic nature. Man is an unkind "kind" or species. The simple joining of two words into one produces *razorblade* and *moun-tainrange*. *Unwish* causes us to think of *wish*, which means *want* or *goal*. We have then a negative, not-goal or without a goal, probably referring to that "busy monster." *Wherewhen* joins adverbs of place and time, a combination that plunges us into the space-time con-tinuum of twentieth-century physics. This interpretation is supported by *curving*, that is, the idea that space is curved, with unwish returning to unwish in an aimless circle. *Unself* apparently means *no self* or *lack of self*. *Made* and *born* function as nouns (objects of preposi-tions), elliptical expressions standing for world of "things that are made" in contrast to a world of "things that are born"—that is, artificial as opposed to living things. *Hyper* in *hypermagical* has, we find, an unsavory implication: more than the normal, excessive, as in *hypersensitive* and *hypercritical*. So we live in a world that is excessively magical. *Ultra* in *ultraomnipotence* also implies *excessive, beyond reasonable limits*. Or, more literally, it means *beyond*. *Ultramodern* means excessively modern. So *ultraomnipotent* means excessively unlimited power, a paradoxical conception that fits in with the earlier paradoxes: progress—disease; bigness—littleness; razorblade—moun-tainrange. All these contradictions are so self-destructive ("unwish returns on its unself") that there is only one thing to do: depart for the "universe next door."

Allusion

An allusion is a word or phrase that refers to a broader context. It enriches the immediate statement by drawing upon a larger frame of reference—historical, literary, religious, mythological. Our literature is full of allusions to the Bible and classical mythology, as well as to any number of other traditions in our culture. When we say that a person has the patience of Job, we are alluding to the biblical story of Job, and we are assuming that the hearer has some knowledge of that story. The following poem employs a number of allusions.

KARMA

> Christmas was in the air and all was well
> With him, but for a few confusing flaws
> In divers of God's images. Because
> A friend of his would neither buy nor sell,

Was he to answer for the axe that fell?   5
He pondered; and the reason for it was,
Partly, a slowly freezing Santa Claus
Upon the corner, with his beard and bell.

Acknowledging an improvident surprise,
He magnified a fancy that he wished   10
The friend whom he had wrecked were here again.
Not sure of that, he found a compromise;
And from the fullness of his heart he fished
A dime for Jesus who had died for men.

                                        — *E. A. Robinson*

The dictionary tells us that Karma is a term in Buddhism and Hinduism signifying that a person's destiny in one existence is determined by the moral quality of his actions in a preceding existence. This definition implies moral responsibility and at the same time a certain fatalism.

Once into the poem, Robinson mentions "divers of God's images," which is an allusion to Genesis 1:27: "So God created man in his own image, in the image of God created he him. . ." The character in the poem "fished" into his pocket, an allusion to Matthew 4:19, where Jesus says to Peter and Andrew, "Follow me, and I will make you fishers of men." The final line, of course, alludes to the crucifixion of Jesus.

There are also allusions to the business world. In line 4 "neither buy nor sell" suggests a large business transaction. "Dime" in line 14, besides being simply a small monetary unit, implies that the person put a small value upon his remorse, as in "a dime a dozen."

Other allusions reinforce this contrast between our business ethics and our religious tradition. "Christmas was in the air" has a colloquial flavor that is incongruous with the solemn implications of the last line. The Santa Claus is "slowly freezing," an implication of death but not of religious sacrifice. Rather, this impending death implies the indifference of modern society. "Acknowledge an improvident surprise" suggests a defensive reaction, as though the momentary guilt feeling is sinful in terms of business ethics. The word *compromise* has become almost a magical word throughout our society. We learn the necessity of compromising, of "getting along." The bitter irony of the first two lines contrasts the "fullness" of this man's heart with the heart of Jesus. The series of allusions beforehand sharpens the ironic balance here at the end.

Study Poems

SONNET—TO SCIENCE

Science! true daughter of Old Time thou art!
Who alterest all things with thy peering eyes,
Why preyest thou thus upon the poet's heart,
Vulture, whose wings are dull realities?
How should he love thee? or how deem thee wise,   *5*
Who wouldst not leave him in his wandering
To seek for treasure in the jewelled skies,
Albeit he soared with an undaunted wing?
Hast thou not dragged Diana from her car?
And driven the Hamadryad from the wood   *10*
To seek a shelter in some happier star?
Hast thou not torn the Naiad from her flood,
The Elfin from the green grass, and from me
The summer dream beneath the tamarind tree?

           —*Edgar Allan Poe*

Aids to Analysis

Identify the allusions through use of a dictionary or encyclopedia.

THREES

I was a boy when I heard three red words
a thousand Frenchmen died in the streets
for: Liberty, Equality, Fraternity—I asked
why men die for words.

I was older; men with mustaches, sideburns,   *5*
lilacs, told me the high golden words are:
Mother, Home, and Heaven—other older men with
face decorations said: God, Duty, Immortality
—they sang these threes slow from deep lungs.

Years ticked off their say-so on the great clocks   *10*
of doom and damnation, soup and nuts: meteors flashed
their say-so: and out of great Russia came three
dusky syllables workmen took guns and went out to die
for: Bread, Peace, Land.

And I met a marine of the U.S.A., a leatherneck with   *15*
a girl on his knee for a memory in ports circling the

earth and he said: Tell me how to say three things
and I always get by—gimme a plate of ham and eggs—
how much?—and, do you love me, kid?

—*Carl Sandburg*

Aids to Analysis

Discuss the denotations and the connotations of the key words of the poem in
terms of the great effects they had on the people of the poem.

JABBERWOCKY

'Twas brillig, and the slithy toves
    Did gyre and gimble in the wabe;
All mimsy were the borogroves,
    And the mome raths outgrabe.

"Beware the Jabberwock, my son!   5
    The jaws that bite, the claws that catch!
Beware the Jubjub bird, and shun
    The frumious Bandersnatch!"

He took his vorpal sword in hand;
    Long time the manxome foe he sought—   10
So rested he by the Tumtum tree,
    And stood awhile in thought.

And, as in uffish thought he stood,
    The Jabberwock, with eyes of flame,
Came whiffling through the tulgey wood,   15
    And burbled as it came!

One, two! One, two! And through and through
    The vorpal blade went snicker-snack!
He left it dead, and with its head
    He went galumphing back.   20

"And hast thou slain the Jabberwock?
    Come to my arms, my beamish boy!
O frabjous day! Callooh! Callay!"
    He chortled in his joy.

'Twas brillig, and the slithy toves   25
    Did gyre and gimble in the wabe;
All mimsy were the borogroves,
    And the mome raths outgrabe.

—*Lewis Carroll*

Aids to Analysis

1. *See how many of the word coinages you can associate with standard
    words they may have been built from. For instance, "slithy" suggests a
    combination of "slippery" and "lithe."*

2. *Discuss possible connotations and denotations of the coinages.*

THE HARLOT'S HOUSE

> We caught the tread of dancing feet,
> We loitered down the moonlit street,
> And stopped beneath the Harlot's House.
> Inside, above the din and fray,
> We heard the loud musicians play   5
> The "Treues Liebes Herz" of Strauss.
>
> Like strange mechanical grotesques,
> Making fantastic arabesques,
> The shadows raced across the blind.
> We watched the ghostly dancers spin,   10
> To sound of horn and violin,
> Like black leaves wheeling in the wind.
>
> Like wire-pulled Automatons,
> Slim silhouetted skeletons
> Went sidling through the slow quadrille,   15
> Then took each other by the hand,
> And danced a stately saraband;
> Their laughter echoed thin and shrill.
>
> Sometimes a clock-work puppet pressed
> A phantom lover to her breast,   20
> Sometimes they seemed to try and sing.
> Sometimes a horrible Marionette
> Came out and smoked its cigarette
> Upon the steps like a live thing.
>
> Then turning to my love I said,   25
> "The dead are dancing with the dead,
> The dust is whirling with the dust."
> But she, she heard the violin,
> And left my side and entered in:
> Love passed into the House of Lust.   30
>
> Then suddenly the tune went false,
> The dancers wearied of the waltz,
> The shadows ceased to wheel and whirl,

And down the long and silent street,
The dawn with silver-sandaled feet,   35
Crept like a frightened girl.

— *Oscar Wilde*

Aids to Analysis

1. *The speaker summarizes the situation in the harlot's house as "The
    dead are dancing with the dead." Pick out words, phrases, and figures
    of speech with connotations and denotations of deadness and
    artificiality.*

2. *Pick out words which connote life and beauty in contrast to the dead-
    ness and ugliness of the harlot's house. The Strauss waltz alluded to is
    translated "Heart of True Love."*

SPRING AND FALL

TO A YOUNG CHILD

Márgarét, are you grieving
Over Goldengrove unleaving?
Leáves, líke the things of man, you
With your fresh thoughts care for, can you?
Áh! ás the heart grows older   5
It will come to such sights colder
By and by, nor spare a sigh
Though worlds of wanwood leafmeal lie;
And yet you wíll weep and know why.
Now no matter, child, the name: 10
Sórrow's spríngs áre the same.
Nor mouth had, no nor mind, expressed
What heart heard of, ghost guessed:
It ís the blight man was born for,
It is Margaret you mourn for.   15

— *Gerard Manley Hopkins*

Aids to Analysis

1. *Hopkins was a religious poet. What are the religious connotations of
    fall? What other connotations of fall are there in the poem?*

2. *What is the difference in the meaning of "Spring" in the title and
    "springs" in "Sorrow's springs"? (line 11)*

3. *What different meanings are suggested by the title? What common meanings of the title apply to the content of the poem?*

4. *What dictionary meaning of "ghost" best fits the context—that is, what meaning would function best with* mouth, mind, *and* heart *at expressing something or guessing something?*

5. *What is the denotative and connotative effect of the use of "blight" rather than "condition" or "disease"?*

6. *What is the "Fall" in the title besides autumn and the falling of leaves? Notice that the context tells us that the fall is related to leaves falling, to sights immeasurably colder than leaves falling, to a heart growing colder, to a blight natural to man ("born for"), and to the cause of all sorrow.*

7. *Define each of the two parts of the word coinages and then combine the two meanings to arrive at the poetic effect:* Goldengrove, wanwood, leafmeal.

SOMEWHERE I HAVE NEVER TRAVELLED

somewhere i have never travelled, gladly beyond
any experience, your eyes have their silence:
in your most frail gesture are things which enclose me,
or which i cannot touch because they are too near

your slightest look easily will unclose me   5
though i have closed myself as fingers,
you open always petal by petal myself as Spring opens
(touching skilfully, mysteriously) her first rose

or if your wish be to close me, i and
my life will shut very beautifully, suddenly,   10
as when the heart of this flower imagines
the snow carefully everywhere descending;

nothing which we are to perceive in this world equals
the power of your intense fragility: whose texture
compels me with the colour of its countries,   15
rendering death and forever with each breathing

(i do not know what is it about you that closes
and opens; only something in me understands
the voice of your eyes is deeper than all roses)
nobody, not even the rain, has such small hands   20

—*E. E. Cummings*

Aids to Analysis

1.   *What words and phrases suggest strength and delicacy?*

2.   *What words and phrases emphasize a close relationship between man and nature?*

3.   *To evaluate the connotations of various words, try these substitutions: "voyaged" for "travelled"; "open" for "unclose"; "center" for "heart"; "shut" for "close" (line 9); "close" for "shut" (line 10); "composition" for "texture"; "forces" for "compels"; "wee" for "small."*

METAMORPHOSIS

Yillow, yillow, yillow,
Old worm, my pretty quirk,
How the wind spells out
Sep - tem - ber. . . .

Summer is in bones.   5
Cock-robin's at Caracas.
Make o, make o, make o,
Oto - otu - bre.

And the rude leaves fall.
The rain falls. The sky   10
Falls and lies with the worms.
The street lamps

Are those that have been hanged,
Dangling in an illogical
To and to and fro   15
Fro Niz - nil - imbo.

— *Wallace Stevens*

Aids to Analysis

1.   *Which meaning of "metamorphosis" in the dictionary is most suited to the context? How many kinds of metamorphoses take place in the poem?*

2.   *Find at least four standard denotative words varied and buried in the last line.*

3.   *Apply the dictionary definition of "quirk" to "worm."*

4. *What are the denotative and connotative meanings of "hanged" as applied to the lamps?*

5. *What is the connotative effect of calling the robin "cock-robin" and using "Caracas" instead of the usual migratory "south"?*

6. *What dictionary definitions of "rude" fit the context?*

7. *Discuss the effectiveness of the coinages "yillow," "o," and "oto-otubre." Bear in mind the title of the poem and what is occurring in the poem.*

NOW SLEEPS THE CRIMSON PETAL

Now sleeps the crimson petal, now the white:
Nor waves the cypress in the palace walk;
Nor winks the gold fin in the porphyry font:
The fire-fly wakens: waken thou with me.

Now droops the milk-white peacock like a ghost,   5
And like a ghost she glimmers on to me.

Now lies the Earth all Danaë to the stars,
And all thy heart lies open unto me.

Now slides the silent meteor on, and leaves
A shining furrow, as thy thoughts in me.   10

Now folds the lily all her sweetness up,
And slips into the bosom of the lake.
So fold thyself, my dearest, thou, and slip
Into my bosom and be lost in me.

—Alfred, Lord Tennyson

Aids to Analysis

1. *Define "porphyry" and "font."*

2. *Look up "Danaë" in the dictionary or encyclopedia to see what meaning the allusion brings to the poem.*

3. *Many of the words have special connotations that support the overall effect. Discuss the effects of the words used rather than near-synonyms that could have been used: as "winks" rather than "splashes"; "ghost" rather than "ghoul" or "spook"; "glimmers" rather than "glitters" or "glows"; "slides" rather than "zips"; "bosom of the lake" rather than "bottom of the lake."*

Chapter 9

Sound and Rhythm

Patterns of sound and rhythm are obvious marks of verse. Here is a simple example:

> Hickory, dickory, dock,
> The mouse ran up the clock.
> The clock struck one.
> The mouse ran down,
> Hickory, dickory, dock.

We know this is verse immediately by the lilting rhythm and the repetitions of sounds. It has little idea content, no moral, no message. But children and many adults consider it a pleasurable experience. We are intrigued by the repetitions and variations of *Hickory* and *dickory*, of *Hick-* and *dick-*, of *dock* and *clock*, and the last line echoing the first line. The experience is hardly more than the conspicuous patterns of sound and movement. If we try it without the refrain lines, which in themselves are nonsense but fun, we end up with inanity, not even fun, not even acceptable verse:

> The mouse ran up the clock.
> The clock struck one.
> The mouse ran down.

From this example we note two main functions of sound and rhythm besides giving pleasure in themselves: they help to provide external structure, and they reinforce idea and emotion.

As art, a poem must have a structure of some kind. The deeper form of a poem grows out of the theme and the pattern of images, metaphor, idea, and significant words. But patterns of sound and rhythm are necessary means of expression. The importance of such patterns is seen in counting rhymes and in memory rhymes. The pattern of "Eeny meeny" determines who will win or lose. Some of us depend upon "Thirty days hath September" to tell us which months have only thirty days. Most of us tend to be vague about the verse after the *November* rhyme, because the rhymes in the rest of the verse are not sharp.

In more serious poetry, the famous "Nevermore" of Poe's "The Raven" is one of the devices for tying the parts of the poem together and for supporting the idea and emotion of the poem. After the raven's entrance, the poem moves to the inevitable climax, each step being ironically marked by the word "Nevermore." The sound and rhythm of Tennyson's "The Charge of the Light Brigade" are apt for a cavalry charge:

> Half a league, half a league,
> Half a league onward,
> All in the valley of Death
>   Rode the six hundred.

But the gentle melody of love is conveyed (by Burns) in a different style:

> My Mary's asleep by thy murmuring stream,
> Flow gently, sweet Afton, disturb not her dream.

To analyze the effects that sound and rhythm have in a poem, we must look at the basic devices common to patterns of sound and rhythm.

Patterns of Sound

Most of the common elements of sound patterns can be illustrated by this poem by Tennyson:

THE SPLENDOR FALLS

> The splendor falls on castle walls
>   And snowy summits old in story;
> The long light shakes across the lakes,
>   And the wild cataract leaps in glory.
> Blow, bugle, blow, set the wild echoes flying,   5
> Blow, bugle; answer, echoes, dying, dying, dying.

O hark, O hear! how thin and clear,
    And thinner, clearer, farther going!
O sweet and far from cliff and scar
    The horns of Elfland faintly blowing!   *10*
Blow, let us hear the purple glens replying,
Blow, bugle; answer, echoes, dying, dying, dying.

O love, they die in yon rich sky,
    They faint on hill or field or river;
Our echoes roll from soul to soul,   *15*
    And grow for ever and for ever.
Blow, bugle, blow, set the wild echoes flying,
And answer, echoes, answer, dying, dying, dying.

Rhyme

Rhyme is the repetition of identical or nearly identical sounds. Rhyme usually occurs in the last syllable or syllables of two or more lines. The repetition normally involves the stressed vowel sound and any sounds that follow: *shakes — lakes, going — blowing.*

Exact rhyme (or *perfect rhyme*) is the repetition of identical sounds, as *flying — dying* (in other poems, *roam — home*).

Slant rhyme (or *off rhyme, approximate rhyme, consonance, assonance*) is a repetition of similar sounds but not identical sounds. Usually only the final consonants are identical; the vowel sounds are approximate. Slant rhymes in Tennyson's poem are *clear — scar* and *river — forever.*

Feminine rhyme includes two or more syllables. The first accented syllable of the group is the rhyming syllable and is followed by identical sounds: *going — blowing.*

Masculine rhyme is a one-syllable repetition of sound. "The Splendor Falls" does not use an exact masculine rhyme. A typical masculine rhyme is *thing — Spring* in Pope's couplet:

A little learning is a dangerous thing;
Drink deep, or taste not the Pierian Spring.

The Tennyson poem does have a slant masculine rhyme in *clear — scar.*

End rhyme is a rhyme which occurs at the end of a line, as in the Pope couplet above.

Internal rhyme is a rhyme with at least one of the rhyming syllables within the line. The other may be at the end. The first and third lines of each stanza of the Tennyson poem use internal rhyme: *falls — walls.*

Other Kinds of Sound Repetition

Alliteration is the repetition of neighboring consonant sounds, usually at the beginning of words. Examples are the *s* in *snowy summits*, the *l* in *long light*, and the *b* in *Blow, bugle, blow.* Alliteration may be internal as in *Elfland faintly.*

Assonance is the repetition of neighboring accented vowel sounds followed by different consonant sounds. Examples are the *o* in *snowy — old.* Assonance is sometimes used to indicate the similarity as well as the identity of any sounds, as the *ar — ear* in *hark — hear.*

Consonance is the repetition of the same consonant sounds (usually at the end of words) after different accented vowel sounds. Examples are *clear — scar, river — forever.*

Onomatopoeia is the use of a word whose sound echoes or suggests its meaning. There is no example in "The Splendor Falls," but here are some general examples: *tweet, chirp, cluck,* and *quack.* An example in Denise Levertov's "Six Variations" is the use of *shlup* to describe a dog drinking water. Other examples are *clank, wha,* and *pah* in William Carlos Williams' poem with the freight car image, "To Freight Cars in Air."

Much of the effect of "The Splendor Falls" comes from the use of sounds. The meaning of the poem is based on sound — the sound of a bugle which blows, and echoes, and dies, in contrast to a love which rolls or echoes from soul to soul and never dies, but goes on forever. The interplay of rhymes and other sounds reinforces the meaning and effect of the poem. For example, the abruptly ending rhymes (*clear — scar*) set a counterpoint for the prolonged echoing effect of the feminine rhyme (*going — blowing, replying — dying*).

Rhyme, alliteration, and assonance are basic obvious patterns of sound. There are many other kinds of sound repetition used effectively in poetry, many of which we do not even have standard terms for. There is no standard term to describe the pattern of the interplay of *blow — echoes — answers — dying* in

> Blow, bugle, blow, set the wild echoes flying,
> And answer, echoes, answer, dying, dying, dying.

Again there is no standard term to define the thread of *ar* and *ear* sounds that runs through the second stanza: *hark—hear—clear—clearer—farther—far—scar—horns—hear—purple.*

Vowel and Consonant Sounds

There are other sounds to consider besides patterns of repetition. Particular vowels, consonants, and their combinations can have different effects. Depending on such qualities as the ease or force with which they are said, the poem can be fast or slow, flowing or halting, light or heavy, melodious or harsh.

Vowel sounds may be long (as in *bite, beat, bait, boat, boot*) or short (as in *bit, bet, bat, but*). They may be front (as in *beat, bit, bait, bat, bet*) or back (as in *boot, boat, bought*) or middle (as in *but* and *bother*). They may be diphthongs (as in *boil, by, brown*). Long vowel sounds have more force and longer duration than short sounds. Diphthongs take even more time.

Consonants may affect movement depending upon whether they are continuants or stops, voiced or voiceless. As continuants, they may be liquid (as *l, m, n, r*) or fricative (as *s, z, sh, th, v, f, h*). The stops are *b, p, d, t, g, k.* Consonants may also be voiced (as *v, d, b, g*), or they may be voiceless (as *f, t, p, k*).

Liquid consonants as in *lawn, roar,* and *moon* move fluidly with no break in the voice. Stop consonants as in *pub, dot,* and *king* can be spoken only by stopping the voice flow; consequently they suggest force or impediment. Clusters of consonants, as in *twitched* and *basked,* slow and obstruct movement.

It also makes a difference to the movement and tone of the poem which vowel and consonant combinations are used. For instance, the low front vowel sound in *fat* is usually not as pleasant to the ear and the emotions as is the middle vowel sound in *ah* or the back vowel sound in *moon.* The upper front sounds as in *seat* and *sit* usually move more briskly than back sounds as in *so* and *suit.* The front long sound in *weight* tends to carry weight and force.

These lists offer only brief suggestions of the many possibilities of sound effects to look for in a poem. Notice here how some of these vowel and consonant combinations work in "The Splendor Falls":

> The long light shakes across the lakes,
> And the wild cataract leaps in glory.

The lines cannot be read lightly or fast. There are consonant clusters in half of the words (as *shakes, lakes, cataract*). Many vowel sounds are long (as *lakes, leaps, glory, long, across*). This combination of vowel sounds and consonants helps make the lines slow, forceful, and heavy—appropriate to the bugle sound about to come.

By contrast, these two lines are light and fast:

> O hark, O hear! how thin and clear,
> And thinner, clearer, farther going!

There is a predominance of front vowel sounds joined with *r* and *n*, and there is a lack of stop consonants and other consonants. The lines move with speed, lightness, and delicacy—appropriate to the fading sound of a bugle.

Two other lines move slowly and continuously:

> Our echoes roll from soul to soul,
> And grow for ever and for ever.

A sense of solemnity is produced by the long *o*, used five times, four of them in successive accented syllables. The use of continuant consonants (*l, m, r, s, v, f*) with only two stop consonants (*ch* and *g*) adds a sense of continuity, supported by the falling rhyme in *for ever*, used twice. Such sound effects reinforce the sense that the very meaningful love will go on forever, unlike the bugle sound which is dying.

EXERCISE:

Vowel and consonant sounds

Analyze the following passages for their use of vowel and consonant sounds. Note what effect the sounds may have on the movement and tone of the poem. For instance, are the lines fast or slow, flowing or halting, melodious or harsh, light or heavy?

1. How many vowel sounds are long? How many are short? Which consonants tend to impede movement?

> Break, break, break,
> On thy cold gray stones, O Sea!
> And I would that my tongue could utter
> The thoughts that arise in me.   (Tennyson)

2. What vowel and consonant sounds especially support the mood and idea of aloneness?

> Alone, alone, all, all alone,
> Alone on a wide wide sea!
> And never a saint took pity on
> My soul in agony.   (Coleridge)

3.   Comment on the appropriateness of the sounds in supporting the idea of awakening.

>   Wake! For the Sun, who scattered into flight
>   The Stars before him from the Field of Night,
>   Drives Night along with them from Heav'n and strikes
>   The Sultan's Turret with a Shaft of Light.   (FitzGerald)

4.   Compare the speed with which you can read the following three passages. What combinations of vowels and consonants make one passage move more rapidly or slowly than the others?

>   I chatter, chatter, as I flow
>   To join the brimming river,
>   For men may come and men may go,
>   But I go on forever.   (Tennyson)

>   Midst thickest mists
>   And stiffest frosts,
>   He stuffs his fists
>   Against the posts
>   And still insists
>   He sees the ghosts.

>   Peter Piper picked a peck of pickled peppers. If Peter
>   Piper picked a peck of pickled peppers, where's the peck
>   of pickled peppers Peter Piper picked?

Study Poems

REQUIESCAT

>   Strew on her roses, roses,
>   And never a spray of yew!
>   In quiet she reposes;
>   Ah, would that I did too!
>
>   Her mirth the world required;   5
>   She bathed it in smiles of glee.
>   But her heart was tired, tired,
>   And now they let her be.
>
>   Her life was turning, turning,
>   In mazes of heat and sound.   10
>   But for peace her soul was yearning,
>   And now peace laps her round.

Her cabined, ample spirit,
　It fluttered and failed for breath.
Tonight it doth inherit   *15*
　The vasty hall of death.

　　　　　　—*Matthew Arnold*

Aids to Analysis

1.　*Find an example of end rhyme, masculine rhyme, feminine rhyme, and*
slant rhyme.

2.　*Find an instance of alliteration.*

TO NIGHT

I

Swiftly walk o'er the western wave,
　Spirit of Night!
Out of the misty eastern cave,
Where all the long and lone daylight,
Thou wovest dreams of joy and fear,   *5*
Which make thee terrible and dear,—
　Swift be thy flight!

II

Wrap thy form in a mantle grey,
　Star-inwrought!
Blind with thine hair the eyes of Day;   *10*
Kiss her until she be wearied out,
Then wander o'er city, and sea, and land,
Touching all with thine opiate wand—
　Come, long-sought!

III

When I arose and saw the dawn,   *15*
　I sighed for thee;
When light rode high, and the dew was gone,
And noon lay heavy on flower and tree,
And the weary Day turned to his rest,
Lingering like an unloved guest,   *20*
　I sighed for thee.

IV

Thy brother Death came, and cried,
　Wouldst thou me?

Thy sweet child Sleep, the filmy-eyed,
Murmured like a noon-tide bee,   25
Shall I nestle near thy side?
Wouldst thou me? — and I replied,
   No, not thee!

V

Death will come when thou art dead,
   Soon, too soon —   30
Sleep will come when thou art fled;
Of neither would I ask the boon
I ask of thee, belovèd Night —
Swift be thine approaching flight,
   Come soon, soon!   35

             — *Percy Bysshe Shelley*

Aids to Analysis

Study the poem carefully for all uses of sound repetition (rhyme, alliteration, assonance, etc.). What special use of vowel and consonant combinations does the poet make?

Patterns of Rhythm

Rhythm in traditional English poetry is based on meter, a regular pattern of stressed and unstressed syllables. The basic unit of meter is the *foot*. The usual metrical foot consists of one stressed syllable and one or two unstressed syllables. In *scansion*, or the marking of meter, a stressed syllable is here indicated by a slant line (*héy*) and an unstressed syllable by a curved line (*thĕ*). One foot is separated from another by an upright bar:

          ˘   ′   ˘ ′   ˘   ′   ˘ ′ ˘ ′
         That time | of year | thou mayst | in me | behold |

The Metrical Foot

There are four common kinds of feet:
iambic (an iamb)   2 syllables: unstressed, stressed

of course, the door

The woods | decay, | the woods | decay | and fall. |
("Tithonus," Tennyson)

trochaic (a trochee)   2 syllables: stressed, unstressed

winter, stop it

Once up | on a | midnight | dreary, | while I | pondered | weak and |
weary |
("The Raven," Poe)

anapestic (an anapest)   3 syllables: unstressed, unstressed, stressed

entertain, in the night

For the moon | never beams | without bring | ing me dreams. |
("Annabel Lee," Poe)

dactyllic (a dactyl)   3 syllables: stressed, unstressed, unstressed

rapidly, hammer it

Half a league, | half a league |
("The Charge of the Light Brigade,"
Tennyson)

Besides these four basic kinds of feet, three other kinds are frequently used as substitutes in a basic meter. They are never used as
the meter for an entire poem, for the regularity of beat would allow
none of the rise and fall which makes rhythm:
spondaic (a spondee)   2 syllables: stressed, stressed

sunset, backyard

pyrrhic (a pyrrhic)   2 syllables: unstressed, unstressed

in a, in the

monosyllabic (a monosyllable)   1 syllable: stressed

hey

Three spondaic feet and a pyrrhic are used in this couplet, which is
primarily iambic:

When A | jax strives | some rock's | vast weight | to throw, |
The line | too la | bors, and | the words | move slow. |
(Pope)

In the following passage, three monosyllabic feet make up the first line. The second line has a spondaic foot between the anapestic and the iambic:

$$\breve{}\quad\breve{}\quad\acute{,}\text{Break,} \mid \text{br}\acute{\text{e}}\text{ak,} \mid \text{break,} \mid$$
$$\text{On thy cold} \mid \text{gray stones,} \mid \text{O Sea!} \mid$$

(Tennyson)

It is possible to scan some lines differently and still accurately describe the basic pattern of rhythm. Notice, for instance, the following lines:

$$\text{Before} \mid \text{the begin} \mid \text{ning of years} \mid$$
$$\text{There came} \mid \text{to the mak} \mid \text{ing of man} \mid$$
$$\text{Time,} \mid \text{with a gift} \mid \text{of tears} \mid$$
$$\text{Grief,} \mid \text{with a glass} \mid \text{that ran.} \mid$$

(Swinburne)

The words *Time* and *Grief* are preferably called monosyllabic feet because of the iambic-anapestic pattern set up in lines one and two. But to describe the words as parts of trochaic feet would indicate the same overall rhythmic effect:

$$\text{Time, with} \mid \text{a gift} \mid \text{of tears} \mid$$

As another illustration, in the following lines the prevailing dactyl meter leads one to expect the last foot in each line to be dactyllic:

$$\text{Just for a} \mid \text{handful of} \mid \text{silver he} \mid \text{left us,} \mid$$
$$\text{Just for a} \mid \text{ribbon to} \mid \text{stick in his} \mid \text{coat.}$$

(Browning)

The final foot in each line may be thought of as a *truncated* dactyl, with the expected syllable or syllables omitted. Or they may be thought of as a trochaic foot and monosyllabic foot.

The Metrical Line

Rhythm is also measured by the number of feet in a line. A line of one foot is *monometer;* a line of two feet is *dimeter.* Others are *trimeter* (three), *tetrameter* (four), *pentameter* (five), *hexameter* (six), *heptameter* (seven), and *octameter* (eight). The lines given above as examples of the four basic metrical feet may be described by length of line:

"Tithonus"	iambic pentameter
"The Raven"	trochaic heptameter
"Annabel Lee"	anapestic tetrameter
"The Charge of the Light Brigade"	dactyllic dimeter

EXERCISE. Basic Meter

Identify the prevailing kind of foot and the line length.

1. The curfew tolls the knell of parting day. (Gray)

2. Double, double, toil and trouble. (Shakespeare)

3. And the dish ran away with the spoon.

4. This is the forest primeval, the murmuring pines and the hemlocks. (Longfellow)

5. Love took up the glass of time, and turned it in his glowing hands; Every moment, lightly shaken, ran itself in golden sands. (Tennyson)

6. The Assyrian came down like a wolf on the fold. (Byron)

7. No longer mourn for me when I am dead. (Shakespeare)

8. Music, when soft voices die, Vibrates in the memory. (Shelley)

9. And the women were weeping and wringing their hands. (Kingsley)

10. And ten low words oft creep in one dull line. (Pope)

STUDY POEMS

ON SEEING A HAIR OF LUCRETIA BORGIA

Borgia, thou once were almost too august
And high for adoration; — now thou'rt dust;
All that remains of thee these plaits infold,
Calm hair, meandering with pellucid gold!

— Walter Savage Landor

Aids to Analysis

The prevailing meter may be considered iambic, but there are several variations. Read the poem with natural emphasis; then mark the stressed syllables with a slant line (') and the unstressed with a curved line (˘). What kinds of feet do you find?

SLOW, SLOW, FRESH FOUNT

Slow, slow, fresh fount, keep time with my salt tears;
   Yet slower, yet, oh, faintly, gentle springs;
List to the heavy part the music bears,
   Woe weeps out her division when she sings.
      Droop herbs and flowers;   5
      Fall grief in showers;
      Our beauties are not ours;
        Oh, I could still,
Like melting snow upon some craggy hill,
   Drop, drop, drop, drop,   10
Since nature's pride is now a withered daffodil.

                    —*Ben Jonson*

Aids to Analysis

Mark the syllables as stressed or unstressed. How many different kinds of metrical feet and line lengths are there?

Variations in Rhythm

    Few poems have the regularity of meter seen in most of the preceding examples. Mechanical regularity in poems of quality is neither common nor desirable. In analyzing the rhythm of a poem, what we do is identify the basic kind of feet, and then study the variations. In Wordsworth's "The World Is Too Much with Us," we find the basic iambic pentameter that we expect in a sonnet. But there are many variations. Six of these can be seen in Wordsworth's sonnet:

THE WORLD IS TOO MUCH WITH US

The world is too much with us; late and soon,
Getting and spending, we lay waste our powers:
Little we see in Nature that is ours;
We have given our hearts away, a sordid boon!
The Sea that bares her bosom to the moon;   5
The winds that will be howling at all hours,
And are up-gathered now like sleeping flowers;

> For this, for everything, we are out of tune;
> It moves us not. — Great God! I'd rather be
> A Pagan suckled in a creed outworn;   *10*
> So might I, standing on this pleasant lea,
> Have glimpses that would make me less forlorn;
> Have sight of Proteus rising from the sea;
> Or hear old Triton blow his wreathèd horn.

— William Wordsworth

Substitution of one kind of foot for another. A trochee varies the iambic pattern in *Getting* and *Little.* Anapests are used in the first two feet on line four: *We have given our hearts.* The third foot in line nine and the fifth foot in line ten are spondees, and the third foot in line ten is a pyrrhic:

> Ĭt mŏves | ŭs nŏt. – | Great God! | I'd rath | er be |
> A pa | gan suck | led in | a creed | outworn. |

There are others. It is doubtful that any line has an exact iambic meter throughout.

The use of a syllable more or a syllable less at the end of a line. A line having an extra syllable or syllables is called *hypermetrical.* A line lacking a syllable or syllables is called *truncated.*

In line two of Wordsworth's sonnet, the *-ers* of *powers* is an extra unstressed syllable added to the final iambic foot.

> Getting | and spend | ing, we | lay waste | our pow | ers.

This sonnet does not have an example of the omission of an expected syllable, but here is such an omission from Blake's "The Tiger." It begins with a trochaic beat, but the final unstressed syllable is omitted:

> Tiger, | tiger, | burning | bright |

Some students may prefer to call the final syllable a monosyllabic foot, but the effect is not changed. A similar example of omission may be seen in Longfellow's *Evangeline*, with the final unstressed syllable omitted from the dactyllic pattern:

> This is the | forest pri | meval, the | murmuring | pines and the | hemlocks |

Degree of Stress. We have so far described the basic feet as if there were only two degrees of stress — accented and unaccented. But such a measurement is only a rough rule of thumb. There are many degrees of stress. In line one of Wordsworth's sonnet, *late* has a heavier stress than *with*, and *world* has the heaviest of all. Of unstressed syllables, *us* has a heavier stress than *The* and *and*. The word *much* would be unstressed in a prevailing iambic pattern, but the meaning of the line can give *much* enough stress to make the foot spondaic rather than iambic. Of all the many degrees of stress possible, if we add only a half-stress mark (-) to scansion, we could describe the line like this:

The world | is too | much with | us; late | and soon |

Other subtleties are possible. Of the seven stressed syllables, probably none are stressed equally. The same could be said for the unstressed syllables. We could use a dot (*the*) to indicate a weak unstress, but the analysis would become too encumbered with signs to be useful. The main thing is to use some principle of measurement as a means of studying the rhythm of a poem. Then we can note how the rhythm supports the meaning. For example, the falling stress on *us* prepares a contrast for the rising emphasis on *late* and *soon*.

Caesuras. A *caesura*, or a pause in the middle of the line, occurs at breaks between sense units. Caesuras are often marked by punctuation. In scansion, a caesura may be indicated by slanted double lines (//). In Wordsworth's sonnet, lines 1, 2 and 4 each contain a definite caesura:

> The World is too much with us; //late and soon,
> Getting and spending, //we lay waste our powers.
> Little we see in nature that is ours.
> We have given our hearts away, //a sordid boon.

The strong effect of the caesura can be seen in line 9, where there are two:

> It moves us not. //Great God! //I'd rather be

A sense of outrage at the thought of one's seeing but little in Nature and the exclamatory force of the words are reinforced by the abrupt, broken rhythm. This would contrast to the almost unbroken line 13, which is to be glimpsed as a single unit and felt as the unity one should have with Nature.

> Have sight of Proteus rising from the sea

End-stopped or Run-on Lines. An *end-stopped line* ends with a pause in syntax or thought. It stops, and necessarily slows rhythmical movement. A *run-on line* has no pause at the end, but carries its thought to the next line. This process, called *enjambment*, gives a sense of speed and continuity to the lines.

In the Wordsworth sonnet, all the lines except line 9 are end-stopped. They all end with a mark of punctuation to indicate an interruption or an end of thought. Line 9 is a run-on line:

> I'd rather be
> A Pagan suckled in a creed outworn;

Duration of Syllables. Some syllables take more time or are more difficult to say than others, and so they affect the speed of the poem's rhythm. One must study the occurrence of long or short vowels, consonant clusters, and kind of consonant (as stop or continuant) to see what makes a line move fast or slow.

In Wordsworth's sonnet, the accented syllables *world, soon, moves* take longer to say than the accented syllables *we, sea, not.* The accented syllable *waste* with its long *a* and consonant cluster *st* takes both time and difficulty. Before we get our tongues untangled from the word, we have a sense of waste heaped up or littering the area.

We can look closely at just one line to illustrate the difference in duration of syllables:

> Little we see in Nature that is ours;

The first five syllables are fast; the second five are slow. For instance, the unaccented *in* with short *i* and tongue-tip consonant moves so fast it takes only a flick of the tongue to say it (as *'n*). But the unaccented *-ture* of *Nature* requires both time and difficulty. Attention is drawn to the word, which is a key word in the poem and occurs at a point between two important ideas. Note how much faster you can read the five syllables "Little we see in" than the five syllables "Nature that is ours." In keeping with the "little we see" in nature, the idea takes but a little time to say. The phrase has only one consonant that stops the voice flow, the *t* which is one of the easiest consonants to say. It requires only a tick of the tongue off the upper teeth ridge. The consonants *w, s, n,* and *l,* as continuants do not break the voice flow. There is no consonant cluster. Both of the accented vowel sounds, short *i* and long *e,* are upper front vowels spoken with ease and speed.

On the other hand, the last half of the line, "Nature that is ours," moves heavily. Besides the stop consonant *t,* there are three difficult consonant sounds—the *t* in *Nature* (as *ch*), the *th* of *that,* and the *rs* cluster in *ours.* The *ou* of *ours* has the double length of the diphthong. The *a* in *Nature* is longer and heavier than the longest vowel sound of the first half of the line—the *e* of *we* and *see.* In English, *a* is frequently lengthened to a diphthong by the glide to an *uh* sound. The vowel sound of *that,* if accented, takes some difficulty, just because the lower jaw has to drop down for it. For ease, only the *is* in the last five syllables compares with the first five syllables of the line.

Overall, the difference in duration and ease of the two parts of the line is not great. But the first part is brief enough to suggest the gravity of our having lost something.

To contrast duration of syllables, try reading as fast as possible these two lines (both ten-syllable iambic lines) from Matthew Arnold's "To a Friend":

Who prop, thou ask'st, in these bad days, my mind?

. . .

The mellow glory of the Attic stage.

Specialized Rhythm Forms

Besides the foregoing six kinds of variations that may alter the rhythm and effect of any prevailing meter, there are several variations that have become specialized patterns of their own.

Accentual verse uses a specified number of accents in each line, but does not fix the number and position of unstressed syllables. The pattern was used in *Beowulf* and was reintroduced into English prosody by Samuel Taylor Coleridge. In the preface to *Christabel*, Coleridge said "that the meter of Christabel is not, properly speaking, irregular, though it may seem so from its being founded on a new principle: namely, that of counting in each line the accents, not the syllables. Though the latter may vary from seven to twelve, yet in each line the accents will be found to be only four." The first lines of the poem illustrate the accentual rhythm:

"Tis the middle of night by the castle clock,
And the owls have awakened the crowing cock;
Tu — whit! — Tu — whoo!
And hark, again! the crowing cock,
How drowsily it crew.

Syllabic verse uses a specified number of syllables in a line but does not distinguish number of stressed from number of unstressed. The number of syllables may vary from line to line in a stanza, but corresponding lines in any two stanzas have the same number of syllables. Robert Bridge's *Testament of Beauty* is written in lines of twelve syllables. Marianne Moore's "The Fish" is written in stanzas of six lines with the syllable count by line as follows: 1, 3, 8, 1, 5, 8. Dylan Thomas' "Fern Hill" has stanzas with the prevailing syllable pattern of 14, 14, 9, 6, 9, 14, 14, 7, 9.

Free verse is the line or poem that does not have any prevailing meter in the traditional sense. What rhythm it does have comes from such things as balance and variation of phrasing or the rise and fall of emotion. Free verse has been widely used from Whitman on, but it had many forerunners, including Milton and Shelley.

> A child said *What is the grass?* fetching it to me with
> full hands,
> How could I answer the child? I do not know what it is
> any more than he,
>
> I guess it must be the flag of my disposition, out of
> hopeful green stuff woven.
>
> Or I guess it is the handkerchief of the Lord.

EXERCISE: Variations in Rhythm

Scan the following passages. First mark each syllable as stressed or unstressed. Then identify the prevailing foot. Then note the variations from the prevailing foot. Consider whether the variations are appropriate to the sense of the passage.

1.   Bright star! would I were steadfast as thou art. (Keats)

2.   Not mine own fears, nor the prophetic soul
     Of the wide world dreaming on things to come. (Shakespeare)

3.   The woods decay, the woods decay and fall,
     The vapors weep their burthen to the ground;
     Man comes and tills the field and lies beneath,
     And after many a summer dies the swan. (Tennyson)

4.   O wild West Wind, thou breath of Autumn's being. (Shelley)

5.   Rocks, Caves, Lakes, Fens, Bogs, Dens, and shades of death. (Milton)

6.   Mary, Mary, quite contrary,
     How does your garden grow?
     With silver bells and cockleshells,
     And pretty maids all in a row. (Anon.)

7.   We're foot — slog — slog — slog — sloggin' over Africa!
     Foot — foot — foot — foot — sloggin' over Africa —
     (Boots — boots — boots — boots — movin' up and down again!)
         There's no discharge in the war! (Kipling)

8.   All down the hills of Habersham,
         All through the valleys of Hall,

The rushes cried *Abide, abide,*
The willful waterweeds held me thrall,
The laving laurel turned my tide,
The ferns and the fondling grass said *Stay,*
The dewberry dipped for to work delay,
And the little reeds sighed *Abide, abide,*
    Here in the hills of Habersham,
    Here in the valleys of Hall. (Lanier)

Patterns in Stanza

A stanza is a group of lines in a poem that we identify as a distinct unit. At the most obvious level, each stanza is marked off by space from the lines coming before and after it. In traditional verse, a stanza consists of a group of two or more lines that follow an established pattern in meter, rhyme, and length and number of lines.

The stanza, like other aspects of poetic form, is closely integrated with the other elements in a poem. A limerick cannot be written on a serious subject. Each stanzaic form tends to have its distinctive tone. For most people, stanzaic forms are not important in themselves. But it will increase a reader's understanding of poetry if he sees that form and content are more closely related than may appear at a casual reading.

The couplet is a two-line unit with end rhyme. It may have any meter or line length. Note the variety in subject and tone possible with this form.

HAPPY THOUGHT

The world is so full of a number of things,
I'm sure we should all be as happy as kings.

             —R. L. Stevenson

A dog starved at his master's gate
Predicts the ruin of the state. (Blake)

That's my last duchess painted on the wall,
Looking as if she were alive. I call
That piece a wonder, now; Fra Pandolph's hands
Worked busily a day, and there she stands. (Browning)

The *heroic couplet* is a two-line unit of iambic pentameter with end rhyme. It is marked by end-stopped lines, balanced grammatical structure, and epigrammatic expression. It was especially popular in the time of Alexander Pope.

> And, spite of pride, in erring reason's spite,
> One truth is clear, *Whatever is, is right.* (Pope)

The *quatrain* is a stanza of four lines. This is the most common stanza in English verse. It may have various meters, rhyme schemes, and line lengths. It lends itself to easy versifying by amateurs as well as good poets. The following passages illustrate the wide variety of tone possible within this stanza.

> Come, fill the Cup, and in the fire of Spring
> Your Winter-garment of Repentance fling:
> 　　The Bird of Time has but a little way
> To flutter—and the Bird is on the Wing. (FitzGerald)

> Ring out, wild bells, to the wild sky,
> 　　The flying cloud, the frosty light:
> 　　The year is dying in the night;
> Ring out, wild bells, and let him die. (Tennyson)

> My love is like a red, red rose,
> 　　That's newly sprung in June:
> My love is like the melodie
> 　　That's sweetly play'd in tune. (Burns)

The *ballad stanza* is a special quatrain based on alternating lines of iambic tetrameter and iambic trimeter. The usual rhyme scheme is *abab*.

> "I fear thee, ancient Mariner!
> I fear thy skinny hand!
> And thou art long, and lank, and brown,
> As is the ribbed sea-sand." (Coleridge)

The sonnet. Among the fixed forms for whole poems based on a specified rhyme and meter, such as the ballade and the villanelle, by far the most common in English is the sonnet. It has many variations from the standard form. The sonnet is a poem of 14 lines of rhyming iambic pentameter. Two sonnet forms have been widely used: the Italian sonnet and the Shakespearean sonnet.

　　The *Italian* (or *Petrarchan*) *sonnet* is divided into an octave (eight lines) and a sestet (six lines). The eight lines rhyme *abbaabba*. The six lines usually rhyme ·*cdecde*, or *cdccdc*. The sonnet has a two-part idea structure. Normally, the octave sets up a problem or proposition or attitude; the sestet provides a comment or resolution.

The *Shakespearean* (or *English*) *sonnet* is composed of three quatrains and a couplet, with the rhyme scheme *abab cdcd efef gg*. The couplet usually provides a comment on or a resolution of the three-quatrain unit.

EXERCISE: The Sonnet

Identify the rhyme scheme and then label these sonnets as to type.

WHOSO LIST TO HUNT

Whoso list to hunt, I know where is an hind,
  But as for me — alas, I may no more.
  The vain travail hath wearied me so sore.
  I am of them that farthest cometh behind.
Yet may I, by no means, my wearied mind   *5*
  Draw from the deer; but as she fleeth afore,
  Fainting I follow. I leave off therefore,
  Since in a net I seek to hold the wind.
Who list her hunt, I put him out of doubt,
  As well as I, may spend his time in vain.   *10*
  And, graven with diamonds, in letters plain
There is written, her fair neck round about:
  Noli me tangere, for Caesar's I am;
  And wild for to hold, though I seem tame.

                                        —*Thomas Wyatt*

SINCE THERE'S NO HELP

Since there's no help, come let us kiss and part;
Nay, I have done, you get no more of me,
And I am glad, yea glad with all my heart
That thus so cleanly I myself can free;
Shake hands forever, cancel all our vows,   *5*
And when we meet at any time again,
Be it not seen in either of our brows
That we one jot of former love retain.
Now at the last gasp of love's latest breath,
When, his pulse failing, passion speechless lies,   *10*
When faith is kneeling by his bed of death,
And innocence is closing up his eyes,
  Now if thou wouldst, when all have given him over,
  From death to life thou mightst him yet recover.

                                        —*Michael Drayton*

Verse paragraph. The verse paragraph, as its name implies, is marked by an indentation or other break indicating a new stage in the thought development. It is especially useful in blank verse and in free verse, where there is no recurring rhyme pattern and no clear stanzaic form to serve as a formal unit. Some poets who use rhyme have, however, used verse paragraphs, for example, Pope.

Blank verse is unrhymed iambic pentameter. This form has been used by Shakespeare, Milton, Wordsworth, and many other great poets. In the following passage of blank verse, the second verse paragraph begins with "Say first":

> Of Man's first disobedience, and the fruit
> Of that forbidden tree whose mortal taste
> Brought death into the World, and all our woe,
> With loss of Eden, till one greater Man
> Restore us, and regain the blissful seat,   *5*
> Sing, Heavenly Muse, that, on the secret top
> Of Oreb, or of Sinai, didst inspire
> That shepherd who first taught the chosen seed
> In the beginning how the heavens and earth
> Rose out of Chaos: or, if Sion hill   *10*
> Delight thee more, and Siloa's brook that flowed
> Fast by the oracle of God, I thence
> Invoke thy aid to my adventurous song,
> That with no middle flight intends to soar
> Above the Aonian mount, while it pursues   *15*
> Things unattempted yet in prose or rime.
> And chiefly Thou, O Spirit, that dost prefer
> Before all temples the upright heart and pure,
> Instruct me, for Thou know'st; Thou from the first
> Wast present, and, with mighty wings outspread,   *20*
> Dove-like sat'st brooding on the vast Abyss,
> And mad'st it pregnant: what in me is dark
> Illumine, what is low raise and support;
> That, to the highth of this great argument,
> I may assert Eternal Providence,   *25*
> And justify the ways of God to men.
>   Say first . . . (Milton)

Free verse, as we have said, has none of the restrictions of traditional meter, rhyme, or stanzaic form. The rhythm and line length vary from one line to the next. The following passage of free verse contains three verse paragraphs:

It is time to explain myself — let us stand up.

What is known I strip away,
I launch all men and women forward with me into the Unknown.

The clock indicates the moment — but what does eternity
    indicate? (Whitman)

Study Poems

Aids to Analysis

*Most of the various poetic devices of sound and rhythm are used in the
following poems. Test your skill on them.*

SONG

Old Adam, the carrion crow,
  The old crow of Cairo;
He sat in the shower, and let it flow
   Under his tail and over his crest;
    And through every feather   5
    Leaked the wet weather;
   And the bough swung under his nest;
For his beak it was heavy with marrow.
   Is that the wind dying? O no;
   It's only two devils, that blow   10
   Through a murderer's bones, to and fro,
   In the ghosts' moonshine.

Ho! Eve, my grey carrion wife,
  When we have supped on kings' marrow,
Where shall we drink and make merry our life?   15
   Our nest it is Queen Cleopatra's skull,
    'Tis cloven and cracked,
    And battered and hacked,
  But with tears of blue eyes it is full;
Let us drink then, my raven of Cairo!   20
   Is that the wind dying? O no;
   It's only two devils, that blow
   Through a murderer's bones, to and fro,
   In the ghosts' moonshine.

             — Thomas Lovell Beddoes

FULL FATHOM FIVE

Full fathom five thy father lies;
    Of his bones are coral made;
Those are pearls that were his eyes:
    Nothing of him that doth fade
But doth suffer a sea-change   5
Into something rich and strange.
Sea-nymphs hourly ring his knell:
        Ding-dong.
Hark! now I hear them,—Ding-dong, bell.

                            —William Shakespeare

BOOT AND SADDLE

Boot, saddle, to horse, and away!
Rescue my castle before the hot day
Brightens to blue from its silvery gray.

    CHORUS—
        Boot, saddle, to horse, and away!

Ride past the suburbs, asleep as you'd say;   5
Many's the friend there, will listen and pray,
"God's luck to gallants that strike up the lay—

    CHORUS—
        Boot, saddle, to horse, and away!"

Forty miles off, like a roebuck at bay,
Flouts Castle Brancepeth the Roundheads' array;   10
Who laughs, "Good fellows ere this, by my fay,

    CHORUS—
        Boot, saddle, to horse, and away!"

Who? My wife Gertrude; that, honest and gay,

Laughs when you talk of surrendering, "Nay!
I've better counselors; what counsel they?   15

    CHORUS—
        Boot, saddle, to horse, and away!"

                            —Robert Browning

SWEET AND LOW

Sweet and low, sweet and low,
   Wind of the western sea,
Low, low, breathe and blow,
   Wind of the western sea!
Over the rolling waters go,   *5*
Come from the dying moon, and blow,
   Blow him again to me;
While my little one, while my pretty one, sleeps.

Sleep and rest, sleep and rest,
   Father will come to thee soon;   *10*
Rest, rest, on mother's breast,
   Father will come to thee soon;
Father will come to his babe in the nest,
Silver sails all out of the west
   Under the silver moon;   *15*
Sleep, my little one, sleep, my pretty one, sleep.

          —Alfred, Lord Tennyson

SCYTHE SONG

Mowers, weary and brown, and blithe,
     What is the word methinks ye know
Endless over-word that the scythe
     Sings to the blades of the grass below?
Scythes that swing in the grass and clover,   *5*
     Something, still, they say as they pass;
What is the word that, over and over,
     Sings the scythe to the flowers and grass?

Hush, ah hush, the scythes are saying,
     Hush, and heed not, and fall asleep;   *10*
Hush, they say to the grasses swaying;
     Hush, they sing to the clover deep!
Hush—'tis the lullaby Time is singing—
     Hush, and heed not, for all things pass;
Hush, ah hush! and the scythes are swinging   *15*
     Over the clover, over the grass!

          —Andrew Lang

A WIND HAS BLOWN

a wind has blown the rain away and blown
the sky away and all the leaves away,
and the trees stand. I think i too have known
autumn too long

              (and what have you to say,   *5*
wind wind wind — did you love somebody
and have you the petal of somewhere in your heart
pinched from dumb summer?
                   O crazy daddy
of death dance cruelly for us and start   *10*

the last leaf whirling in the final brain
of air!) Let us as we have seen see
doom's integration . . . . a wind has blown the rain

away and the leaves and the sky and the
trees stand: *15*
            the trees stand. The trees,
suddenly wait against the moon's face.

                      —E. E. Cummings

WEEP YOU NO MORE, SAD FOUNTAINS

Weep you no more, sad fountains;
    What need you flow so fast?
Look how the snowy mountains
    Heaven's sun doth gently waste.
But my sun's heav'nly eyes   *5*
        View not your weeping,
        That now lies sleeping
Softly, now softly lies
        Sleeping.

Sleep is a reconciling,   *10*
    A rest that peace begets.
Doth not the sun rise smiling
    When fair at e'en he sets?
Rest you then, rest, sad eyes,
        Melt not in weeping   *15*
        While she lies sleeping
Softly, now softly lies
        Sleeping.

       —Anonymous

LINES

I

When the lamp is shattered,
The light in the dust lies dead—
    When the cloud is scattered,
The rainbow's glory is shed.
    When the lute is broken,   5
Sweet tones are remembered not;
    When the lips have spoken,
Loved accents are soon forgot.

II

    As music and splendour
Survive not the lamp and the lute,   10
    The heart's echoes render
No song when the spirit is mute—
    No song but sad dirges,
Like the wind through a ruined cell,
    Or the mournful surges   15
That ring the dead seaman's knell.

III

When hearts have once mingled
Love first leaves the well-built nest;
    The weak one is singled
To endure what it once possest.   20
    O Love! who bewailest
The frailty of all things here,
    Why choose you the frailest
For your cradle, your home, and your bier?

IV

Its passions will rock thee   25
As the storms rock the ravens on high:
    Bright reason will mock thee,
Like the sun from a wintry sky.
    From thy nest every rafter
Will rot, and thine eagle home   30
    Leave thee naked to laughter,
When leaves fall and cold winds come.

—*Percy Bysshe Shelley*

WHAN THAT APRILLE WITH HIS SHOURES SOOTE

Whan that Aprille with his shoures soote
The droghte of Marche hath perced to the roote,
And bathed every veyne in swich licour,
Of which vertu engendred is the flour;
Whan Zephirus eek with his swete breeth   5
Inspiréd hath in every holt and heeth
The tendre croppes, and the yonge sonne
Hath in the Ram his halfe cours y-ronne,
And smale fowles maken melodye,
That slepen al the night with open yë,   10
(So priketh hem nature in hir corages),
Than longen folk to goon on pilgrimages
(And palmers for to seken straunge strondes)
To ferne halwes, couthe in sondry londes;
And specially, from every shires ende   15
Of Engelond, to Caunterbury they wende,
The holy blisful martir for to seke,
That hem hath holpen, whan that they were seke.
   Bifel that, in that sesoun on a day,
In Southwerk at the Tabard as I lay   20
Redy to wenden on my pilgrimage
To Caunterbury with ful devout corage,
At night was come in-to that hostelrye
Wel nyne and twenty in a companye,
Of sondry folk, by aventure y-falle   25
In felawshipe, and pilgrims were they alle,
That toward Caunterbury wolden ryde:
The chambres and the stables weren wyde,
And wel we weren esed atte beste.
And shortly, whan the sonne was to reste,   30
So hadde I spoken with hem everichon,
That I was of hir felawshipe anon,
And made forward erly for to ryse,
To take our wey, ther as I yow devyse.

—Geoffrey Chaucer

WHEN THE HOUNDS OF SPRING

When the hounds of spring are on winter's traces,
   The mother of months in meadow or plain
Fills the shadows and windy places
   With lisp of leaves and ripple of rain;
And the brown bright nightingale amorous   5
Is half assuaged for Itylus,

For the Thracian ships and the foreign faces,
  The tongueless vigil, and all the pain.

Come with bows bent and with emptying of quivers,
  Maiden most perfect, lady of light,   *10*
With a noise of winds and many rivers,
  With a clamor of waters, and with might;
Bind on thy sandals, O thou most fleet,
Over the splendor and speed of thy feet;
For the faint east quickens, the wan west shivers,   *15*
  Round the feet of the day and the feet of the night.

Where shall we find her, how shall we sing to her,
  Fold our hands round her knees, and cling?
O that man's heart were as fire and could spring to her,
  Fire, or the strength of the streams that spring!   *20*
For the stars and the winds are unto her
As raiment, as songs of the harp-player;
For the risen stars and the fallen cling to her,
  And the southwest-wind and the west-wind sing.

For winter's rains and ruins are over,   *25*
  And all the season of snows and sins;
The days dividing lover and lover,
  The light that loses, the night that wins;
And time remembered is grief forgotten,
And frosts are slain and flowers begotten,   *30*
And in green underwood and cover
  Blossom by blossom the spring begins.

The full streams feed on flower of rushes,
  Ripe grasses trammel a traveling foot,
The faint fresh flame of the young year flushes   *35*
  From leaf to flower and flower to fruit;
And fruit and leaf are as gold and fire,
And the oat is heard above the lyre,
And the hoofed heel of a satyr crushes
  The chestnut-husk at the chestnut-root.   *40*

And Pan by noon and Bacchus by night,
  Fleeter of foot than the fleet-foot kid,
Follows with dancing and fills with delight
  The Maenad and the Bassarid;
And soft as lips that laugh and hide   *45*
The laughing leaves of the trees divide,
And screen from seeing and leave in sight
  The god pursuing, the maiden hid.

The ivy falls with the Bacchanal's hair
  Over her eyebrows hiding her eyes;   *50*
The wild vine slipping down leaves bare
  Her bright breast shortening into sighs;
The wild vine slips with the weight of its leaves,
But the berried ivy catches and cleaves
To the limbs that glitter, the feet that scare   *55*
  The wolf that follows, the fawn that flies.

          —Algernon Charles Swinburne

Part III

Cultural Contexts

Introduction

A poem is written at a particular time and is therefore influenced by the cultural milieu in which the poet wrote. A poem has a cultural significance as well as an aesthetic form, which is to say that a poem implies its cultural context. The words and ideas that make a poem have a history. They are a part of time, and part of their time.

A poem also is written within a tradition. The three most important traditions in Western civilization are the Hebraic-Christian, the Greco-Roman, and the empirical or scientific. These traditions enter into the texture of a great deal of our poetry. Milton's poetry includes both the religious and the classical traditions. We are likely to misinterpret Wordsworth's earlier poetry, which is most of his greatest poetry, if we do not know that it is permeated by eighteenth-century psychological theory.

As we know, words change their meaning with time. A word in one time and cultural context has a different meaning in another context. "Nature" for the Neoclassic writer implied, among other things, a reflection of a rational order. For the Romantic writer, nature was likely to be a source of mysterious inspiration. For the eighteenth century, society was the norm. The standards for society could be determined by studying the universal and regular patterns found in human nature. For the Romantic, on the other hand, social institutions were anathema. The emphasis was upon the individual emotion, which had its source in man's peculiar relationship with nature. Pope, the Neoclassic poet, said, "True Wit is Nature to advantage dress'd,/What oft was thought, but ne'er so well express'd." Wordsworth, the Romantic, said, "Nature never did betray/The heart that loved her." Pope's "Nature" seems to be universal common sense, and Wordsworth's "nature" is, among other things, love and loyalty.

A careful reader must respect dates. The more we know about a poet, the more useful his dates are likely to be in interpreting his poetry. Tennyson is concerned in Sections 55 and 56 of In Memoriam with the theory of evolution and its effect on religious faith. The poem was published in 1850. Darwin's Origin of Species was published in 1859. These dates tell us that Tennyson —and therefore presumably others—was aware of biological evolution before Charles Darwin published his famous work. We know then that, though we may interpret Tennyson's poem in terms of evolution, we may not interpret it in terms of Darwinian theory.

The average reader of poetry cannot be expected to know all the details about all the poets and the times in which they wrote. Not even most teachers of poetry know that much. But it is desirable that we acquire a general knowledge of cultural developments, so that we have some idea of the difference between one century and the next. In 1800 the representative poets were concerned with spiritual aspiration; by 1900 the representative voices were much more disillusioned and realistic. We cannot read Wordsworth's poetry at the beginning of the century and Hardy's at the end of the century from exactly the same point of view. Wordsworth says that "Nature never did betray/The heart that loved her." Hardy says that "Crass Casualty obstructs the sun and rain."

The following summary is intended to be a general introduction to the cultural context in which English and American poetry has been written for about the last four hundred years. It deals in broad outline with some of the major ideas, themes, and influences that lie behind this poetry. From this survey you can begin to understand some of the differences that exist between one period and another. Perhaps equally important, you can get a sense of continuity in the poetic tradition.

The medieval background sets many of the themes that carry into the modern period.

The Medieval Background. *In the Middle Ages the individual was aware of his place within the tradition. His position in the social and economic system was set by birth. Although he had a short life expectancy—being constantly prey to plague, famine, and war—he was not subject to the kind of psychological and spiritual uncertainty that man has known since the breakdown of the medieval synthesis.*

Many of the most important themes in poetry since the Middle Ages would have been impossible in this earlier era. Modern poetry has seen the continuing effects of the struggle between science and religion, the opposition between the individual and society, the truths of the intellect opposed by the truths of the emotions.

Many poets since the Middle Ages have been concerned with the problem of developing cultural coherence. We find them in all periods since the Middle Ages searching the past and the present alike for meaning. The Bible and the writers of ancient Greece are important influences in poets as far apart in time as Milton (seventeenth century), Shelley (nineteenth century), and T. S. Eliot (twentieth century). Though they are vitally concerned with contemporary issues, poets have a strong sense of the past and tradition. They are constantly searching for a meaningful coherence in human life. The loss of the medieval coherence has therefore had profound implications for poetry because so much poetry reflects man's attempt to find meaning in his life.

Chapter 10

The Renaissance (1500–1660)

The Renaissance, which includes the sixteenth century and about half of the seventeenth in England, made the shift from the other-worldly view of the Middle Ages to a secular concern for the individual realizing himself in this world. Increasing secularization was brought about primarily by science, which gave man an ever-growing control of his world, by capitalism, which gave him a chance to take advantage of these new worldly opportunities, and by the Greek and Roman classics, which emphasized the human over the divine.

Early in the Renaissance, man's view of himself was essentially medieval. It was geocentric and theocentric. God controlled a tightly ordered universe, and man's primary duty was to prepare himself for the next life. As a consequence, all knowledge had a religious, other-worldly orientation. What we know as astronomy, physics, chemistry, physiology, psychology, philosophy, sociology, botany — and all the other divisions of man's knowledge — were alike devoted to one purpose: the demonstration of Divine Law. Everything in the universe from God down to the lowest forms of inanimate substance fit into one gigantic cosmic system.

The earth was the center of the universe with the planets, moon, stars, and sun revolving on spheres around the earth. All parts of this cosmic system were related. The stars influenced men's temperaments and destinies. The moon, for instance, was the chief agent for change and mutability. Juliet, afraid of fickleness, says to Romeo,

> O, swear not by the moon, th' inconstant moon,
> That monthly changes in her circled orb,
> Lest that thy love prove likewise variable.

The physical universe was made up of four elements: earth, air, fire, and water. These elements were mixed in varying degrees to form the different substances and beings. If well mixed, they produced stable substances like gold or excellent characters like Brutus in *Julius Caesar:*

> the elements
> So mix'd in him that Nature might stand up
> And say to all the world, "This was a man!"

The elements, according to the psychology of humors, could explain man's temperament. Yellow bile or choler, related to fire, made a man hot-tempered. Blood, related to air, made him sanguine, an ardent lover or soldier. Phlegm, related to water, made him sluggish and morose. Black bile, related to earth, made him melancholy.

Everything had its proper place in this system, a chain of being which joined the lowest to the highest in an uninterrupted series of links. From the lowest inanimate object up through the plants, animals, man, angels, and on up to God, each thing had its assigned and necessary place. Ulysses' speech in Shakespeare's *Troilus and Cressida* expresses the fear that one of these links in the chain of being might get out of its proper place, or "degree," and so turn the system to chaos.

> The heavens themselves, the planets and this centre,
> Observe degree, priority and place,
> Insisture, course, proportion, season, form,
> Office and custom, in all line of order;
> And therefore is the glorious planet Sol   5
> In noble eminence enthroned and sphered
> Amidst the other; whose medicinable eye
> Corrects the ill aspects of planets evil,
> And posts like the commandment of a king,
> Sans check to good and bad: but when the planets   10
> In evil mixture to disorder wander,
> What plagues and what portents! what mutiny!
> What raging of the sea! shaking of earth!
> Commotion in the winds! frights, changes, horrors,
> Divert and crack, rend and deracinate,   15
> The unity and married calm of states
> Quite from their fixture! O, when degree is shaked,
> Which is the ladder to all high designs,
> The enterprise is sick! How could communities,
> Degrees in schools and brotherhoods in cities,   20
> Peaceful commerce from dividable shores,
> The primogenitive and due of birth,
> Prerogative of age, crowns, sceptres, laurels,
> But by degree, stand in authentic place?
> Take but degree away, untune that string,   25
> And, hark, what discord follows!

Man the microcosm, the little world, the cosmos in miniature, was midway between beasts and angels. He had the senses and the appetites of the brutes. He had an angelic soul to exercise control over this lower nature as God controlled the macrocosm under him. In this precarious middle state man was caught in the midst of warring forces: reason, passion, and will; the soul and the body; the four humors; the four elements; the planetary influences. As these forces struggled among themselves for dominance, man was caught in their disturbance. The struggle between these contending forces was attributed to sin, which had corrupted man and the universe since the Fall of Adam and Eve.

> I am a little world made cunningly
> Of elements, and an angelic sprite;
> But black sin hath betrayed to endless night
> My world's both parts, and, oh, both parts must die. (Donne)

Neoplatonic influences infused much of the Renaissance world view. Neoplatonism held that the soul of man struggled to rise above matter. It reached for perfection out of the imperfections and shadows of material existence. In human love, the aim was spirituality rather than fleshly passion.

It should be remembered, however, that the Neoplatonic idea of love is only one aspect of the subject. There was also a strong fleshly element in Renaissance love poetry. Whereas a love poem by Thomas Campion begins "Follow your saint," Christopher Marlowe begins his "Passionate Shepherd" with the line, "Come live with me and be my Love. . ."

By the end of the sixteenth century, then, the mood is in sharp contrast to medieval otherworldliness. In addition to those worldly influences already mentioned—capitalism, scientific induction, the classics—the new secularism was affected by the emerging spirit of nationalism. This developing emphasis upon the State and man's relationship to a worldly social organization gradually displaced the older system based upon the Church and the ideal of the Heavenly City. Secular rulers, such as Henry VIII and Elizabeth I, replaced the Pope as the head of the national church. The rise of Protestantism tended to weaken the authority of the church over the individual and therefore in the long run it promoted individualism. Shakespeare's Cassius showed that God and the stars had given over some of their influence to an individual-oriented destiny.

> The fault, dear Brutus, is not in our stars,
> But in ourselves, that we are underlings.

Man became much more interested in time as he turned from spiritual to worldly interests. He became acutely aware of the brevity of life. The theme of mutability recurs in Renaissance poetry. One of the favorite themes in Shakespeare's sonnets, as in those of his contemporaries, is the mutability of things (see, for example, Shakespeare's Sonnet 64). The fear of Time's ravages prompted a special interest in fame. Shakespeare's Sonnet 55 shows man triumphing over Time by achievement or memorial.

> Not marble, nor the gilded monuments
> Of princes shall outlive this powerful rhyme;
> But you shall shine more bright in these contents
> Than unswept stone besmear'd with sluttish time.

Compensation for this concern with the ravages of time also took two other forms entirely the opposite of each other. One was the *carpe diem* attitude: live for the moment because the pleasures of life are all too fleeting.

> Had we but world enough and time,
> This coyness, lady, were no crime. (Marvell)

Opposed to this point of view was a response to the still influential medieval otherworldliness.

> Beauty is but a flower
> Which wrinkles will devour;
> Brightness falls from the air;
> Queens have died young and fair;
> Dust hath closed Helen's eye.
> I am sick, I must die.
>   Lord, have mercy on us! (Nashe)

A special way of escaping from the world and time was the pastoral convention. This was a fictitious rural world, borrowed largely from the Greeks and the Romans, of shepherds and shepherdesses, living in love, freedom, and simplicity away from the bustling real world. This was a literary convention, a self-conscious and sometimes affected pretense of escape from the vital, bustling, and often violent world in which the poets actually lived. The pastoral tradition reflected then, as it has throughout its long tradition in poetry, more a dream of peace and happiness than a real desire to escape from the conflicts of life.

IT WAS A LOVER

It was a lover and his lass,
 With a hey, and a ho, and a hey nonino,
That o'er the green corn-field did pass,
 In spring time, the only pretty ring time,
 When birds do sing, hey ding a ding, ding!   5
Sweet lovers love the spring.

Between the acres of the rye,
 With a hey, and a ho, and a hey nonino,
Those pretty country folks would lie,
 In spring time, the only pretty ring time,   10
 When birds do sing, hey ding a ding, ding!
Sweet lovers love the spring.

This carol they began that hour,
 With a hey, and a ho, and a hey nonino,
How that a life was but a flower   15
 In spring time, the only pretty ring time,
 When birds do sing, hey ding a ding, ding!
Sweet lovers love the spring.

And therefore take the present time,
 With a hey, and a ho, and a hey nonino,   20
For love is crownèd with the prime
 In spring time, the only pretty ring time,
 When birds do sing, hey ding a ding, ding!
Sweet lovers love the spring.

                    —*William Shakespeare*

The Renaissance was, then, a period of strong and frequently opposing forces, many of which remained unreconciled. The new world jostled the old, and the resulting conflicts are reflected in the irony and paradox which mark the poetry of John Donne and others of the metaphysical school.

At the round earth's imagined corners, blow
Your trumpets, angels, and arise, arise
From death, you numberless infinities
Of souls, and to your scattered bodies go.

Dominant Motifs

Order in the Universe, the State, Man. The Four Elements (Earth, Air, Fire, Water). The Four Humors (Blood, Phlegm, Yellow Bile or

Choler, Black Bile). Man as Microcosm. Planetary Influence. Chain of Being. Pastoral Convention. Time—Fame. Time—Mutability. Time —*Carpe Diem.* Conflicts of Reason and Passion. Conflicts of Soul and Body. Neoplatonism.

Study Poems

ONE DAY I WROTE HER NAME UPON THE STRAND

One day I wrote her name upon the strand,
But came the waves and washéd it away;
Again I wrote it with a second hand,
But came the tide, and made my pains his prey.
"Vain man," said she, "that dost in vain essay   5
A mortal thing so to immortalize,
For I myself shall like to this decay,
And eke my name be wipéd out likewise."
"Not so," quoth I; "let baser things devise
To die in dust, but you shall live by fame;   10
My verse your virtues rare shall eternize,
And in the heavens write your glorious name:
Where, whenas death shall all the world subdue,
Our love shall live, and later life renew."

—*Edmund Spenser*

THE GOOD-MORROW

I wonder, by my troth, what thou and I
Did, till we loved? Were we not weaned till then,
But sucked on country pleasures, childishly?
Or snorted we in the seven sleepers' den?
'Twas so; but this, all pleasures fancies be.   5
If ever any beauty I did see,
Which I desired, and got, 'twas but a dream of thee.

And now good-morrow to our waking souls,
Which watch not one another out of fear;
For love all love of other sights controls,   10
And makes one little room an everywhere.
Let sea-discoverers to new worlds have gone,
Let maps to other, worlds on worlds have shown,
Let us possess one world; each hath one, and is one.

My face in thine eye, thine in mine appears,   15
And true plain hearts do in the faces rest;

Where can we find two better hemispheres
Without sharp North, without declining West?
Whatever dies was not mixed equally;
If our two loves be one, or thou and I   *20*
Love so alike that none do slacken, none can die.

                      —John Donne

MAN

    My God, I heard this day
That none doth build a stately habitation
    But he that means to dwell therein.
    What house more stately hath there been,
Or can be, than is man, to whose creation   *5*
    All things are in decay?

    For man is everything,
And more: he is a tree, yet bears no fruit;
    A beast, yet is, or should be, more;
    Reason and speech we only bring;   *10*
Parrots may thank us if they are not mute,
    They go upon the score.

    Man is all symmetry,
Full of proportions, one limb to another,
    And all to all the world besides.   *15*
    Each part may call the farthest brother,
For head with foot hath private amity,
    And both with moons and tides.

    Nothing hath got so far
But man hath caught and kept it as his prey: *20*
    His eyes dismount the highest star;
    He is in little all the sphere;
Herbs gladly cure our flesh, because that they
    Find their acquaintance there.

    For us the winds do blow,   *25*
The earth doth rest, heav'n move, and fountains flow.
    Nothing we see but means our good,
    As our delight, or as our treasure;
The whole is either our cupboard of food,
    Or cabinet of pleasure.   *30*

    The stars have us to bed;
Night draws the curtain, which the sun withdraws;
    Music and light attend our head;
    All things unto our flesh are kind

In their descent and being, to our mind   35
    In their ascent and cause.

    Each thing is full of duty:
Waters united are our navigation;
    Distinguishéd, our habitation;
    Below, our drink; above, our meat;   40
Both are our cleanliness. Hath one such beauty?
    Then how are all things neat!

    More servants wait on man
Than he'll take notice of; in every path
    He treads down that which doth befriend him   45
    When sickness makes him pale and wan.
Oh, mighty love! Man is one world and hath
    Another to attend him.

    Since then, my God, thou hast
So brave a palace built, O dwell in it,   50
    That it may dwell with thee at last!
    Till then afford us so much wit
That as the world serves us we may serve thee,
    And both thy servants be.

                   —*George Herbert*

TO THE VIRGINS, TO MAKE MUCH OF TIME

Gather ye rose-buds while ye may,
    Old Time is still a-flying:
And this same flower that smiles today,
    Tomorrow will be dying.

The glorious lamp of heaven, the Sun,   5
    The higher he's a-getting
The sooner will his race be run,
    And nearer he's to setting.

That age is best which is the first,
    When youth and blood are warmer;   10
But being spent, the worse, and worst
    Times, still succeed the former.

Then be not coy, but use your time,
    And while ye may, go marry;
For having lost but once your prime,   15
    You may for ever tarry.

                —*Robert Herrick*

HERO AND LEANDER

Both robb'd of air, we lie in one ground,
Both whom one fire had burn'd, one water drown'd.

—John Donne

ON TIME

Fly envious Time, till thou run out thy race,
Call on the lazy leaden-stepping hours,
Whose speed is but the heavy plummet's pace;
And glut thy self with what thy womb devours,
Which is no more than what is false and vain,   5
And merely mortal dross;
So little is our loss,
So little is thy gain.
For when as each thing bad thou hast entombed,
And last of all, thy greedy self consumed,   10
Then long eternity shall greet our bliss
With an individual kiss;
And joy shall overtake us as a flood,
When every thing that is sincerely good
And perfectly divine,   15
With truth, and peace, and love shall ever shine
About the supreme throne
Of him, to whose happy-making sight alone,
When once our heavenly-guided soul shall climb,
Then all this earthy grossness quit,   20
Attired with stars, we shall forever sit,
    Triumphing over death, and chance, and thee O Time.

—John Milton

Chapter 11

The Restoration and Eighteenth Century (1660–1800)

The key word in this period, which is also called the Neoclassical period, is order. The period was marked by an increasingly secular point of view. The predominant tone of this period was a loss of interest in the attempt to reconcile the new secularism with the old religious system. Whereas the Renaissance, with its rising Protestantism and its attempt to transfer a religious idea like love into a secular idea, still had one foot in the medieval universe, the Neoclassical period unabashedly turned to secular interests. Its literature, like its science and its theology (deism), made man and his society the center of interest. Still, as man moved from the religious-centered life, he felt the need of order.

> The general Order, since the whole began,
> Is kept in Nature, and is kept in man. (Pope)

For models of order man turned to science and natural law. Pope's praise of Isaac Newton shows God as working through natural law.

INTENDED FOR SIR ISAAC NEWTON

> Nature and Nature's laws lay hid in Night:
> God said, *Let* Newton be*!* and all was Light.

Another model of order was the literature of ancient Greece and Rome. Pope in *An Essay on Criticism* looked to the ancient classics for guidance:

Be Homer's works your study and delight,
Read them by day, and meditate by night;
Thence form your judgment, thence your maxims bring,
And trace the Muses upward to their spring.
Still with itself compared, his text peruse,   5
And let your comment be the Mantuan Muse.
　When first young Maro in his boundless mind
A work to outlast immortal Rome designed,
Perhaps he seemed above the critic's law,
And but from nature's fountains scorned to draw;   10
But when to examine every part he came,
Nature and Homer were, he found, the same.
Convinced, amazed, he checks the bold design;
And rules as strict his laboured work confine,
As if the Stagirite o'erlooked each line.   15
Learn hence for ancient rules a just esteem;
To copy nature is to copy them.

Form became all-important. The iambic pentameter couplet was the favorite verse pattern because it demonstrated a balanced control over the poet's material. Whatever emotion there is, is restrained. Wit predominates over feeling.

Man was considered a social being rather than a religious spirit. Deism illustrates the manner in which theology, philosophy, and science joined to provide a firm foundation for this secularism. Suppose God is conceived of as a clock-maker. In his omnipotence, he had manufactured the universe like an incredibly perfect mechanism, had wound it up, and set it going. From this point of creation it ran itself according to the natural laws built into it. The universe was stable, society was stable, and all was orderly, as illustrated by scientific law. "Whatever is, is right!" was Pope's claim in *An Essay on Man*. In religion, therefore, the typical eighteenth-century view appeals to common-sense interpretation of natural phenomena rather than to inspiration.

This secularism was further strengthened by the empirical philosophy of John Locke, whose doctrine taught that ideas come from sensations. In its practical application, this philosophy means that man is the product of his environment, with no special insights into higher realms of being.

Know then thyself, presume not God to scan;
The proper study of mankind is man. (Pope)

Man's aim was to live in conformity with natural law. Consequently, the universal or general was valued over the individual or particular because man's goal should be to follow those principles which were in conformity with the general laws of nature.

> The first Almighty Cause
> Acts not by partial, but by general laws;
> The exceptions few. (Pope)

It was an age of didacticism. Since the truths taught were those already universally accepted, writers preferred "common sense" couched in pithy phrases over lyricism or flights of imagination. The balance and restraint of common sense were safer guides than either emotions or abstract intellectual speculation. Moderation was the watchword.

> Avoid extremes, and shun the fault of such,
> Who still are pleased too little or too much. (Pope)

The didactic impulse found expression in satire, which covered any subject from religion to literature and assumed a point of view that could be one of general moral outrage or personal abuse. Satire was extremely popular during this Neoclassic period, and almost no subject was barred, as is shown by this attack on the King himself:

HERE LIES OUR MASTER, CHARLES THE KING

> Here lies our master, Charles the King,
> Whose word no man relies on,
> Who never said a foolish thing,
> And never did a wise one.

> —*John Wilmot, Earl of Rochester*

An undercurrent of reaction against Neoclassic principles is also noticeable in the eighteenth century. Dryden and Pope are the most representative poets of the period, but attitudes are emerging to prepare the way for the Romantic movement later in the century which will revolt against the established standards of form and tradition. Emotion became increasingly important in the later eighteenth century. While Gray's *Elegy Written in a Country Churchyard* shows Neoclassic influence in its incisive statements of universal observations, its mood is Romantic in its emotional assertion of individual worth regardless of rank or public recognition. Neither Pope nor Addison would have approved of the feeling for nature and for simple rural people that Gray expresses in his *Elegy*.

Can storied urn or animated bust
Back to its mansion call the fleeting breath?
Can Honour's voice provoke the silent dust,
Or Flattery soothe the dull cold ear of Death?

Perhaps in this neglected spot is laid   5
Some heart once pregnant with celestial fire;
Hands that the rod of empire might have swayed,
Or waked to ecstasy the living lyre.

But Knowledge to their eyes her ample page
Rich with the spoils of time did ne'er unroll;   10
Chill Penury repressed their noble rage,
And froze the genial current of the soul.

Full many a gem of purest ray serene,
The dark unfathomed caves of ocean bear:
Full many a flower is born to blush unseen,   15
And waste its sweetness on the desert air.

Man the individual gradually drew apart from the social mechanism, leading to the cult of primitivism and the political theory of the rights of man as distinct from the need for social order. For some writers, Nature unrestrained replaced the concept of Nature methodized. Instead of Pope's call for balance and order, we find Blake writing:

Piping down the valleys wild,
    Piping songs of pleasant glee.

While Joseph Addison with cool reason would the "great Original proclaim," William Cowper uttered a more personal and emotional God:

God moves in a mysterious way,
    His wonders to perform;
He plants his footsteps in the sea,
    And rides upon the storm.

These tendencies brought the Neoclassic Age to an end. Burns said that the common man was better than any lord. Idealistic Englishmen were willing to risk their lives in France, where a rebellious peasantry overthrew the tradition-bound aristocracy. At his most extreme, William Blake seemed to want to abolish all social, political, and religious institutions.

> Bring me my bow of burning gold:
>> Bring me my arrows of desire:
> Bring me my spear: O clouds, unfold!
>> Bring me my chariot of fire.

Dominant Motifs

Stable Universe. Science and Natural Law. Classical Models. Balance and Restraint. Heroic Couplet. Form. Deism. Society over the Individual. General over the Particular. Common Sense. Undercurrent of Romantic Emotion.

Study Poems

A SONG FOR ST. CECILIA'S DAY

I

From harmony, from heav'nly harmony,
  This universal frame began:
  When Nature underneath a heap
    Of jarring atoms lay,
  And could not heave her head,   *5*
The tuneful voice was heard from high:
  "Arise, ye more than dead."
Then cold, and hot, and moist, and dry,
In order to their stations leap,
    And Music's pow'r obey.   *10*
From harmony, from heav'nly harmony,
  This universal frame began:
  From harmony to harmony
Through all the compass of the notes it ran
The diapason closing full in Man.   *15*

II

What passion cannot Music raise and quell!
    When Jubal struck the corded shell,
  His list'ning brethren stood around,
  And, wond'ring, on their faces fell
  To worship that celestial sound.   *20*
Less than a god they thought there could not dwell
    Within the hollow of that shell
    That spoke so sweetly and so well.
What passion cannot Music raise and quell!

III

The Trumpet's loud clangour   *25*
   Excites us to arms,
With shrill notes of anger,
   And mortal alarms.
The double double double beat
   Of the thund'ring Drum   *30*
Cries: "Hark! the foes come;
Charge, charge, 'tis too late to retreat."

IV

   The soft complaining Flute
   In dying notes discovers
   The woes of hopeless lovers,   *35*
Whose dirge is whisper'd by the warbling Lute.

V

   Sharp Violins proclaim
Their jealous pangs, and desperation,
Fury, frantic indignation,
Depth of pains, and height of passion,   *40*
   For the fair, disdainful dame.

VI

   But oh! what art can teach,
   What human voice can reach,
The sacred Organ's praise?
   Notes inspiring holy love,   *45*
Notes that wing their heav'nly ways
   To mend the choirs above.

VII

Orpheus could lead the savage race;
And trees unrooted left their place,
   Sequacious of the lyre;   *50*
But bright Cecilia rais'd the wonder high'r:
When to her Organ vocal breath was giv'n,
An angel heard, and straight appear'd,
   Mistaking earth for heav'n.

GRAND CHORUS

As from the pow'r of sacred lays   *55*
   The spheres began to move,
And sung the great Creator's praise
   To all the blest above;

So, when the last and dreadful hour
This crumbling pageant shall devour,   *60*
The Trumpet shall be heard on high,
The dead shall live, the living die,
And Music shall untune the sky.

—*John Dryden*

A HINTED WISH

You told me, Maro, whilst you live
You'd not a single penny give,
But that, whene'er you chanced to die,
You'd leave a handsome legacy:
You must be mad beyond redress   *5*
If my next wish you cannot guess.

—*translated from Martial*
by Samuel Johnson

EPIGRAM ENGRAVED ON THE COLLAR OF A DOG WHICH I GAVE HIS ROYAL HIGHNESS

I am his Highness' dog at Kew;
Pray tell me, sir, whose dog are you?

—*Alexander Pope*

THE SPACIOUS FIRMAMENT ON HIGH

The spacious firmament on high,
With all the blue ethereal sky,
And spangled heavens, a shining frame,
Their great Original proclaim.
Th' unwearied Sun from day to day   *5*
Does his Creator's power display;
And publishes to every land
The work of an Almighty hand.

Soon as the evening shades prevail,
The Moon takes up the wondrous tale;   *10*
And nightly to the listening Earth
Repeats the story of her birth:
Whilst all the stars that round her burn,
And all the planets in their turn,

Confirm the tidings as they roll,   *15*
And spread the truth from pole to pole.

What though in solemn silence all
Move round the dark terrestrial ball;
What though no real voice nor sound
Amidst their radiant orbs be found?   *20*
In Reason's ear they all rejoice,
And utter forth a glorious voice;
Forever singing as they shine,
"The Hand that made us is divine."

—Joseph Addison

ODE TO EVENING

If aught of oaten stop, or pastoral song,
May hope, chaste Eve, to soothe thy modest ear,
   Like thy own solemn springs,
   Thy springs and dying gales,

O nymph reserved, while now the bright-haired sun   *5*
Sits in yon western tent, whose cloudy skirts,
   With brede ethereal wove,
   O'erhang his wavy bed:

Now air is hushed, save where the weak-eyed bat,
With short shrill shriek, flits by on leathern wing, *10*
   Or where the beetle winds
   His small but sullen horn,

As oft he rises 'midst the twilight path,
Against the pilgrim borne in heedless hum:
   Now teach me, maid composed,   *15*
   To breathe some softened strain,

Whose numbers, stealing through thy darkening vale,
May not unseemly with its stillness suit,
   As, musing slow, I hail
   Thy genial loved return!   *20*

For when thy folding-star arising shows
His paly circlet, at his warning lamp
   The fragrant Hours, and elves
   Who slept in flowers the day,

And many a nymph who wreaths her brows with sedge,   *25*
And sheds the fresh'ning dew, and, lovelier still,
   The pensive Pleasures sweet,
   Prepare thy shadowy car.

Then lead, calm vot'ress, where some sheety lake
Cheers the lone heath, or some time-hallowed pile   *30*
   Or upland fallows gray
   Reflect its last cool gleam.

But when chill blust'ring winds, or driving rain,
Forbid my willing feet, be mine the hut
   That from the mountain's side   *35*
   Views wilds, and swelling floods,

And hamlets brown, and dim-discovered spires,
And hears their simple bell, and marks o'er all
   Thy dewy fingers draw
   The gradual dusky veil.   *40*

While Spring shall pour his show'rs, as oft he wont,
And bathe thy breathing tresses, meekest Eve;
   While Summer loves to sport
   Beneath thy ling'ring light;

While sallow Autumn fills thy lap with leaves;   *45*
Or Winter, yelling through the troublous air,
   Affrights thy shrinking train,
   And rudely rends thy robes;

So long, sure-found beneath the sylvan shed,
Shall Fancy, Friendship, Science, rose-lipped Health,   *50*
   Thy gentlest influence own,
   And hymn thy fav'rite name!

               — *William Collins*

FROM *AN ESSAY ON MAN*

   Go, wondrous creature; mount where science guides,
Go, measure earth, weigh air, and state the tides;
Instruct the planets in what orbs to run,
Correct old Time, and regulate the sun;
Go, soar with Plato to th' empyreal sphere,   *5*
To the first good, first perfect, and first fair;
Or tread the mazy round his followers trod,

And quitting sense call imitating God;
As eastern priests in giddy circles run,
And turn their heads to imitate the sun.   *10*
Go, teach Eternal Wisdom how to rule—
Then drop into thyself, and be a fool!
   Superior beings, when of late they saw
A mortal man unfold all nature's law,
Admired such wisdom in an earthly shape,   *15*
And showed a Newton, as we show an ape.
   Could he, whose rules the rapid comet bind,
Describe or fix one movement of his mind?
Who saw its fires here rise, and there descend,
Explain his own beginning, or his end?   *20*
Alas! what wonder! Man's superior part
Unchecked may rise, and climb from art to art;
But when his own great work is but begun,
What reason weaves, by passion is undone.
   Trace science, then, with modesty thy guide;   *25*
First strip off all her equipage of pride;
Deduct what is but vanity or dress,
Or learning's luxury, or idleness,
Or tricks to show the stretch of human brain,
Mere curious pleasure, or ingenious pain;   *30*
Expunge the whole, or lop th' excrescent parts
Of all our vices have created arts;
Then see how little the remaining sum,
Which served the past, and must the times to come!

                       —Alexander Pope

A MAN'S A MAN FOR A' THAT

Is there, for honest poverty,
  That hings his head, an' a' that?
The coward slave, we pass him by,
  We dare be poor for a' that!
    For a' that, an' a' that,   *5*
      Our toils obscure, an' a' that;
    The rank is but the guinea's stamp;
      The man's the gowd for a' that.

What tho' on hamely fare we dine,
  Wear hodden-gray, an' a' that;   *10*
Gie fools their silks, and knaves their wine,
  A man's a man for a' that.
    For a' that, an' a' that,
      Their tinsel show, an' a' that;

The honest man, tho' e'er sae poor,   *15*
  Is king o' men for a' that.

Ye see yon birkie, ca'd a lord,
  Wha struts, an' stares, an' a' that;
Tho' hundreds worship at his word,
  He's but a coof for a' that.   *20*
    For a' that, an' a' that,
      His riband, star, an' a' that
    The man o' independent mind,
      He looks and laughs at a' that.

A prince can mak a belted knight,   *25*
  A marquis, duke, an' a' that;
But an honest man's aboon his might,
  Guid faith he mauna fa' that!
    For a' that, an' a' that,
      Their dignities, an' a' that,   *30*
    The pith o' sense, an' pride o' worth,
      Are higher rank than a' that.

Then let us pray that come it may,
  As come it will for a' that,
That sense and worth, o'er a' the earth,   *35*
  May bear the gree, an' a' that.
    For a' that, an' a' that,
      It's coming yet, for a' that,
    That man to man, the warld o'er,
      Shall brothers be for a' that.   *40*

        —Robert Burns

ON THE UNIFORMITY AND PERFECTION OF NATURE

On one fix'd point all nature moves,
Nor deviates from the track she loves;
Her system, drawn from reason's source,
She scorns to change her wonted course.

Could she descend from that great plan   *5*
To work unusual things for man,
To suit the insect of an hour—
This would betray a want of power,

Unsettled in its first design
And erring, when it did combine   *10*

The parts that form the vast machine,
The figures sketch'd on nature's scene.

Perfections of the great first cause
Submit to no contracted laws,
But all-sufficient, all-supreme,   15
Include no trivial views in them.

Who looks through nature with an eye
That would the scheme of heaven descry,
Observes her constant, still the same,
In all her laws, through all her frame.   20

No imperfection can be found
In all that is, above, around, —
All, nature made, in reason's sight
Is order all, and *all is right.*

—*Philip Freneau*

Chapter 12

The Nineteenth Century

In English literature the nineteenth century is usually divided into the Romantic period, which runs to 1832, and the Victorian period, which continues to the end of the century or, according to some interpreters, to 1914. In American literature the first half of the century or a little beyond, through Whitman, is sometimes designated as the Romantic period and the last part of the century as the Realistic period. We do not need to be so specific here, however. A few generalizations will apply to the poetry of both countries in the nineteenth century and will serve as a working background.

The nineteenth century begins with the "triumph" of Romanticism, and the Romantic impulse remains a strong influence throughout the century. To simplify a very complex subject, we may say that Romanticism is dominated by a profound concern with nature and by philosophic idealism. Whatever was natural was good and whatever was unnatural, that is, artificial, was suspect. Man, insofar as he was a product of nature and nature's laws and insofar as he was uncorrupted by society, was good. He was good because his natural emotions were good. He might, however, be corrupted by traditions and institutions. Even learning might interfere with the process of natural development.

THE TABLES TURNED

Up! up! my Friend, and quit your books;
Or surely you'll grow double:
Up! up! my Friend, and clear your looks;
Why all this toil and trouble?

The sun, above the mountain's head,   5
A freshening lustre mellow

Through all the long green fields has spread,
His first sweet evening yellow.

Books! 'tis a dull and endless strife:
Come, hear the woodland linnet,   10
How sweet his music! on my life,
There's more of wisdom in it.

And hark! how blithe the throstle sings!
He, too, is no mean preacher:
Come forth into the light of things,   15
Let Nature be your Teacher.

She has a world of ready wealth,
Our minds and hearts to bless—
Spontaneous wisdom breathed by health,
Truth breathed by cheerfulness.   20

One impulse from a vernal wood
May teach you more of man,
Of moral evil and of good,
Than all the sages can.

Sweet is the lore which Nature brings;   25
Our meddling intellect
Mis-shapes the beauteous forms of things:—
We murder to dissect.

Enough of Science and of Art;
Close up those barren leaves;   30
Come forth, and bring with you a heart
That watches and receives.

—William Wordsworth

This theme of inspiration from nature reinforced the idea that the
individual was inspired by a mysterious spiritual force, as in Shelley's
"Hymn to Intellectual Beauty":

The awful shadow of some unseen Power
Floats though unseen among us—visiting
This various world with as inconstant wing
As summer winds that creep from flower to flower—

Such ideas of inspiration helped to produce a strong individualism
based on emotional and spiritual insight. Liberty was therefore a

creed of Romanticism, freedom from political and social restraints that prevented the spirit of man from fulfilling itself. Freed of artificial restraints, man would love his fellows and promote their welfare. This love of freedom is to be found, for example, in William Blake's "The Garden of Love."

THE GARDEN OF LOVE

I went to the Garden of Love,
And saw what I never had seen:
A chapel was built in the midst,
Where I used to play on the green.

And the gates of this chapel were shut,   5
And "Thou shalt not" writ over the door;
So I turned to the Garden of Love,
That so many sweet flowers bore:

And I saw it was filléd with graves,
And tombstones where flowers should be;   10
And priests in black gowns were walking their rounds,
And binding with briars my joys and desires.

Through nature the poets turned their eyes to a higher realm of being and to higher truths than the facts of daily existence. Philosophic idealism, the tradition of Plato and the German idealists, gave intellectual coherence to the movement. The disciplined intellect was almost as important for the Romantic poets as the emotions. They distinguished between the disciplined intellect and the sterile imitation of established intellectual traditions. Wordsworth, Coleridge, and Shelley were philosophic poets in that they tried to create a philosophic synthesis that found expression in poetry. Keats, though not so learned as these three, evolved an aesthetic theory within a coherent intellectual framework. In forming their synthesis, Wordsworth and Keats even took account of utilitarianism, which is seemingly incompatible with idealism. Utilitarianism, the pleasure-pain philosophy, had its basis in sensation. And so the Romantic poets, with their interest in man's response to nature, began by observing sensory reactions. This was an important part of the total truth of human perception. The importance of sensory reactions to the total truth of human perception can be seen in Wordsworth's *The Prelude:*

Dust as we are, the immortal spirit grows
Like harmony in music; there is a dark
Inscrutable workmanship that reconciles
Discordant elements, makes them cling together
In one society. How strange, that all   5
The terrors, pains, and early miseries,
Regrets, vexations, lassitudes interfused
Within my mind, should e'er have borne a part,
And that a needful part, in making up
The calm existence that is mine when I   10
Am worthy of myself! Praise to the end!
Thanks to the means which Nature deigned to employ;
Whether her fearless visitings, or those
That came with soft alarm, like hurtless light
Opening the peaceful clouds; or she would use   15
Severer interventions, ministry
More palpable, as best might suit her aim.

Idealism is concerned with spiritual or nonmaterial entities which, because they are immaterial, are not subject to time and change. Such precepts as truth, beauty, and love have for the idealists a permanent reality that transcends the material world. Art is important for this reason. Its form is eternal and its subjects are universal, transcending time and place. This relationship between idealism, nature, and art is illustrated in the opening lines of Keats' *Endymion*.

A thing of beauty is a joy for ever:
Its loveliness increases; it will never
Pass into nothingness; but still will keep
A bower quiet for us, and a sleep
Full of sweet dreams, and health, and quiet breathing.   5
Therefore, on every morrow, are we wreathing
A flowery band to bind us to the earth,
Spite of despondence, of the inhuman dearth
Of noble natures, of the gloomy days,
Of all the unhealthy and o'er-darkened ways   10
Made for our searching: yes, in spite of all,
Some shape of beauty moves away the pall
From our dark spirits. Such the sun, the moon,
Trees old, and young, sprouting a shady boon
For simple sheep; and such are daffodils   15
With the green world they live in; and clear rills
That for themselves a cooling covert make
'Gainst the hot season; the mid forest brake,
Rich with a sprinkling of fair musk-rose blooms:

And such too is the grandeur of the dooms   *20*
We have imagined for the mighty dead;
All lovely tales that we have heard or read:
An endless fountain of immortal drink,
Pouring unto us from the heaven's brink.

Most Romantic poets believed that there was a special faculty, the imagination, by which we comprehend these higher truths. Imagination was thought of as the power by which man sees the spiritual unity underlying the variety and change in material existence. It was much more than merely the faculty for creating images. The concept of imagination fit in with the interest in nature because it was through nature that the imagination perceived the eternal truths manifested. For example, nature teaches joy, a spontaneous response to her beauty and life. The imagination can respond fully to this joy only if freed of the restraints and cares that society imposes.

As the nineteenth century passed into its fourth decade, several new forces began to conflict with a waning Romanticism. In response to pressing social questions, writers grew concerned over immediate contemporary issues. They were doubtful whether a poet should be first an artist or first a social commentator. At one extreme was the aesthetic movement, which was especially noticeable in the last forty years of the century in England, and had been foreshadowed earlier in America by Edgar Allan Poe. The aesthetes held that poets should be concerned only with beauty as the object of poetry. An example of this aesthetic point of view is Poe's theory about "The Raven" that "Beauty is the sole legitimate province of the poem." At the other extreme was the poetry of social protest, such as Elizabeth Barrett Browning's "The Cry of the Children," which inveighed against the social and economic conditions that were matters of increasing concern in this century.

In between these extremes were the poets who were concerned both as artists and as men. Tennyson, one of the most musical of poets, dealt with such knotty problems as the warfare between science and religion and the necessity for higher moral integrity. The resulting spiritual tension is evident in section 55 from *In Memoriam:*

The wish, that of the living whole
  No life may fail beyond the grave,
  Derives it not from what we have
The likest God within the soul?

Are God and Nature then at strife,   *5*
  That Nature lends such evil dreams?

So careful of the type she seems,
So careless of the single life,

That I, considering everywhere
  Her secret meaning in her deeds,   *10*
  And finding that of fifty seeds
She often brings but one to bear,

I falter where I firmly trod,
  And falling with my weight of cares
  Upon the great world's altar-stairs   *15*
That slope through darkness up to God,

I stretch lame hands of faith, and grope,
  And gather dust and chaff, and call
  To what I feel is Lord of all,
And faintly trust the larger hope.   *20*

Realism was also an emerging force. William Ernest Henley, for example, wrote with the stark detail we find in a realistic movie:

WAITING

A square, squat room (a cellar on promotion),
Drab to the soul, drab to the very daylight;
Plasters astray in unnatural-looking tinware;
Scissors and lint and apothecary's jars.

Here, on a bench a skeleton would writhe from,   *5*
Angry and sore, I wait to be admitted;
Wait till my heart is lead upon my stomach,
While at their ease two dressers do their chores.

One has a probe — it feels to me a crowbar.
A small boy sniffs and shudders after bluestone.   *10*
A poor old tramp explains his poor old ulcers.
Life is (I think) a blunder and a shame.

We also see realism combining with a visionary democratic idealism in Whitman, where Romantic individualism and realistic detail are joined in the poetry of an expanding America. Browning, Rossetti, Meredith, and Dickinson brought psychological realism to their poetry. Arnold was concerned with the cultural and social consequences of the breakdown in religious faith and moral values.

By the end of the century in England a certain logic in the development becomes apparent. Wordsworth, at the beginning of the century, had seen nature as benevolent. Hardy, toward the end of the century, saw nature from a bitterly ironic point of view, as seen in "The Darkling Thrush":

> The land's sharp features seemed to be
>   The Century's corpse outleant,
> His crypt the cloudy canopy,
>   The wind his death-lament.
> The ancient pulse of germ and birth   *5*
>   Was shrunken hard and dry,
> And every spirit upon earth
>   Seemed fervorless as I.

Optimism had turned to pessimism. Faith gave way to disenchantment. Nature had changed from being a spiritual force to becoming the object of descriptive and therefore impersonal observation. With the spiritual basis thus removed, the idealist pursuit of beauty became by the end of the century a cult of perverse elegance known as Decadence. This change is illustrated by comparing Keats' "Beauty is truth, truth beauty" with the following poem:

A LAST WORD

> Let us go hence—the night is now at hand;
>   The day is overworn, the birds all flown;
>   And we have reaped the crops the gods have sown,
> Despair and death; deep darkness o'er the land,
> Broods like an owl; we cannot understand   *5*
>   Laughter or tears, for we have only known
>   Surpassing vanity: vain things alone
> Have driven our perverse and aimless band.
>
> Let us go hence, somewhither strange and cold,
>   To Hollow Lands where just men and unjust   *10*
>   Find end of labor, where's rest for the old,
> Freedom to all from love and fear and lust.
> Twine our torn hands! O pray the earth enfold
> Out life-sick hearts and turn them into dust.

> *—Ernest Dowson*

In America the realistic influence increased in importance and shaded towards naturalism. Stephen Crane and the early E. A. Robinson are the most significant voices here. They express a harsh, even brutal disenchantment.

A MAN SAID TO THE UNIVERSE

A man said to the universe:
"Sir, I exist!"
"However," replied the universe,
"The fact has not created in me
A sense of obligation."   5

                    —*Stephen Crane*

In reading poetry of the last half of the nineteenth century, keep in mind the great intellectual currents underlying and permeating the developments of this period: Darwin's theory of evolution; Marx's theories of economics, history, and politics; Comte's sociology; and in general the naturalistic view of man's history.

Dominant Motifs. Nature. Imagination. Idealism. Individualism. Liberty. Utilitarianism. Social Criticism. Aestheticism. Realism. Religious Faith and Doubt. Naturalism.

Study Poems

LINES WRITTEN IN EARLY SPRING

I heard a thousand blended notes,
While in a grove I sate reclined,
In that sweet mood when pleasant thoughts
Bring sad thoughts to the mind.

To her fair works did Nature link   5
The human soul that through me ran;
And much it grieved my heart to think
What man has made of man.

Through primrose tufts, in that green bower,
The periwinkle trailed its wreaths;   10
And 'tis my faith that every flower
Enjoys the air it breathes.

The birds around me hopped and played,
Their thoughts I cannot measure—
But the least motion which they made,   15
It seemed a thrill of pleasure.

The budding twigs spread out their fan,
To catch the breezy air;
And I must think, do all I can,
That there was pleasure there.   *20*

If this belief from heaven be sent,
If such be Nature's holy plan,
Have I not reason to lament
What man has made of man?

                              —*William Wordsworth*

PROMETHEUS

TITAN! to whose immortal eyes
    The sufferings of mortality,
    Seen in their sad reality,
Were not as things that gods despise;
What was thy pity's recompense?   *5*
A silent suffering, and intense;
The rock, the vulture, and the chain,
All that the proud can feel of pain,
The agony they do not show,
The suffocating sense of woe,   *10*
    Which speaks but in its loneliness,
And then is jealous lest the sky
Should have a listener, nor will sigh
    Until its voice is echoless.

Titan! to thee the strife was given   *15*
    Between the suffering and the will,
    Which torture where they cannot kill;
And the inexorable Heaven,
And the deaf tyranny of Fate,
The ruling principle of Hate,   *20*
Which for its pleasure doth create
The things it may annihilate,
Refused thee even the boon to die:
The wretched gift eternity
Was thine—and thou hast borne it well.   *25*
All that the Thunderer wrung from thee
Was but the menace which flung back
On him the torments of thy rack;
The fate thou didst so well foresee,
But would not to appease him tell;   *30*
And in thy Silence was his Sentence,

And in his Soul a vain repentance,
And evil dread so ill dissembled,
That in his hand the lightnings trembled.

Thy Godlike crime was to be kind,   *35*
   To render with thy precepts less
   The sum of human wretchedness,
And strengthen Man with his own mind;
But baffled as thou wert from high,
Still in thy patient energy,   *40*
In the endurance, and repulse
   Of thine impenetrable Spirit,
Which Earth and Heaven could not convulse,
   A mighty lesson we inherit:
Thou art a symbol and a sign   *45*
   To Mortals of their fate and force;
Like thee, Man is in part divine,
   A troubled stream from a pure source;
And Man in portions can foresee
His own funereal destiny;   *50*
His wretchedness, and his resistance,
And his sad unallied existence;
To which his Spirit may oppose
Itself—and equal to all woes,
   And a firm will, and a deep sense,   *55*
Which even in torture can descry
   Its own concenter'd recompense,
Triumphant where it dares defy,
And making Death a Victory.

            —George Gordon, Lord Byron

ISRAFEL

And the angel Israfel, whose heart-strings are a lute,
and who has the sweetest voice of all God's creatures. —KORAN

In Heaven a spirit doth dwell
   "Whose heart-strings are a lute":
None sing so wildly well
As the angel Israfel,
And the giddy stars (so legends tell)   *5*
Ceasing their hymns, attend the spell
   Of his voice, all mute.

Tottering above
   In her highest noon,
   The enamoured moon   *10*
Blushes with love,

While, to listen, the red levin
   (With the rapid Pleiads, even,
   Which were seven)
Pauses in Heaven.   *15*

And they say (the starry choir
   And the other listening things)
That Israfeli's fire
Is owing to that lyre
   By which he sits and sings—   *20*
The trembling living wire
   Of those unusual strings.

But the skies that angel trod,
   Where deep thoughts are a duty—
Where Love's a grown-up God—   *25*
   Where the Houri glances are
Imbued with all the beauty
   Which we worship in a star.

Therefore, thou art not wrong,
   Israfeli, who despisest   *30*
An unimpassioned song;
To thee the laurels belong,
   Best bard, because the wisest!
Merrily live, and long!

The ecstasies above   *35*
   With thy burning measures suit—
Thy grief, thy joy, thy hate, thy love,
   With the fervour of thy lute—
   Well may the stars be mute!

Yes, Heaven is thine; but this   *40*
   Is a world of sweets and sours;
   Our flowers are merely—flowers,
And the shadow of thy perfect bliss
   Is the sunshine of ours.

If I could dwell   *45*
Where Israfel
   Hath dwelt, and he where I,
He might not sing so wildly well
   A mortal melody,
While a bolder note than this might swell   *50*
   From my lyre within the sky.

       —*Edgar Allan Poe*

WEST LONDON

Crouched on the pavement close by Belgrave Square,
A tramp I saw, ill, moody, and tongue-tied;
A babe was in her arms, and at her side
A girl; their clothes were rags, their feet were bare.
Some labouring men, whose work lay somewhere there,   5
Passed opposite; she touched her girl, who hied
Across and begged, and came back satisfied.
The rich she had let pass with frozen stare.
Thought I: "Above her state this spirit towers;
She will not ask of aliens, but of friends,   10
Of sharers in a common human fate.
She turns from that cold succor, which attends
The unknown little from the unknowing great,
And points us to a better time than ours."

—*Matthew Arnold*

IN TENEBRIS

I
      Wintertime nighs;
But my bereavement-pain
It cannot bring again:
      Twice no one dies.

      Flower-petals flee;   5
But, since it once hath been,
No more that severing scene
      Can harrow me.

      Birds faint in dread:
I shall not lose old strength   10
In the lone frost's black length:
      Strength long since fled!

      Leaves freeze to dun;
But friends can not turn cold
This season as of old   15
      For him with none.

      Tempests may scath;
But love can not make smart
Again this year his heart
      Who no heart hath.   20

Black is night's cope;
But death will not appal
One who, past doubtings all,
Waits in unhope.

—Thomas Hardy

NON SUM QUALIS ERAM BONAE
SUB REGNO CYNARAE

Last night, ah, yesternight, betwixt her lips and mine
There fell thy shadow, Cynara! thy breath was shed
Upon my soul between the kisses and the wine;
And I was desolate and sick of an old passion,
    Yea, I was desolate and bowed my head: 5
I have been faithful to thee, Cynara! in my fashion.

All night upon mine heart I felt her warm heart beat,
Night-long within mine arms in love and sleep she lay;
Surely the kisses of her bought red mouth were sweet;
But I was desolate and sick of an old passion, 10
    When I awoke and found the dawn was gray:
I have been faithful to thee, Cynara! in my fashion.

I have forgot much, Cynara! gone with the wind,
Flung roses, roses riotously with the throng,
Dancing, to put thy pale, lost lilies out of mind; 15
But I was desolate and sick of an old passion,
    Yea, all the time, because the dance was long:
I have been faithful to thee, Cynara! in my fashion.

I cried for madder music and for stronger wine,
But when the feast is finished and the lamps expire, 20
Then falls thy shadow, Cynara! the night is thine;
And I am desolate and sick of an old passion,
    Yea hungry for the lips of my desire:
I have been faithful to thee, Cynara! in my fashion.

—Ernest Dowson

Note: The title means "I am not what I was under the reign of good Cynara"; from Horace (*Odes*, IV, i), in which the poet asks Venus not to disturb him, because he is older and not what he was when he loved the girl Cynara.

IMPRESSION DU MATIN

The Thames nocturne of blue and gold
  Changed to a harmony in gray;
  A barge with ocher-colored hay
Dropped from the wharf: and chill and cold

The yellow fog came creeping down   *5*
  The bridges, till the houses' walls
  Seemed changed to shadows, and St. Paul's
Loomed like a bubble o'er the town.

Then suddenly arose the clang
  Of waking life; the streets were stirred   *10*
  With country wagons; and a bird
Flew to the glistening roofs and sang.

But one pale woman all alone,
  The daylight kissing her wan hair,
  Loitered beneath the gas lamps' flare,   *15*
With lips of flame and heart of stone.

                   —Oscar Wilde

GOD FASHIONED THE SHIP OF THE WORLD CAREFULLY

God fashioned the ship of the world carefully.
With the infinite skill of an All-Master
Made He the hull and the sails,
Held He the rudder
Ready for adjustment.   *5*
Erect stood He, scanning His work proudly.
Then—at fateful time—a wrong called,
And God turned, heeding.
Lo, the ship, at this opportunity, slipped slyly,
Making cunning noiseless travel down the ways. *10*
So that, for ever rudderless, it went upon the seas
Going ridiculous voyages,
Making quaint progress,
Turning as with serious purpose
Before stupid winds.   *15*
And there were many in the sky
Who laughed at this thing.

                   —Stephen Crane

Chapter 13

The Twentieth Century

Twentieth-century poets have been strongly aware of the complexity and fragmentation of their society. Cultural values seemed to have broken up, and everywhere thoughtful people expressed concern about the symptoms of cultural decline. Materialism was more pronounced than ever. Science had made people skeptical of old ideas and old faiths. Technology had created an urban society that was neither inspiring nor beautiful.

In this century, the poet of experience is no longer expansive and optimistic like Whitman or spiritually exalted like Emily Dickinson. Instead he expresses disenchantment with his new world, as we see in this early poem by T. S. Eliot:

MORNING AT THE WINDOW

They are rattling breakfast plates in basement kitchens,
And along the trampled edges of the street
I am aware of the damp souls of housemaids
Sprouting despondently at area gates.

The brown waves of fog toss up to me   5
Twisted faces from the bottom of the street,
And tear from a passer-by with muddy skirts
An aimless smile that hovers in the air
And vanishes along the level of the roofs.

In the face of an increasing materialism, the poet begins to express an alienation from his society, an alienation that reflects to some extent the psychological reality that lies beneath the surface of modern life. Although some poets, such as Carl Sandburg in "Chicago," could feel a certain rapport with the new urban power, the tone of alienation, isolation, or withdrawal is very pronounced in twentieth-century poetry.

THE EAGLE AND THE MOLE

Avoid the reeking herd,
Shun the polluted flock,
Live like that stoic bird,
The eagle of the rock.

The huddled warmth of crowds   5
Begets and fosters hate;
He keeps, above the clouds,
His cliff inviolate.

When flocks are folded warm,
And herds to shelter run,   10
He sails above the storm,
He stares into the sun.

If in the eagle's track
Your sinews cannot leap,
Avoid the lathered pack,   15
Turn from the steaming sheep.

If you would keep your soul
From spotted sight or sound,
Live like the velvet mole;
Go burrow underground.   20

And there hold intercourse
With roots of trees and stones,
With rivers at their source,
And disembodied bones.

—Elinor Wylie

Much of twentieth-century poetry is a search for personal and social identity. Many poets felt that it was not fitting that man live alienated from his society, and yet society was not producing a set of values which the poet could accept. In the absence of an acceptable value system within the society at large, the poet felt that he must search for his own set of values if he was to have a base from which to write.

This search for values took two major directions, both of which tend to make modern poetry difficult. Some poets, of whom Eliot is the most famous, looked to the past. For them, tradition was the answer. Religious, social, and literary tradition could provide the coherence that the modern world lacked. In Eliot's *The Waste Land*, for example, the mythological, religious, and literary allusions reach far into the past for traditional values.

The other major direction in the search for values was a turning to the self, one large expression of which was the wide popularity of the philosophy of existentialism. A related expression was the exaltation of individual experience as the prime value in a disordered world, a pronounced emphasis on sensation. The individual self is asserted because it is alive and has experiences worth asserting. Dylan Thomas, for example, says that man's senses, rather than his mind or his soul, unify experience.

WHEN ALL MY FIVE AND COUNTRY SENSES SEE

When all my five and country senses see,
The fingers will forget green thumbs and mark
How, through the halfmoon's vegetable eye,
Husk of young stars and handfull zodiac,
Love in the frost is pared and wintered by,   5
The whispering ears will watch love drummed away
Down breeze and shell to a discordant beach,
And, lashed to syllables, the lynx tongue cry
That her fond wounds are mended bitterly.
My nostrils see her breath burn like a bush.   10

My one and noble heart has witnesses
In all love's countries, that will grope awake;
And when blind sleep drops on the spying senses,
The heart is sensual, though five eyes break.

Twentieth-century poetry, like the twentieth-century novel and drama, is noted for its experimentation. This experimentation is part of breaking with the past and searching for new insights and new ways to express these insights. In poetry this search takes noticeable form in freer rhythms, in condensed phrasing with odd syntax and abrupt transitions, in an allusive and symbolic language that draws freely upon any area of human experience, whether the reference is generally understood or not.

The result of these developments has been a good deal of excitement about poetry at various times throughout the century. Much modern poetry is a challenge to read, though it should be noted that most of it is not really any harder to understand than much of the poetry of the past. If we think of past poetry as Longfellow's "Psalm of Life," then most modern poetry is difficult. But if we think of past poetry in terms of Browning's "Childe Roland to the Dark Tower Came," then modern poetry does not seem particularly difficult by comparison — more condensed, yes, but not more difficult as to theme and meaning. And when we consider interpreting the poem in relation to its total context, modern poetry is not harder to understand than most of the good poetry of the past.

Dominant Motifs. Anti-materialism. Disenchantment. Search for Values. Fragmentation. Existentialism. Alienation. Tradition. Private Symbols. Experimentation. Symbolic and Allusive Language.

Study Poems

AN IRISH AIRMAN FORESEES HIS DEATH

I know that I shall meet my fate
Somewhere among the clouds above;
Those that I fight I do not hate,
Those that I guard I do not love;
My country is Kiltartan Cross,   5
My countrymen Kiltartan's poor,
No likely end could bring them loss
Or leave them happier than before.
Nor law, nor duty bade me fight,
Nor public men, nor cheering crowds,   10
A lonely impulse of delight
Drove to this tumult in the clouds;
I balanced all, brought all to mind,
The years to come seemed waste of breath,
A waste of breath the years behind   15
In balance with this life, this death.

—William Butler Yeats

SHINE, PERISHING REPUBLIC

While this America settles in the mould of its vulgarity, heavily
    thickening to empire,
And protest, only a bubble in the molten mass, pops and sighs out,
    and the mass hardens,

I sadly smiling remember that the flower fades to make fruit, the
    fruit rots to make earth.
Out of the mother; and through the spring exultances, ripeness and
    decadence; and home to the mother.

You make haste haste on decay: not blameworthy; life is good, be
    it stubbornly long or suddenly   5
A mortal splendor: meteors are not needed less than mountains:
    shine, perishing republic.

But for my children, I would have them keep their distance from
    the thickening center; corruption
Never has been compulsory, when the cities lie at the monster's
    feet there are left the mountains.

And boys, be in nothing so moderate as in love of man, a clever
    servant, insufferable master.
There is the trap that catches noblest spirits, that caught—they say—
    God, when he walked on earth.   10

                              —*Robinson Jeffers*

ANYONE LIVED IN A PRETTY HOW TOWN

anyone lived in a pretty how town
(with up so floating many bells down)
spring summer autumn winter
he sang his didn't he danced his did.

Women and men(both little and small)   5
cared for anyone not at all
they sowed their isn't they reaped their same
sun moon stars rain

children guessed(but only a few
and down they forgot as up they grew   10
autumn winter spring summer)
that noone loved him more by more

when by now and tree by leaf
she laughed his joy she cried his grief
bird by snow and stir by still   15
anyone's any was all to her

someones married their everyones
laughed their cryings and did their dance
(sleep wake hope and then) they
said their nevers they slept their dream   20

stars rain sun moon
(and only the snow can begin to explain
how children are apt to forget to remember
with up so floating many bells down)

one day anyone died i guess   25
(and noone stooped to kiss his face)
busy folk buried them side by side
little by little and was by was

all by all and deep by deep
and more by more they dream their sleep   30
noone and anyone earth by april
wish by spirit and if by yes.

Women and men(both dong and ding)
summer autumn winter spring
reaped their sowing and went their came   35
sun moon stars rain

                              —*E. E. Cummings*

THE END OF THE WORLD

Quite unexpectedly as Vasserot
The armless ambidextrian was lighting
A match between his great and second toe,
And Ralph the lion was engaged in biting
The neck of Madame Sossman while the drum   5
Pointed, and Teeny was about to cough
In waltz-time swinging Jocko by the thumb—
Quite unexpectedly the top blew off:

And there, there overhead, there, there hung over
Those thousands of white faces, those dazed eyes,   10
There in the starless dark the poise, the hover,
There with vast wings across the canceled skies,
There in the sudden blackness the black pall
Of nothing, nothing, nothing—nothing at all.

                              —*Archibald MacLeish*

EFFORT AT SPEECH BETWEEN TWO PEOPLE

Speak to me. Take my hand. What are you now?
I will tell you all. I will conceal nothing.

When I was three, a little child read a story about a rabbit
who died, in the story, and I crawled under a chair :
a pink rabbit : it was my birthday, and a candle   *5*
burnt a sore spot on my finger, and I was told to be happy.

Oh, grow to know me. I am not happy. I will be open:
Now I am thinking of white sails against a sky like music,
like glad horns blowing, and birds tilting, and an arm
   about me.
There was one I loved, who wanted to live, sailing.   *10*

Speak to me. Take my hand. What are you now?
When I was nine, I was fruitily sentimental,
fluid : and my widowed aunt played Chopin,
and I bent my head to the painted woodwork, and wept.
I want now to be close to you. I would   *15*
link the minutes of my days close, somehow, to your days.

I am not happy. I will be open.
I have liked lamps in evening corners, and quiet poems.
There has been fear in my life. Sometimes I speculate
on what a tragedy his life was, really.   *20*

Take my hand. Fist my mind in your hand. What are
   you now?
When I was fourteen, I had dreams of suicide,
I stood at a steep window, at sunset, hoping toward
   death :
if the light had not melted clouds and plains to beauty,
if light had not transformed that day, I would have leapt. *25*
I am unhappy. I am lonely. Speak to me.

I will be open. I think he never loved me:
he loved the bright beaches, the little lips of foam
that ride small waves, he loved the veer of gulls:
he said with a gay mouth : I love you. Grow to know   *30*
   me.

What are you now? If we could touch one another,
if these our separate entities could come to grips,
clenched like a Chinese puzzle . . . yesterday
I stood in a crowded street that was live with people,
and no one spoke a word, and the morning shone.   *35*
Everyone silent, moving . . . Take my hand. Speak to
   me.

                      —Muriel Rukeyser

IDENTITY

To locate a person hidden in this room,
Who stands—in fact—before us, dispersed in a shape
Of primitive coinage, with arms, legs and a nose,
We need no deeper philosophy than subtraction,
Which takes from ten, the height of the room, his height   5
Of full six feet, leaving his selfhood suspended
(Where the brain beats, hoarding awareness and memory)
Some four feet from the ceiling, like a bird
Hovering in the wind, more like a bubble
Or unexpected balloon: a magician's secret   10
No greater in strangeness than a maid's way with a man.

—Hyam Plutzik

Part IV

The Critical View

Introduction

The critical statements in this section will serve as an introduction to some of the major problems of critical theory and judgment. These statements include some of the most famous questions ever raised about the nature of poetry and the problem of evaluation.

These questions continue to be important. Aristotle's theory of imitation, for example, raises a highly significant issue: What is the subject matter of poetry? One tradition says that the subject matter of poetry is human action (see Arnold's statement). Another tradition judges the subject matter of poetry by emotional reaction (see Hazlitt). These two points of view generally define the classical and the romantic theories of poetry.

The two complete essays deal with some of the old issues, but with a modern emphasis. Yvor Winters wants us to think about evaluation. He is not content that we allow each person his own choice. Winters contends that there is a difference between good poetry and bad and that we can define the difference. Stauffer's purpose is to point out the distinctive nature of poetry so that we can read it without certain prejudices and misapprehensions.

Chapter 14

Readings In Criticism

The Nature of Poetry

Donald Stauffer

Few people have ever been brave enough to define poetry. Not many among those few have felt happy with their definitions. Yet most of us have experienced poetry, and many of us believe that we can recognize it when we see it, just as we can recognize life when we see it, although we cannot satisfactorily define it. Like life, poetry exists in so many forms and on so many levels that it triumphantly defies description. Keats has written of poetry as the realms of gold, and has noted its many goodly states and kingdoms, its many islands held in fealty to Apollo. The metaphor is a good one, though it hardly goes far enough. There are more poems than there are islands in the Caribbean, or the Mediterranean; and they vary more in shape, size, color, contour, and human habitability.

Furthermore, any individual poem, as Keats wrote of Homer's *Iliad*, may in itself be a complete domain, illimitable as the Pacific, ruled by its own king and creator, a wide expanse arched over by a pure and serene air. Or—and here is the rub—it may not be like that at all. It may be as small and limited as an epigram by Martial, as precipitous and rocky as a lyric by Donne, as barely above sea level as a poem by Edgar Guest. And it might be quite different from any now known. Surely there is good reason to avoid a definition of poetry. The clearer and more concise the definition is, the more poems it leaves out.

If we are to understand the nature of poetry, we must view the realms of gold from many points of vantage. We must travel on various single quests across many islands. At the start we must take certain bearings and ask certain questions. Are we to consider the *medium* of words in which poetry is composed? Or the *subjects* which poetry treats? Or the *purposes* for which the subjects are being used? Or the *forms* created in that verbal medium in order to give expression to certain subjects and purposes? The first of these possibilities will occupy us in later paragraphs. The second need not detain us, for the answer, if we judge by actual practice, is that any subject matter may furnish raw materials for poets, from Chaucer, who used warts and running sores, to T. S. Eliot, who uses statistics. The last two possibilities present the further question: Are we to consider poetry or poems? Poetry, of course, may serve as a generic name for a group of poems or for all poems taken together. Often, however, the word is used to describe the spirit or mood which may find expression in a poem but may also find expression in, say, a painting or a piece of music. Many critical battles and misunderstandings have arisen because one man was viewing the qualities of the *poetic spirit* and his opponent was seeing only the qualities of a *poem*. We might at this point decide on a procedure: to consider first those elements which most usually combine in the poetic spirit; and then, more narrowly, the technical and formal elements which shape words into a poem.

Poetry labors under the further handicap of being the most misunderstood of all the arts. And yet of all the arts, poetry should afford to the greatest number of people the most delight. Actually it does nothing of the kind. Instead, the average adolescent or adult (for children know what poetry is) feels uncomfortable or irritated or bored when he confronts a poem. Partly this defect in sympathy may be attributed to the many easy substitutes that now satisfy everyone's natural craving for esthetic experience—the comic strips and the movies, the detective stories and the weekly magazines, the soap opera on the radio and the trip in the car. A debased currency will always drive out the genuine article, and there are plenty of ways today to get others to do our thinking and our feeling for us. Partly the misunderstanding springs from the amount of rapid reading we do, skimming newspapers and billboards and novels, so that we are impatient when anything demands close scrutiny. We have also had little practice in taking in through the ear esthetically ordered words. The eye has displaced the ear as the instrument for literary communication, although it is quite possible that the radio, some day in the future, may help to restore the enjoyment of poetry as a verbal pattern of meaningful *sounds*.

But the main cause of the popular uneasiness before poetry lies in the very medium which this art uses — the medium of words. We are accustomed to using words almost solely for the practical purposes of living. We cannot understand without an effort — or better still, without long experience — that in poetry words are used in a different way and serve different purposes. Poetry alone among the arts suffers this serious handicap. We understand that almost all the other arts are not aiming at the practical. No one supposes that ballet dancers are building up their muscles for military service or are running to the store to buy a loaf of bread. A painting and a symphony concert cannot readily be considered to be of immediate practical usefulness, and there is little likelihood of approaching them with dangerously wrong expectations. But let us imagine for a moment that from childhood we had constantly used square or rectangular surfaces solely as dining tables, writing tables, or checkerboards. A painting might then fill us with contempt because it would be so poorly designed to satisfy what we felt to be its natural functions. Or suppose from the cradle up we had sipped our milk and drunk our coffee from receptacles resembling saxophones. Would it not then seem to us ludicrous to see a man blowing into his cup in order to make it produce inedible and therefore unedifying saxophonic sounds?

We need not resort to such far-fetched parables when we turn to poetry. We are already in the midst of a comedy, or tragedy, of errors. Continually we use words to say: "Please pass the butter," or "I think free trade is obviously the solution," or "I hear Marjorie has given up Steve for Dick." And when the words of poetry fail to say similar things satisfying similar purposes, we are irked or bewildered. Or worse, we try to force them into our ordinary modes of practical or logical thought. We are constantly coming out with the wrong answers. We call poetry a means of escape — as if we actually lived all the time, or even most of the time, in the practical and active world, and never among dreams, aspirations, values, and the sheer sensations of being alive. Even when we know that there are other ways of life than the business of the world, we fail to look for them in poetry, for the barrier of words is still there, and words in our experience are used for immediate utilitarian purposes. And therefore we collect a small handful of commonplace notions and facts from the rich mines of poetry. We feel that we have settled Hardy's business when we label him pessimistic and fatalistic, we consider *Macbeth* simply as a tract to show that too much ambition is a bad thing, we read *Childe Harold's Pilgrimage* because it deals with travels through Europe and an actual battle of Waterloo, or we abstain from *Paradise Lost* because Milton was a Puritan who took the story of Adam and Eve literally. Poetry, we feel, contains some history and some facts, but the *World Almanac* organizes them more efficiently.

Another of our misapprehensions is that reason is the prime distinction of man and that poetry is inferior intellectually to mathematics or philosophy. One of America's most notable critics, John Crowe Ransom, finds the distinguishing mark of poetry to lie in the logical irrelevancy of its local details; to most readers this would immediately appear a flaw in poetry resulting from the ignorance or perversity of poets. That there are other modes of thought and of knowledge than the logical and the practical is not one of our habitual assumptions. My purpose here is to present an approach to poetry as poetry. I am trying to show how poets use words. The notion is difficult to express and to grasp, but it is also, I think inevitably, the basic assumption for any further profitable discussion. Stated in its simplest terms, my position rests on the assumption that a poem is like a person. We can classify persons as Vermonters or Italians, just as we can classify poems as elegies, ballads, and the rest; but perhaps such categories do little to help us understand either personality or poetry. The first safe generalization to make about persons is that each one of them is individual, unmistakable, unduplicable, and that if he were not — if there were any identical substitute for him — he would not be a person. The same is true of a poem, of any poem. I have tried to express this notion in the statement: "Poetry is exact." The phrase is not good enough: its very failure proves the point I am attempting to establish. A poem, through its overtones, its suggestions, the relations between its words and motifs, and its other complexities, may express with complete adequacy a definite and unique experience. But the limited language of analysis, in such a phrase as "Poetry is exact," does not satisfactorily "cover" its subject. Even in this first sketching of the idea, without amplification or illustration or qualification, I must at least point out that the exactness of poetic language is not the logical invariability of a mathematical proposition; rather, it is the unmistakability by which we recognize one person as different from another, depending upon a multiplicity of traits, features, and qualities, material and immaterial, which defy complete analysis. The mere fact that the words of a poem can *not* be analyzed and described exhaustively does not make it less exact: instead, it constitutes the peculiar "exactness," the particularity, the uniqueness, of that poem. Wherever we find poetry, we find also this pleasure in recognizing the unique.

The same voice is not speaking in

> The curfew tolls the knell of parting day

that speaks in

> For God's sake, hold your tongue and let me love,

and there is no good in trying to make them sound alike. Even when the same poet speaks, he may speak in various moods. We should not bring the temper of the "Elegy in a Country Churchyard" to a reading of

> Ruin seize thee, ruthless King!
> Confusion on thy banners wait!

All of this is only a way of saying that the first enjoyment we may get from poetry comes from accepting it for what it is and not for something else. We do not enjoy a friend by reducing him to a set of categories: age, 30; hair, dark brown; nationality, U.S.; religion, Methodist. And the better we know the friend, the less we are satisfied to ticket him as 30% justice; 30% cantankerousness; 20% amiability; 15% laziness; and 5% hot temper. Instead, we take pleasure in recognizing that

> I must confess it could not choose but be
> Profane to think thee anything but thee.

A poem, just as clearly, is a fusion of innumerable elements, large and small, in many fields of experience, obvious or subtle or even not consciously noticed or describable. Experienced fully as a poem, it is not made up of separable or interchangeable parts, and its exactness lies in this unique wholeness.

We may grasp completely the meaning of a scientific law such as "For every action there is an equal and opposite reaction" when that law is stated in other words. But we have lost something when we take the last line of Dante's *Divine Comedy*,

> *L'amor che move il sole e l'altre stelle,*

and translate it literally as

> The love which moves the sun and the other stars.

Furthermore, in the Italian, that line gains its full illumination, its precision of meaning, only in its relation to all the rest of the poem with its great weight and glory of details.

The poetic world is the world seen through the eyes of an individual and expressed in his words. Even when that world appears most abstracted and generalized, the poetic view is still unique, and cannot be changed or added to or translated into other terms, as can the propositions in the communal and rational world of science. A poem is an individual imaginative experience recorded as faithfully as possible by an individual poet.

Suppose we accept as the necessary first approach to poetry this recognition that poetic exactness consists in the unique individuality of each complete poetic expression. Does it follow, then, that any further observations on the nature of poetry are rendered impossible because each separate poem is a law unto itself? Does anarchy or multiplicity crowd out order? By no means. But the order cannot be mechanical, for a poem is comparable to a living organism. I have no desire to set up shop as Procrustes and reduce all poems to a long or short bed. On the contrary I am aware that the art of poetry is not the exclusive possession of any century or school or age or race or nation. The range of poetry is immense, and good poems are inexhaustible in number and in variety.

Everything that I have to say here amounts to a single argument regarding the nature of poetry—that a poem is like a person. Now a person does not lose his personality because he is subject to certain general laws: of gravity, of chemistry, of heredity, or of Nemesis. If one considers the laws governing poetry not as grim fiats, but as descriptions of what usually happens in a poem, as generalizations based on experience, they need not seem stern and inflexible and forbidding. The nature of poetry is fluid, so that the laws of poetry, like the laws of nature, may be deduced as great guiding principles within which individual entities move easily, in accordance with their own particular natures, and with no sense of let or hindrance. The biological laws of intussusception and of senescence apply equally to an Anopheles mosquito, an oak tree, and an elephant, but they do not compel the mosquito to be the elephant. Similarly, the qualities of poetry which I am proposing here are found as constants in all poetry, yet are uniquely embodied in each particular poem. No one law of poetry reveals all its secrets; and only open, comprehensive, tolerant minds will save us from clamping poetry in too narrow a cage.

Secondly, I maintain that poetry is intense. To create any work of art requires strenuous effort; only an experience of more than average intensity is strong enough to compel an artist to reproduce that experience as exactly as poetry requires. The more traditional way of stating the fact of poetic intensity would be to say that poetry is emotional or passionate. Calling poetry emotional, however, suggests to some people that poetry gushes and sentimentalizes. So it does, when it wishes, and still it remains poetry: far too many modern critics and readers assume that sentiment and even sentimentality are no fit parts of human experience. But romantic sentiment is not the only way of expressing feeling; restraint and understatement can produce equally powerful emotional effects. Profound thought, no less than smiles and tears, may stamp passion upon a poem; and following the convolutions of a controlled argument may produce an exhilaration and an awareness which cannot be distinguished from emotion. Nevertheless, to avoid the popular limitations set upon the word "emotion," I have chosen to speak of the *intensity* of poetry. Even the idea of intensity must be considered closely to prevent misunderstanding. It might imply that the sensation of poetry is comparable to an electric shock or an exploding firecracker; and much of the discussion, in consequence, is devoted to showing how intensity may be secured through diffusion as well as through compression, through simple serious statement as well as through distortion and hyperbole, through repetition as well as through epigram. For again, though the goal of intensity is single for all poems, it may be reached by various individual paths.

A man does not write a poem in a typhoon or on the bier of his child. He must be at least detached enough from any intense experience to express satisfactorily its meaning for him. Poetry is significant. The care to put exact words in right places, the intensity evoked by the poet and felt by the reader—these could not exist if the poet did not believe that he was being exact and intense about *something*. In part, then, I am attacking the idea of art as an end in itself, an ivory tower walled off from and raised beyond the world of common sense. In part also, since poetry presents one man's consciousness as he regards his material, and since his material is usually human life, I maintain that poetry almost inescapably contains judgments on human values. The discussion, therefore, again argues the venerable case, now somewhat unfashionable, that the end of art is to teach, and that the significance of poetry is primarily a moral significance. Poetry may even be considered as the most effective of moral agents, since it presents not bloodless propositions, but one man's answer to particular situations. In other words, it affords useful examples, for each of us must reach his own moral decisions under similar circumstances of particularity. Such a position demands that many warning signs be set up to show that moral beliefs need not be expressed directly; that poetry is not narrow, rigid, and crude in dogmatism; and that a poem, though it strives toward meaning as intently as a sermon, a legal brief, or a scientific journal, possesses a significance different in kind and different in expression.

In developing this argument, a fourth conclusion naturally follows: "Poetry is concrete." Its significance is embodied in the symbols of all the senses; and moral statements, abstract speculations, convictions, hopes, and tenuous emotions, are all set forth to walk in images and actions. Like the ordinary man, the poet naturally grasps an idea in terms of an example. He "sees" his thought. His pictures and vivid instances convey his sense of the immediacy, the tangibility, the actuality, of the world and of his own existence. The gorgeous galleries of poetry afford ample illustrations that the typical poet thinks in images. Even philosophical or reflective or didactic poetry possesses, to a remarkable degree, this quality of concreteness.

"But poetry is also complex." The earlier principles are, I think, applicable to all poetry; each is quite able to get along independently; each differs from the others; yet how are they to subsist simultaneously in the same poem? Words must be set down in a satisfying and inevitable order; figures and panoramas and symbols must be summoned up before the mind's eye; the dance of the words and figures must not be meaningless, but must rouse in the reader a sense of significance; and thought, words, images, must not clog each other, nor interfere with the sense of heightened experience, of intensity, which gives to art its life and joyousness. The various modes of living—in sensation, in intellect, in emotion, in desire, in conscience—must be allowed full and harmonious interplay. This is the miracle of poetry. This is the mystery of unity-achieved-through-variety which again makes inevitable the comparison: a poem is like a person. The four first statements express merely a few of the great guiding general principles in poetry; there are innumerable smaller laws and local ordinances and temporary edicts and proclamations in time of emergency. Fortunately the immense domains of poetry can never be reduced to mathematical or legal order; and this fifth statement is not so much a law as a description, a recognition, of the complexity of poetry. In art, and perhaps only in art, are the full possibilities of man's existence imaginatively realized, so that life may be apprehended, for a moment, at its highest and its most complete.

Poetry is also rhythmic. A poem maintains its life by walking the knife-edge between rhythmical formlessness on one side and mechanical meter on the other.

And finally, "Poetry is formal." The word is forbidding in its stiffness, but here we are dealing with the most purely esthetic aspects of our subject, the most strictly poetic. And we are finding that poetry is not only a way of looking at the world, but a way of speaking about it. No one can enjoy a poem to the full who does not take it on its own incomparable terms, not only in its unique words and images and rhythms, but also in its form. The structures of poems are as beautiful in themselves as the structures of music or architecture. That poems may appeal to us on so many additional levels is no adequate reason for neglecting or minimizing the delight they afford through the sheer beauty of their forms. We may agree with Plato and with Spenser that

> Soule is forme, and doth the bodie make.

But conversely, we arrive at the highest and purest pleasures of poetry by observing the control, the shape, the harmony which the artist's activity has brought into being.

The nature of poetry is not mechanical. Its laws are not edicts, but observations; they are not forced upon poetry, but derived from it. In all fairness, I should offer here, in very brief compass, an illustration. Let us take a short poem by Housman:

> Into my heart an air that kills
>   From yon far country blows:
> What are those blue remembered hills,
>   What spires, what farms are those?
>
> That is the land of lost content,
>   I see it shining plain,
> The happy highways where I went
>   And cannot come again.

The voice is unmistakably Housman's: even a parody of it, though it might catch salient traits, would destroy some of the nuances that give it *exactness*. No word can be changed without changing the effect of the whole. If we substitute "distant countries" for "yon far country," we not only destroy Housman's characteristic sense of the past underlying the present, which he manages to suggest through the use of the slightly archaic word "yon," but we also lose the almost concrete action of pointing which "yon" gives, and we weaken the unity of the stanza by canceling the echoing "far" and "farms." We might say also that literally the air is not "killing" anything; the image would be closer to possible sensations if we substituted "an air that chills." But "kills" is the more exact word, for it can suggest the emotional *intensity* of Housman's intuition, which he has made even more poignant by the statement, meaningless in the actual world of matter, that the killing air blows into his heart. This intensity he makes specific by speaking of the content, the shining happiness, which now is lost. Few of us would miss his *significance*—that youth is irrecoverable, or the ecstasy, once past, cannot be recaptured; many of us would feel that judgments of value are also implicit: that content and happiness are good, and that if we cannot have them, it is good at least to see clearly what we have lost, and to recognize time as evil, truth and self-control as good. Any such values are not stated in abstract propositions, but with *concreteness*, in controlled and harmonized images, so that we are made to feel the air, the country, the hills, the spires, the farms, the land, and the highways of Shropshire, perhaps even the plains. *Complexity* is evident enough in the working together of these disparate elements. "Far," for instance, conveys in the thought the years between past and present; in the emotion, regret; in the image, the distant panorama; in the sound, a link with "farms" and other words.

[handwritten annotation: hard to believe? — believe?]

Complexity arises from those ambiguities which, to a greater or less degree, all readers find in a poem. If they heard it read orally, many readers might sense as the prime meaning of the sixth line, "I see *its* shining *plain*"; and is this panoramic overtone lacking even when we see that it is not grammatically permissible in the printed version? "Spires," for me at least, is better than "towers" because it makes me think of "aspiring" and "suspiration." Such complexities are not controlled, but will vary from reader to reader; so long as they remain relevant to the whole, they enrich the poem.

We respond to the complex nature of poetry, our imaginations becoming eager and alert, because of the formal qualities of the poem itself. *Rhythm* has a powerful emotional effect, rousing and quieting at the same time, so that we take delight, usually an unconscious delight, in points in the pattern — the alternate rhymes, and the alternating line lengths which compel a pause after each even-numbered line to fill it up to the rhythmical length of its odd-numbered predecessor. Variations from the rhythmical pattern are here not only pleasing in themselves but aid in successful expression: the two inverted first feet — "Ínto my heart" and "Whát are those blue" — suggest spontaneous emotion, and the extra accented syllables — "yón fár coúntry," "Whát spíres, whát fárms" — add power to the thought and emotion, extension to the landscape. And finally, the perfect *form* of the whole, the echoes, repetitions, and balances, the contrast between the question of the first stanza and the answer of the second, make all these materials into a poem. And the poem, as distinct from its poetic qualities and potentialities, consists precisely in *these* words, *this* rhythm, *this* form. Therein lies its esthetic delight, so that we would not trade the eight lines themselves for eight bushel baskets of such analyses as this. Nevertheless, developing one's power to analyze increases one's capacity to enjoy.

Inspiration

—from Plato's Ion

SOCRATES-I perceive, Ion; and I will proceed to explain to you what I imagine to be the reason of this. The gift which you possess of speaking excellently about Homer is not an art, but, as I was just saying, an inspiration; there is a divinity moving you, like that contained in the stone which Euripides calls a magnet, but which is commonly known as the stone of Heraclea. This stone not only attracts iron rings, but also imparts to them a similar power of attracting other rings; and sometimes you may see a number of pieces of iron and rings suspended from one another so as to form quite a long chain: and all of them derive their power of suspension from the original stone. In like manner the Muse first of all inspires men herself; and from these inspired persons a chain of other persons is suspended, who take the inspiration. For all good poets, epic as well as lyric, compose their beautiful poems not by art, but because they are inspired and possessed. And as the Corybantian revellers when they dance are not in their right mind, so the lyric poets are not in their right mind when they are composing their beautiful strains: but when falling under the power of music and metre they are inspired and possessed; like Bacchic maidens who draw milk and honey from the rivers when they are under the influence of Dionysus but not when they are in their right mind. And the soul of the lyric poet does the same, as they themselves say; for they tell us that they bring songs from honeyed fountains, culling them out of the gardens and dells of the Muses; they, like the bees, winging their way from flower to flower. And this is true. For the poet is a light and winged and holy thing, and there is no invention in him until he has been inspired and is out of his senses, and the mind is no longer in him: when he has not attained to this state, he is powerless and is unable to utter his oracles. Many are the noble words in which poets speak concerning the actions of men: but like yourself when speaking about Homer, they do not speak of them by any rules of art: they are simply inspired to utter that to which the Muse impels them, and that only; and when inspired, one of them will make dithyrambs, another hymns of praise, another choral strains, another epic or iambic verses—and he who is good at one is not good at any other kind of verse: for not by art does the poet sing, but by power divine. . . .

Style

—from Aristotle's Poetics

The perfection of style is to be clear without being mean. The clearest style is that which uses only current or proper words; at the same time it is mean:— witness the poetry of Cleophon and of Sthenelus. That diction, on the other hand, is lofty and raised above the commonplace which employs unusual words. By unusual, I mean strange (or rare) words, metaphorical, lengthened,—anything, in short, that differs from the normal idiom. 2. Yet a style wholly composed of such words is either a riddle or a jargon; a riddle, if it consists of metaphors; a jargon, if it consists of strange (or rare) words. For the essence of a riddle is to express true facts under impossible combinations. Now this cannot be done by any arrangement of ordinary words, but by the use of metaphor it can. Such is the riddle:— "A man I saw who on another man had glued the bronze by aid of fire," and others of the same kind. A diction that is made up of strange (or rare) terms is a jargon. 3. A certain infusion, therefore, of these elements is necessary to style; for the strange (or rare) word, the metaphorical, the ornamental, and the other kinds above mentioned, will raise it above the commonplace and mean, while the use of proper words will make it perspicuous. 4. But nothing contributes more to produce a clearness of diction that is remote from commonness than the lengthening, contraction, and alteration of words. For by deviating in exceptional cases from the normal idiom, the language will gain distinction; while, at the same time, the partial conformity with usage will give perspicuity.

Imitation

—from Aristotle's Poetics

With respect to critical difficulties and their solutions, the number and nature of the sources from which they may be drawn may be thus exhibited.

The poet being an imitator, like a painter or any other artist, must of necessity imitate one of three objects,—things as they were or are, things as they are said or thought to be, or things as they ought to be. 2. The vehicle of expression is language,—either current terms or, it may be, rare words or metaphors. There are also many modifications of language, which we concede to the poets. 3. Add to this, that the standard of correctness is not the same in poetry and politics, any more than in poetry and any other art. Within the art of poetry itself there are two kinds of faults,—those which touch its essence, and those which are accidental. 4. If a poet has proposed to himself to imitate something [but has imitated it incorrectly], through want of capacity, the error is inherent in the poetry. But if the failure is due to the thing he has proposed to do—if he has represented a horse as throwing out both his off legs at once, or introduced technical inaccuracies in medicine, for example, or in any other art—the error is not essential to the poetry. These are the points of view from which we should consider and answer the objections raised by the critics.

5. First we will suppose the poet has represented things impossi-

ble according to the laws of his own art. It is an error; but the error may be justified, if the end of the art be thereby attained (the end being that already mentioned),—if, that is, the effect of this or any other part of the poem is thus rendered more striking. A case in point is the pursuit of Hector. If, however, the end might have been as well, or better, attained without violating the special rules of the poetic art, the error is not justified: for every kind of error should, if possible, be avoided.

How to Criticize Poetry

—*from* An Essay on Criticism
Alexander Pope

First follow Nature, and your judgment frame
By her just standard, which is still the same:
Unerring NATURE, still divinely bright,
One clear, unchanged, and universal light,
Life, force, and beauty, must to all impart,
At once the source, and end, and test of Art.
Art from that fund each just supply provides,
Works without show, and without pomp presides:
In some fair body thus th' informing soul
With spirits feeds, with vigour fills the whole,
Each motion guides, and every nerve sustains;
Itself unseen, but in the effects, remains.
Some, to whom Heaven in wit has been profuse,
Want as much more, to turn it to its use;
For wit and judgment often are at strife,
Though meant each other's aid, like man and wife.
'Tis more to guide, than spur the Muse's steed;
Restrain his fury, than provoke his speed;
The wingéd courser, like a generous horse,
Shows most true mettle when you check his course.

Those RULES of old discovered, not devised,
Are Nature still, but Nature methodized;
Nature, like Liberty, is but restrained
By the same Laws which first herself ordained.

Hear how learned Greece her useful rules indites,
When to repress, and when indulge our flights:
High on Parnassus' top her sons she showed,

And pointed out those arduous paths they trod;
Held from afar, aloft, th' immortal prize,
And urged the rest by equal steps to rise.
Just precepts thus from great examples given,
She drew from them what they derived from Heaven.
The generous Critic fanned the Poet's fire,
And taught the world with reason to admire.
Then Criticism the Muses' handmaid proved,
To dress her charms, and make her more beloved:
But following wits from that intention strayed,
Who could not win the mistress, wooed the maid;
Against the Poets their own arms they turned,
Sure to hate most the men from whom they learned.
So modern 'Pothecaries, taught the art
By Doctor's bills to play the Doctor's part,
Bold in the practice of mistaken rules,
Prescribe, apply, and call their masters fools.
Some on the leaves of ancient authors prey,
Nor time nor moths e'er spoiled so much as they.
Some drily plain, without invention's aid,
Write dull receipts how poems may be made.
These leave the sense, their learning to display,
And those explain the meaning quite away.
   You then whose judgment the right course would steer,
Know well each ANCIENT'S proper character;
His Fable, Subject, scope in every page;
Religion, Country, genius of his Age:
Without all these at once before your eyes,
Cavil you may, but never criticise.
Be Homer's works your study and delight,
Read them by day, and meditate by night;
Thence form your judgment, thence your maxims bring,
And trace the Muses upward to their spring.
Still with itself compared, his text peruse;
And let your comment be the Mantuan Muse.

   When first young Maro in his boundless mind
A work t' outlast immortal Rome designed,
Perhaps he seemed above the critic's law,
And but from Nature's fountains scorned to draw:
But when t' examine every part he came,
Nature and Homer were, he found, the same.
Convinced, amazed, he checks the bold design;
And rules as strict his laboured work confine,
As if the Stagirite o'erlooked each line.
Learn hence for ancient rules a just esteem;
To copy nature is to copy them.

The General and the Particular

—from Rasselas
Samuel Johnson

"The business of a poet," said Imlac, "is to examine, not the individual, but the species; to remark general properties and large appearances: he does not number the streaks of the tulip, or describe the different shades in the verdure of the forest. He is to exhibit in his portraits of nature such prominent and striking features, as recall the original to every mind; and must neglect the minuter discriminations, which one may have remarked, and another have neglected, for those characteristics which are alike obvious to vigilance and carelessness.

"But the knowledge of nature is only half the task of a poet; he must be acquainted likewise with all the modes of life. His character requires that he estimate the happiness and misery of every condition; observe the power of all the passions in all their combinations, and trace the changes of the human mind as they are modified by various institutions and accidental influences of climate or custom, from the spriteliness of infancy to the despondence of decrepitude. He must divest himself of the prejudices of his age or country; he must consider right and wrong in their abstracted and invariable state; he must disregard present laws and opinions, and rise to general and transcendental truths, which will always be the same: he must therefore content himself with the slow progress of his name; contemn the applause of his own time, and commit his claims to the justice of posterity. He must write as the interpreter of nature, and the legislator of mankind, and consider himself as presiding over the thoughts and manners of future generations; as a being superiour to time and place.

"His labour is not yet at an end: he must know many languages and many sciences; and, that his stile may be worthy of his thoughts, must, by incessant practice, familiarize to himself every delicacy of speech and grace of harmony."

Poetic Imagination

—from Biographia Literaria
Samuel Taylor Coleridge

What is poetry? is so nearly the same question with, what is a poet? that the answer to the one is involved in the solution of the other. For it is a distinction resulting from the poetic genius itself, which sustains and modifies the images, thoughts, and emotions of the poet's own mind. The poet, described in ideal perfection, brings the whole soul of man into activity, with the subordination of its faculties to each other, according to their relative worth and dignity. He diffuses a tone and spirit of unity that blends and (as it were) fuses each into each, by that synthetic and magical power to which we have exclusively appropriated the name of imagination. This power, first put in action by the will and understanding, and retained under their irremissive, though gentle and unnoticed, control (*laxis effertur habenis*), reveals itself in the balance or reconciliation of opposite or discordant qualities: of sameness, with difference; of the general, with the concrete; the idea, with the image; the individual, with the representative; the sense of novelty and freshness, with old and familiar objects; a more than usual state of emotion, with more than usual order; judgment ever awake and steady self-possession with enthusiasm and feeling profound or vehement; and while it blends and harmonizes the natural and the artificial, still subordinates art to nature; the manner to the matter; and our admiration of the poet to our sympathy with the poetry. "Doubtless," as Sir John Davies observes of the soul (and his words may with slight alteration be applied, and even more appropriately, to the poetic imagination)—

> Doubtless this could not be, but that she turns
> Bodies to spirit by sublimation strange,
> As fire converts to fire, the things it burns,
> As we our food into our nature change.
>
> From their gross matter she abstracts their forms,
> And draws a kind of quintessence from things;
> Which to her proper nature she transforms
> To bear them light on her celestial wings.
>
> Thus does she, when from individual states
> She doth abstract the universal kinds;
> Which then re-clothed in divers names and fates
> Steal access through our senses to our minds.

Finally, good sense is the body of poetic genius, fancy its drapery, motion its life, and imagination the soul that is everywhere, and in each; and forms all into one graceful and intelligent whole.

Poetry and Emotional Need

—from "On Poetry in General"
William Hazlitt

Poetry is the language of the imagination and the passions. It relates to whatever gives immediate pleasure and pain to the human mind. It comes home to the bosoms and businesses of men; for nothing but what so comes home to them in the most general and intelligible shape, can be a subject for poetry. Poetry is the universal language which the heart holds with nature and itself. He who has a contempt for poetry, cannot have much respect for himself, or for anything else. It is not a mere frivolous accomplishment (as some persons have been led to imagine), the trifling amusement of a few idle readers or leisure hours—it has been the study and delight of mankind in all ages. Many people suppose that poetry is something to be found only in books, contained in lines of ten syllables, with like endings: but wherever there is a sense of beauty, or power, or harmony, as in the motion of a wave of the sea, in the growth of a flower that "spreads its sweet leaves to the air, and dedicates its beauty to the sun,"—*there* is poetry, in its birth. If history is a grave study, poetry may be said to be a graver: its materials lie deeper, and are spread wider. History treats, for the most part, of the cumbrous and unwieldy masses of things, the empty cases in which the affairs of the world are packed, under the heads of intrigue or war, in different states, and from century to century: but there is no thought or feeling that can have entered into the mind of man, which he would be eager to communicate to others, or which they would listen to with delight, that is not a fit subject for poetry. It is not a branch of authorship: it is "the stuff of which our life is made." The rest is "mere oblivion," a dead letter: for all that is worth remembering in life, is the poetry of it. Fear is poetry, hope is poetry, love is poetry, hatred is poetry; contempt, jealousy, remorse, admiration, wonder, pity, despair, or madness, are all poetry. Poetry is that fine particle within us, that expands, rarefies, refines, raises our whole being: without it "man's life is poor as beast's." Man is a poetical animal: and those of us who do not study the principles of poetry, act upon them all our lives, like Molière's *Bourgeois Gentilhomme*, who had always spoken prose without knowing it. The child is a poet in fact, when he first plays at hide-and-seek, or repeats the story of Jack the Giant-killer; the shepherd-boy is a poet, when he first crowns his mistress with a garland of flowers; the countryman, when he stops to look at the rainbow; the city-apprentice, when he gazes after the Lord Mayor's show; the miser, when he hugs his gold; the courtier, who builds his hopes upon a smile; the savage, who paints his idol with blood; the slave, who worships a tyrant, or the tyrant, who fancies himself a god;—the vain, the ambitious, the proud, the choleric man, the hero and the coward, the beggar and the king, the rich and the poor, the young and the old, all live in a world of their own making; and the poet does no more than describe what all the others think and act.

Poets as Legislators of the World

—from A Defense of Poetry
Percy Bysshe Shelley

The most unfailing herald, companion, and follower of the awakening of a great people to work a beneficial change in opinion or institution, is poetry. At such periods there is an accumulation of the power of communicating and receiving intense and impassioned conceptions respecting man and nature. The persons in whom this power resides may often, as far as regards many portions of their nature, have little apparent correspondence with that spirit of good of which they are the ministers. But even whilst they deny and abjure, they are yet compelled to serve, the power which is seated on the throne of their own soul. It is impossible to read the compositions of the most celebrated writers of the present day without being startled with the electric life which burns within their words. They measure the circumference and sound the depths of human nature with a comprehensive and all-penetrating spirit, and they are themselves perhaps the most sincerely astonished at its manifestations; for it is less their spirit than the spirit of the age. Poets are the hierophants of an unapprehended inspiration; the mirrors of the gigantic shadows which futurity casts upon the present; the words which express what they understand not; the trumpets which sing to battle, and feel not what they inspire; the influence which is moved not, but moves. Poets are the unacknowledged legislators of the world.

Poetry and Action

—from Preface to Poems, *1853*
Matthew Arnold

What are the eternal objects of Poetry, among all nations and at all times? They are actions; human actions; possessing an inherent interest in themselves, and which are to be communicated in an interesting manner by the art of the Poet. Vainly will the latter imagine that he has everything in his own power; that he can make an intrinsically inferior action equally delightful with a more excellent one by his treatment of it; he may indeed compel us to admire his skill, but his work will possess, within itself, an incurable defect.

The Poet, then, has in the first place to select an excellent action; and what actions are the most excellent? Those, certainly, which most powerfully appeal to the great primary human affections: to those elementary feelings which subsist permanently in the race, and which are independent of time. These feelings are permanent and the same; that which interests them is permanent and the same also. The modernness or antiquity of an action, therefore, has nothing to do with its fitness for poetical representation; this depends upon its inherent qualities. To the elementary part of our nature, to our passions, that which is great and passionate is eternally interesting; and interesting solely in proportion to its greatness and to its passion. A great human action of a thousand years ago is more interesting to it than a smaller human action of to-day, even though upon the representation of this last the most consummate skill may have been expended, and though it has the advantage of appealing by its modern language, familiar manners, and contemporary allusions, to all our transient feelings and interests. These, however, have no right to demand of a poetical work that it shall satisfy them; their claims are to be directed elsewhere. Poetical works belong to the domain of our permanent passions: let them interest these, and the voice of all subordinate claims upon them is at once silenced.

Achilles, Prometheus, Clytemnestra, Dido—what modern poem presents personages as interesting, even to us moderns, as these personages of an "exhausted past"? We have the domestic epic dealing with the details of modern life which pass daily under our eyes; we have poems representing modern personages in contact with the problems of modern life, moral, intellectual, and social; these works have been produced by poets the most distinguished of their nation and time; yet I fearlessly assert that *Hermann and Dorothea, Childe Harold,* "Jocelyn," *The Excursion,* leave the reader cold in comparison with the effect produced upon him by the later books of the *Iliad,* by the *Orestea,* or by the episode of Dido. And why is this? Simply because in the three latter cases the action is greater, the personages nobler, the situations more intense: and this is the true basis of the interest in a poetical work, and this alone.

It may be urged, however, that past actions may be interesting in themselves, but that they are not to be adopted by the modern Poet, because it is impossible for him to have them clearly present to his own mind, and he cannot therefore feel them deeply, nor represent them forcibly. But this is not necessarily the case. The externals of a past action, indeed, he cannot know with the precision of a contemporary; but his business is with its essentials. The outward man of Oedipus or of Macbeth, the houses in which they lived, the ceremonies of their courts, he cannot accurately figure to himself; but neither do they essentially concern him. His business is with their inward man; with their feelings and behavior in certain tragic situations, which engage their passions as men; these have in them nothing local and casual; they are as accessible to the modern Poet as to a contemporary.

The date of an action, then, signifies nothing: the action itself, its selection and construction, this is what is all-important. This the Greeks understood far more clearly than we do. The radical difference between their poetical theory and ours consists, as it appears to me, in this: that, with them, the poetical character of the action in itself, and the conduct of it, was the first consideration; with us, attention is fixed mainly on the value of the separate thoughts and images which occur in the treatment of an action. They regarded the whole; we regard the parts. With them, the action predominated over the expression of it; with us, the expression predominates over the action. Not that they failed in expression, or were inattentive to it; on the contrary, they are the highest models of expression, the unapproached masters of the *grand style*: but their expression is so excellent because it is so admirably kept in its right degree of prominence; because it is so simple and so well subordinated; because it draws its force directly from the pregnancy of the matter which it conveys. For what reason was the Greek tragic poet confined to so limited a range of subjects? Because there are so few actions which unite in themselves, in the highest degree, the conditions of excellence: and it was not thought that on any but an excellent subject could an excellent Poem be constructed. A few actions, therefore, eminently adapted for tragedy, maintained almost exclusive possession of the Greek tragic stage. Their significance appeared inexhaustible; they were as permanent · problems, perpetually offered to the genius of every fresh poet. This too is the reason of what appears to us moderns a certain baldness of expression in Greek tragedy; or the triviality with which we often reproach the remarks of the chorus, where it takes part in the dialogue: that the action itself, the situation of Orestes, or Merope, or Alcmaeon, was to stand the central point of interest, unforgotten, absorbing, principal; that no accessories were for a moment to distract the spectator's attention from this, that the tone of the parts was to be perpetually kept down, in order not to impair the grandiose effect of the whole. The terrible old mythic story on which the drama was founded stood, before he entered the theatre, traced in its bare outlines upon the spectator's mind; it stood in his memory, as a group of statuary, faintly seen, at the end of a long and dark vista: then came the Poet, embodying outlines, developing situations, not a word wasted, not a sentiment capriciously thrown in: stroke upon stroke, the drama proceeded: the light deepened upon the group; more and more it revealed itself to the riveted gaze of the spectator: until at last, when the final words were spoken, it stood before him in broad sunlight, a model of immortal beauty.

This was what a Greek critic demanded; this was what a Greek poet endeavoured to effect. It signified nothing to what time an action belonged; we do not find that the *Persae* occupied a particularly high rank among the dramas of Aeschylus, because it represented a matter of contemporary interest: this was not what a cultivated Athenian required; he required that the permanent elements of his nature should be moved; and dramas of which the action, though taken from a long-distant mythic time, yet was calculated to accomplish this in a higher degree than that of the *Persae*, stood higher in his estimation accordingly. The Greeks felt, no doubt, with their exquisite sagacity of taste, that an action of present times was too near them, too much mixed up with what was accidental and passing, to form a sufficiently grand, detached, and self-subsistent object for a tragic poem: such objects belonged to the domain of the comic poet, and of the lighter kinds of poetry. For the more serious kinds, for *pragmatic* poetry, to use an excellent expression of Polybius, they were more difficult and severe in the range of subjects which they permitted. Their theory and practice alike, the admirable treatise of Aristotle, and the unrivalled works of their poets, exclaim with a thousand tongues—"All depends upon the subject; choose a fitting action, penetrate yourself with the feeling of its situations; this done, everything else will follow."

But for all kinds of poetry alike there was one point on which they were rigidly exacting; the adaptability of the subject to the kind of poetry selected, and the careful construction of the poem.

How different a way of thinking from this is ours! We can hardly at the present day understand what Menander meant, when he told a man who inquired as to the progress of his comedy that he had finished it, not having yet written a single line, because he had constructed the action of it in his mind. A modern critic would have assured him that the merit of his piece depended on the brilliant things which arose under his pen as he went along. We have poems which seem to exist merely for the sake of single lines and passages; not for the sake of producing any total-impression. We have critics who seem to direct their attention merely to detached expressions, to the language about the action, not to the action itself. I verily think that the majority of them do not in their hearts believe that there is such a thing as a total-impression to be derived from a poem at all, or to be demanded from a poet; they think the term a commonplace of metaphysical criticism. They will permit the Poet to select any action he pleases, and to suffer that action to go as it will, provided he gratifies them with occasional bursts of fine writing, and with a shower of isolated thoughts and images. That is, they permit him to leave their poetical sense ungratified, provided that he gratifies their rhetorical sense and their curiosity. Of his neglecting to gratify these, there is little danger; he needs rather to be warned against the danger of attempting to gratify these alone; he needs rather to be perpetually reminded to prefer his action to everything else; so to treat this, as to permit its inherent excellences to develop themselves, without interruption from the intrusion of his personal peculiarities: most fortunate, when he most entirely succeeds in effacing himself, and in enabling a noble action to subsist as it did in nature.

Preliminary Problems

Yvor Winters

First Problem

Is it possible to say that Poem A (one of Donne's *Holy Sonnets*, or one of the poems of Jonson or of Shakespeare) is better than Poem B (Collins' *Ode to Evening*) or vice versa?

If not, is it possible to say that either of these is better than Poem C (*The Cremation of Sam Magee*, or something comparable)?

If the answer is no in both cases, then any poem is as good as any other. If this is true, then all poetry is worthless; but this obviously is not true, for it is contrary to all our experience.

If the answer is yes in both cases, then there follows the question of whether the answer implies merely that one poem is better than another for the speaker, or whether it means that one poem is intrinsically better than another. If the former, then we are impressionists, which is to say relativists; and are either mystics of the type of Emerson, or hedonists of the type of Stevens and Ransom. If the latter, then we assume that constant principles govern the poetic experience, and that the poem (as likewise the judge) must be judged in relationship to those principles. It is important, therefore, to discover the consequences of assuming each of these positions.

If our answer to the first question is no and to the second yes, then we are asserting that we can distinguish between those poems which are of the canon and those which are not, but that within the canon all judgment is impossible. This view, if adopted, will require serious elucidation, for on the face of it, it appears inexplicable. On the other hand, one cannot deny that within the canon judgment will become more difficult, for the nearer two poems may be to the highest degrees of excellence, the harder it will be to choose between them. Two poems, in fact, might be so excellent that there would be small profit in endeavoring to say that one was better, but one could arrive at this conclusion only after a careful examination of both.

Second Problem

If we accept the view that one poem can be regarded as better than another, the question then arises whether this judgment is a matter of inexplicable intuition, or whether it is a question of intuition that can be explained, and consequently guided and improved by rational elucidation.

If we accept the view that the judgment in question is inexplicable, then we are again forced to confess ourselves impressionists and relativists, unless we can show that the intuitions of all men agree at all times, or that the intuitions of one man are invariably right and those of all others wrong whenever they differ. We obviously can demonstrate neither of these propositions.

If we start, then, with the proposition that one poem may be intrinsically superior to another, we are forced to account for differences of opinion regarding it. If two critics differ, it is possible that one is right and the other wrong, more likely that both are partly right and partly wrong, but in different respects: neither the native gifts nor the education of any man have ever been wholly adequate to many of the critical problems he will encounter, and no two men are ever the same in these respects or in any others. On the other hand, although the critic should display reasonable humility and caution, it is only fair to add that few men possess either the talent or the education to justify their being taken very seriously, even of those who are nominally professional students of these matters.

But if it is possible by rational elucidation to give a more or less clear account of what one finds in a poem and why one approves or disapproves, then communication between two critics, though no doubt imperfect, becomes possible, and it becomes possible that they may in some measure correct each other's errors and so come more near to a true judgment of the poem.

REDlisted poetry - 'sonnet - 14 lines; rhyme scheme
2. Haiku - always deals with nature, 14 syll. & 3 lm
3. limericks   5. satire
4. epic

Third Problem

If rational communication about poetry is to take place, it is
necessary first to determine what we mean by a poem.

A poem is first of all a statement in words.

But it differs from all such statements of a purely philosophical or
theoretical nature, in that it has by intention a controlled content of
feeling. In this respect, it does not differ from many works written in
prose, however.

A poem differs from a work written in prose by virtue of its being
composed in verse. The rhythm of verse permits the expression of
more powerful feeling than is possible in prose when such feeling is
needed, and it permits at all times the expression of finer shades of
feeling.

A poem, then, is a statement in words in which special pains are
taken with the expression of feeling. This description is merely intended to distinguish the poem from other kinds of writing; it is not
offered as a complete description.

Fourth Problem

What, however, are words?

They are audible sounds, or their visual symbols, invented by man
to communicate his thoughts and feelings. Each word has a conceptual
content, however slight; each word, exclusive, perhaps, of the parti-
cles, communicates vague associations of feeling.

The word *fire* communicates a concept; it also connotes very
vaguely certain feelings, depending on the context in which we happen
to place it—depending, for example, on whether we happen to think of
a fire on a hearth, in a furnace, or in a forest. These feelings may be
rendered more and more precise as we render the context more and
more precise; as we come more and more near to completing and
perfecting our poem.

Fifth Problem

But if the poem, as compared to prose, pays especial attention to
feeling, are we to assume that the rational content of the poem is
unimportant to its success?

The rational content cannot be eliminated from words; consequently the rational content cannot be eliminated from poetry. It is
there. If it is unsatisfactory in itself, a part of the poem is unsatisfactory; the poem is thus damaged beyond argument. If we deny this, we
must surely explain ourselves very fully.

If we admit this, we are faced with another problem: is it conceivable that rational content and feeling-content may both be perfect, and yet that they may be unrelated to each other, or imperfectly related? To me this is inconceivable, because the emotional content of words is generated by our experience with the conceptual content, so that a relationship is necessary.

This fact of the necessity of such relationship may fairly return us for a moment to the original question: whether imperfection of rational content damages the entire poem. If there is a necessary relationship between concept and feeling, and concept is unsatisfactory, then feeling must be damaged by way of the relationship.

Sixth Problem

If there is a relationship between concept and feeling, what is the nature of that relationship?

To answer this, let us return to the basic unit, the word. The concept represented by the word, motivates the feeling which the word communicates. It is the concept of fire which generates the feelings communicated by the word, though the sound of the word may modify these feelings very subtly, as may other accidental qualities, especially if the word be used skillfully in a given context. The accidental qualities of a word, however, such as its literary history, for example, can only modify, cannot essentially change, for these will be governed ultimately by the concept; that is, *fire* will seldom be used to signify *plum-blossom*, and so will have few opportunities to gather connotations from the concept, *plum-blossom*. The relationship, in the poem, between rational statement and feeling, is thus seen to be that of motive to emotion.

Seventh Problem

But has not this reasoning brought us back to the proposition that all poems are equally good? For if each word motivates its own feeling, because of its intrinsic nature, will not any rational statement, since it is composed of words, motivate the feeling exactly proper to it?

This is not true, for a good many reasons, of which I shall enumerate only a few of the more obvious. In making a rational statement, in purely theoretical prose, we find that our statement may be loose or exact, depending upon the relationships of the words to each other. The precision of a word depends to some extent upon its surroundings. This is true likewise with respect to the connotations of words. Two words, each of which has several usably close rational synonyms, may reinforce and clarify each other with respect to their connotations or they may not do so.

Let me illustrate with a simple example from Browning's *Serenade at the Villa:*

> So wore night; the East was gray,
>   White the broad-faced hemlock flowers.

The lines are marred by a crowding of long syllables and difficult consonants, but they have great beauty in spite of the fault. What I wish to point out, for the sake of my argument, is the relationship between the words *wore* and *gray*. The verb *wore* means literally that the night passed, but it carries with it connotations of exhaustion and attrition which belong to the condition of the protagonist; and grayness is a color which we associate with such a condition. If we change the phrase to read: "Thus night passed," we shall have the same rational meaning, and a meter quite as respectable, but no trace of the power of the line: the connotation of *wore* will be lost, and the connotation of *gray* will remain merely in a state of ineffective potentiality. The protagonist in seeing his feeling mirrored in the landscape is not guilty of motivating his feeling falsely, for we know his general motive from the poem as a whole; he is expressing a portion of the feeling motivated by the total situation through a more or less common psychological phenomenon. If the poem were such, however, that we did not know why the night *wore* instead of *passed*, we should have just cause for complaint; in fact, most of the strength of the word would probably be lost. The second line contains other fine effects, immediately with reference to the first line, ultimately with reference to the theme; I leave the reader to analyze them for himself, but he will scarcely succeed without the whole poem before him.

Concepts, as represented by particular words, are affected by connotations due to various and curious accidents. A word may gather connotations from its use in folk-poetry, in formal poetry, in vulgar speech, or in technical prose: a single concept might easily be represented by four words with these distinct histories; and any one of the words might prove to be proper in a given poetic context. Words gain connotation from etymological accidents. Something of this may be seen in the English word *outrage*, in which is commonly felt, in all likelihood, something associated with *rage*, although there is no rage whatever in the original word. Similarly the word *urchin*, in modern English, seldom connotes anything related to hedgehogs, or to the familiars of the witches, by whose intervention the word arrived at its modern meaning and feeling. Yet the connotation proper to any stage in the history of such a word might be resuscitated, or a blend of connotations effected, by skillful use. Further, the connotation of a word may be modified very strongly by its function in the metrical structure, ...

This is enough to show that exact motivation of feeling by concept is not inherent in any rational statement. Any rational statement will govern the general possibilities of feeling derivable from it, but the task of the poet is to adjust feeling to motive precisely. He has to select words containing not only the right relationships within themselves, but the right relationships to each other. The task is very difficult; and this is no doubt the reason why the great poetry of a great poet is likely to be very small in bulk.

Eighth Problem

Is it not possible, however, to escape from this relationship of motive to emotion by confining ourselves very largely to those words which denote emotion: love, envy, anger, and the like?

This is not possible, for these words, like others, represent concepts. If we should confine ourselves strictly to such a vocabulary, we should merely write didactic poetry: poetry about love in general, or about anger in general. The emotion communicated would result from our apprehension of the ideas in question. Such poetry is perfectly legitimate, but it is only one kind of poetry, and it is scarcely the kind which the Romantic theorist is endeavoring to define.

Such poetry has frequently been rendered particular by the use of allegory. The playful allegorizing of minor amoristic themes which one encounters in the Renaissance and which is possibly descended from certain neo-Platonic elements in medieval poetry may serve as illustration. Let us consider these and the subsequent lines by Thomas Lodge:

> Love in my bosom like a bee
>   Doth suck his sweet;
> Now with his wings he plays with me,
>   Now with his feet.

Love itself is a very general idea and might include many kinds of experience; the idea is limited by this allegory to the sentimental and sensual, but we still have an idea, the subdivision of the original idea, and the feeling must be appropriate to the concept. The concept is rendered concrete by the image of Cupid, whose actions, in turn, are rendered visible by comparison to the bee: it is these actions which make the poem a kind of anticipatory meditation on more or less sensual love, a meditation which by its mere tone of expression keeps the subject in its proper place as a very minor one. Sometimes the emphasis is on the mere description of the bee, sometimes on the description of Cupid, sometimes on the lover's feeling; but the feeling motivated in any passage is governed by this emphasis. The elements, once they are united in the poem, are never really separated, of course. In so far as the poet departs from his substantial theme in the direction of mere bees and flowers, he will achieve what Ransom calls irrelevance; but if there is much of this the poem will be weakened. Whether he so departs or not, the relation of motive to emotion must remain the same, within each passage. . . .

A common Romantic practice is to use words denoting emotions, but to use them loosely and violently, as if the very carelessness expressed emotion. Another is to make a general statement, but seem to refer it to a particular occasion, which, however, is never indicated: the poet thus seems to avoid the didactic, yet he is not forced to understand the particular motive. Both these faults may be seen in these lines from Shelley:

> Out of the day and night
> A joy has taken flight;
> Fresh spring, and summer, and winter hoar,
> Move my faint heart with grief, but with delight
> No more—oh, never more.

The poet's intention is so vague, however, that he achieves nothing but stereotypes of a very crude kind.

The Romantics often tried other devices. For example, it would be possible to write a poem on fear in general, but to avoid in some measure the effect of the purely didactic by illustrating the emotion along the way with various experiences which might motivate fear. There is a danger here, though it is merely a danger, that the general idea may not dominate the poem, and that the poem may thus fall apart into a group of poems on particular experiences. There is the alternative danger, that the particular quality of the experiences may be so subordinated to the illustrative function of the experiences, that within each illustration there is merely a stereotyped and not a real relationship of motive to feeling: this occurs in Collins' *Ode to Fear*, though a few lines in the Epode come surprisingly to life. But the methods which I have just described really offer no semblance of an escape from the theory of motivation which I am defending.

Another Romantic device, if it is conscious enough to be called a device, is to offer instead of a defensible motive a false one, usually culled from landscape. This kind of writing represents a tacit admission of the principle of motivation which I am defending, but a bad application of the principle. It results in the kind of writing which I have called pseudo-reference . . . . One cannot believe, for example, that Wordsworth's passions were charmed away by a look at the daffodils, or that Shelley's were aroused by the sight of the leaves blown about in the autumn wind. A motive is offered, and the poet wants us to accept it, but we recognize it as inadequate. In such a poem there may be fragments of good description, which motivate a feeling more or less purely appropriate to the objects described, and these fragments may sustain our liking for the poem: this happens in Collins' *Ode to Evening*; but one will find also an account of some kind of emotion essentially irrelevant to the objects described, along with the attempt, more or less explicit, to deduce the emotion from the object.

There remains the method of the Post-Romantics, whether French Symbolists or American Experimentalists: the method of trying to extinguish the rational content of language while retaining the content of association. . . .

Ninth Problem

The relationship in the poem of rational meaning to feeling we have seen to be that of motive to emotion; and we have seen that this must be a satisfactory relationship. How do we determine whether such a relationship is satisfactory? We determine it by an act of moral judgment. The question then arises whether moral judgments can be made, whether the concept of morality is or is not an illusion.

If morality can be considered real, if a theory of morality can be said to derive from reality, it is because it guides us toward the greatest happiness which the accidents of life permit: that is, toward the fullest realization of our nature, in the Aristotelian or Thomistic sense. But is there such a thing, abstractly considered, as full realization of our nature?

To avoid discussion of too great length, let us consider the opposite question: is there such a thing as obviously unfulfilled human nature? Obviously there is. We need only turn to the feeble-minded, who cannot think and so cannot perceive or feel with any clarity; or to the insane, who sometimes perceive and feel with great intensity, but whose feelings and perceptions are so improperly motivated that they are classed as illusions. At slightly higher levels, the criminal, the dissolute, the unscrupulously selfish, and various types of neurotics are likely to arouse but little disagreement as examples.

Now if we are able to recognize the fact of insanity—if in fact we are forced to recognize it—that is, the fact of the obvious maladjustment of feeling to motive, we are forced to admit the possibility of more accurate adjustment, and, by necessary sequence, of absolutely accurate adjustment, even though we admit the likelihood that most people will attain to a final adjustment but very seldom indeed. We can guide ourselves toward such an adjustment in life, as in art, by means of theory and the critical examination of special instances; but the final act of judgment is in both life and art a unique act—it is a relationship between two elements, the rational understanding and the feeling, of which only one is classificatory and of which the other has infinite possibilities of variation.

Tenth Problem

If the final act of adjustment is a unique act of judgment, can we say that it is more or less right, provided it is demonstrably within the general limits prescribed by the theory of morality which has led to it? The answer to this question is implicit in what has preceded; in fact the answer resembles exactly that reached at the end of the first problem examined. We can say that it is more or less nearly right. If extreme deviation from right judgment is obvious, then there is such a thing as right judgment. The mere fact that life may be conducted in a fairly satisfactory manner, by means of inaccurate judgment within certain limits, and that few people ever bother to refine their judgment beyond the stage which enables them to remain largely within those limits, does not mean that accurate judgment has no reality. Implicit in all that has preceded is the concept that in any moral situation, there is a right judgment as an ultimate possibility; that the human judge, or actor, will approximate it more or less nearly; that the closeness of his approximation will depend upon the accuracy of his rational understanding and of his intuition, and upon the accuracy of their interaction upon each other.

Eleventh Problem

Nothing has thus far been said about human action, yet morality is supposed to guide human action. And if art is moral, there should be a relationship between art and human action.

The moral judgment, whether good, bad, or indifferent, is commonly the prelude and instigation to action. Hastily or carefully, intelligently or otherwise, one arrives at some kind of general idea of a situation calling for action, and one's idea motivates one's feeling: the act results. The part played by will, or the lack of it, between judgment and act, the possibility that action may be frustrated by some constitutional or habitual weakness or tendency, such as cowardice or a tendency to anger, in a person of a fine speculative or poetic judgment, are subjects for a treatise on ethics or psychology; a treatise on poetry stops with the consideration of the speculative judgment, which reaches its best form and expression in poetry. In the situations of daily life, one does not, as a rule, write a poem before acting: one makes a more rapid and simple judgment. But if the poem does not individually lead to a particular act, it does not prevent action. It gives us a better way of judging representative acts than we should otherwise have. It is thus a civilizing influence: it trains our power of judgment, and should, I imagine, affect the quality of daily judgments and actions.

Twelfth Problem

What, then, is the nature of the critical process?

It will consist (1) of the statement of such historical or biographical knowledge as may be necessary in order to understand the mind and method of the writer; (2) of such analysis of his literary theories as we may need to understand and evaluate what he is doing; (3) of a rational critique of the paraphrasable content (roughly, the motive) of the poem; (4) of a rational critique of the feeling motivated — that is, of the details of style, as seen in language and technique; and (5) of the final act of judgment, a unique act, the general nature of which can be indicated, but which cannot be communicated precisely, since it consists in receiving from the poet his own final and unique judgment of his matter and in judging that judgment. It should be noted that the purpose of the first four processes is to limit as narrowly as possible the region in which the final unique act is to occur.

In the actual writing of criticism, a given task may not require all of these processes, or may not require that all be given equal emphasis; or it may be that in connection with a certain writer, whether because of the nature of the writer or because of the way in which other critics have treated him previously, one or two of these processes must be given so much emphasis that others must be neglected for lack of space. These are practical matters to be settled as the occasions arise.

Part V

Poems for Study

Chapter 15

**Review Analysis
and Evaluation**

We have considered a number of different devices useful in analyzing a poem and a number of different levels of interpretation. It is now time to apply this knowledge and skill to a variety of poems that cover several centuries of English and American poetry.

As a last word in introduction, we have chosen several poems to be studied as whole poems rather than as illustrations in various techniques of analysis. The exercises include most of the analytical problems we have studied.

Besides serving as a review of analytical techniques, these poems and exercises will also give you an opportunity to begin the process of evaluating a poem, that is, determining whether or not it is a good poem. We say "begin" the process of evaluation, because critical standards are difficult to define and even more difficult to get agreement about. Critical judgment is such a complex matter that many people say that appreciating poetry is a matter of taste, and that is all that can be said on the subject.

Perhaps this is a valid critical attitude, but before you accept it as your own, you should test the possibility of forming value judgments by determining how effective a poem is within those areas discussed in this book. The analytical principles covered in this book offer a tangible basis for critical evaluation. Working within these areas, we can state a useful critical principle: *The elements of a poem should be coherent and appropriate within the poetic context.* Applying this principle means asking questions concerning coherence and appropriateness within these areas: structural patterns, syntax and situation, imagery, metaphor, irony, symbol, words, and sound and rhythm.

Sample Evaluation Questions

1. *Is the tiger an appropriate symbol in "The Tiger"?*

2. *Are the other images in "The Tiger" coherently related to the central symbol?*

3. *Are the problems of syntax and vocabulary too difficult in "Thou Art Indeed Just, Lord"?*

4. *"Kubla Khan" is a "fragment," reportedly part of a dream. To what extent is it a complete poem?*

5. *Is the ironic tone of "The Latest Decalogue" appropriate to the religious subject?*

6. *There is a notable lack of imagery to communicate abstractions in Shelley's "To—." How does the poet compensate for this deficiency?*

7. *What incoherence is there in the image pattern in "The Skaters"?*

8. *Is the sprightly rhythm of "Because I Could Not Stop for Death" inappropriate to such a serious subject as death?*

9. *In "When God Decided to Invent," what is the effect of Cummings' using "because" instead of a conventional noun?*

10. *Is Shelley successful in conveying his theme in "Ozymandias" without direct statement? If so, what means has he used?*

11. *Evaluate the coherence of the idea structure of "The Road Not Taken." For example, are the phrases "really about the same" and "equally lay" consistent with the last two lines?*

TO A WATERFOWL

Whither, midst falling dew,
While glow the heavens with the last steps of day,
Far, through their rosy depths, dost thou pursue
Thy solitary way?

Vainly the fowler's eye   5
Might mark thy distant flight to do thee wrong,
As, darkly seen against the crimson sky,
Thy figure floats along.

Seek'st thou the plashy brink
Of weedy lake, or marge of river wide,   *10*
Or where the rocking billows rise and sink
    On the chafed ocean-side?

There is a Power whose care
Teaches thy way along that pathless coast—
The desert and illimitable air—   *15*
    Lone wandering, but not lost.

All day thy wings have fanned,
At that far height, the cold, thin atmosphere,
Yet stoop not, weary, to the welcome land,
    Though the dark night is near.   *20*

And soon that toil shall end;
Soon shalt thou find a summer home, and rest,
And scream among thy fellows; reeds shall bend,
    Soon, o'er thy sheltered nest.

Thou'rt gone, the abyss of heaven   *25*
Hath swallowed up thy form; yet, on my heart
Deeply hath sunk the lesson thou hast given,
    And shall not soon depart.

He who, from zone to zone,
Guides through the boundless sky thy certain flight,   *30*
In the long way that I must tread alone,
    Will lead my steps aright.

                        —*William Cullen Bryant*

Aids to Analysis

This poem has often been criticized for having an intrusive moral statement at the end. The following questions are designed to help you to evaluate this criticism as you analyze the poem.

1. *Mark the stages in the narrative pattern. Is there a clear progression?*

2. *The last two stanzas state the theme. Study the preceding stanzas to see if each marks a clear progression in thought to lead us to connect the waterfowl and the speaker. For instance,* Whither *in stanza 1 and* Vainly *in stanza 2 indicate that a human observer sees some significance in the bird's flight.*

3. *Once you have decided on the relevance of the last two stanzas, determine whether or not they are needed. That is, is the theme clear without these last two stanzas?*

SONG OF THE NIGHT AT DAYBREAK

All my stars forsake me,
And the dawn-winds shake me;
Where shall I betake me?

Whither shall I run
Till the set of the sun,   5
Till the day be done?

To the mountain-mine,
To the boughs o' the pine,
To the blind man's eyne,

To a brow that is   10
Bowed upon the knees,
Sick with memories.

—*Alice Meynell*

Aids to Analysis

1. *Who is the speaker?*

2. *What is the dominant image in the poem? Is this image coherent throughout?*

3. *There is a shift from inanimate images in lines 7–8 to human images in lines 9–12. What development in theme is marked by this shift in imagery? Does this shift weaken the coherence of the image pattern and the idea pattern of the poem?*

4. *Is the vocabulary appropriate to the subject and mood? For example,* set *(instead of* setting*),* be *(instead of* is*),* eyne *(instead of* eyes*).*

5. *Are rhymes such as* forsake me—betake me, is—knees—memories *appropriate to the seriousness of the subject?*

ON FIRST LOOKING INTO CHAPMAN'S HOMER

Much have I travelled in the realms of gold,
  And many goodly states and kingdoms seen;
  Round many western islands have I been
Which bards in fealty to Apollo hold.
Oft of one wide expanse had I been told   5
  That deep-browed Homer ruled as his demesne;
  Yet did I never breathe its pure serene

Till I heard Chapman speak out loud and bold:
Then felt I like some watcher of the skies
   When a new planet swims into his ken;   *10*
Or like stout Cortez when with eagle eyes
   He stared at the Pacific—and all his men
Looked at each other with a wild surmise—
   Silent, upon a peak in Darien.

                      —John Keats

Aids to Analysis

1.   *Identify the image pattern. Identify the idea pattern. Are they coherently related?*

2.   *Is the metaphor of exploration appropriately applied to reading?*

3.   *How serious a weakness in the poem is the factual error about Balboa's, not Cortez', discovery of the Pacific?*

HYMN TO THE NIGHT

I heard the trailing garments of the Night
   Sweep through her marble halls!
I saw her sable skirts all fringed with light
   From the celestial walls!

I felt her presence, by its spell of might,   *5*
   Stoop o'er me from above;
The calm, majestic presence of the Night,
   As of the one I love.

I heard the sounds of sorrow and delight,
   The manifold, soft chimes,   *10*
That fill the haunted chambers of the Night,
   Like some old poet's rhymes.

From the cool cisterns of the midnight air
   My spirit drank repose;
The fountain of perpetual peace flows there,—   *15*
   From those deep cisterns flows.

O holy Night! from thee I learn to bear
   What man has borne before!
Thou layest thy finger on the lips of Care,
   And they complain no more.   *20*

Peace! Peace! Orestes-like I breathe this prayer!
  Descend with broad-winged flight,
The welcome, the thrice-prayed for, the most fair,
  The best-beloved Night!

—*Henry Wadsworth Longfellow*

Aids to Analysis

1. *Are the images sufficient to communicate the abstractions? For instance, just what is it that "man has borne before"?*

2. *Is the simile in line 8 consistent with the apostrophe to Night in line 17?*

3. *Does the allusion "Orestes-like" fit the situation of the speaker?*

4. *Is the metaphor "haunted chambers of the Night" consistent with the metaphors "calm, majestic presence of the Night" and "holy Night"?*

5. *Point out any examples you find of effective images and figures of speech.*

THE ARSENAL AT SPRINGFIELD

This is the Arsenal. From floor to ceiling,
  Like a huge organ, rise the burnished arms;
But from their silent pipes no anthem pealing
  Startles the villages with strange alarms.

Ah! what a sound will rise, how wild and dreary,   5
  When the death-angel touches those swift keys!
What loud lament and dismal Miserere
  Will mingle with their awful symphonies!

I hear even now the infinite fierce chorus,
  The cries of agony, the endless groan,   10
Which, through the ages that have gone before us,
  In long reverberations reach our own.

On helm and harness rings the Saxon hammer,
  Through Cimbric forest roars the Norseman's song,
And loud, amid the universal clamor,   15
  O'er distant deserts sounds the Tartar gong.

I hear the Florentine, who from his palace
  Wheels out his battle-bell with dreadful din,

And Aztec priests upon their teocallis
   Beat the wild war-drum made of serpent's skin;   *20*

The tumult of each sacked and burning village;
   The shout that every prayer for mercy drowns;
The soldiers' revels in the midst of pillage;
   The wail of famine in beleaguered towns;

The bursting shell, the gateway wrenched asunder,   *25*
   The rattling musketry, the clashing blade;
And ever and anon, in tones of thunder,
   The diapason of the cannonade.

Is it, O man, with such discordant noises,
   With such accursed instruments as these,   *30*
Thou drownest Nature's sweet and kindly voices,
   And jarrest the celestial harmonies?

Were half the power that fills the world with terror,
   Were half the wealth bestowed on camps and courts,
Given to redeem the human mind from error,   *35*
   There were no need of arsenals or forts:

The warrior's name would be a name abhorréd!
   And every nation, that should lift again
Its hand against a brother, on its forehead
   Would wear forevermore the curse of Cain!   *40*

Down the dark future, through long generations,
   The echoing sounds grow fainter and then cease;
And like a bell, with solemn, sweet vibrations,
   I hear once more the voice of Christ say, "Peace!"

Peace! and no longer from its brazen portals   *45*
   The blast of War's great organ shakes the skies!
But beautiful as songs of the immortals,
   The holy melodies of love arise.

            —Henry Wadsworth Longfellow

Aids to Analysis

1.   *The dominant images of stanza 1 are images of war and of sacred music. Are these clearly related to the last stanza? Are they carried through the poem consistently? For example, see stanza 7.*

2. *Is the question introduced in stanza 8 coherently related to the preceding images? Explain your answer.*

3. *There is a turn of thought beginning with line 33. Evaluate the last four stanzas in terms of the overall coherence of the poem.*

INVICTUS

Out of the night that covers me,
    Black as the Pit from pole to pole,
I thank whatever gods may be
    For my unconquerable soul.

In the fell clutch of circumstance   5
    I have not winced nor cried aloud.
Under the bludgeonings of chance
    My head is bloody, but unbowed.

Beyond this place of wrath and tears
    Looms but the Horror of the shade,   10
And yet the menace of the years
    Finds, and shall find, me unafraid.

It matters not how strait the gate,
    How charged with punishments the scroll,
I am the master of my fate: 15
    I am the captain of my soul.

           —William Ernest Henley

Aids to Analysis

1. *Is the image in line 2 factually accurate? That is, is it possible for the night to be as "Black as the Pit from pole to pole"?*

2. *What is the meaning of "but" in line 10? Is this meaning appropriate here?*

3. *Is the speaker's claim to being "master" of his fate substantiated in the poem? In answering this question, consider his situation in life described by such images as "the fell clutch of circumstance," "the bludgeonings of chance," "bloody" head, and "the Horror of the shade."*

As a final aid, we have prepared questions for Tennyson's *Ulysses*. The fact that the poem is longer than most of the poems dealt with so far should not be a serious hindrance to understanding. Simply follow the analytical principle of breaking the whole into its parts. This principle is useful in analyzing a poem of any length.

The questions are extensive. They are designed to help you analyze a major poem and at the same time make a final review of many of the subjects we have covered from idea pattern to cultural contexts. The questions will also help to bring out the coherence and appropriateness of the poem's various elements.

ULYSSES

It little profits that an idle king,
By this still hearth, among these barren crags,
Match'd with an aged wife, I mete and dole
Unequal laws unto a savage race,
That hoard, and sleep, and feed, and know not me.   5
I cannot rest from travel; I will drink
Life to the lees. All times I have enjoyed
Greatly, have suffered greatly, both with those
That loved me, and alone; on shore, and when
Thro' scudding drifts the rainy Hyades   10
Vexed the dim sea. I am become a name;
For always roaming with a hungry heart
Much have I seen and known—cities of men
And manners, climates, councils, governments,
Myself not least, but honour'd of them all—   15
And drunk delight of battle with my peers,
Far on the ringing plains of windy Troy.
I am a part of all that I have met;
Yet all experience is an arch wherethro'
Gleams that untravelled world, whose margin fades   20
For ever and for ever when I move.
How dull it is to pause, to make an end,
To rust unburnished, not to shine in use!
As though to breathe were life! Life piled on life
Were all too little, and of one to me   25
Little remains: but every hour is saved
From that eternal silence, something more,
A bringer of new things; and vile it were
For some three suns to store and hoard myself,
And this gray spirit yearning in desire   30
To follow knowledge like a sinking star,
Beyond the utmost bound of human thought.
   This is my son, mine own Telemachus;
To whom I leave the sceptre and the isle—

Well-loved of me, discerning to fulfill   35
This labor, by slow prudence to make mild
A rugged people, and through soft degrees
Subdue them to the useful and the good.
Most blameless is he, centered in the sphere
Of common duties, decent not to fail   40
In offices of tenderness, and pay
Meet adoration to my household gods,
When I am gone. He works his work, I mine.
   There lies the port; the vessel puffs her sail;
There gloom the dark broad seas. My mariners,   45
Souls that have toiled, and wrought, and thought with me—
That ever with a frolic welcome took
The thunder and the sunshine, and opposed
Free hearts, free foreheads—you and I are old;
Old age hath yet his honor and his toil;   50
Death closes all; but something ere the end,
Some work of noble note, may yet be done,
Not unbecoming men that strove with gods.
The lights begin to twinkle from the rocks;
The long day wanes; the slow moon climbs; the deep   55
Moans round with many voices. Come, my friends,
'Tis not too late to seek a newer world.
Push off, and sitting well in order smite
The sounding furrows; for my purpose holds
To sail beyond the sunset, and the baths   60
Of all the western stars, until I die.
It may be that the gulfs will wash us down;
It may be we shall touch the Happy Isles,
And see the great Achilles, whom we knew.
Though much is taken, much abides; and though   65
We are not now that strength which in old days
Moved earth and heaven, that which we are, we are—
One equal temper of heroic hearts,
Made weak by time and fate, but strong in will
To strive, to seek, to find, and not to yield.   70

               —*Alfred, Lord Tennyson*

Aids to Analysis

*A quick reading of the poem shows it to be a dramatic monologue. We know,
then, that the first steps are to identify the speaker, to clarify the situation,
and to outline the narrative pattern.*

1.   Speaker and Situation.
     a.   Check the title. What was Ulysses famous for?

       b.   *How does this legend serve as background to the poem?*
       c.   *What is his present situation (lines 1–7)?*
       d.   *What is his attitude toward the situation expressed in the opening lines?*

2.   Narrative pattern. *Define the narrative-dramatic situation in each of the three verse paragraphs.*

3.   Idea pattern. *Trace the idea pattern of the poem in terms of the three verse paragraphs.*
       a.   *In paragraph 1, what is the difference between Ulysses' present situation and his past experience? How does his past experience explain his attitude toward his current situation?*
       b.   *In paragraph 2, what is Ulysses' attitude toward his son?*
       c.   *Paragraph 3 is a direct statement of his fixed purpose. Where is his purpose most clearly stated? This paragraph reemphasizes the past achievements, but it also introduces a new problem. What is this problem? What bearing does this problem have on the theme of the poem?*

4.   Vocabulary. *Define "profits" (line 1), "mete and dole" (line 3), "Hyades" (line 10), "meet" (line 42), and "Achilles" (line 64).*

5.   Syntax. *What is the grammatical function of "king" (line 1)? What is the meaning of the following phrases: "but . . . things" (lines 26–28), and "opposed . . . foreheads" (lines 48–49)?*

6.   Imagery. *Ulysses thinks of himself as a famous warrior and traveler. Find images to support these characteristics.*

7.   Metaphor. *What are the indications that the imagery of travel and battle is to be interpreted figuratively? What do these metaphors tell us about the theme of the poem?*

8.   Other figures. *Identify the following kinds of figures and tell their meaning: "still hearth" (line 2), "hungry heart" (line 12), "drunk delight of battle" (line 16), "rust unburnished" (line 23), "three suns" (line 29), "the thunder and the sunshine" (line 48), the strength that "Moved earth and heaven" (lines 66–67).*

9.   Symbol. *What evidence is there that Ulysses is a symbolic figure?*

10.   Sound and Rhythm.
       a.   *What is the dominant meter?*
       b.   *What is the stanzaic pattern?*
       c.   *In line 5 what is the effect of the long vowels, the diphthongs, and the stop consonants? Compare this effect with that in line 70.*

d.   *Point out instances of alliteration, assonance, and consonance in lines 16–17. Point out several other instances in the poem of the close relationship between sound and meaning.*

e.   *What devices contribute to the distinctive rhythmical movement in these passages: lines 19–21 and lines 55–56?*

11.   Cultural Context. *This poem is commonly considered a representative Victorian poem.*

a.   *What ideals does the speaker represent?*

b.   *What is his attitude toward such matters as the family, the virtue of patience, and the idea of progress?*

c.   *How does he reconcile the conflict between the individual and his social responsibility?*

Chapter 16

The Continuing Tradition

WILLIAM SHAKESPEARE

Sonnet 56

Sweet love, renew thy force; be it not said
Thy edge should blunter be than appetite,
Which but to day by feeding is allay'd,
To morrow sharpen'd in his former might:
So, love, be thou; although to day thou fill   5
Thy hungry eyes even till they wink with fullness,
To-morrow see again, and do not kill
The spirit of love with a perpetual dulness.
Let this sad interim like the ocean be
Which parts the shore, where two contracted new   10
Come daily to the banks, that, when they see
Return of love, more blest may be the view;
   Or call it winter, which being full of care
    Makes summer's welcome thrice more wish'd, more rare.

Sonnet 60

Like as the waves make towards the pebbled shore,
So do our minutes hasten to their end;
Each changing place with that which goes before,
In sequent toil all forwards do contend.
Nativity, once in the main of light,   5
Crawls to maturity, wherewith being crown'd,
Crooked eclipses 'gainst his glory fight,
And Time that gave doth now his gift confound.
Time doth transfix the flourish set on youth

And delves the parallels in beauty's brow,   *10*
Feeds on the rarities of nature's truth,
And nothing stands but for his scythe to mow:
    And yet to times in hope my verse shall stand,
    Praising thy worth, despite his cruel hand.

Sonnet 64

When I have seen by Time's fell hand defaced
The rich proud cost of outworn buried age;
When sometime lofty towers I see down-razed
And brass eternal slave to mortal rage;
When I have seen the hungry ocean gain   *5*
Advantage on the kingdom of the shore,
And the firm soil win of the wat'ry main,
Increasing store with loss and loss with store;
When I have seen such interchange of state,
Or state itself confounded to decay;   *10*
Ruin hath taught me thus to ruminate,
That Time will come and take my love away.
    This thought is as a death, which cannot choose
    But weep to have that which it fears to lose.

Sonnet 71

No longer mourn for me when I am dead
Than you shall hear the surly sullen bell
Give warning to the world that I am fled
From this vile world, with vilest worms to dwell:
Nay, if you read this line, remember not   *5*
The hand that writ it; for I love you so,
That I in your sweet thoughts would be forgot
If thinking on me then should make you woe.
O, if, I say, you look upon this verse
When I perhaps compounded am with clay,   *10*
Do not so much as my poor name rehearse,
But let your love even with my life decay,
    Lest the wise world should look into your moan,
    And mock you with me after I am gone.

Sonnet 138

When my love swears that she is made of truth
I do believe her, though I know she lies,
That she might think me some untutor'd youth,
Unlearned in the world's false subtleties.

Thus vainly thinking that she thinks me young,   *5*
Although she knows my days are past the best,
Simply I credit her false-speaking tongue:
On both sides thus is simple truth suppress'd.
But wherefore says she not she is unjust?
And wherefore say not I that I am old?   *10*
O, love's best habit is in seeming trust,
And age in love loves not to have years told:
   Therefore I lie with her and she with me,
   And in our faults by lies we flatter'd be.

Let's Talk of Graves

Let's talk of graves, of worms, and epitaphs;
Make dust our paper, and with rainy eyes
Write sorrow on the bosom of the earth,
Let's choose executors and talk of wills:
And yet not so, for what can we bequeath   *5*
Save our deposed bodies to the ground?
Our lands, our lives, and all are Bolingbroke's,
And nothing can we call our own but death
And that small model of the barren earth
Which serves as paste and cover to our bones.   *10*
For God's sake let us sit upon the ground
And tell sad stories of the death of kings:
How some have been deposed, some slain in war,
Some haunted by the ghosts they have deposed,
Some poisoned by their wives; some sleeping kill'd;   *15*
All murder'd; for within the hollow crown
That rounds the mortal temples of a king
Keeps Death his court and there the antic sits,
Scoffing his state and grinning at his pomp,
Allowing him a breath, a little scene,   *20*
To monarchize, be fear'd, and kill with looks,
Infusing him with self and vain conceit,
As if this flesh which walls about our life
Were brass impregnable, and humour'd thus
Comes at the last and with a little pin   *25*
Bores through his castle wall, and farewell king!

Richard II *(Act III sc. ii)*

All the World's a Stage

      All the world's a stage,
And all the men and women merely players:
They have their exits and their entrances,

And one man in his time plays many parts,
His acts being seven ages. At first the infant,   *5*
Mewling and puking in the nurse's arms.
Then the whining school-boy, with his satchel
And shining morning face, creeping like snail
Unwillingly to school. And then the lover,
Sighing like furnace, with a woeful ballad   *10*
Made to his mistress' eyebrow. Then a soldier,
Full of strange oaths, and bearded like the pard,
Jealous in honour, sudden and quick in quarrel,
Seeking the bubble reputation
Even in the cannon's mouth. And then the justice,   *15*
In fair round belly with good capon lined,
With eyes severe and beard of formal cut,
Full of wise saws and modern instances;
And so he plays his part. The sixth age shifts
Into the lean and slipper'd pantaloon,   *20*
With spectacles on nose and pouch on side,
His youthful hose, well saved, a world too wide
For his shrunk shank; and his big manly voice,
Turning again toward childish treble, pipes
And whistles in his sound. Last scene of all,   *25*
That ends this strange eventful history,
Is second childishness and mere oblivion,
Sans teeth, sans eyes, sans taste, sans every thing.

As You Like It (*Act II sc. vii*)

Had It Pleased Heaven

       Had it pleased Heaven
To try me with affliction; had they rain'd
All kinds of sores and shames on my bare head,
Steep'd me in poverty to the very lips,
Given to captivity me and my utmost hopes,   *5*
I should have found in some place of my soul
A drop of patience; but, alas, to make me
A fixed figure for the time of scorn
To point his slow unmoving finger at!
Yet could I bear that too; well, very well: *10*
But there, where I have garner'd up my heart,
Where either I must live, or bear no life;
The fountain from the which my current runs,
Or else dries up; to be discarded thence!
Or keep it as a cistern for foul toads   *15*
To knot and gender in! Turn thy complexion there,
Patience, thou young and rose-lipp'd cherubin,—
Ay, there, look grim as hell!

Othello (*Act IV sc. ii*)

Our Revels Now Are Ended

Our revels now are ended. These our actors,
As I foretold you, were all spirits, and
Are melted into air, into thin air:
And, like the baseless fabric of this vision,
The cloud-capp'd towers, the gorgeous palaces,   *5*
The solemn temples, the great globe itself,
Yea, all which it inherit, shall dissolve,
And, like this insubstantial pageant faded,
Leave not a rack behind. We are such stuff
As dreams are made on, and our little life   *10*
Is rounded with a sleep.

                                  The Tempest *(Act IV sc. i)*

JOHN DONNE

The Sun Rising

   Busy old fool, unruly sun,
     Why dost thou thus
Through windows and through curtains call on us?
Must to thy motions lovers' seasons run?
    Saucy pedantic wretch, go chide   *5*
     Late schoolboys and sour prentices,
  Go tell court-huntsmen that the king will ride,
  Call country ants to harvest offices;
Love, all alike, no season knows, nor clime,
Nor hours, days, months, which are the rags of time.   *10*

   Thy beams, so reverend, and strong
     Why shouldst thou think?
I could eclipse and cloud them with a wink,
But that I would not lose her sight so long;
    If her eyes have not blinded thine,   *15*
     Look, and tomorrow late tell me
  Whether both the Indias of spice and mine
  Be where thou left'st them, or lie here with me.
Ask for those kings whom thou saw'st yesterday,
And thou shalt hear, all here in one bed lay.   *20*

   She is all states, and all princes I;
     Nothing else is.

Princes do but play us; compared to this,
All honor's mimic, all wealth alchemy.
    Thou, sun, art half as happy as we,   *25*
      In that the world's contracted thus;
    Thine age asks ease, and since thy duties be
    To warm the world, that's done in warming us.
Shine here to us, and thou art everywhere;
This bed thy center is, these walls thy sphere.   *30*

The Canonization

For God's sake hold your tongue, and let me love,
  Or chide my palsy, or my gout,
My five gray hairs, or ruin'd fortune flout,
    With wealth your state, your mind with arts improve,
      Take you a course, get you a place,   *5*
      Observe his honor, or his grace,
Or the King's real, or his stamped face
  Contemplate, what you will, approve,
  So you will let me love.

Alas, alas, who's injur'd by my love?   *10*
  What merchant's ships have my sighs drown'd?
Who says my tears have overflow'd his ground?
    When did my colds a forward spring remove?
      When did the heats which my veins fill
      Add one more to the plaguy bill?   *15*
Soldiers find wars, and lawyers find out still
  Litigious men, which quarrels move,
  Though she and I do love.

Call us what you will, we are made such by love;
  Call her one, me another fly,   *20*
We are tapers too, and at our own cost die,
    And we in us find th' eagle and the dove.
      The phoenix riddle hath more wit
      By us, we two being one, are it.
So, to one neutral thing both sexes fit,   *25*
  We die and rise the same, and prove
  Mysterious by this love.

We can die by it, if not live by love,
  And if unfit for tombs and hearse
Our legend be, it will be fit for verse;   *30*
  And if no piece of chronicle we prove,
      We'll build in sonnets pretty rooms;
      As well as well-wrought urn becomes

The greatest ashes, as half-acre tombs,
  And by these hymns, all shall approve   35
Us *Canoniz'd* for Love:

And thus invoke us; You whom reverend love
  Made one another's hermitage;
You, to whom love was peace, that now is rage;
  Who did the whole world's soul contract, and drove   40
    Into the glasses of your eyes
      (So made such mirrors, and such spies,
That they did all to you epitomize,)
  Countries, towns, Courts: Beg from above
A pattern of your love!   45

The Ecstasy

Where, like a pillow on a bed,
  A pregnant bank swelled up to rest
The violet's reclining head,
  Sat we two, one another's best.
Our hands were firmly cèmented   5
  With a fast balm, which thence did spring;
Our eye-beams twisted, and did thread
  Our eyes upon one double string;
So to entergraft our hands, as yet
  Was all the means to make us one,   10
And pictures in our eyes to get
  Was all our propagation.
As 'twixt two equal armies, Fate
  Suspends uncertain victory,
Our souls, which to advance their state   15
  Were gone out, hung 'twixt her and me.
And whilst our souls negotiate there,
  We like sepulchral statues lay;
All day, the same our postures were,
  And we said nothing, all the day.   20
If any, so by love refined
  That he soul's language understood,
And by good love were grown all mind,
  Within convenient distance stood,
He, though he knew not which soul spake,   25
  Because both meant, both spake the same,
Might thence a new concoction take
  And part far purer than he came.
This ecstasy doth unperplex,
  We said, and tell us what we love: 30

We see by this it was not sex,
    We see, we saw not what did move;
But as all several souls contain
    Mixture of things, they know not what,
Love these mixed souls doth mix again   *35*
    And makes both one, each this and that.
A single violet transplant,
    The strength, the color, and the size,
All which before was poor and scant,
    Redoubles still, and multiplies.   *40*
When love with one another so
    Interinanimates two souls,
That abler soul, which thence doth flow,
    Defects of loneliness controls.
We then, who are this new soul, know   *45*
    Of what we are composed, and made,
For th' atomies of which we grow
    Are souls, whom no change can invade.
But O alas! so long, so far,
    Our bodies why do we forbear?   *50*
They are ours, though they are not we; we are
    Th' intelligences, they the spheres.
We owe them thanks, because they thus
    Did us, to us, at first convey,
Yielded their forces, sense, to us,   *55*
    Nor are dross to us, but allay.
On man heaven's influence works not so,
    But that it first imprints the air;
So soul into the soul may flow,
    Though it to body first repair.   *60*
As our blood labours to beget
    Spirits, as like souls as it can;
Because such fingers need to knit
    That subtle knot, which makes us man;
So must pure lovers' souls descend   *65*
    T'affections, and to faculties,
Which sense may reach and apprehend,
    Else a great prince in prison lies.
To our bodies turn we then, that so
    Weak men on love reveal'd may look;   *70*
Love's mysteries in souls do grow,
    But yet the body is his book.
And if some lover, such as we,
    Have heard this dialogue of one,
Let him still mark us, he shall see   *75*
    Small change when we're to bodies gone.

Love's Deity

I long to talk with some old lover's ghost
   Who died before the god of love was born;
I cannot think that he who then loved most,
   Sunk so low as to love one which did scorn.
But since this god produced a destiny   5
And that vice-nature, custom, lets it be,
   I must love her that loves not me.

Sure, they which made him god, meant not so much,
   Nor he in his young godhead practiced it.
But when an even flame two hearts did touch,   10
   His office was indulgently to fit
Actives to passives. Correspondency
Only, his subject was; it cannot be
   Love, till I love her who loves me.

But every modern god will not extend   15
   His vast prerogative as far as Jove.
To rage, to lust, to write to, to commend,
   All is the purlieu of the god of love.
O! were we wakened by this tyranny
To ungod this child again, it could not be   20
   I should love her who loves not me.

Rebel and atheist too, why murmur I,
   As though I felt the worse that love could do?
Love may make me leave loving, or might try
   A deeper plague, to make her love me too;   25
Which, since she loves before, I'm loath to see.
Falsehood is worse than hate; and that must be,
   If she whom I love, should love me.

I Am a Little World Made Cunningly

I am a little world made cunningly
Of elements, and an angelic sprite,
But black sin hath betrayed to endless night
My world's both parts, and oh, both parts must die.
You which beyond that heaven which was most high   5
Have found new spheres, and of new lands can write,
Pour new seas in mine eyes, that so I might
Drown my world with my weeping earnestly,
Or wash it if it must be drowned no more;
But oh it must be burnt! Alas, the fire   10
Of lust and envy have burnt it heretofore,

And made it fouler; let their flames retire,
And burn me, O Lord, with a fiery zeal
Of Thee and Thy house, which doth in eating heal.

At the Round Earth's Imagined Corners

At the round earth's imagined corners, blow
Your trumpets, angels, and arise, arise
From death, you numberless infinities
Of souls, and to your scattered bodies go;
All whom the flood did, and fire shall o'erthrow,   5
All whom war, dearth, age, agues, tyrannies,
Despair, law, chance, hath slain, and you whose eyes
Shall behold God, and never taste death's woe.
But let them sleep, Lord, and me mourn a space,
For if, above all these, my sins abound,   10
'Tis late to ask abundance of Thy grace
When we are there; here on this lowly ground,
Teach me how to repent; for that's as good
As if Thou hadst sealed my pardon with Thy blood.

GEORGE HERBERT

Virtue

Sweet day, so cool, so calm, so bright,
The bridal of the earth and sky;
The dew shall weep thy fall tonight,
    For thou must die.

Sweet rose, whose hue angry and brave   5
Bids the rash gazer wipe his eye;
Thy root is ever in its grave,
    And thou must die.

Sweet spring, full of sweet days and roses,
A box where sweets compacted lie;   10
My music shows ye have your closes,
    And all must die.

Only a sweet and virtuous soul,
Like seasoned timber, never gives;
But though the whole world turn to coal,   15
    Then chiefly lives.

The Collar

I struck the board, and cried "No more;
  I will abroad!
  What! shall I ever sigh and pine?
My lines and life are free; free as the road,
  Loose as the wind, as large as store.   *5*
    Shall I be still in suit?
Have I no harvest but a thorn
  To let me blood, and not restore
What I have lost with cordial fruit?
  Sure there was wine   *10*
Before my sighs did dry it; there was corn
  Before my tears did drown it;
Is the year only lost to me?
  Have I no bays to crown it,
No flowers, no garlands gay? all blasted,   *15*
  All wasted?
Not so, my heart; but there is fruit,
  And thou hast hands.
  Recover all thy sigh-blown age
On double pleasures; leave thy cold dispute   *20*
  Of what is fit and not; forsake thy cage,
    Thy rope of sands
Which petty thoughts have made; and made to thee
  Good cable, to enforce and draw,
    And be thy law,   *25*
While thou didst wink and wouldst not see.
    Away! take heed;
    I will abroad.
  Call in thy death's-head there, tie up thy fears;
    He that forbears   *30*
  To suit and serve his need
    Deserves his load."
But as I rav'd and grew more fierce and wild
  At every word,
Methought I heard one calling "Child,"   *35*
  And I replied, "My Lord."

Temptation

Broken in pieces all asunder,
    Lord, hunt me not,
    A thing forgot,
Once a poor creature, now a wonder,
  A wonder tortured in the space   *5*
  Betwixt this world and that of grace.

My thoughts are all a case of knives,
  Wounding my heart
  With scattered smart,
As watering pots give flowers their lives.   *10*
  Nothing their fury can control
  While they do wound and pink my soul.

All my attendants are at strife,
  Quitting their place
  Unto my face: *15*
Nothing performs the task of life:
  Th' elements are let loose to fight,
  And while I live, try out their right.

O help, my God! let not their plot
  Kill them and me,   *20*
  And also thee,
Who art my life: dissolve the knot,
  As the sun scatters by his light
  All the rebellions of the night.

Then shall those powers, which work for grief   *25*
  Enter thy pay,
  And day by day
Labor thy praise, and my relief;
  With care and courage building me,
  Till I reach heaven, and much more, thee.   *30*

JOHN MILTON

How Soon Hath Time

How soon hath Time, the subtle thief of youth,
  Stolen on his wing my three and twentieth year!
  My hasting days fly on with full career,
  But my late spring no bud or blossom show'th.
Perhaps my semblance might deceive the truth,   *5*
  That I to manhood am arrived so near,
  And inward ripeness doth much less appear,
  That some more timely-happy spirits endu'th.
Yet be it less or more, or soon or slow,
  It shall be still in strictest measure even   *10*
  To that same lot, however mean or high,
Toward which Time leads me, and the will of Heaven;
  All is, if I have grace to use it so,
  As ever in my great Taskmaster's eye.

When I Consider How My Light Is Spent

When I consider how my light is spent
   Ere half my days in this dark world and wide,
   And that one talent which is death to hide
   Lodged with me useless, though my soul more bent
To serve therewith my Maker, and present   *5*
   My true account, lest he returning chide,
   "Doth God exact day-labour, light denied?"
   I fondly ask. But Patience, to prevent
That murmur, soon replies, "God doth not need
   Either man's work or his own gifts. Who best   *10*
   Bear his mild yoke, they serve him best. His state
Is kingly: thousands at his bidding speed,
   And post o'er land and ocean without rest;
   They also serve who only stand and wait."

Methought I Saw

Methought I saw my late espoused saint
   Brought to me like Alcestis from the grave,
   Whom Jove's great son to her glad husband gave,
   Rescued from death by force, though pale and faint.
Mine, as whom washed from spot of child-bed taint,   *5*
   Purification in the Old Law did save,
   And such, as yet once more I trust to have
   Full sight of her in Heaven without restraint,
Came vested all in white, pure as her mind;
   Her face was veiled, yet to my fancied sight,   *10*
   Love, sweetness, goodness, in her person shined
So clear, as in no face with more delight.
   But O, as to embrace me she inclined,
   I waked, she fled, and day brought back my night.

Better to Reign in Hell *(from Paradise Lost)*

"Is this the region, this the soil, the clime,"
Said then the lost Archangel, "this the seat
That we must change for Heaven, this mournful gloom
For that celestial light? Be it so, since he
Who now is sovran can dispose and bid   *5*
What shall be right. Farthest from him is best,
Whom reason hath equalled, force hath made supreme
Above his equals. Farewell happy fields
Where joy for ever dwells: Hail horrors, hail

Infernal world, and thou profoundest Hell　　　　　*10*
Receive thy new possessor: one who brings
A mind not to be changed by place or time.
The mind is its own place, and in itself
Can make a Heaven of Hell, a Hell of Heaven.
What matter where, if I be still the same,　　　　　*15*
And what I should be, all but less than he
Whom thunder hath made greater? Here at least
We shall be free; the Almighty hath not built
Here for his envy, will not drive us hence:
Here we may reign secure, and in my choice　　　　*20*
To reign is worth ambition, though in Hell:
Better to reign in Hell than serve in Heaven.
But wherefore let we then our faithful friends,
The associates and co-partners of our loss,
Lie thus astonished on the oblivious pool,　　　　　*25*
And call them not to share with us their part
In this unhappy mansion; or once more
With rallied arms to try what may be yet
Regained in Heaven, or what more lost in Hell?"

Adam's Fall *(from Paradise Lost)*

On th' other side, Adam, soon as he heard
The fatal trespass done by Eve, amazed,
Astonied stood and blank, while horror chill
Ran through his veins, and all his joints relaxed.
From his slack hand the garland wreathed for Eve　　　*5*
Down dropt, and all the faded roses shed.
Speechless he stood and pale, till thus at length
First to himself he inward silence broke:—
　　"O fairest of creation, last and best
Of all God's works, creature in whom excelled　　　*10*
Whatever can to sight or thought be formed,
Holy, divine, good, amiable, or sweet!
How art thou lost! how on a sudden lost,
Defaced, deflowered, and now to death devote!
Rather, how hast thou yielded to transgress　　　　*15*
The strict forbiddance, how to violate
The sacred fruit forbidden? Some cursèd fraud
Of enemy hath beguiled thee, yet unknown,
And me with thee hath ruined; for with thee
Certain my resolution is to die.　　　　　　　　　*20*
How can I live without thee; how forgo

Thy sweet converse, and love so dearly joined,
To live again in these wild woods forlorn?
Should God create another Eve, and I
Another rib afford, yet loss of thee   *25*
Would never from my heart. No, no! I feel
The link of nature draw me: flesh of flesh,
Bone of my bone thou art, and from thy state
Mine never shall be parted, bliss or woe."

Samson's Blindness *(from Samson Agonistes)*

Why was my breeding ordered and prescribed
As of a person separate to God,
Designed for great exploits, if I must die
Betrayed, captived, and both my eyes put out,
Made of my enemies the scorn and gaze,   *5*
To grind in brazen fetters under task
With this heaven-gifted strength? O glorious strength,
Put to the labour of a beast, debased
Lower than bond-slave! Promise was that I
Should Israel from Philistian yoke deliver;   *10*
Ask for this great deliverer now, and find him
Eyeless in Gaza, at the mill with slaves,
Himself in bonds under Philistian yoke.
Yet stay; let me not rashly call in doubt
Divine prediction. What if all foretold   *15*
Had been fulfilled but through mine own default?
Whom have I to complain of but myself,
Who this high gift of strength committed to me,
In what part lodged, how easily bereft me,
Under the seal of silence could not keep,   *20*
But weakly to a woman must reveal it,
O'ercome with importunity and tears?
O impotence of mind in body strong!
But what is strength without a double share
Of wisdom? Vast, unwieldy, burdensome,   *25*
Proudly secure, yet liable to fall
By weakest subtleties; not made to rule,
But to subserve where wisdom bears command.
God, when he gave me strength, to show withal,
How slight the gift was, hung it in my hair.   *30*
But peace! I must not quarrel with the will
Of highest dispensation, which herein
Haply had ends above my reach to know.
Suffices that to me strength is my bane,

And proves the source of all my miseries—   *35*
So many, and so huge, that each apart
Would ask a life to wail. But, chief of all,
O loss of sight, of thee I must complain!
Blind among enemies! O worse than chains,
Dungeon, or beggary, or decrepit age!   *40*
Light, the prime work of God, to me is extinct,
And all her various objects of delight
Annulled, which might in part my grief have eased.
Inferior to the vilest now become
Of man or worm, the vilest here excel me: *45*
They creep, yet see, I, dark in light, exposed
To daily fraud, contempt, abuse, and wrong,
Within doors, or without, still as a fool,
In power of others, never in my own;
Scarce half I seem to live, dead more than half.   *50*
O dark, dark, dark, amid the blaze of noon,
Irrecoverably dark, total eclipse
Without all hope of day!
O first-created beam, and thou great Word,
"Let there be light, and light was over all;"   *55*
Why am I thus bereaved thy prime decree
The Sun to me is dark
And silent as the Moon,
When she deserts the night
Hid in her vacant interlunar cave.   *60*
Since light so necessary is to life,
And almost life itself, if it be true
That light is in the soul,
She all in every part; why was the sight
To such a tender ball as the eye confined?   *65*
So obvious and so easy to be quenched,
And not as feeling through all parts diffused,
That she might look at will through every pore?
Then had I not been thus exiled from light;
As in the land of darkness yet in light,   *70*
To live a life half dead, a living death,
And buried; but O yet more miserable!
Myself, my sepulchre, a moving grave,
Buried, yet not exempt
By privilege of death and burial   *75*
From worst of other evils, pains and wrongs,
But made hereby obnoxious more
To all the miseries of life,
Life in captivity
Among inhuman foes.   *80*

THOMAS GRAY

Elegy Written in a Country Churchyard

The Curfew tolls the knell of parting day,
  The lowing herd winds slowly o'er the lea,
The plowman homeward plods his weary way,
  And leaves the world to darkness and to me.

Now fades the glimmering landscape on the sight,   5
  And all the air a solemn stillness holds,
Save where the beetle wheels his droning flight,
  And drowsy tinklings lull the distant folds;

Save that from yonder ivy-mantled tower
  The moping owl does to the moon complain   10
Of such, as wand'ring near her secret bower,
  Molest her ancient solitary reign.

Beneath those rugged elms, that yew-tree's shade,
  Where heaves the turf in many a mold'ring heap,
Each in his narrow cell for ever laid,   15
  The rude Forefathers of the hamlet sleep.

The breezy call of incense-breathing Morn,
  The swallow twitt'ring from the straw-built shed,
The cock's shrill clarion, or the echoing horn,
  No more shall rouse them from their lowly bed.   20

For them no more the blazing hearth shall burn,
  Or busy housewife ply her evening care:
No children run to lisp their sire's return,
  Or climb his knees the envied kiss to share.

Oft did the harvest to their sickle yield,   25
  Their furrow oft the stubborn glebe has broke;
How jocund did they drive their team afield!
  How bowed the woods beneath their sturdy stroke!

Let not Ambition mock their useful toil,
  Their homely joys, and destiny obscure;   30
Nor Grandeur hear with a disdainful smile,
  The short and simple annals of the poor.

The boast of heraldry, the pomp of power,
  And all that beauty, all that wealth e'er gave,

Await alike th' inevitable hour.   *35*
   The paths of glory lead but to the grave.

Nor you, ye proud, impute to these the fault,
   If Memory o'er their tomb no trophies raise,
Where through the long-drawn aisle and fretted vault
   The pealing anthem swells the note of praise.   *40*

Can storied urn or animated bust
   Back to its mansion call the fleeting breath?
Can Honor's voice provoke the silent dust,
   Or Flattery soothe the dull cold ear of Death?

Perhaps in this neglected spot is laid   *45*
   Some heart once pregnant with celestial fire;
Hands that the rod of empire might have swayed,
   Or waked to ecstasy the living lyre.

But Knowledge to their eyes her ample page
   Rich with the spoils of time did ne'er unroll;   *50*
Chill Penury repressed their noble rage,
   And froze the genial current of the soul.

Full many a gem of purest ray serene,
   The dark unfathomed caves of ocean bear:
Full many a flower is born to blush unseen,   *55*
   And waste its sweetness on the desert air.

Some village Hampden, that, with dauntless breast
   The little tyrant of his fields withstood;
Some mute inglorious Milton here may rest,
   Some Cromwell guiltless of his country's blood.   *60*

Th' applause of listening senates to command,
   The threats of pain and ruin to despise,
To scatter plenty o'er a smiling land,
   And read their history in a nation's eyes,

Their lot forbade: nor circumscribed alone   *65*
   Their growing virtues, but their crimes confined;
Forbade to wade through slaughter to a throne,
   And shut the gates of mercy on mankind.

The struggling pangs of conscious truth to hide,
   To quench the blushes of ingenuous shame,   *70*
Or heap the shrine of Luxury and Pride
   With incense kindled at the Muse's flame.

Far from the madding crowd's ignoble strife,
   Their sober wishes never learned to stray;
Along the cool sequestered vale of life   *75*
   They kept the noiseless tenor of their way.

Yet ev'n these bones from insult to protect
   Some frail memorial still erected nigh,
With uncouth rimes and shapeless sculpture decked,
   Implores the passing tribute of a sigh.   *80*

Their name, their years, spelt by th' unlettered muse,
   The place of fame and elegy supply:
And many a holy text around she strews,
   That teach the rustic moralist to die.

For who to dumb Forgetfulness a prey,   *85*
   This pleasing anxious being e'er resigned,
Left the warm precincts of the cheerful day,
   Nor cast one longing ling'ring look behind?

On some fond breast the parting soul relies,
   Some pious drops the closing eye requires;   *90*
Ev'n from the tomb the voice of Nature cries,
   Ev'n in our Ashes live their wonted Fires.

For thee, who mindful of th' unhonored Dead
   Dost in these lines their artless tale relate;
If chance, by lonely contemplation led,   *95*
   Some kindred Spirit shall inquire thy fate,

Haply some hoary-headed Swain may say,
   "Oft have we seen him at the peep of dawn
Brushing with hasty steps the dews away
   To meet the sun upon the upland lawn.   *100*

"There at the foot of yonder nodding beech,
   That wreathes its old fantastic roots so high,
His listless length at noontide would he stretch,
   And pore upon the brook that babbles by.

"Hard by yon wood, now smiling as in scorn,   *105*
   Mutt'ring his wayward fancies he would rove,
Now drooping, woeful wan, like one forlorn,
   Or crazed with care, or crossed in hopeless love.

"One morn I missed him on the customed hill,
   Along the heath and near his fav'rite tree;   *110*

Another came; nor yet beside the rill,
   Nor up the lawn, nor at the wood was he;

"The next with dirges due in sad array
   Slow through the church-way path we saw him borne.
Approach and read (for thou canst read) the lay   *115*
   Graved on the stone beneath yon agèd thorn."

The Epitaph

Here rests his head upon the lap of Earth
   A Youth to Fortune and to Fame unknown.
Fair Science frown'd not on his humble birth,
   And Melancholy mark'd him for her own.   *120*

Large was his bounty, and his soul sincere,
   Heav'n did a recompense as largely send:
He gave to Mis'ry all he had, a tear,
   He gain'd from Heav'n ('twas all he wish'd) a friend.

No farther seek his merits to disclose,   *125*
   Or draw his frailties from their dread abode,
(There they alike in trembling hope repose,)
   The bosom of his Father and his God.

WILLIAM BLAKE

Introduction

Piping down the valleys wild,
Piping songs of pleasant glee,
On a cloud I saw a child,
And he laughing said to me:

"Pipe a song about a Lamb!"   *5*
So I piped with merry cheer.
"Piper, pipe that song again";
So I piped: he wept to hear.

"Drop thy pipe, thy happy pipe;
Sing thy songs of happy cheer":   *10*
So I sung the same again,
While he wept with joy to hear.

"Piper, sit thee down and write
In a book that all may read."
So he vanished from my sight,   *15*
And I plucked a hollow reed,

And I made a rural pen,
And I stained the water clear,
And I wrote my happy songs
Every child may joy to hear.   *20*

Nurse's Song—I

When the voices of children are heard on the green
And laughing is heard on the hill,
My heart is at rest within my breast
    And everything else is still.

"Then come home, my children, the sun is gone down   *5*
And the dews of night arise;
Come, come, leave off play, and let us away
Till the morning appears in the skies."

"No, no, let us play, for it is yet day
And we cannot go to sleep;   *10*
Besides, in the sky the little birds fly
And the hills are all cover'd with sheep."

"Well, well, go and play till the light fades away
And then go home to bed."
The little ones leaped and shouted and laugh'd   *15*
    And all the hills echoèd.

Holy Thursday—I

'Twas on a Holy Thursday, their innocent faces clean,
The children walking two and two, in red and blue and green,
Gray-headed beadles walk'd before, with wands as white as snow,
Till into the high dome of Paul's they like Thames' waters flow.

O what a multitude they seem'd, these flowers of London town!   *5*
Seated in companies they sit with radiance all their own.
The hum of multitudes was there, but multitudes of lambs,
Thousands of little boys and girls raising their innocent hands.

Now like a mighty wind they raise to Heaven the voice of song,
Or like harmonious thunderings the seats of Heaven among.   *10*
Beneath them sit the aged men, wise guardians of the poor;
Then cherish pity, lest you drive an angel from your door.

The Chimney Sweeper—I

When my mother died I was very young,
And my father sold me while yet my tongue
Could scarcely cry "'weep! 'weep! 'weep! 'weep!"
So your chimneys I sweep, and in soot I sleep.

There's little Tom Dacre, who cried when his head,   5
That curled like a lamb's back, was shaved: so I said,
"Hush, Tom! never mind it, for when your head's bare
You know that the soot cannot spoil your white hair."

And so he was quiet, and that very night,
As Tom was a-sleeping, he had such a sight!   10
That thousands of sweepers, Dick, Joe, Ned, and Jack,
Were all of them locked up in coffins of black.

And by came an Angel who had a bright key,
And he opened the coffins and set them all free;
Then down a green plain leaping, laughing, they run,   15
And wash in a river, and shine in the Sun.

Then naked and white, all their bags left behind,
They rise upon clouds and sport in the wind;
And the Angel told Tom, if he'd be a good boy,
He'd have God for his father, and never want joy.   20

And so Tom awoke; and we rose in the dark,
And got with our bags and our brushes to work.
Though the morning was cold, Tom was happy and warm;
So if all do their duty they need not fear harm.

The Little Black Boy

My mother bore me in the southern wild,
And I am black, but O my soul is white;
White as an angel is the English child,
But I am black, as if bereav'd of light.

My mother taught me underneath a tree,   5.
And sitting down before the heat of day,
She took me on her lap and kissed me,
And, pointing to the east, began to say:

"Look on the rising sun—there God does live,
And gives his light, and gives his heat away;   10
And flowers and trees and beasts and men receive
Comfort in morning, joy in the noon day.

"And we are put on earth a little space,
That we may learn to bear the beams of love;
And these black bodies and this sun-burnt face   *15*
Is but a cloud, and like a shady grove.

"For when our souls have learn'd the heat to bear,
The cloud will vanish; we shall hear his voice,
Saying: 'Come out from the grove, my love and care,
And round my golden tent like lambs rejoice.'"   *20*

Thus did my mother say, and kissed me;
And thus I say to little English boy:
When I from black, and he from white cloud free,
And round the tent of God like lambs we joy,

I'll shade him from the heat, till he can bear   *25*
To lean in joy upon our father's knee;
And then I'll stand and stroke his silver hair,
And be like him, and he will then love me.

Nurse's Song — II

When the voices of children are heard on the green
And whisp'rings are in the dale,
The days of my youth rise fresh in my mind,
My face turns green and pale.

Then come home, my children, the sun is gone down,   *5*
And the dews of night arise;
Your spring and your day are wasted in play,
And your winter and night in disguise.

Holy Thursday — II

Is this a holy thing to see
In a rich and fruitful land,
Babes reduced to misery,
Fed with cold and usurous hand?

Is that trembling cry a song?   *5*
Can it be a song of joy?
And so many children poor?
It is a land of poverty!

And their sun does never shine,
And their fields are bleak and bare,   *10*

And their ways are filled with thorns:
It is eternal winter there.

For where'er the sun does shine,
And where'er the rain does fall,
Babe can never hunger there,   15
Nor poverty the mind appall.

The Chimney Sweeper—II

A little black thing among the snow,
Crying "'weep! 'weep!" in notes of woe!
"Where are the father and mother? Say!"—
"They are both gone up to church to pray.

"Because I was happy upon the heath,   5
And smiled among the winter's snow,
They clothed me in the clothes of death,
And taught me to sing the notes of woe.

"And because I am happy, and dance and sing,
They think they have done me no injury,   10
And are gone to praise God and His priest and king,
Who make up a heaven of our misery."

London

I wander through each chartered street,
Near where the chartered Thames does flow,
And mark in every face I meet
Marks of weakness, marks of woe.

In every cry of every man,   5
In every infant's cry of fear,
In every voice, in every ban,
The mind-forged manacles I hear.

How the chimney-sweeper's cry
Every black'ning church appalls;   10
And the hapless soldier's sigh
Runs in blood down palace walls.

But most through midnight streets I hear
How the youthful harlot's curse
Blasts the new-born infant's tear,   15
And blights with plagues the marriage hearse.

The Human Abstract

Pity would be no more
If we did not make somebody Poor;
And Mercy no more could be
If all were as happy as we.

And mutual fear brings peace   5
Till the selfish loves increase;
Then Cruelty knits a snare,
And spreads his baits with care.

He sits down with holy fears,
And waters the ground with tears;   10
Then Humility takes its root
Underneath his foot.

Soon spreads the dismal shade
Of Mystery over his head;
And the Caterpillar and Fly   15
Feed on the Mystery.

And it bears the fruit of Deceit,
Ruddy and sweet to eat;
And the Raven his nest has made
In its thickest shade.   20

The Gods of the earth and sea
Sought through Nature to find this Tree;
But their search was all in vain:
There grows one in the Human Brain.

A Poison Tree

I was angry with my friend:
I told my wrath, my wrath did end.
I was angry with my foe:
I told it not, my wrath did grow.

And I water'd it in fears,   5
Night and morning with my tears;
And I sunnèd it with smiles,
And with soft deceitful wiles.

And it grew both day and night,
Till it bore an apple bright;   10
And my foe beheld it shine,
And he knew that it was mine,

And into my garden stole
When the night had veil'd the pole:
In the morning glad I see   15
My foe outstretch'd beneath the tree.

To See a World

To see a World in a grain of sand,
And a Heaven in a wild flower,
Hold Infinity in the palm of your hand,
And eternity in an hour.

And Did Those Feet in Ancient Time

And did those feet in ancient time
Walk upon England's mountains green?
And was the holy Lamb of God
On England's pleasant pastures seen?

And did the Countenance Divine   5
Shine forth upon our clouded hills?
And was Jerusalem builded here
Among these dark Satanic Mills?

Bring me my Bow of burning gold!
Bring me my arrows of desire!   10
Bring me my Spear: O clouds, unfold!
Bring me my Chariot of fire!

I will not cease from Mental Fight,
Nor shall my Sword sleep in my hand,
Till we have built Jerusalem   15
In England's green and pleasant land.

ROBERT BURNS

Green Grow the Rashes

Chorus

Green grow the rashes, O;
Green grow the rashes, O;
The sweetest hours that e'er I spend
Are spent amang the lasses, O!

There's nought but care on ev'ry han',   5
   In ev'ry hour that passes, O:
What signifies the life o' man,
   An' 'twere na for the lasses, O?

The war'ly race may riches chase,
   An' riches still may fly them, O;   10
An' tho' at last they catch them fast,
   Their hearts can ne'er enjoy them, O.

But gie me a canny hour at e'en,
   My arms about my dearie, O;
An' war'ly cares, an' war'ly men,   15
   May a' gae tapsalteerie, O!

For you sae douce, ye sneer at this:
   Ye're nought but senseless asses, O:
The wisest man the warl' e'er saw,
   He dearly loved the lasses, O.   20

Auld Nature swears, the lovely dears
   Her noblest work she classes, O:
Her prentice han' she tried on man,
   An' then she made the lasses, O.

Willie Brew'd a Peck o' Maut

O, Willie brew'd a peck o' maut,
And Rob an' Allan cam to see:
Three blyther hearts that lee-lang night
Ye wad na found in Christendie.

Chorus

   We are na fou, we're nae that fou,   5
   But just a drappie in our ee;
   The cock may craw, the day may daw,
   And ay we'll taste the barley bree.

Here are we met, three merry boys,
Three merry boys, I trow, are we;   10
And monie a night we've merry been,
And monie mae we hope to be!

It is the moon, I ken her horn,
That's blinkin in the lift sae hie;
She shines sae bright to wyle us hame,   15
But, by my sooth, she'll wait a wee!

Wha first shall rise to gang awa',
A cuckold, coward loun is he!
Wha first beside his chair shall fa',
He is the king amang us three!   *20*

    Chorus

    We are na fou, we're nae that fou,
    But just a drappie in our ee;
    The cock may craw, the day may daw,
    And ay we'll taste the barley bree.

A Red, Red Rose

O my luve is like a red, red rose,
   That's newly sprung in June;
O my luve is like the melodie
   That's sweetly played in tune.

As fair art thou, my bonie lass,   *5*
   So deep in luve am I;
And I will luve thee still, my dear,
   Till a' the seas gang dry.

Till a' the seas gang dry, my dear,
   And the rocks melt wi' the sun;   *10*
And I will luve thee still, my dear,
   While the sands o' life shall run.

And fare thee weel, my only luve,
   And fare thee weel a while;
And I will come again, my luve,   *15*
   Tho' it were ten thousand mile!

O, Wert Thou in the Cauld Blast

O, wert thou in the cauld blast,
   On yonder lea, on yonder lea,
My plaidie to the angry airt,
   I'd shelter thee, I'd shelter thee.
Or did misfortune's bitter storms   *5*
   Around thee blaw, around thee blaw,
Thy bield should be my bosom,
   To share it a', to share it a'.

Or were I in the wildest waste,
   Sae black and bare, sae black and bare,   *10*

The desert were a paradise,
   If thou wert there, if thou wert there.
Or were I monarch o' the globe,
   Wi' thee to reign, wi' thee to reign,
The brightest jewel in my crown   *15*
   Wad be my queen, wad be my queen.

WILLIAM WORDSWORTH

My Heart Leaps Up When I Behold

My heart leaps up when I behold
   A rainbow in the sky:
So was it when my life began;
So is it now I am a man;
So be it when I shall grow old,   *5*
   Or let me die!
The Child is father of the Man;
And I could wish my days to be
Bound each to each by natural piety.

I Wandered Lonely As a Cloud

I wandered lonely as a cloud
That floats on high o'er vales and hills,
When all at once I saw a crowd,
A host, of golden daffodils;
Beside the lake, beneath the trees,   *5*
Fluttering and dancing in the breeze.

Continuous as the stars that shine
And twinkle on the milky way,
They stretched in never-ending line
Along the margin of a bay: *10*
Ten thousand saw I at a glance,
Tossing their heads in sprightly dance.

The waves beside them danced; but they
Outdid the sparkling waves in glee:
A poet could not but be gay,   *15*
In such a jocund company:
I gazed—and gazed—but little thought
What wealth the show to me had brought:

For oft, when on my couch I lie
In vacant or in pensive mood,   *20*
They flash upon that inward eye
Which is the bliss of solitude;
And then my heart with pleasure fills,
And dances with the daffodils.

Composed upon Westminster Bridge, September 3, 1802

Earth has not anything to show more fair:
Dull would he be of soul who could pass by
A sight so touching in its majesty:
This city now doth, like a garment, wear
The beauty of the morning; silent, bare,   *5*
Ships, towers, domes, theatres, and temples lie
Open unto the fields, and to the sky;
All bright and glittering in the smokeless air.
Never did sun more beautifully steep
In his first splendor, valley, rock, or hill;   *10*
Ne'er saw I, never felt, a calm so deep!
The river glideth at his own sweet will:
Dear God! the very houses seem asleep;
And all that mighty heart is lying still!

It Is a Beauteous Evening, Calm and Free

It is a beauteous evening, calm and free,
The holy time is quiet as a nun
Breathless with adoration; the broad sun
Is sinking down in its tranquillity;
The gentleness of heaven broods o'er the sea: *5*
Listen! the mighty being is awake,
And doth with his eternal motion make
A sound like thunder—everlastingly.
Dear Child! dear Girl! that walkest with me here,
If thou appear untouched by solemn thóught,   *10*
Thy nature is not therefore less divine:
Thou liest in Abraham's bosom all the year;
And worship'st at the temple's inner shrine,
God being with thee when we know it not.

Lines Composed
a Few Miles Above Tintern Abbey

Five years have passed; five summers, with the length
Of five long winters! and again I hear
These waters, rolling from their mountain-springs
With a soft inland murmur. — Once again
Do I behold these steep and lofty cliffs,   *5*
That on a wild secluded scene impress
Thoughts of more deep seclusion; and connect
The landscape with the quiet of the sky.
The day is come when I again repose
Here, under this dark sycamore, and view   *10*
These plots of cottage-ground, these orchard-tufts,
Which at this season, with their unripe fruits,
Are clad in one green hue, and lose themselves
'Mid groves and copses. Once again I see
These hedge-rows, hardly hedge-rows, little lines   *15*
Of sportive wood run wild: these pastoral farms,
Green to the very door; and wreaths of smoke
Sent up, in silence, from among the trees!
With some uncertain notice, as might seem
Of vagrant dwellers in the houseless woods,   *20*
Or of some hermit's cave, where by his fire
The hermit sits alone.
                      These beauteous forms,
Through a long absence, have not been to me
As is a landscape to a blind man's eye:
But oft, in lonely rooms, and 'mid the din   *25*
Of towns and cities, I have owed to them,
In hours of weariness, sensations sweet,
Felt in the blood, and felt along the heart;
And passing even into my purer mind,
With tranquil restoration: — feelings too   *30*
Of unremembered pleasure: such, perhaps,
As have no slight or trivial influence
On that best portion of a good man's life,
His little, nameless, unremembered, acts
Of kindness and of love. Nor less, I trust,   *35*
To them I may have owed another gift,
Of aspect more sublime; that blessèd mood,
In which the burthen of the mystery,
In which the heavy and the weary weight
Of all this unintelligible world,   *40*
Is lightened: — that serene and blessèd mood,
In which the affections gently lead us on, —
Until, the breath of this corporeal frame
And even the motion of our human blood

Almost suspended, we are laid asleep   *45*
In body, and become a living soul:
While with an eye made quiet by the power
Of harmony, and the deep power of joy,
We see into the life of things.
                            If this
Be but a vain belief, yet, oh! how oft—   *50*
In darkness and amid the many shapes
Of joyless daylight; when the fretful stir
Unprofitable, and the fever of the world,
Have hung upon the beatings of my heart—
How oft, in spirit, have I turned to thee,   *55*
O sylvan Wye! thou wanderer thro' the woods,
How often has my spirit turned to thee!
   And now, with gleams of half-extinguished thought,
With many recognitions dim and faint,
And somewhat of a sad perplexity,   *60*
The picture of the mind revives again:
While here I stand, not only with the sense
Of present pleasure, but with pleasing thoughts
That in this moment there is life and food
For future years. And so I dare to hope,   *65*
Though changed, no doubt, from what I was when first
I came among these hills; when like a roe
I bounded o'er the mountains, by the sides
Of the deep rivers, and the lonely streams,
Wherever nature led: more like a man   *70*
Flying from something that he dreads, than one
Who sought the thing he loved. For nature then
(The coarser pleasures of my boyish days,
And their glad animal movements all gone by)
To me was all in all.—I cannot paint   *75*
What then I was. The sounding cataract
Haunted me like a passion: the tall rock,
The mountain, and the deep and gloomy wood,
Their colours and their forms, were then to me
An appetite; a feeling and a love,   *80*
That had no need of a remoter charm,
By thought supplied, nor any interest
Unborrowed from the eye.—That time is past,
And all its aching joys are now no more,
And all its dizzy raptures. Not for this   *85*
Faint I, nor mourn nor murmur; other gifts
Have followed; for such loss, I would believe,
Abundant recompense. For I have learned
To look on nature, not as in the hour
Of thoughtless youth; but hearing oftentimes   *90*
The still, sad music of humanity,

Nor harsh nor grating, though of ample power
To chasten and subdue. And I have felt
A presence that disturbs me with the joy
Of elevated thoughts; a sense sublime   95
Of something far more deeply interfused,
Whose dwelling is the light of setting suns,
And the round ocean and the living air,
And the blue sky, and in the mind of man;
A motion and a spirit, that impels   100
All thinking things, all objects of all thought,
And rolls through all things. Therefore am I still
A lover of the meadows and the woods,
And mountains; and of all that we behold
From this green earth; of all the mighty world   105
Of eye, and ear,—both what they half create,
And what perceive; well pleased to recognize
In nature and the language of the sense,
The anchor of my purest thoughts, the nurse,
The guide, the guardian of my heart, and soul   110
Of all my moral being.
                         Nor perchance,
If I were not thus taught, should I the more
Suffer my genial spirits to decay:
For thou art with me here upon the banks
Of this fair river; thou my dearest Friend,   115
My dear, dear Friend; and in thy voice I catch
The language of my former heart, and read
My former pleasures in the shooting lights
Of thy wild eyes. Oh! yet a little while
May I behold in thee what I was once,   120
My dear, dear Sister! and this prayer I make,
Knowing that Nature never did betray
The heart that loved her; 'tis her privilege,
Through all the years of this our life, to lead
From joy to joy: for she can so inform   125
The mind that is within us, so impress
With quietness and beauty, and so feed
With lofty thoughts, that neither evil tongues,
Rash judgments, nor the sneers of selfish men,
Nor greetings where no kindness is, nor all   130
The dreary intercourse of daily life,
Shall e'er prevail against us, or disturb
Our cheerful faith that all which we behold
Is full of blessings. Therefore let the moon
Shine on thee in thy solitary walk;   135
And let the misty mountain-winds be free
To blow against thee: and, in after years,
When these wild ecstasies shall be matured

Into a sober pleasure; when thy mind
Shall be a mansion for all lovely forms,   *140*
Thy memory be as a dwelling-place
For all sweet sounds and harmonies; oh! then,
If solitude, or fear, or pain, or grief,
Should be thy portion, with what healing thoughts
Of tender joy wilt thou remember me,   *145*
And these my exhortations! Nor, perchance —
If I should be where I no more can hear
Thy voice, nor catch from thy wild eyes these gleams
Of past existence — wilt thou then forget
That on the banks of this delightful stream   *150*
We stood together; and that I, so long
A worshipper of Nature, hither came
Unwearied in that service: rather say
With warmer love — oh! with far deeper zeal
Of holier love. Nor wilt thou then forget,   *155*
That after many wanderings, many years
Of absence, these steep woods and lofty cliffs,
And this green pastoral landscape, were to me
More dear, both for themselves and for thy sake!

SAMUEL TAYLOR COLERIDGE

The Rime of the Ancient Mariner

Part I

An ancient Mariner meeteth three Gallants bidden to a wedding-feast, and detaineth one.

It is an ancient Mariner,
And he stoppeth one of three.
"By thy long grey beard and glittering eye,
Now wherefore stopp'st thou me?

The Bridegroom's doors are opened wide,   *5*
And I am next of kin;
The guests are met, the feast is set:
May'st hear the merry din."

He holds him with his skinny hand,
"There was a ship," quoth he.   *10*
"Hold off! unhand me, greybeard loon!"
Eftsoons his hand dropt he.

He holds him with his glittering eye —
The Wedding-Guest stood still,
And listens like a three years' child: 15
The Mariner hath his will.

The Wedding-Guest sat on a stone:
He cannot choose but hear;
And thus spake on that ancient man,
The bright-eyed Mariner.   20

"The ship was cheered, the harbour cleared,
Merrily did we drop
Below the kirk, below the hill,
Below the lighthouse top.

The Sun came up upon the left,   25
Out of the sea came he!
And he shone bright, and on the right
Went down into the sea.

Higher and higher every day,
Till over the mast at noon — "   30
The Wedding Guest here beat his breast,
For he heard the loud bassoon.

The bride hath paced into the hall,
Red as a rose is she;
Nodding their heads before her goes   35
The merry minstrelsy.

The Wedding Guest he beat his breast,
Yet he cannot choose but hear;
And thus spake on that ancient man,
The bright-eyed Mariner.   40

"And now the STORM-BLAST came, and he
Was tyrannous and strong:
He struck with his o'ertaking wings,
And chased us south along.

With sloping masts and dipping prow,   45
As who pursued with yell and blow
Still treads the shadow of his foe,
And forward bends his head,
The ship drove fast, loud roared the blast,
And southward aye we fled.   50

And now there came both mist and snow,
And it grew wondrous cold:

And ice, mast-high, came floating by,
As green as emerald.

And through the drifts the snowy clifts   55
Did send a dismal sheen:
Nor shapes of men nor beasts we ken —
The ice was all between.

The ice was here, the ice was there,
The ice was all around: 60
It cracked and growled, and roared and howled,
Like noises in a swound!

At length did cross an Albatross,
Thorough the fog it came;
As if it had been a Christian soul,   65
We hailed it in God's name.

It ate the food it ne'er had eat,
And round and round it flew.
The ice did split with a thunder-fit;
The helmsman steered us through!   70

And a good south wind sprung up behind;
The Albatross did follow,
And every day, for food or play,
Came to the mariners' hollo!

In mist or cloud, on mast or shroud,   75
It perched for vespers nine;
Whiles all the night, through fog-smoke white,
Glimmered the white Moon-shine."

"God save thee, ancient Mariner!
From the fiends that plague thee thus! —   80
Why look'st thou so?" — "With my crossbow
I shot the Albatross.

Part II

The Sun now rose upon the right:
Out of the sea came he,
Still hid in mist, and on the left   85
Went down into the sea.

And the good south wind still blew behind,
But no sweet bird did follow,
Nor any day for food or play
Came to the mariners' hollo!   90

*His shipmates
cry out against
the ancient
Mariner for
killing the bird
of good luck.*

And I had done a hellish thing,
And it would work 'em woe:
For all averred, I had killed the bird
That made the breeze to blow.
Ah wretch! said they, the bird to slay,   95
That made the breeze to blow!

*But when the
fog cleared off,
they justify the
same, and thus
make them-
selves accom-
plices in the
crime.*

Nor dim nor red, like God's own head,
The glorious Sun uprist:
Then all averred, I had killed the bird
That brought the fog and mist.   100
'Twas right, said they, such birds to slay,
That bring the fog and mist.

*The fair breeze
continues;
the ship enters
the Pacific
Ocean, and
sails north-
ward, even
till it reaches
the Line.*

The fair breeze blew, the white foam flew,
The furrow followed free;
We were the first that ever burst   105
Into that silent sea.

*The ship hath
been suddenly
becalmed.*

Down dropped the breeze, the sails dropped down,
'Twas sad as sad could be;
And we did speak only to break
The silence of the sea!   110

All in a hot and copper sky,
The bloody Sun, at noon,
Right up above the mast did stand,
No bigger than the Moon.

Day after day, day after day,   115
We stuck, nor breath nor motion;
As idle as a painted ship
Upon a painted ocean.

*And the Alba-
tross begins to
be avenged.*

Water, water, everywhere
And all the boards did shrink;   120
Water, water, everywhere,
Nor any drop to drink.

The very deep did rot: O Christ!
That ever this should be!
Yea, slimy things did crawl with legs   125
Upon the slimy sea.

About, about, in reel and rout
The death-fires danced at night;
The water, like a witch's oils,
Burnt green, and blue, and white.   130

A Spirit had followed them; one of the invisible inhabitants of this planet, neither departed souls nor angels; concerning whom the learned Jew, Josephus, and the Platonic Constantinopolitan, Michael Psellus, may be consulted. They are very numerous, and there is no climate or element without one or more.

And some in dreams assurèd were
Of the Spirit that plagued us so:
Nine fathom deep he had followed us
From the land of mist and snow.

And every tongue, through utter drought,   *135*
Was withered at the root;
We could not speak, no more than if
We had been choked with soot.

The shipmates, in their sore distress, would fain throw the whole guilt on the ancient Mariner; in sign whereof they hang the dead sea-bird round his neck.

Ah! well-a-day! what evil looks
Had I from old and young!   *140*
Instead of the cross, the Albatross
About my neck was hung.

Part III

There passed a weary time. Each throat
Was parched, and glazed each eye.
A weary time! a weary time!   *145*
How glazed each weary eye!

The ancient Mariner beholdeth a sign in the element afar off.

When looking westward, I beheld
A something in the sky.

At first it seemed a little speck,
And then it seemed a mist;   *150*
It moved and moved, and took at last
A certain shape, I wist.

A speck, a mist, a shape, I wist!
And still it neared and neared:
As if it dodged a water-sprite,   *155*
It plunged and tacked and veered.

At its nearer approach, it seemeth him to be a ship; and at a dear ransom he freeth his speech from the bonds of thirst.

With throats unslaked, with black lips baked,
We could not laugh nor wail;
Through utter drought all dumb we stood!
I bit my arm, I sucked the blood,   *160*
And cried, A sail! a sail!

With throats unslaked, with black lips baked,
Agape they heard me call:

A flash of joy;

Gramercy! they for joy did grin,
And all at once their breath drew in,   *165*
As they were drinking all.

And horror follows. For can it be a ship that

See! See! (I cried) she tacks no more!
Hither to work us weal;

*comes onward
without wind or
tide?*

Without a breeze, without a tide,
She steadies with upright keel!   *170*

The western wave was all a-flame.
The day was well nigh done!
Almost upon the western wave
Rested the broad bright Sun;
When that strange shape drove suddenly   *175*
Betwixt us and the Sun.

*It seemeth
him but the
skeleton of
a ship.*

And straight the Sun was flecked with bars,
(Heaven's Mother send us grace!)
As if through a dungeon-grate he peered
With broad and burning face.   *180*

*And its ribs
are seen as
bars on the
face of the
setting Sun.
The Specter-
Woman and
her Deathmate,
and no
other on
board the
skeleton-ship.*

Alas! (thought I, and my heart beat loud)
How fast she nears and nears!
Are those *her* sails that glance in the Sun,
Like restless gossameres?

Are those *her* ribs through which the Sun   *185*
Did peer, as through a grate?
And is that Woman all her crew?
Is that a DEATH? and are there two?
Is DEATH that woman's mate?

*Like vessel,
like crew!*

Her lips were red, *her* looks were free,   *190*
Her locks were yellow as gold:

*Death and
Life-in-Death
have diced for
the ship's
crew, and she
(the latter)
winneth the
ancient
Mariner.*

Her skin was as white as leprosy,
The Night-mare LIFE-IN-DEATH was she,
Who thicks man's blood with cold.

The naked hulk alongside came,   *195*
And the twain were casting dice;
"The game is done! I've won! I've won!"
Quoth she, and whistles thrice.

*No twilight
within the
courts of the
Sun.*

The Sun's rim dips; the stars rush out:
At one stride comes the dark;   *200*
With far-heard whisper, o'er the sea,
Off shot the specter bark.

*At the rising
of the Moon,*

We listened and looked sideways up!
Fear at my heart, as at a cup,
My life-blood seemed to sip!   *205*
The stars were dim, and thick the night,
The steersman's face by his lamp gleamed white;
From the sails the dew did drip—

Till clomb above the eastern bar
The hornèd Moon, with one bright star   210
Within the nether tip.

*One after
another,*

One after one, by the star-dogged Moon,
Too quick for groan or sigh,
Each turned his face with a ghastly pang,
And cursed me with his eye.   215

*His shipmates
drop down
dead.*

Four times fifty living men,
(And I heard nor sign nor groan)
With heavy thump, a lifeless lump,
They dropped down one by one.

*But Life-in-
Death begins
her work on
the ancient
Mariner.*

The souls did from their bodies fly,—   220
They fled to bliss or woe!
And every soul, it passed me by,
Like the whizz of my crossbow!"

Part IV

*The Wedding-
Guest feareth
that a spirit is
talking to him;*

"I fear thee, ancient Mariner!
I fear thy skinny hand!   225
And thou art long, and lank, and brown,
As is the ribbed sea-sand.

I fear thee and thy glittering eye,
And thy skinny hand, so brown."—

*But the ancient
Mariner as-
sureth him of
his bodily life,
and proceedeth
to relate his hor-
rible penance.*

"Fear not, fear not, thou Wedding-Guest!   230
This body dropt not down.

Alone, alone, all, all alone,
Alone on a wide wide sea!
And never a saint took pity on
My soul in agony.   235

*He despiseth
the creatures of
the calm,*

The many men, so beautiful!
And they all dead did lie:
And a thousand thousand slimy things
Lived on; and so did I.

*And envieth
that they should
live, and so
many lie dead.*

I looked upon the rotting sea,   240
And drew my eyes away;
I looked upon the rotting deck,
And there the dead men lay.

I looked to Heaven, and tried to pray;
But or ever a prayer had gusht,   245

A wicked whisper came, and made
My heart as dry as dust.

I closed my lids, and kept them close,
And the balls like pulses beat;
For the sky and the sea, and the sea and the sky,   *250*
Lay like a load on my weary eye,
And the dead were at my feet.

*But the curse
liveth for him
in the eye of
the dead men.*

The cold sweat melted from their limbs,
Nor rot nor reek did they:
The look with which they looked on me   *255*
Had never passed away.

An orphan's curse would drag to hell
A spirit from on high;
But oh! more horrible than that
Is the curse in a dead man's eye!   *260*
Seven days, seven nights, I saw that curse,
And yet I could not die.

*In his loneliness
and fixedness he
yearneth towards
the journeying
Moon, and the
stars that still
sojourn, yet still
move onward;
and everywhere
the blue sky
belongs to them,
and is their
appointed rest,
and their
native country
and their own
natural homes,
which they enter
unannounced,
as lords that
are certainly
expected and
yet there is a
silent joy at
their arrival.*

The moving Moon went up the sky,
And no where did abide:
Softly she was going up,   *265*
And a star or two beside —

Her beams bemocked the sultry main,
Like April hoar-frost spread;
But where the ship's huge shadow lay,
The charméd water burnt alway   *270*
A still and awful red.

*By the light
of the Moon he
beholdeth
God's crea-
tures of the
great calm.*

Beyond the shadow of the ship,
I watched the water-snakes:
They moved in tracks of shining white,
And when they reared, the elfish light   *275*
Fell off in hoary flakes.

Within the shadow of the ship
I watched their rich attire:
Blue, glossy green, and velvet black,
They coiled and swam; and every track   *280*
Was a flash of golden fire.

*Their beauty
and their happi-
ness.*

O happy living things! no tongue
Their beauty might declare:
A spring of love gushed from my heart,

*He blesseth
them in his
heart.*

And I blessed them unaware: 285
Sure my kind saint took pity on me,
And I blessed them unaware.

*The spell begins
to break.*

The selfsame moment I could pray;
And from my neck so free
The Albatross fell off, and sank   290
Like lead into the sea.

Part V

Oh sleep! it is a gentle thing,
Beloved from pole to pole!
To Mary Queen the praise be given!
She sent the gentle sleep from Heaven,   295
That slid into my soul.

*By grace of the
holy Mother,
the ancient
Mariner is re-
freshed with
rain.*

The silly buckets on the deck,
That had so long remained,
I dreamt that they were filled with dew;
And when I awoke, it rained.   300

My lips were wet, my throat was cold,
My garments all were dank;
Sure I had drunken in my dreams,
And still my body drank.

I moved, and could not feel my limbs: 305
I was so light—almost
I thought that I had died in sleep,
And was a blessèd ghost.

*He heareth
sounds and
seeth strange
sights and com-
motions in the
sky and the
element.*

And soon I saw a roaring wind:
It did not come anear;   310
But with its sound it shook the sails,
That were so thin and sere.

The upper air burst into life!
And a hundred fire-flags sheen,
To and fro they were hurried about!   315
And to and fro, and in and out,
The wan stars danced between.

And the coming wind did roar more loud,
And the sails did sigh like sedge;
And the rain poured down from one black cloud;   320
The Moon was at its edge.

The thick black cloud was cleft, and still
The Moon was at its side:
Like waters shot from some high crag,
The lightning fell with never a jag,   *325*
A river steep and wide.

The bodies of
the ship's crew
are inspired,
and the ship
moves on;

The loud wind never reached the ship,
Yet now the ship moved on!
Beneath the lightning and the Moon
The dead men gave a groan.   *330*

They groaned, they stirred, they all uprose,
Nor spake, nor moved their eyes;
It had been strange, even in a dream,
To have seen those dead men rise.

The helmsman steered, the ship moved on;   *335*
Yet never a breeze up-blew;
The mariners all 'gan work the ropes,
Where they were wont to do;
They raised their limbs like lifeless tools—
We were a ghastly crew.   *340*

The body of my brother's son
Stood by me, knee to knee:
The body and I pulled at one rope,
But he said nought to me."

"I fear thee, ancient Mariner!"   *345*

But not by the
souls of the
men, nor by
demons of
earth or
middle air, but
by a blessed
troop of
angelic spirits,
sent down by
the invocation
of the guar-
dian saint.

"Be calm, thou Wedding-Guest!
'Twas not those souls that fled in pain,
Which to their corses came again,
But a troop of spirits blessed:

For when it dawned—they dropped their arms,   *350*
And clustered round the mast;
Sweet sounds rose slowly through their mouths,
And from their bodies passed.

Around, around, flew each sweet sound,
Then darted to the Sun;   *355*
Slowly the sounds came back again,
Now mixed, now one by one.

Sometimes adropping from the sky
I heard the skylark sing;
Sometimes all little birds that are,   *360*
How they seemed to fill the sea and air
With their sweet jargoning!

And now 'twas like all instruments,
Now like a lonely flute;
And now it is an angel's song,   365
That makes the heavens be mute.

It ceased; yet still the sails made on
A pleasant noise till noon,
A noise like of a hidden brook
In the leafy month of June,   370
That to the sleeping woods all night
Singeth a quiet tune.

Till noon we quietly sailed on,
Yet never a breeze did breathe:
Slowly and smoothly went the ship,   375
Moved onward from beneath.

*The lonesome
Spirit from the
south pole car-
ries on the ship
as far as the
Line, in obedi-
ence to the an-
gelic troop, but
still requireth
vengeance.*

Under the keel nine fathom deep,
From the land of mist and snow,
The Spirit slid: and it was he
That made the ship to go.   380
The sails at noon left off their tune,
And the ship stood still also.

The Sun, right up above the mast,
Had fixed her to the ocean:
But in a minute she 'gan stir,   385
With a short uneasy motion —
Backwards and forwards half her length
With a short uneasy motion.

Then, like a pawing horse let go,
She made a sudden bound: 390
It flung the blood into my head,
And I fell down in a swound.

*The Polar
Spirit's fellow
demons, the
invisible inhabi-
tants of the ele-
ment, take part
in his wrong;
and two of them
relate, one to
the other, that
penance long
and heavy for
the ancient
Mariner hath
been accorded
to the Polar
Spirit, who re-
turneth south-
ward.*

How long in that same fit I lay,
I have not to declare;
But ere my living life returned,   395
I heard and in my soul discerned
Two voices in the air.

'Is it he?' quoth one, 'Is this the man?
By him who died on cross,
With his cruel bow he laid full low   400
The harmless Albatross.

The spirit who bideth by himself
In the land of mist and snow,

He loved the bird that loved the man
Who shot him with his bow.'   405

The other was a softer voice,
As soft as honey-dew:
Quoth he, 'The man hath penance done,
And penance more will do.'

Part VI

First Voice

'But tell me, tell me! speak again,   410
Thy soft response renewing—
What makes that ship drive on so fast?
What is the ocean doing?'

Second Voice

'Still as a slave before his lord,
The ocean hath no blast;   415
His great bright eye most silently
Up to the Moon is cast—

If he may know which way to go;
For she guides him smooth or grim.
See, brother, see! how graciously   420
She looketh down on him.'

First Voice

'But why drives on that ship so fast,
Without or wave or wind?'

*The Mariner
hath been cast
into a trance;
for the angelic
power causeth
the vessel to
drive northward
faster than hu-
man life could
endure.*

Second Voice

'The air is cut away before,
And closes from behind.   425

Fly, brother, fly! more high, more high!
Or we shall be belated:
For slow and slow that ship will go,
When the Mariner's trance is abated.'

*The supernatu-
ral motion is re-
tarded; the
Mariner awakes,
and his penance
begins anew.*

I woke, and we were sailing on   430
As in a gentle weather:
'Twas night, calm night, the Moon was high;
The dead men stood together.

All stood together on the deck,
For a charnel-dungeon fitter: 435
All fixed on me their stony eyes,
That in the Moon did glitter.

The pang, the curse, with which they died,
Had never passed away:
I could not draw my eyes from theirs,   440
Nor turn them up to pray.

*The curse is
finally expiated.*
And now this spell was snapt: once more
I viewed the ocean green,
And looked far forth, yet little saw
Of what had else been seen —   445

Like one that on a lonesome road
Doth walk in fear and dread,
And having once turned round walks on,
And turns no more his head;
Because he knows a frightful fiend   450
Doth close behind him tread.

But soon there breathed a wind on me,
Nor sound nor motion made:
Its path was not upon the sea,
In ripple or in shade.   455

It raised my hair, it fanned my cheek
Like a meadow-gale of spring —
It mingled strangely with my fears,
Yet it felt like a welcoming.

Swiftly, swiftly flew the ship,   460
Yet she sailed softly too:
Sweetly, sweetly blew the breeze —
On me alone it blew.

*And the ancient
Mariner be-
holdeth his na-
tive country.*
Oh! dream of joy! is this indeed
The lighthouse top I see?   465
Is this the hill? is this the kirk?
Is this mine own countree?

We drifted o'er the harbour-bar,
And I with sobs did pray —
O let me be awake, my God!   470
Or let me sleep alway.

The harbour-bay was clear as glass,
So smoothly was it strewn!
And on the bay the moonlight lay,
And the shadow of the Moon.   *475*

The rock shone bright, the kirk no less,
That stands above the rock:
The moonlight steeped in silentness
The steady weathercock.

The angelic spirits leave the dead bodies,

And the bay was white with silent light,   *480*
Till rising from the same,
Full many shapes, that shadows were,
In crimson colors came.

And appear in their own forms of light.

A little distance from the prow
Those crimson shadows were: *485*
I turned my eyes upon the deck—
Oh, Christ! what saw I there!

Each corse lay flat, lifeless and flat,
And, by the holy rood!
A man all light, a seraph-man,   *490*
On every corse there stood.

This seraph-band, each waved his hand:
It was a heavenly sight!
They stood as signals to the land,
Each one a lovely light;   *495*

This seraph-band, each waved his hand,
No voice did they impart—
No voice; but oh! the silence sank
Like music on my heart.

But soon I heard the dash of oars,   *500*
I heard the Pilot's cheer;
My head was turned perforce away,
And I saw a boat appear.

The Pilot and the Pilot's boy,
I heard them coming fast: *505*
Dear Lord in Heaven! it was a joy
That dead men could not blast.

I saw a third—I heard his voice:
It is the Hermit good!
He singeth loud his godly hymns   *510*
That he makes in the wood.

He'll shrieve my soul, he'll wash away
The Albatross's blood.

Part VII

The Hermit of
the wood

This Hermit good lives in that wood
Which slopes down to the sea.   *515*
How loudly his sweet voice he rears!
He loves to talk with the marineres
That come from a far countree.

He kneels at morn, and noon, and eve —
He hath a cushion plump: *520*
It is the moss that wholly hides
The rotted old oak-stump.

The skiff-boat neared: I heard them talk,
'Why this is strange, I trow!
Where are those lights so many and fair,   *525*
That signal made but now?'

Approacheth
the ship with
wonder.

'Strange, by faith!' the Hermit said —
'And they answered not our cheer!
The planks look warped! and see those sails,
How thin they are and sere!   *530*
I never saw aught like to them,
Unless perchance it were

Brown skeletons of leaves that lag
My forest-brook along;
When the ivy-tod is heavy with snow,   *535*
And the owlet whoops to the wolf below,
That eats the she-wolf's young.'

'Dear Lord! it hath a fiendish look —'
(The Pilot made reply)
'I am a-feared' — 'Push on, push on!'   *540*
Said the Hermit cheerily.

The boat came closer to the ship,
But I nor spake nor stirred;
The boat came close beneath the ship,
And straight a sound was heard.   *545*

The ship
suddenly sinketh.

Under the water it rumbled on,
Still louder and more dread:
It reached the ship, it split the bay;
The ship went down like lead.

Stunned by that loud and dreadful sound,   *550*
Which sky and ocean smote,
Like one that hath been seven days drowned

*The ancient
Mariner is saved
in the Pilot's
boat.*
My body lay afloat;
But swift as dreams, myself I found
Within the Pilot's boat.   *555*

Upon the whirl, where sank the ship,
The boat spun round and round;
And all was still, save that the hill
Was telling of the sound.

I moved my lips — the Pilot shrieked   *560*
And fell down in a fit;
The holy Hermit raised his eyes,
And prayed where he did sit.

I took the oars: the Pilot's boy,
Who now doth crazy go,   *565*
Laughed loud and long, and all the while
His eyes went to and fro.
'Ha! ha!' quoth he, 'full plain I see,
The Devil knows how to row.'

And now, all in my own countree,   *570*
I stood on the firm land!
The Hermit stepped forth from the boat,
And scarcely he could stand.

*The ancient
Mariner earn-
estly entreateth
the Hermit to
shrive him; and
the penance of
life falls on
him.*
'O shrieve me, shrieve me, holy man!'
The Hermit crossed his brow.   *575*
'Say quick,' quoth he, 'I bid thee say —
What manner of man are thou?'

Forthwith this frame of mine was wrenched
With a woeful agony,
Which forced me to begin my tale;   *580*
And then it left me free.

*And ever and
anon through-
out his future
life an agony
constraineth
him to travel
from land to
land,*
Since then, at an uncertain hour,
That agony returns:
And till my ghastly tale is told,
This heart within me burns.   *585*

I pass, like night, from land to land;
I have strange power of speech;
That moment that his face I see,

I know the man that must hear me:
To him my tale I teach.   *590*

What loud uproar bursts from that door!
The wedding-guests are there:
But in the garden-bower the bride
And bride-maids singing are:
And hark the little vesper bell,   *595*
Which biddeth me to prayer!

O Wedding-Guest! this soul hath been
Alone on a wide wide sea:
So lonely 'twas, that God himself
Scarce seemèd there to be.   *600*

O sweeter than the marriage-feast,
'Tis sweeter far to me,
To walk together to the kirk
With a goodly company! —

To walk together to the kirk,   *605*
And all together pray,
While each to his great Father bends,
Old men, and babes, and loving friends,
And youths and maidens gay!

And to teach, by his own ex-ample, love and reverence to all things that God made and loveth.

Farewell, farewell! but this I tell   *610*
To thee, thou Wedding-Guest!
He prayeth well, who loveth well
Both man and bird and beast.

He prayeth best, who loveth best
All things both great and small;   *615*
For the dear God who loveth us,
He made and loveth all."

The Mariner, whose eye is bright,
Whose beard with age is hoar,
Is gone: and now the Wedding-Guest   *620*
Turned from the bridegroom's door.

He went like one that hath been stunned,
And is of sense forlorn:
A sadder and a wiser man,
He rose the morrow morn.   *625*

PERCY BYSSHE SHELLEY

England in 1819

An old, mad, blind, despised, and dying king,—
Princes, the dregs of their dull race, who flow
Through public scorn—mud from a muddy spring;
Rulers who neither see, nor feel, nor know,
But leech-like to their fainting country cling,   5
Till they drop, blind in blood, without a blow;
A people starved and stabbed in the untilled field,—
An army, which liberticide and prey
Makes as a two-edged sword to all who wield—
Golden and sanguine laws which tempt and slay,—   10
Religion Christless, Godless—a book sealed;
A Senate,—Time's worst statute unrepealed,—
Are graves, from which a glorious Phantom may
Burst, to illumine our tempestuous day.

The Indian Serenade

I arise from dreams of thee
In the first sweet sleep of night,
When the winds are breathing low,
And the stars are shining bright:
I arise from dreams of thee,   5
And a spirit in my feet
Hath led me—who knows how?
To thy chamber window, Sweet!

The wandering airs they faint
On the dark, the silent stream—   10
The Champak odors fail
Like sweet thoughts in a dream;
The nightingale's complaint,
It dies upon her heart;—
As I must on thine,   15
Oh, belovèd as thou art!

Oh lift me from the grass!
I die! I faint! I fail!
Let thy love in kisses rain
On my lips and eyelids pale.   20
My cheek is cold and white, alas!
My heart beats loud and fast;—
Oh! press it to thine own again,
Where it will break at last.

Love's Philosophy

The fountains mingle with the river
And the rivers with the ocean,
The winds of heaven mix for ever
With a sweet emotion;
Nothing in the world is single;   5
All things by a law divine
In one another's being mingle—
Why not I with thine?

See the mountains kiss high heaven,
And the waves clasp one another;   10
No sister-flower would be forgiven
If it disdained its brother:
And the sunlight clasps the earth,
And the moonbeams kiss the sea—
What are all these kissings worth,   15
If thou kiss not me?

To—

Music, when soft voices die,
Vibrates in the memory—
Odors, when sweet violets sicken,
Live within the sense they quicken.
Rose leaves, when the rose is dead,   5
Are heaped for the belovéd's bed;
And so thy thoughts, when thou are gone,
Love itself shall slumber on.

Mutability

The flower that smiles today
          Tomorrow dies;
All that we wish to stay
          Tempts and then flies.
What is this world's delight?   5
Lightning that mocks the night,
          Brief even as bright.

Virtue, how frail it is!
          Friendship how rare!
Love, how it sells poor bliss   10
          For proud despair!
But we, though soon they fall,
Survive their joy, and all
          Which ours we call.

Whilst skies are blue and bright,   *15*
   Whilst flowers are gay,
Whilst eyes that change ere night
   Make glad the day;
Whilst yet the calm hours creep,
Dream thou—and from thy sleep   *20*
   Then wake to weep.

Ode to the West Wind

I

O wild West Wind, thou breath of Autumn's being,
Thou, from whose unseen presence the leaves dead
Are driven, like ghosts from an enchanter fleeing,

Yellow, and black, and pale, and hectic red,
Pestilence-stricken multitudes: O thou,   *5*
Who chariotest to their dark wintry bed

The wingèd seeds, where they lie cold and low,
Each like a corpse within its grave, until
Thine azure sister of the Spring shall blow

Her clarion o'er the dreaming earth, and fill   *10*
(Driving sweet buds like flocks to feed in air)
With living hues and odors plain and hill:

Wild Spirit, which art moving everywhere;
Destroyer and preserver, hear, oh, hear!

II

Thou on whose stream, 'mid the steep sky's commotion,   *15*
Loose clouds like earth's decaying leaves are shed,
Shook from the tangled boughs of Heaven and Ocean,

Angels of rain and lightning: there are spread
On the blue surface of thine aery surge,
Like the bright hair uplifted from the head   *20*

Of some fierce Maenad, even from the dim verge
Of the horizon to the zenith's height,
The locks of the approaching storm. Thou dirge

Of the dying year, to which this closing night
Will be the dome of a vast sepulchre   *25*
Vaulted with all thy congregated might

Of vapors, from whose solid atmosphere
Black rain, and fire, and hail will burst: oh, hear!

III

Thou who didst waken from his summer dreams
The blue Mediterranean, where he lay,   30
Lulled by the coil of his crystàlline streams,

Beside a pumice isle in Baiae's bay,
And saw in sleep old palaces and towers
Quivering within the wave's intenser day,

All overgrown with azure moss and flowers   35
So sweet, the sense faints picturing them! Thou
For whose path the Atlantic's level powers

Cleave themselves into chasms, while far below
The sea-blooms and the oozy woods which wear
The sapless foliage of the ocean, know   40

Thy voice, and suddenly grow gray with fear,
And tremble and despoil themselves: oh, hear!

IV

If I were a dead leaf thou mightest bear;
If I were a swift cloud to fly with thee;
A wave to pant beneath thy power, and share   45

The impulse of thy strength, only less free
Than thou, O uncontrollable! If even
I were as in my boyhood, and could be

The comrade of thy wanderings over Heaven,
As then, when to outstrip thy skiey speed   50
Scarce seemed a vision; I would ne'er have striven

As thus with thee in prayer in my sore need.
Oh, lift me as a wave, a leaf, a cloud!
I fall upon the thorns of life! I bleed!

A heavy weight of hours has chained and bowed   55
One too like thee: tameless, and swift, and proud.

V

Make me thy lyre, even as the forest is:

What if my leaves are falling like its own!
The tumult of thy mighty harmonies

Will take from both a deep, autumnal tone,   60
Sweet though in sadness. Be thou, Spirit fierce,
My spirit! Be thou me, impetuous one!

Drive my dead thoughts over the universe
Like withered leaves to quicken a new birth!
And, by the incantation of this verse,   65

Scatter, as from an unextinguished hearth
Ashes and sparks, my words among mankind!
Be through my lips to unawakened earth

The trumpet of a prophecy! O, Wind,
If Winter comes, can Spring be far behind?   70

This Is the Day (from *Prometheus Unbound*)

This is the day, which down the void abysm
At the Earth-born's spell yawns for Heaven's despotism,
    And Conquest is dragged captive through the deep:
Love, from its awful throne of patient power
In the wise heart, from the last giddy hour   5
    Of dread endurance, from the slippery, steep,
And narrow verge of crag-like agony, springs
And folds over the world its healing wings.

Gentleness, Virtue, Wisdom, and Endurance,
These are the seals of that most firm assurance   10
    Which bars the pit over Destruction's strength;
And if, with infirm hand, Eternity,
Mother of many acts and hours, should free
    The serpent that would clasp her with his length;
These are the spells by which to re-assume   15
An empire o'er the disentangled doom.

 To suffer woes which Hope thinks infinite;
To forgive wrongs darker than death or night;
    To defy Power, which seems omnipotent;
To love, and bear; to hope till Hope creates   20
From its own wreck the thing it contemplates:
    Neither to change, nor falter, nor repent;
This, like thy glory, Titan! is to be
Good, great and joyous, beautiful and free;
This is alone Life, Joy, Empire, and Victory!   25

JOHN KEATS

On the Grasshopper and Cricket

The poetry of earth is never dead:
When all the birds are faint with the hot sun,
And hide in cooling trees, a voice will run
From hedge to hedge about the new-mown mead;
That is the Grasshopper's—he takes the lead   5
In summer luxury,—he has never done
With his delights; for when tired out with fun
He rests at ease beneath some pleasant weed.
The poetry of earth is ceasing never:
On a lone winter evening, when the frost   10
Has wrought a silence, from the stove there shrills
The Cricket's song, in warmth increasing ever,
And seems to one in drowsiness half lost,
The Grasshopper's among some grassy hills.

The Devon Maid

Where be ye going, you Devon maid?
    And what have ye there in the basket?
Ye tight little fairy, just fresh from the dairy,
    Will ye give me some cream if I ask it?

I love your Meads, and I love your flowers,   5
    And I love your junkets mainly,
But 'hind the door I love kissing more,
    O look not so disdainly.

I love your hills and I love your dales,
    And I love your flocks a-bleating—   10
But O, on the heather to lie together,
    With both our hearts a-beating!

I'll put your basket all safe in a nook;
    Your shawl I'll hang on the willow;
And we will sigh in the daisy's eye,   15
    And kiss on a grass green pillow.

Bright Star

Bright star, would I were steadfast as thou art—
Not in lone splendor hung aloft the night

And watching, with eternal lids apart,
Like nature's patient, sleepless Eremite,
The moving waters at their priestlike task   *5*
Of pure ablution round earth's human shores,
Or gazing on the new soft fallen mask
Of snow upon the mountains and the moors—
No—yet still steadfast, still unchangeable,
Pillowed upon my fair love's ripening breast,   *10*
To feel forever its soft fall and swell,
Awake forever in a sweet unrest,
Still, still to hear her tender-taken breath,
And so live ever—or else swoon to death.

Ode on a Grecian Urn

I

Thou still unravish'd bride of quietness,
    Thou foster-child of silence and slow time,
Sylvan historian, who canst thus express
    A flowery tale more sweetly than our rhyme:
What leaf-fring'd legend haunts about thy shape   *5*
    Of deities or mortals, or of both,
        In Tempe or the dales of Arcady?
    What men or gods are these? What maidens loth?
What mad pursuit? What struggle to escape?
        What pipes and timbrels? What wild ecstasy? *10*

II

Heard melodies are sweet, but those unheard
    Are sweeter; therefore, ye soft pipes, play on;
Not to the sensual ear, but, more endear'd,
    Pipe to the spirit ditties of no tone:
Fair youth, beneath the trees, thou canst not leave *15*
    Thy song, nor ever can those trees be bare;
        Bold Lover, never, never canst thou kiss,
Though winning near the goal—yet, do not grieve;
    She cannot fade, though thou hast not thy bliss,
        For ever wilt thou love, and she be fair!   *20*

III

Ah, happy, happy boughs! that cannot shed
    Your leaves, nor ever bid the Spring adieu;
And, happy melodist, unwearièd,
    For ever piping songs for ever new;
More happy love! more happy, happy love!   *25*
    For ever warm and still to be enjoy'd,
        For ever panting, and for ever young;

All breathing human passion far above,
  That leaves a heart high-sorrowful and cloy'd,
    A burning forehead, and a parching tongue.   *30*

IV

Who are these coming to the sacrifice?
  To what green altar, O mysterious priest,
Lead'st thou that heifer lowing at the skies,
  And all her silken flanks with garlands drest?
What little town by river or sea shore,   *35*
  Or mountain-built with peaceful citadel,
    Is emptied of this folk, this pious morn?
And, little town, thy streets for evermore
  Will silent be; and not a soul to tell
    Why thou art desolate, can e'er return.   *10*

V

O Attic shape! Fair attitude! with brede
  Of marble men and maidens overwrought,
With forest branches and the trodden weed;
  Thou, silent form, dost tease us out of thought
As doth eternity: Cold Pastoral!   *45*
  When old age shall this generation waste,
    Thou shalt remain, in midst of other woe
  Than ours, a friend to man, to whom thou say'st,
"Beauty is truth, truth beauty,"—that is all
  Ye know on earth, and all ye need to know.   *50*

Ode to a Nightingale

I

My heart aches, and a drowsy numbness pains
  My sense, as though of hemlock I had drunk,
Or emptied some dull opiate to the drains
  One minute past, and Lethe-wards had sunk:
'Tis not through envy of thy happy lot,   *5*
  But being too happy in thine happiness—
    That thou, light-wingèd Dryad of the trees,
      In some melodious plot
  Of beechen green, and shadows numberless,
    Singest of summer in full-throated ease.   *10*

II

O, for a draught of vintage! that hath been
  Cooled a long age in the deep-delvèd earth,
Tasting of Flora and the country green,

Dance, and Provençal song, and sunburnt mirth!
O for a beaker full of the warm South,   *15*
  Full of the true, the blushful Hippocrene,
    With beaded bubbles winking at the brim,
      And purple-stainéd mouth;
  That I might drink, and leave the world unseen,
    And with thee fade away into the forest dim: *20*

III

Fade far away, dissolve, and quite forget
  What thou among the leaves hast never known,
The weariness, the fever, and the fret
  Here, where men sit and hear each other groan;
Where palsy shakes a few, sad, last gray hairs,   *25*
    Where youth grows pale, and specter-thin, and dies;
      Where but to think is to be full of sorrow
        And leaden-eyed despairs,
    Where Beauty cannot keep her lustrous eyes,   *30*
      Or new Love pine at them beyond tomorrow.

IV

Away! away! for I will fly to thee,
  Not charioted by Bacchus and his pards,
But on the viewless wings of Poesy,
  Though the dull brain perplexes and retards:
Already with thee! tender is the night,   *35*
    And haply the Queen-Moon is on her throne,
      Clustered around by all her starry Fays;
        But here there is no light,
    Save what from heaven is with the breezes blown
      Through verdurous glooms and winding mossy ways. *40*

V

I cannot see what flowers are at my feet,
  Nor what soft incense hangs upon the boughs,
But, in embalmed darkness, guess each sweet
  Wherewith the seasonable month endows
The grass, the thicket, and the fruit-tree wild;   *45*
    White hawthorn, and the pastoral eglantine;
      Fast fading violets cover'd up in leaves;
        And mid-May's eldest child,
    The coming musk-rose, full of dewy wine,
      The murmurous haunt of flies on summer eves.   *50*

VI

Darkling I listen; and, for many a time
  I have been half in love with easeful Death,
Call'd him soft names in many a muséd rhyme,
  To take into the air my quiet breath;
Now more than ever seems it rich to die,   55
  To cease upon the midnight with no pain,
    While thou art pouring forth thy soul abroad
      In such an ecstasy!
  Still wouldst thou sing, and I have ears in vain —
    To thy high requiem become a sod.   60

VII

Thou wast not born for death, immortal Bird!
  No hungry generations tread thee down;
The voice I hear this passing night was heard
  In ancient days by emperor and clown:
Perhaps the self-same song that found a path   65
  Through the sad heart of Ruth, when, sick for home,
    She stood in tears amid the alien corn;
      The same that oft-times hath
  Charm'd magic casements, opening on the foam
    Of perilous seas, in faery lands forlorn.   70

VIII

Forlorn! the very word is like a bell
  To toll me back from thee to my sole self!
Adieu! the fancy cannot cheat so well
  As she is fam'd to do, deceiving elf.
Adieu! adieu! thy plaintive anthem fades   75
  Past the near meadows, over the still stream,
    Up the hill-side; and now 'tis buried deep
      In the next valley-glades:
  Was it a vision, or a waking dream?
    Fled is that music: — Do I wake or sleep?   80

Ode on Melancholy

I

No, no, go not to Lethe, neither twist
  Wolf's-bane, tight-rooted, for its poisonous wine;
Nor suffer thy pale forehead to be kiss'd
  By nightshade, ruby grape of Proserpine;
Make not your rosary of yew-berries,   5

Nor let the beetle, nor the death-moth be
   Your mournful Psyche, nor the downy owl
A partner in your sorrow's mysteries;
   For shade to shade will come too drowsily,
     And drown the wakeful anguish of the soul.   *10*

II

But when the melancholy fit shall fall
   Sudden from heaven like a weeping cloud,
That fosters the droop-headed flowers all,
   And hides the green hill in an April shroud;
Then glut thy sorrow on a morning rose,   *15*
   Or on the rainbow of the salt sand-wave,
     Or on the wealth of globed peonies;
Or if thy mistress some rich anger shows,
   Emprison her soft hand, and let her rave,
     And feed deep, deep upon her peerless eyes.   *20*

III

She dwells with Beauty—Beauty that must die;
   And Joy, whose hand is ever at his lips
Bidding adieu; and aching Pleasure nigh,
   Turning to poison while the bee-mouth sips:
Ay, in the very temple of Delight   *25*
   Veil'd Melancholy has her sovran shrine,
     Though seen of none save him whose strenuous tongue
Can burst Joy's grape against his palate fine;
   His soul shall taste the sadness of her might,
     And be among her cloudy trophies hung.   *30*

EDGAR ALLAN POE

The City in the Sea

Lo! Death has reared himself a throne
In a strange city lying alone
Far down within the dim West,
Where the good and the bad and the worst
   and the best
Have gone to their eternal rest.   *5*
There shrines and palaces and towers
(Time-eaten towers that tremble not)
Resemble nothing that is ours.
Around, by lifting winds forgot,

Resignedly beneath the sky   *10*
The melancholy waters lie.

No rays from the holy heaven come down
On the long night-time of that town;
But light from out the lurid sea
Streams up the turrets silently,   *15*
Gleams up the pinnacles far and free:
Up domes, up spires, up kingly halls;
Up fanes, up Babylon-like walls,
Up shadowy long-forgotten bowers
Of sculptured ivy and stone flowers,   *20*
Up many and many a marvelous shrine
Whose wreathed friezes intertwine
The viol, the violet, and the vine.

Resignedly beneath the sky
The melancholy waters lie.   *25*
So blend the turrets and shadows there
That all seem pendulous in air,
While from a proud tower in the town
Death looks gigantically down.

There open fanes and gaping graves   *30*
Yawn level with the luminous waves;
But not the riches there that lie
In each idol's diamond eye,—
Not the gayly-jewelled dead,
Tempt the waters from their bed;   *35*
For no ripples curl, alas,
Along that wilderness of glass;
No swellings tell that winds may be
Upon some far-off happier sea;
No heavings hint that winds have been   *40*
On seas less hideously serene!

But lo, a stir is in the air!
The wave—there is a movement there!
As if the towers had thrust aside,
In slightly sinking, the dull tide;   *45*
As if their tops had feebly given
A void within the filmy Heaven!
The waves have now a redder glow,
The hours are breathing faint and low;
And when, amid no earthly moans,   *50*
Down, down that town shall settle hence,
Hell, rising from a thousand thrones,
Shall do it reverence.

To One in Paradise

Thou wast all that to me, love,
  For which my soul did pine:
A green isle in the sea, love,
  A fountain and a shrine,
All wreathed with fairy fruits and flowers,   *5*
  And all the flowers were mine.

Ah, dream too bright to last!
  Ah, starry Hope, that didst arise
But to be overcast!
  A voice from out the Future cries,   *10*
"On! on!"—but o'er the Past
  (Dim gulf!) my spirit hovering lies
Mute, motionless, aghast!

For, alas! alas! with me
  The light of Life is o'er!   *15*
  No more—no more—no more—
(Such language holds the solemn sea
  To the sands upon the shore)
Shall bloom the thunder-blasted tree,
  Or the stricken eagle soar!   *20*

And all my days are trances,
  And all my nightly dreams
Are where thy gray eye glances,
  And where thy footstep gleams—
In what ethereal dances,   *25*
  By what eternal streams.

The Haunted Palace

I

In the greenest of our valleys
  By good angels tenanted,
Once a fair and stately palace—
  Radiant palace—reared its head.
In the monarch Thought's dominion,   *5*
  It stood there;
Never seraph spread a pinion
  Over fabric half so fair!

II

Banners yellow, glorious, golden,
  On its roof did float and flow   *10*

(This — all this — was in the olden
　　Time long ago),
And every gentle air that dallied,
　　In that sweet day,
Along the ramparts plumed and pallid,　　　　　*15*
　　A wingéd odor went away.

III

Wanderers in that happy valley
　　Through two luminous windows saw
Spirits moving musically
　　To a lute's well-tunéd law,　　　　　*20*
Round about a throne, where, sitting
　　(Porphyrogene!)
In state his glory well befitting,
　　The ruler of the realm was seen.

IV

And all with pearl and ruby glowing　　　　　*25*
　　Was the fair palace-door,
Through which came flowing, flowing, flowing,
　　And sparkling evermore,
A troop of Echoes, whose sweet duty
　　Was but to sing,　　　　　*30*
In voices of surpassing beauty,
　　The wit and wisdom of their king.

V

But evil things, in robes of sorrow,
　　Assailed the monarch's high estate;
(Ah, let us mourn! for never morrow　　　　　*35*
　　Shall dawn upon him, desolate!)
And, round about his home, the glory
　　That blushed and bloomed
Is but a dim-remembered story
　　Of the old time entombed.　　　　　*40*

VI

And travelers now within that valley
　　Through the red-litten windows see
Vast forms that move fantastically
　　To a discordant melody,
While, like a ghastly rapid river,　　　　　*45*
　　Through the pale door,
A hideous throng rush out forever,
　　And laugh — but smile no more.

Annabel Lee

It was many and many a year ago,
  In a kingdom by the sea,
That a maiden there lived whom you may know
  By the name of Annabel Lee;—
And this maiden she lived with no other thought   5
  Than to love and be loved by me.

I was a child and *she* was a child,
  In this kingdom by the sea,
But we loved with a love that was more than love—
  I and my Annabel Lee—   10
With a love that the wingèd seraphs in Heaven
  Coveted her and me.

And this was the reason that, long ago,
  In this kingdom by the sea,
A wind blew out of a cloud, chilling   15
  My beautiful Annabel Lee;
So that her high-born kinsmen came
  And bore her away from me,
To shut her up in a sepulcher
  In this kingdom by the sea.   20

The angels, not half so happy in Heaven,
  Went envying her and me:—
Yes!—that was the reason (as all men know,
  In this kingdom by the sea)
That the wind came out of the cloud, by night,   25
  Chilling and killing my Annabel Lee.

But our love it was stronger by far than the love
  Of those who were older than we—
Of many far wiser than we—
And neither the angels in Heaven above,   30
  Nor the demons down under the sea,
Can ever dissever my soul from the soul
  Of the beautiful Annabel Lee:—

For the moon never beams without bringing me dreams
  Of the beautiful Annabel Lee;   35
And the stars never rise but I feel the bright eyes
  Of the beautiful Annabel Lee;
And so, all the night-tide, I lie down by the side
Of my darling,—my darling,—my life and my bride,
  In her sepulcher there by the sea—   40
  In her tomb by the sounding sea.

ALFRED, LORD TENNYSON

From *In Memoriam*

Prologue

Strong Son of God, immortal Love,
    Whom we, that have not seen thy face,
    By faith, and faith alone, embrace,
Believing where we cannot prove;

Thine are these orbs of light and shade;   *5*
    Thou madest Life in man and brute;
    Thou madest Death; and lo, thy foot
Is on the skull which thou hast made.

Thou wilt not leave us in the dust:
    Thou madest man, he knows not why,   *10*
    He thinks he was not made to die;
And thou hast made him: thou art just.

Thou seemest human and divine,
    The highest, holiest manhood, thou.
    Our wills are ours, we know not how;   *15*
Our wills are ours, to make them thine.

Our little systems have their day;
    They have their day and cease to be;
    They are but broken lights of thee,
And thou, O Lord, art more than they.   *20*

We have but faith: we cannot know,
    For knowledge is of things we see;
    And yet we trust it comes from thee,
A beam in darkness: let it grow.

Let knowledge grow from more to more,   *25*
    But more of reverence in us dwell;
    That mind and soul, according well,
May make one music as before,

But vaster. We are fools and slight;
    We mock thee when we do not fear: *30*
    But help thy foolish ones to bear;
Help thy vain worlds to bear thy light.

Forgive what seem'd my sin in me,
    What seem'd my worth since I began;

For merit lives from man to man,   *35*
And not from man, O Lord, to thee.

Forgive my grief for one removed,
   Thy creature, whom I found so fair.
   I trust he lives in thee, and there
I find him worthier to be loved.   *40*

Forgive these wild and wandering cries,
   Confusions of a wasted youth;
   Forgive them where they fail in truth,
And in thy wisdom make me wise.

Dark House, by Which Once More I Stand

Dark house, by which once more I stand
   Here in the long unlovely street,
   Doors, where my heart was used to beat
So quickly, waiting for a hand,

A hand that can be clasp'd no more —   *5*
   Behold me, for I cannot sleep,
   And like a guilty thing I creep
At earliest morning to the door.

He is not here; but far away
   The noise of life begins again,   *10*
   And ghastly thro' the drizzling rain
On the bald street breaks the blank day.

The Time Draws Near the Birth of Christ

The time draws near the birth of Christ:
   The moon is hid, the night is still;
   The Christmas bells from hill to hill
Answer each other in the mist.

Four voices of four hamlets round,   *5*
   From far and near, on mead and moor,
   Swell out and fail, as if a door
Were shut between me and the sound;

Each voice four changes on the wind,
   That now dilate, and now decrease,   *10*
   Peace and goodwill, goodwill and peace,
Peace and goodwill, to all mankind.

This year I slept and woke with pain,
  I almost wished no more to wake,
  And that my hold on life would break   *15*
Before I heard those bells again;

But they my troubled spirit rule,
  For they controlled me when a boy;
  They bring me sorrow touched with joy,
The merry, merry bells of Yule.   *20*

Oh Yet We Trust

Oh yet we trust that somehow good
  Will be the final goal of ill,
  To pangs of nature, sins of will,
Defects of doubt, and taints of blood;

That nothing walks with aimless feet;   *5*
  That not one life shall be destroy'd,
  Or cast as rubbish to the void,
When God hath made the pile complete;

That not a worm is cloven in vain;
  That not a moth with vain desire   *10*
  Is shrivell'd in a fruitless fire,
Or but subserves another's gain.

Behold, we know not anything;
  I can but trust that good shall fall
  At last—far off—at last, to all,   *15*
And every winter change to spring.

So runs my dream; but what am I?
  An infant crying in the night:
  An infant crying for the light:
And with no language but a cry.   *20*

You Say, but with No Touch of Scorn

You say, but with no touch of scorn,
  Sweet-hearted, you, whose light-blue eyes
  Are tender over drowning flies,
You tell me, doubt is Devil-born.

I know not: one indeed I knew 5
   In many a subtle question versed,
   Who touched a jarring lyre at first,
But ever strove to make it true:

Perplexed in faith, but pure in deeds,
   At last he beat his music out. 10
   There lives more faith in honest doubt,
Believe me, than in half the creeds.

He fought his doubts and gathered strength,
   He would not make his judgment blind,
   He faced the specters of the mind 15
And laid them: thus he came at length

To find a stronger faith his own;
   And Power was with him in the night,
   Which makes the darkness and the light,
And dwells not in the light alone, 20

But in the darkness and the cloud,
   As over Sinai's peaks of old,
   While Israel made their gods of gold,
Although the trumpet blew so loud.

Who Loves Not Knowledge?

Who loves not Knowledge? Who shall rail
   Against her beauty? May she mix
   With men and prosper! Who shall fix
Her pillars? Let her work prevail.

But on her forehead sits a fire; 5
   She sets her forward countenance
   And leaps into the future chance,
Submitting all things to desire.

Half-grown as yet, a child, and vain—
   She cannot fight the fear of death. 10
   What is she, cut from love and faith,
But some wild Pallas from the brain

Of demons? fiery-hot to burst
   All barriers in her onward race
   For power. Let her know her place; 15
She is the second, not the first.

A higher hand must make her mild,
  If all be not in vain, and guide
  Her footsteps, moving side by side
With Wisdom, like the younger child;   *20*

For she is earthly of the mind,
  But Wisdom heavenly of the soul.
  O friend, who camest to thy goal
So early, leaving me behind,

I would the great world grew like thee,   *25*
  Who grewest not alone in power
  And knowledge, but by year and hour
In reverence and in charity.

O Living Will That Shalt Endure

O living will that shalt endure
  When all that seems shall suffer shock,
  Rise in the spiritual rock,
Flow thro' our deeds and make them pure,

That we may lift from out of dust   *5*
  A voice as unto him that hears,
  A cry above the conquer'd years
To one that with us works, and trust,

With faith that comes of self-control,
  The truths that never can be proved   *10*
  Until we close with all we loved,
And all we flow from, soul in soul.

ROBERT BROWNING

My Last Duchess

Ferrara

That's my last Duchess painted on the wall,
Looking as if she were alive. I call
That piece a wonder, now: Frà Pandolf's hands
Worked busily a day, and there she stands.
Will't please you sit and look at her? I said   *5*

"Frà Pandolf" by design, for never read
Strangers like you that pictured countenance,
The depth and passion of its earnest glance,
But to myself they turned (since none puts by
The curtain I have drawn for you, but I)   *10*
And seemed as they would ask me, if they durst,
How such a glance came there; so, not the first
Are you to turn and ask thus. Sir, 'twas not
Her husband's presence only, called that spot
Of joy into the Duchess' cheek: perhaps   *15*
Frà Pandolf chanced to say, "Her mantle laps
Over my lady's wrist too much," or "Paint
Must never hope to reproduce the faint
Half-flush that dies along her throat": such stuff
Was courtesy, she thought, and cause enough   *20*
For calling up that spot of joy. She had
A heart—how shall I say?—too soon made glad,
Too easily impressed: she liked whate'er
She looked on, and her looks went everywhere.
Sir, 'twas all one! My favor at her breast,   *25*
The dropping of the daylight in the West,
The bough of cherries some officious fool
Broke in the orchard for her, the white mule
She rode with round the terrace—all and each
Would draw from her alike the approving speech,   *30*
Or blush, at least. She thanked men,—good! but thanked
Somehow—I know not how—as if she ranked
My gift of a nine-hundred-years-old name
With anybody's gift. Who'd stoop to blame
This sort of trifling? Even had you skill   *35*
In speech—(which I have not)—to make your will
Quite clear to such an one, and say, "Just this
Or that in you disgusts me; here you miss,
Or there exceed the mark"—and if she let
Herself be lessoned so, nor plainly set   *40*
Her wits to yours, forsooth, and made excuse,
—E'en then would be some stooping, and I choose
Never to stoop. Oh Sir, she smiled, no doubt,
Whene'er I passed her; but who passed without
Much the same smile? This grew; I gave commands;   *45*
Then all smiles stopped together. There she stands
As if alive. Will't please you rise? We'll meet
The company below, then. I repeat,
The Count your master's known munificence
Is ample warrant that no just pretence   *50*
Of mine for dowry will be disallowed;
Though his fair daughter's self, as I avowed
At starting, is my object. Nay, we'll go

Together down, sir! Notice Neptune, though,
Taming a sea-horse, thought a rarity,   *55*
Which Claus of Innsbruck cast in bronze for me!

"Childe Roland to the Dark Tower Came"

I

My first thought was, he lied in every word,
 That hoary cripple, with malicious eye
 Askance to watch the working of his lie
On mine, and mouth scarce able to afford
Suppression of the glee, that pursed and scored   *5*
 Its edge, at one more victim gained thereby.

II

What else should he be set for, with his staff?
 What, save to waylay with his lies, ensnare
 All travellers who might find him posted there,
And ask the road? I guessed what skull-like laugh   *10*
Would break, what crutch 'gin write my epitaph
 For pastime in the dusty thoroughfare,

III

If at his counsel I should turn aside
 Into that ominous tract which, all agree,
 Hides the Dark Tower. Yet acquiescingly   *15*
I did turn as he pointed: neither pride
Nor hope rekindling at the end descried,
 So much as gladness that some end might be.

IV

For, what with my whole world-wide wandering,
 What with my search drawn out thro' years, my hope   *20*
 Dwindled into a ghost not fit to cope
With that obstreperous joy success would bring,
I hardly tried now to rebuke the spring
 My heart made, finding failure in its scope.

V

As when a sick man very near to death   *25*
 Seems dead indeed, and feels begin and end
 The tears, and takes the farewell of each friend,
And hears one bid the other go, draw breath
Freelier outside ("since all is o'er," he saith,
 "And the blow fallen no grieving can amend"),   *30*

VI

While some discuss if near the other graves
    Be room enough for this, and when a day
    Suits best for carrying the corpse away,
With care about the banners, scarves and staves:
And still the man hears all, and only craves   *35*
    He may not shame such tender love and stay.

VII

Thus, I had so long suffered in this quest,
    Heard failure prophesied so oft, been writ
    So many times among "The Band"—to wit,
The knights who to the Dark Tower's search addressed   *40*
Their steps—that just to fail as they, seemed best,
    And all the doubt was now—should I be fit?

VIII

So, quiet as despair, I turned from him,
    That hateful cripple, out of his highway
    Into the path he pointed. All the day   *45*
Had been a dreary one at best, and dim
Was settling to its close, yet shot one grim
    Red leer to see the plain catch its estray.

IX

For mark! no sooner was I fairly found
    Pledged to the plain, after a pace or two,   *50*
    Than, pausing to throw backward a last view
O'er the safe road, 'twas gone; grey plain all round:
Nothing but plain to the horizon's bound.
    I might go on; nought else remained to do.

X

So, on I went. I think I never saw   *55*
    Such starved ignoble nature; nothing throve:
    For flowers—as well expect a cedar grove!
But cockle, spurge, according to their law
Might propagate their kind, with none to awe,
    You'd think; a burr had been a treasure-trove.   *60*

XI

No! penury, inertness and grimace,
    In some strange sort, were the land's portion. "See

Or shut your eyes," said Nature peevishly,
    "It nothing skills: I cannot help my case:
    'Tis the Last Judgment's fire must cure this place,   *65*
        Calcine its clods and set my prisoners free."

XII

If there pushed any ragged thistle-stalk
    Above its mates, the head was chopped; the bents
    Were jealous else. What made those holes and rents
In the dock's harsh swarth leaves, bruised as to balk   *70*
All hope of greenness? 't is a brute must walk
    Pashing their life out, with a brute's intents.

XIII

As for the grass, it grew as scant as hair
    In leprosy; thin dry blades pricked the mud
    Which underneath looked kneaded up with blood.   *75*
One stiff blind horse, his every bone a-stare,
Stood stupified, however he came there:
    Thrust out past service from the devil's stud!

XIV

Alive? he might be dead for aught I know,
    With that red gaunt and colloped neck a-strain,   *80*
    And shut eyes underneath the rusty mane;
Seldom went such grotesqueness with such woe;
I never saw a brute I hated so;
    He must be wicked to deserve such pain.

XV

I shut my eyes and turned them on my heart.   *85*
    As a man calls for wine before he fights,
    I asked one draught of earlier, happier sights,
Ere fitly I could hope to play my part.
Think first, fight afterwards—the soldier's art:
    One taste of the old time sets all to rights.   *90*

XVI

Not it! I fancied Cuthbert's reddening face
    Beneath its garniture of curly gold,
    Dear fellow, till I almost felt him fold
An arm in mine to fix me to the place,
That way he used. Alas, one night's disgrace!   *95*
    Out went my heart's new fire and left it cold.

XVII

Giles then, the soul of honour—there he stands
 Frank as ten years ago when knighted first.
 What honest man should dare (he said) he durst.
Good—but the scene shifts—faugh! what hangman hands
Pin to his breast a parchment? His own bands
 Read it. Poor traitor, spit upon and curst!

XVIII

Better this present than a past like that;
 Back therefore to my darkening path again!
 No sound, no sight as far as eye could strain.   *105*
Will the night send a howlet or a bat?
I asked: when something on the dismal flat
 Came to arrest my thoughts and change their train.

XIX

A sudden little river crossed my path
 As unexpected as a serpent comes.   *110*
 No sluggish tide congenial to the glooms;
This, as it frothed by, might have been a bath
For the fiend's glowing hoof—to see the wrath
 Of its black eddy bespate with flakes and spumes.

XX

So petty yet so spiteful! All along,   *115*
 Low scrubby alders kneeled down over it;
 Drenched willows flung them headlong in a fit
Of mute despair, a suicidal throng:
The river which had done them all the wrong,
 Whate'er that was, rolled by, deterred no whit.   *120*

XXI

Which, while I forded,—good saints, how I feared
 To set my foot upon a dead man's cheek,
 Each step, or feel the spear I thrust to seek
For hollows, tangled in his hair or beard!
—It may have been a water-rat I speared,   *125*
 But, ugh! it sounded like a baby's shriek.

XXII

Glad was I when I reached the other bank.
 Now for a better country. Vain presage!
 Who were the strugglers, what war did they wage,
Whose savage trample thus could pad the dank   *130*

Soil to a plash? Toads in a poisoned tank,
   Or wild cats in a red-hot iron cage —

XXIII

The fight must so have seemed in that fell cirque.
   What penned them there, with all the plain to choose?
   No foot-print leading to that horrid mews,   *135*
None out of it. Mad brewage set to work
Their brains, no doubt, like galley-slaves the Turk
   Pits for his pastime, Christians against Jews.

XXIV

And more than that — a furlong on — why, there!
   What bad use was that engine for, that wheel,   *140*
   Or brake, not wheel — that harrow fit to reel
Men's bodies out like silk? with all the air
Of Tophet's tool, on earth left unaware,
   Or brought to sharpen its rusty teeth of steel.

XXV

Then came a bit of stubbed ground, once a wood,   *145*
   Next a marsh, it would seem, and now mere earth
   Desperate and done with; (so a fool finds mirth,
Makes a thing and then mars it, till his mood
Changes and off he goes!) within a rood —
   Bog, clay and rubble, sand and stark black dearth.   *150*

XXVI

Now blotches rankling, coloured gay and grim,
   Now patches where some leanness of the soil's
   Broke into moss or substances like boils;
Then came some palsied oak, a cleft in him
Like a distorted mouth that splits its rim   *155*
   Gaping at death, and dies while it recoils.

XXVII

And just as far as ever from the end!
   Nought in the distance but the evening, nought
   To point my footstep further! At the thought,
A great black bird, Apollyon's bosom-friend,   *160*
Sailed past, nor beat his wide wing dragon-penned
   That brushed my cap — perchance the guide I sought.

XXVIII

For, looking up, aware I somehow grew,
   'Spite of the dusk, the plain had given place

All round to mountains—with such name to grace   *165*
Mere ugly heights and heaps now stolen in view.
How thus they had surprised me,—solve it, you!
    How to get from them was no clearer case.

XXIX

Yet half I seemed to recognize some trick
    Of mischief happened to me, God knows when—   *170*
    In a bad dream perhaps. Here ended, then,
Progress this way. When, in the very nick
Of giving up, one time more, came a click
    As when a trap shuts—you're inside the den!

XXX

Burningly it came on me all at once,   *175*
    This was the place! those two hills on the right,
    Crouched like two bulls locked horn in horn in fight;
While to the left, a tall scalped mountain . . . Dunce,
Dotard, a-dozing at the very nonce,
    After a life spent training for the sight!   *180*

XXXI

What in the midst lay but the Tower itself?
    The round squat turret, blind as the fool's heart,
    Built of brown stone, without a counterpart
In the whole world. The tempest's mocking elf
Points to the shipman thus the unseen shelf   *185*
    He strikes on, only when the timbers start.

XXXII

Not see? because of night perhaps?—why, day
    Came back again for that! before it left,
    The dying sunset kindled through a cleft:
The hills, like giants at a hunting, lay,   *190*
Chin upon hand, to see the game at bay,—
    "Now stab and end the creature—to the heft!"

XXXIII

Not hear? when noise was everywhere! it tolled
    Increasing like a bell. Names in my ears,
    Of all the lost adventurers my peers,—   *195*
How such a one was strong, and such was bold,
And such was fortunate, yet each of old
    Lost, lost! one moment knelled the woe of years.

XXXIV

There they stood, ranged along the hillsides, met
    To view the last of me, a living frame   *200*
    For one more picture! in a sheet of flame
I saw them and I knew them all. And yet
Dauntless the slug-horn to my lips I set,
    And blew. *"Childe Roland to the Dark Tower came."*

WALT WHITMAN

To the Man-of-War-Bird

Thou who has slept all night upon the storm,
Waking renew'd on thy prodigious pinions,
(Burst the wild storm? above it thou ascended'st,
And rested on the sky, thy slave that cradled thee,)
Now a blue point, far, far in heaven floating,   *5*
As to the light emerging here on deck I watch thee,
(Myself a speck, a point on the world's floating vast.)
Far, far at sea,
After the night's fierce drifts have strewn the shore with wrecks,
With reappearing day as now so happy and serene,   *10*
The rosy and elastic dawn, the flashing sun,
The limpid spread of air cerulean,
Thou also reappearest.

Thou born to match the gale, (thou art all wings,)
To cope with heaven and earth and sea and hurricane,   *15*
Thou ship of air that never furl'st thy sails,
Days, even weeks untired and onward, through spaces, realms
               gyrating,
At dusk that look'st on Senegal, at morn America,
That sport'st amid the lightning-flash and thunder-cloud,
In them, in thy experiences, had'st thou my soul,   *20*
What joys! what joys were thine!

When, Lilacs Last In The Dooryard Bloom'd

I

When lilacs last in the dooryard bloom'd,
And the great star early droop'd in the western sky in the night,
I mourn'd, and yet shall mourn with ever-returning spring.

Ever-returning spring, trinity sure to me you bring,
Lilac blooming perennial and drooping star in the west,   5
And thought of him I love.

II

O powerful western fallen star!
O shades of night—O moody, tearful night!
O great star disappear'd—O the black murk that hides the star!
O cruel hands that hold me powerless—O helpless soul of me!
O harsh surrounding cloud that will not free my soul.

III

In the dooryard fronting an old farm-house near the white-wash'd palings,
Stands the lilac-bush tall-growing with heart-shaped leaves of rich green,
With many a pointed blossom rising delicate, with the perfume strong I
      love,
With every leaf a miracle—and from this bush in the dooryard,
With delicate-color'd blossoms and heart-shaped leaves of rich green,
A sprig with its flower I break.

IV

In the swamp in secluded recesses,
A shy and hidden bird is warbling a song.
Solitary the thrush,   20
The hermit withdrawn to himself, avoiding the settlements,
Sings by himself a song.

Song of the bleeding throat,
Death's outlet song of life, (for well dear brother I know,
If thou wast not granted to sing thou would'st surely die.) 25

V

Over the breast of the spring, the land, amid cities,
Amid lanes and through old woods, where lately the violets peep'd from
      the ground, spotting the gray debris,
Amid the grass in the fields each side of the lanes, passing the endless
      grass,
Passing the yellow-spear'd wheat, every grain from its shroud in the
      dark-brown fields uprisen,
Passing the apple-tree blows of white and pink in the orchards,   30
Carrying a corpse to where it shall rest in the grave,
Night and day journeys a coffin.

VI

Coffin that passes through lanes and streets,
Through day and night with the great cloud darkening the land,

With the pomp of the inlooped flags with the cities draped in black,
With the show of the States themselves as of crepe-veiled women
    standing,
With processions long and winding and the flambeaus of the night,
With the countless torches lit, with the silent sea of faces and the
    unbared heads,
With the waiting depot, the arriving coffin, and the sombre faces,
With dirges through the night, with the thousand voices rising
    strong and solemn,   *40*
With all the mournful voices of the dirges poured around the coffin,
The dim-lit churches and the shuddering organs—where amid
    these you journey,
With the tolling tolling bells' perpetual clang,
Here, coffin that slowly passes,
I give you my sprig of lilac.

    VII

(Nor for you, for one alone,
Blossoms and branches green to coffins all I bring,
For fresh as the morning, thus would I chant a song for you O sane
    and sacred death.

All over bouquets of roses,
O death, I cover you over with roses and early lilies,   *50*
But mostly and now the lilac that blooms the first,
Copious I break, I break the sprigs from the bushes,
With loaded arms I come, pouring for you,
For you and the coffins all of you O death.)

    VIII

O western orb sailing the heaven,   *55*
Now I know what you must have meant as a month since I walk'd,
As I walk'd in silence the transparent shadowy night,
As I saw you had something to tell as you bent to me night after
    night,
As you droop'd from the sky low down as if to my side, (while the
    other stars all look'd on,)
As we wander'd together the solemn night, (for something I know
    not what kept me from sleep,)   *60*
As the night advanced, and I saw on the rim of the west how full
    you were of woe,
As I stood on the rising ground in the breeze in the cool transparent
    night,
As I watch'd where you pass'd and was lost in the netherward
    black of the night,
As my soul in its trouble dissatisfied sank, as where you sad orb,
Concluded, dropt in the night, and was gone.   *65*

IX

Sing on there in the swamp,
O singer bashful and tender, I hear your notes, I hear your call,
I hear, I come presently, I understand you,
But a moment I linger, for the lustrous star has detained me,
The star my departing comrade holds and detains me.   *70*

X

O how shall I warble myself for the dead one there I loved?
And how shall I deck my song for the large sweet soul that has
    gone?
And what shall my perfume be for the grave of him I love?
Sea-winds blown from east and west,
Blown from the Eastern sea and blown from the Western sea, till
    there on the prairies meeting,   *75*
These and with these and the breath of my chant,
I'll perfume the grave of him I love.

XI

O what shall I hang on the chamber walls?
And what shall the pictures be that I hang on the walls,
To adorn the burial-house of him I love?   *80*

Pictures of growing spring and farms and homes,
With the Fourth-month eve at sundown, and the gray smoke lucid
    and bright,
With floods of the yellow gold of the gorgeous, indolent, sinking
    sun, burning, expanding the air,
With the fresh sweet herbage under foot, and the pale green leaves
    of the trees prolific,
In the distance the flowing glaze, the breast of the river, with a
    wind-dapple here and there,   *85*
With ranging hills on the banks, with many a line against the sky,
    and shadows,
And the city at hand with dwellings so dense, and stacks of
    chimneys,
And all the scenes of life and the workshops, and the workmen
    homeward returning.

XII

Lo, body and soul—this land,
My own Manhattan with spires, and the sparkling and hurrying
    tides, and the ships,   *90*
The varied and ample land, the South and the North in the light,
    Ohio's shores and flashing Missouri,
And ever the far-spreading prairies cover'd with grass and corn.

Lo, the most excellent sun so calm and haughty,
The violet and purple morn with just-felt breezes,
The gentle soft-born measureless light,   *95*
The miracle spreading bathing all, the fulfill'd noon,
The coming eve delicious, the welcome night and the stars,
Over my cities shining all, enveloping man and land.

XIII

Sing on, sing on you gray-brown bird,
Sing from the swamps, the recesses, pour your chant from the
    bushes,   *100*
Limitless out of the dusk, out of the cedars and pines.

Sing on dearest brother, warble your reedy song,
Loud human song, with voice of uttermost woe.

O liquid and free and tender!
O wild and loose to my soul—O wondrous singer!   *105*
You only I hear—yet the star holds me, (but will soon depart),
Yet the lilac with mastering odor holds me.

XIV

Now while I sat in the day and look'd forth,
In the close of the day with its light and the fields of spring, and the
    farmers preparing their crops,
In the large unconscious scenery of my land with its lakes and
    forests,   *110*
In the heavenly aerial beauty, (after the perturb'd winds and the
    storms,)
Under the arching heavens of the afternoon swift passing, and the
    voices of children and women,
The many-moving sea-tides, and I saw the ships how they sail'd,
And the summer approaching with richness, and the fields all busy
    with labor,
And the infinite separate houses, how they all went on, each with its
    meals and minutia of daily usages,   *115*
And the streets how their throbbings throbb'd, and the cities pent—
    lo, then and there,
Falling upon them all and among them all, enveloping me with the
    rest,
Appear'd the cloud, appear'd the long black trail,
And I knew death, its thought, and the sacred knowledge of death.

Then with the knowledge of death as walking one side of me, *120*
And the thought of death close-walking the other side of me,

And I in the middle as with companions, and as holding the hands of
    companions,
I fled forth to the hiding receiving night that talks not,
Down to the shores of the water, the path by the swamp in the dimness,
To the solemn shadowy cedars and ghostly pines so still.   *125*

And the singer so shy to the rest receiv'd me,
The gray-brown bird I know receiv'd us comrades three,
And he sang the carol of death, and a verse for him I love.

From deep secluded recesses,
From the fragrant cedars and the ghostly pines so still,   *130*
Came the carol of the bird.
And the charm of the carol rapt me,
As I held as if by their hands my comrades in the night,
And the voice of my spirit tallied the song of the bird.

Come lovely and soothing death,   *135*
Undulate round the world, serenely arriving, arriving,
In the day, in the night, to all, to each,
Sooner or later delicate death.

Praised be the fathomless universe
For life and joy, and for objects and knowledge curious,
And for love, sweet love — but praise! praise! praise!
For the sure-enwinding arms of cool-enfolding death.

Dark mother always gliding near with soft feet,
Have none chanted for thee a chant of fullest welcome?
Then I chant it for thee, I glorify thee above all,   *145*
I bring thee a song that when thou must indeed come, come un-
*   falteringly.*

Approach strong deliveress,
When it is so, when thou hast taken them I joyously sing the dead,
Lost in the loving floating ocean of thee,
Laved in the flood of thy bliss O death.   *150*

From me to thee glad serenades,
Dances for thee I propose saluting thee, adornments and feastings
*   for thee,*
And the sights of the open landscape and the high-spread sky are
*   fitting,*
And life and the fields, and the huge and thoughtful night.

The night in silence under many a star,   *155*
The ocean shore and the husky whispering wave whose voice I
*   know,*

And the soul turning to thee O vast and well-veiled death,
And the body gratefully nestling close to thee.

Over the tree-tops I float thee a song,
Over the rising and sinking waves, over the myriad fields and the
*   prairies wide,*   *160*
Over the dense-packed cities all and the teeming wharves and ways,
I float this carol with joy, with joy to thee O death.

XV

To the tally of my soul,
Loud and strong kept up the gray-brown bird,
With pure deliberate notes spreading filling the night.   *165*

Loud in the pines and cedars dim,
Clear in the freshness moist and the swamp-perfume,
And I with my comrades there in the night.

While my sight that was bound in my eyes unclosed,
As to long panoramas of visions.   *170*

And I saw askant the armies,
I saw as in noiseless dreams hundreds of battle-flags,
Borne through the smoke of the battles and pierced with missiles I
      saw them,
And carried hither and yon through the smoke, and torn and
      bloody,
And at last but a few shreds left on the staffs, (and all in silence,)
And the staffs all splintered and broken.

I saw battle-corpses, myriads of them,
And the white skeletons of young men, I saw them,
I saw the debris and debris of all the slain soldiers of the war,
But I saw they were not as was thought,   *180*
They themselves were fully at rest, they suffered not,
The living remained and suffered, the mother suffered,
And the wife and the child and the musing comrade suffered,
And the armies that remained suffered.

XVI

Passing the visions, passing the night,   *185*
Passing, unloosing the hold of my comrades' hands,
Passing the song of the hermit bird and the tallying song of my
      soul,
Victorious song, death's outlet song, yet varying ever-altering song,
As low and wailing, yet clear the notes, rising and falling, flooding
      the night,

Sadly sinking and fainting, as warning and warning, and yet again
    bursting with joy,   *190*
Covering the earth and filling the spread of the heaven,
As that powerful psalm in the night I heard from recesses,
Passing, I leave thee lilac with heart-shaped leaves,
I leave thee there in the door-yard, blooming, returning with
    spring.

I cease from my song for thee,   *195*
From my gaze on thee in the west, fronting the west, communing
    with thee,
O comrade lustrous with silver face in the night.

Yet each to keep and all, retrievements out of the night,
The song, the wondrous chant of the gray-brown bird,
And the tallying chant, the echo aroused in my soul,   *200*
With the lustrous and drooping star with the countenance full of
    woe,
With the holders holding my hand hearing the call of the bird,
Comrades mine and I in the midst, and their memory ever to keep,
    for the dead I loved so well,
For the sweetest, wisest soul of all my days and lands—and this for
    his dear sake,
Lilac and star and bird twined with the chant of my soul,
There in the fragrant pines and the cedars dusk and dim.

MATTHEW ARNOLD

To Marguerite—Continued

Yes! in the sea of life enisled,
With echoing straits between us thrown,
Dotting the shoreless watery wild,
We mortal millions live *alone*.
The islands feel the enclasping flow,   *5*
And then their endless bounds they know.

But when the moon their hollows lights,
And they are swept by balms of spring,
And in their glens, on starry nights,
The nightingales divinely sing;   *10*
And lovely notes, from shore to shore,
Across the sounds and channels pour—

Oh! then a longing like despair
Is to their farthest caverns sent;

For surely once, they feel, we were   *15*
Parts of a single continent!
Now round us spreads the watery plain—
Oh might our marges meet again!

Who order'd, that their longing's fire
Should be, as soon as kindled, cool'd?   *20*
Who renders vain their deep desire?—
A God, a God their severance ruled!
And bade betwixt their shores to be
The unplumb'd, salt, estranging sea.

Dover Beach

The sea is calm to-night.
The tide is full, the moon lies fair
Upon the straits;—on the French coast, the light
Gleams and is gone; the cliffs of England stand,
Glimmering and vast, out in the tranquil bay.   *5*
Come to the window, sweet is the night-air!

Only, from the long line of spray
Where the sea meets the moon-blanch'd land,
Listen! you hear the grating roar
Of pebbles which the waves draw back, and fling,   *10*
At their return, up the high strand,
Begin, and cease, and then again begin,
With tremulous cadence slow, and bring
The eternal note of sadness in.

Sophocles long ago   *15*
Heard it on the Aegean, and it brought
Into his mind the turbid ebb and flow
Of human misery; we
Find also in the sound a thought,
Hearing it by this distant northern sea.   *20*

The Sea of Faith
Was once, too, at the full, and round earth's shore
Lay like the folds of a bright girdle furl'd.
But now I only hear
Its melancholy, long, withdrawing roar,   *25*
Retreating, to the breath
Of the night-wind, down the vast edges drear
And naked shingles of the world.

Ah, love, let us be true
To one another! for the world, which seems   *30*
To lie before us like a land of dreams,

So various, so beautiful, so new,
Hath really neither joy, nor love, nor light,
Nor certitude, nor peace, nor help for pain;
And we are here as on a darkling plain   35
Swept with confused alarms of struggle and flight,
Where ignorant armies clash by night.

The Forsaken Merman

Come, dear children, let us away;
Down and away below!
Now my brothers call from the bay,
Now the great winds shoreward blow,
Now the salt tides seaward flow;   5
Now the wild white horses play,
Champ and chafe and toss in the spray.
Children dear, let us away!
This way, this way!

Call her once before you go —   10
Call once yet!
In a voice that she will know:
"Margaret! Margaret!"
Children's voices should be dear
(Call once more) to a mother's ear;   15
Children's voices, wild with pain —
Surely she will come again!
Call her once and come away;
This way, this way!
"Mother dear, we cannot stay!   20
The wild white horses foam and fret."
Margaret! Margaret!

Come, dear children, come away down;
Call no more!
One last look at the white-walled town,   25
And the little gray church on the windy shore,
Then come down!
She will not come though you call all day;
Come away, come away!

Children dear, was it yesterday   30
We heard the sweet bells over the bay?
In the caverns where we lay,
Through the surf and through the swell,
The far-off sound of a silver bell?

Sand-strewn caverns, cool and deep,   *35*
Where the winds are all asleep;
Where the spent lights quiver and gleam,
Where the salt weed sways in the stream,
Where the sea-beasts, ranged all round,
Feed in the ooze of their pasture-ground;   *40*
Where the sea-snakes coil and twine,
Dry their mail and bask in the brine;
Where great whales come sailing by,
Sail and sail, with unshut eye,
Round the world for ever and aye?   *45*
When did music come this way?
Children dear, was it yesterday?

Children dear, was it yesterday
(Call yet once) that she went away?
Once she sate with you and me,   *50*
On a red gold throne in the heart of the sea,
And the youngest sate on her knee.
She combed its bright hair, and she tended it well,
When down swung the sound of a far-off bell.
She sighed, she looked up through the clear green sea;   *55*
She said: "I must go, for my kinsfolk pray
In the little gray church on the shore to-day.
'Twill be Easter-time in the world—ah me!
And I lose my poor soul, Merman! here with thee."
I said: "Go up, dear heart, through the waves;   *60*
Say thy prayer, and come back to the kind seacaves!"
She smiled, she went up through the surf in the bay.
Children dear, was it yesterday?

  Children dear, were we long alone?
"The sea grows stormy, the little ones moan;   *65*
Long prayers," I said, "in the world they say;
Come!" I said; and we rose through the surf in the bay.
We went up the beach, by the sandy down
Where the sea-stocks bloom, to the white-walled town;
Through the narrow paved streets, where all was still,   *70*
To the little gray church on the windy hill.
From the church came a murmur of folk at their prayers,
But we stood without in the cold blowing airs.
We climbed on the graves, on the stones worn with rains,
And we gazed up the aisle through the small leaded panes.
She sate by the pillar; we saw her clear:
"Margaret, hist! come quick, we are here!
Dear heart," I said, "we are long alone;
The sea grows stormy, the little ones moan."

But, ah, she gave me never a look,   80
For her eyes were sealed to the holy book!
Loud prays the priest; shut stands the door.
Come away, children, call no more!
Come away, come down, call no more!

   Down, down, down!   85
Down to the depths of the sea!
She sits at her wheel in the humming town,
Singing most joyfully.
Hark what she sings: "O joy, O joy,
For the humming street, and the child with its toy!   90
For the priest, and the bell, and the holy well;
For the wheel where I spun,
And the blessed light of the sun!"
And so she sings her fill,
Singing most joyfully,   95
Till the spindle drops from her hand,
And the whizzing wheel stands still.
She steals to the window, and looks at the sand,
And over the sand at the sea;
And her eyes are set in a stare;   100
And anon there breaks a sigh,
And anon there drops a tear,
From a sorrow-clouded eye,
And a heart sorrow-laden,
A long, long sigh;   105
For the cold strange eyes of a little Mermaiden
And the gleam of her golden hair.

   Come away, away, children;
Come, children, come down!
The hoarse wind blows coldly;   110
Lights shine in the town.
She will start from her slumber
When gusts shake the door;
She will hear the winds howling,
Will hear the waves roar.   115
We shall see, while above us
The waves roar and whirl,
A ceiling of amber,
A pavement of pearl.
Singing: "Here came a mortal,   120
But faithless was she!
And alone dwell forever
The kings of the sea."

But, children, at midnight,
When soft the winds blow,   125

When clear falls the moonlight,
When spring-tides are low;
When sweet airs come seaward
From heaths starred with broom,
And high rocks throw mildly   130
On the blanched sands a gloom;
Up the still, glistening beaches,
Up the creeks we will hie,
Over banks of bright seaweed
The ebb-tide leaves dry.   135
We will gaze, from the sand-hills,
At the white, sleeping town;
At the church on the hillside —
And then come back down,
Singing: "There dwells a loved one,   140
But cruel is she!
She left lonely forever
The kings of the sea."

EMILY DICKINSON

I Like a Look of Agony

I like a look of agony,
Because I know it's true;
Men do not sham convulsion,
Nor simulate a throe.

The eyes glaze once, and that is death.   5
Impossible to feign
The beads upon the forehead
By homely anguish strung.

A Narrow Fellow in the Grass

A narrow fellow in the grass
Occasionally rides;
You may have met him — did you not
His notice sudden is.

The grass divides as with a comb,   5
A spotted shaft is seen;
And then it closes at your feet
And opens further on.

He likes a boggy acre,
A floor too cool for corn.   10
Yet when a boy, and barefoot,
I more than once, at noon,

Have passed, I thought, a whip-lash
Unbraiding in the sun,
When, stooping to secure it,   15
It wrinkled, and was gone.

Several of nature's people
I know, and they know me;
I feel for them a transport
Of cordiality;   20

But never met this fellow,
Attended or alone,
Without a tighter breathing,
And zero at the bone.

A Death-Blow Is a Life-Blow

A death-blow is a life-blow to some
Who, till they died, did not alive become;
Who, had they lived, had died, but when
They died, vitality begun.

The Brain Within Its Groove

The brain within its groove
Runs evenly and true;
But let a splinter swerve,
'Twere easier for you
To put the water back   5
When floods have slit the hills,
And scooped a turnpike for themselves,
And blotted out the mills!

I Know That He Exists

I know that he exists
Somewhere, in silence.
He has hid his rare life
From our gross eyes.

'Tis an instant's play, 5
'Tis a fond ambush,
Just to make bliss
Earn her own surprise!

But should the play
Prove piercing earnest, 10
Should the glee glaze
In death's stiff stare,

Would not the fun
Look too expensive?
Would not the jest 15
Have crawled too far?

There Came a Wind Like a Bugle

There came a wind like a bugle;
It quivered through the grass,
And a green chill upon the heat
So ominous did pass
We barred the windows and the doors 5
As from an emerald ghost;
The doom's electric moccasin
That very instant passed.
On a strange mob of panting trees,
And fences fled away, 10
And rivers where the houses ran
The living looked that day.
The bell within the steeple wild
The flying tidings whirled.
How much can come 15
And much can go
And yet abide the world!

Pain Has an Element of Blank

Pain has an element of blank;
It cannot recollect
When it began, or if there were
A day when it was not.

It has no future but itself, 5
Its infinite realms contain
Its past, enlightened to perceive
New periods of pain.

I Stepped from Plank to Plank

I stepped from plank to plank
　　A slow and cautious way;
The stars about my head I felt,
　　About my feet the sea.

I knew not but the next   5
　　Would be my final inch,—
This gave me that precarious gait
　　Some call experience.

Apparently with No Surprise

Apparently with no surprise
To any happy flower,
The frost beheads it at its play
In accidental power.
The blond assassin passes on,   5
The sun proceeds unmoved
To measure off another day
For an approving God.

The Soul Selects Her Own Society

The soul selects her own society,
Then shuts the door;
To her divine majority
Present no more.

Unmoved, she notes the chariot's pausing   5
At her low gate;
Unmoved, an emperor be kneeling
Upon her mat.

I've known her from an ample nation
Choose one;   10
Then close the valves of her attention
Like stone.

A Face Devoid of Love or Grace

A face devoid of love or grace,
A hateful, hard, successful face,
A face with which a stone
Would feel as thoroughly at ease
As were they old acquaintances,—   5
First time together thrown.

GERARD MANLEY HOPKINS

The Windhover

To Christ Our Lord

I caught this morning morning's minion, king-
    dom of daylight's dauphin, dapple-dawn-drawn Falcon, in his
        riding
Of the rolling level underneath him steady air, and striding
High there, how he rung upon the rein of a wimpling wing
In his ecstasy! then off, off forth on swing,   5
    As a skate's heel sweeps smooth on a bow-bend: the hurl and
        gliding
Rebuffed the big wind. My heart in hiding
Stirred for a bird,—the achieve of, the mastery of the thing!

Brute beauty and valor and act, oh, air, pride, plume, here
    Buckle! AND the fire that breaks from thee then, a billion   *10*
Times told lovelier, more dangerous, O my chevalier!

    No wonder of it: shéer plód makes plough down sillion
Shine, and blue-bleak embers, ah my dear,
    Fall, gall themselves, and gash gold-vermilion.

Felix Randal

Felix Randal the farrier, O he is dead then? my duty all ended,
Who have watched his mold of man, big-boned and hardy-
    handsome
Pining, pining, till time when reason rambled in it and some
Fatal four disorders, fleshed there, all contended?

Sickness broke him. Impatient he cursed at first, but mended   5
Being anointed and all; though a heavenlier heart began some
Months earlier, since I had our sweet reprieve and ransom
Tendered to him. Ah well, God rest him all road ever he offended!

This seeing the sick endears them to us, us too it endears.
My tongue had taught thee comfort, touch had quenched thy tears,
Thy tears that touched my heart, child, Felix, poor Felix Randal;

How far from then forethought of, all thy more boisterous years,
When thou at the random grim forge, powerful amidst peers,
Didst fettle for the great grey drayhorse his bright and battering
    sandal!

I Wake and Feel the Fell of Dark

I wake and feel the fell of dark, not day.
What hours, O what black hoürs we have spent
This night! what sights you, heart, saw; ways you went!
And more must, in yet longer light's delay.
    With witness I speak this. But where I say   *5*
Hours I mean years, mean life. And my lament
Is cries countless, cries like dead letters sent
To dearest him that lives alas! away.

    I am gall, I am heartburn. God's most deep decree
Bitter would have me taste: my taste was me;   *10*
Bones built in me, flesh filled, blood brimmed the curse.
    Selfyeast of spirit a dull dough sours. I see
The lost are like this, and their scourge to be
As I am mine, their sweating selves; but worse.

The Caged Skylark

As a dare-gale skylark scanted in a dull cage
    Man's mounting spirit in his bone-house, mean house, dwells—
    That bird beyond the remembering his free fells;
This in drudgery, day-laboring-out life's age.

Though aloft on turf or perch or poor low stage,   *5*
    Both sing sometimes the sweetest, sweetest spells,
    Yet both droop deadly sometimes in their cells
Or wring their barriers in bursts of fear or rage.

Not that the sweet-fowl, song-fowl, needs no rest—
Why, hear him, hear him babble and drop down to his nest,
    But his own nest, wild nest, no prison.

Man's spirit will be flesh-bound when found at best,
But uncumbered: meadow-down is not distressed
    For a rainbow footing it nor he for his bones risen.

A. E. HOUSMAN

Reveille

Wake: the silver dusk returning
    Up the beach of darkness brims,

And the ship of sunrise burning
    Strands upon the eastern rims.

Wake: the vaulted shadow shatters,   *5*
    Trampled to the floor it spanned,
And the tent of night in tatters
    Straws the sky-pavilioned land.

Up, lad, up, 'tis late for lying,
    Hear the drums of morning play;   *10*
Hark, the empty highways crying,
    "Who'll beyond the hills away?"

Towns and countries woo together,
    Forelands beacon, belfries call;
Never lad that trod on leather   *15*
    Lived to feast his heart with all.

Up, lad: thews that lie and cumber
    Sunlit pallets never thrive;
Morns abed and daylight slumber
    Were not meant for man alive.   *20*

Clay lies still, but blood's a rover;
    Breath's a ware that will not keep.
Up, lad: when the journey's over
    There'll be time enough to sleep.

On Wenlock Edge

On Wenlock Edge the wood's in trouble;
    His forest fleece the Wrekin heaves;
The gale, it plies the saplings double,
    And thick on Severn snow the leaves.

'Twould blow like this through holt and hanger   *5*
    When Uricon the city stood:
'Tis the old wind in the old anger,
    But then it threshed another wood.

Then, 'twas before my time, the Roman
    At yonder heaving hill would stare: *10*
The blood that warms an English yeoman,
    The thoughts that hurt him, they were there.

There, like the wind through woods in riot,
    Through him the gale of life blew high;

The tree of man was never quiet: *15*
   Then 'twas the Roman, now 'tis I.

The gale, it plies the saplings double,
   It blows so hard, 'twill soon be gone:
To-day the Roman and his trouble
   Are ashes under Uricon.   *20*

From Far, from Eve and Morning

From far, from eve and morning
   And yon twelve-winded sky,
The stuff of life to knit me
   Blew hither; here am I.

Now — for a breath I tarry   *5*
   Nor yet disperse apart —
Take my hand quick and tell me,
   What have you in your heart.

Speak now, and I will answer;
   How shall I help you, say;
Ere to the wind's twelve quarters
   I take my endless way.

With Rue My Heart Is Laden

With rue my heart is laden
   For golden friends I had,
For many a rose-lipt maiden
   And many a lightfoot lad.

By brooks too broad for leaping   *5*
   The lightfoot boys are laid;
The rose-lipt girls are sleeping
   In fields where roses fade.

Along the Field As We Came By

   Along the field as we came by
A year ago, my love and I,
The aspen over stile and stone
Was talking to itself alone.
"Oh, who are these that kiss and pass?   *5*
A country lover and his lass;
Two lovers looking to be wed;
And time shall put them both to bed,

But she shall lie with earth above,
And he beside another love." *10*

    And sure enough beneath the tree
There walks another love with me,
And overhead the aspen heaves
Its rainy-sounding silver leaves;
And I spell nothing in their stir, *15*
But now perhaps they speak to her,
And plain for her to understand
They talk about a time at hand
When I shall sleep with clover clad,
And she beside another lad. *20*

Could Man Be Drunk Forever

Could man be drunk forever
    With liquor, love, or fights,
Lief should I rouse at morning
    And lief lie down of nights.

But men at whiles are sober *5*
    And think by fits and starts,
And if they think, they fasten
    Their hands upon their hearts.

Terence, This Is Stupid Stuff

    "Terence, this is stupid stuff:
You eat your victuals fast enough;
There can't be much amiss, 'tis clear,
To see the rate you drink your beer.
But, oh, good Lord, the verse you make, *5*
It gives a chap the belly-ache.
The cow, the old cow, she is dead;
It sleeps well, the horned head:
We poor lads, 'tis our turn now
To hear such tunes as killed the cow. *10*
Pretty friendship 'tis to rime
Your friends to death before their time
Moping melancholy mad.
Come, pipe a tune to dance to, lad."

    Why, if 'tis dancing you would be, *15*
There's brisker pipes than poetry.
Say, for what were hop-yards meant,
Or why was Burton built on Trent?

Oh, many a peer of England brews
Livelier liquor than the Muse,   *20*
And malt does more than Milton can
To justify God's ways to man.
Ale, man, ale's the stuff to drink
For fellows whom it hurts to think;
Look into the pewter pot   *25*
To see the world as the world's not.
And faith, 'tis pleasant till 'tis past:
The mischief is that 'twill not last.
Oh, I have been to Ludlow fair
And left my necktie God knows where,   *30*
And carried half way home, or near,
Pints and quarts of Ludlow beer:
Then the world seemed none so bad,
And I myself a sterling lad;
And down in lovely muck I've lain,   *35*
Happy till I woke again.
Then I saw the morning sky—
Heighho, the tale was all a lie;
The world, it was the old world yet,
I was I, my things were wet,   *40*
And nothing now remained to do
But begin the game anew.

Therefore, since the world has still
Much good, but much less good than ill,
And while the sun and moon endure   *45*
Luck's a chance, but trouble's sure.
I'd face it as a wise man would,
And train for ill and not for good.
'Tis true, the stuff I bring for sale
Is not so brisk a brew as ale: *50*
Out of a stem that scored the hand
I wrung it in a weary land.
But take it—if the smack is sour,
The better for the embittered hour;
It should do good to heart and head   *55*
When your soul is in my soul's stead;
And I will friend you, if I may,
In the dark and cloudy day.

There was a king reigned in the East:
There, when kings will sit to feast,   *60*
They get their fill before they think
With poisoned meat and poisoned drink.
He gathered all that springs to birth
From the many-venomed earth;

First a little, thence to more,   *65*
He sampled all her killing store;
And easy, smiling, seasoned sound,
Sate the king when healths went round.
They put arsenic in his meat
And stared aghast to watch him eat;   *70*
They poured strychnine in his cup
And shook to see him drink it up:
They shook, they stared as white's their shirt:
Them it was their poison hurt.
—I tell the tale that I heard told,   *75*
Mithridates, he died old.

The Chestnut Casts His Flambeaux

The chestnut casts his flambeaux, and the flowers
    Stream from the hawthorn on the wind away,
The doors clap to, the pane is blind with showers.
    Pass me the can, lad; there's an end of May.

There's one spoilt spring to scant our mortal lot,   *5*
    One season ruined of our little store.
May will be fine next year as like as not:
    Oh ay, but then we shall be twenty-four.

We for a certainty are not the first
    Have sat in taverns while the tempest hurled   *10*
Their hopeful plans to emptiness, and cursed
    Whatever brute and blackguard made the world.

It is in truth iniquity on high
    To cheat our sentenced souls of aught they crave,
And mar the merriment as you and I   *15*
    Fare on our long fool's-errand to the grave.

Iniquity it is; but pass the can.
    My lad, no pair of kings our mothers bore;
Our only portion is the estate of man:
    We want the moon, but we shall get no more.   *20*

If here today the cloud of thunder lours
    Tomorrow it will hie on far behests;
The flesh will grieve on other bones than ours
    Soon, and the soul will mourn in other breasts.

The troubles of our proud and angry dust   *25*
    Are from eternity, and shall not fail.

Bear them we can, and if we can we must.
Shoulder the sky, my lad, and drink your ale.

WILLIAM BUTLER YEATS

The Song Of Wandering Aengus

I went out to the hazel wood,
Because a fire was in my head,
And cut and peeled a hazel wand,
And hooked a berry to a thread;
And when white moths were on the wing,   5
And moth-like stars were flickering out,
I dropped the berry in a stream
And caught a little silver trout.

When I had laid it on the floor,
I went to blow the fire a-flame,   10
But something rustled on the floor,
And some one called me by my name:
It had become a glimmering girl
With apple blossom in her hair
Who called me by my name and ran   15
And faded through the brightening air.

Though I am old with wandering
Through hollow lands and hilly lands,
I will find out where she has gone,
And kiss her lips and take her hands;   20
And walk among long dappled grass,
And pluck till time and times are done,
The silver apples of the moon,
The golden apples of the sun.

No Second Troy

Why should I blame her that she filled my days
With misery, or that she would of late
Have taught to ignorant men most violent ways,
Or hurled the little streets upon the great,
Had they but courage equal to desire?   5
What could have made her peaceful with a mind
That nobleness made simple as a fire,
With beauty like a tightened bow, a kind

That is not natural in an age like this,
Being high and solitary and most stern?   *10*
Why, what could she have done, being what she is?
Was there another Troy for her to burn?

Sailing to Byzantium

I

That is no country for old men. The young
In one another's arms, birds in the trees
— Those dying generations — at their song,
The salmon-falls, the mackerel-crowded seas,
Fish, flesh, or fowl, commend all summer long   *5*
Whatever is begotten, born, and dies.
Caught in that sensual music all neglect
Monuments of unaging intellect.

II

An aged man is but a paltry thing,
A tattered coat upon a stick, unless   *10*
Soul clap its hands and sing, and louder sing
For every tatter in its mortal dress,
Nor is there singing school but studying
Monuments of its own magnificence;
And therefore I have sailed the seas and come   *15*
To the holy city of Byzantium.

III

O sages standing in God's holy fire
As in the gold mosaic of a wall,
Come from the holy fire, perne in a gyre,
And be the singing-masters of my soul.   *20*
Consume my heart away; sick with desire
And fastened to a dying animal
It knows not what it is; and gather me
Into the artifice of eternity.

IV

Once out of nature I shall never take   *25*
My bodily form from any natural thing,
But such a form as Grecian goldsmiths make
Of hammered gold and gold enamelling
To keep a drowsy Emperor awake;
Or set upon a golden bough to sing   *30*
To lords and ladies of Byzantium
Of what is past, or passing, or to come.

Leda and the Swan

A sudden blow: the great wings beating still
Above the staggering girl, her thighs caressed
By the dark webs, her nape caught in his bill,
He holds her helpless breast upon his breast.

How can those terrified vague fingers push   5
The feathered glory from her loosening thighs?
And how can body, laid in that white rush,
But feel the strange heart beating where it lies?

A shudder in the loins engenders there
The broken wall, the burning roof and tower   10
And Agamemnon dead.
                     Being so caught up,
So mastered by the brute blood of the air,
Did she put on his knowledge with his power
Before the indifferent beak could let her drop?

Among School Children

I

I walk through the long schoolroom questioning;
A kind old nun in a white hood replies;
The children learn to cipher and to sing,
To study reading-books and histories,
To cut and sew, be neat in everything   5
In the best modern way—the children's eyes
In momentary wonder stare upon
A sixty-year-old smiling public man.

II

I dream of a Ledaean body, bent
Above a sinking fire, a tale that she   10
Told of a harsh reproof, or trivial event
That changed some childish day to tragedy—
Told, and it seemed that our two natures blent
Into a sphere from youthful sympathy,
Or else, to alter Plato's parable,   15
Into the yolk and white of the one shell.

III

And thinking of that fit of grief or rage
I look upon one child or t'other there

And wonder if she stood so at that age —
For even daughters of the swan can share 20
Something of every paddler's heritage —
And had that colour upon cheek or hair,
And thereupon my heart is driven wild:
She stands before me as a living child.

IV

Her present image floats into the mind — 25
Did Quattrocento finger fashion it
Hollow of cheek as though it drank the wind
And took a mess of shadows for its meat?
And I though never of Ledaean kind
Had pretty plumage once — enough of that, 30
Better to smile on all that smile, and show
There is a comfortable kind of old scarecrow.

V

What youthful mother, a shape upon her lap
Honey of generation had betrayed,
And that must sleep, shriek, struggle to escape 35
As recollection or the drug decide,
Would think her son, did she but see that shape
With sixty or more winters on its head,
A compensation for the pang of his birth,
Or the uncertainty of his setting forth? 40

VI

Plato thought nature but a spume that plays
Upon a ghostly paradigm of things;
Solider Aristotle played the taws
Upon the bottom of a king of kings;
World-famous golden-thighed Pythagoras 45
Fingered upon a fiddle-stick or strings
What a star sang and careless Muses heard:
Old clothes upon old sticks to scare a bird.

VII

Both nuns and mothers worship images,
But those the candles light are not as those 50
That animate a mother's reveries,
But keep a marble or a bronze repose.
And yet they too break hearts — O Presences
That passion, piety or affection knows,
And that all heavenly glory symbolize — 55
O self-born mockers of man's enterprise;

VIII

Labour is blossoming or dancing where
The body is not bruised to pleasure soul,
Nor beauty born out of its own despair,
Nor blear-eyed wisdom out of midnight oil.   *60*
O chestnut tree, great rooted blossomer,
Are you the leaf, the blossom or the bole?
O body swayed to music, O brightening glance,
How can we know the dancer from the dance?

The Circus Animals' Desertion

I

I sought a theme and sought for it in vain,
I sought it daily for six weeks or so.
Maybe at last, being but a broken man,
I must be satisfied with my heart, although
Winter and summer till old age began   *5*
My circus animals were all on show,
Those stilted boys, that burnished chariot,
Lion and woman and the Lord knows what.

II

What can I but enumerate old themes?
First that sea-rider Oisin led by the nose   *10*
Through three enchanted islands, allegorical dreams,
Vain gaiety, vain battle, vain repose,
Themes of the embittered heart, or so it seems,
That might adorn old songs or courtly shows;
But what cared I that set him on to ride,   *15*
I, starved for the bosom of his faery bride?

And then a counter-truth filled out its play,
The Countess Cathleen was the name I gave it;
She, pity-crazed, had given her soul away,
But masterful Heaven had intervened to save it.   *20*
I thought my dear must her own soul destroy,
So did fanaticism and hate enslave it,
And this brought forth a dream and soon enough
This dream itself had all my thought and love.

And when the Fool and Blind Man stole the bread   *25*
Cuchulain fought the ungovernable sea;
Heart-mysteries there, and yet when all is said
It was the dream itself enchanted me:

Character isolated by a deed
To engross the present and dominate memory.   *30*
Players and painted stage took all my love,
And not those things that they were emblems of.

III

Those masterful images because complete
Grew in pure mind, but out of what began?
A mound of refuse or the sweepings of a street,   *35*
Old kettles, old bottles, and a broken can,
Old iron, old bones, old rags, that raving slut
Who keeps the till. Now that my ladder's gone,
I must lie down where all the ladders start,
In the foul rag-and-bone shop of the heart.   *40*

Chapter 17

The Range of Modern Poetry

ROBERT FROST

The Road Not Taken

Two roads diverged in a yellow wood,
And sorry I could not travel both
And be one traveler, long I stood
And looked down one as far as I could
To where it bent in the undergrowth;   5

Then took the other, as just as fair,
And having perhaps the better claim,
Because it was grassy and wanted wear;
Though as for that the passing there
Had worn them really about the same,   10

And both that morning equally lay
In leaves no step had trodden black.
Oh, I kept the first for another day!
Yet knowing how way leads on to way,
I doubted if I should ever come back.   15

I shall be telling this with a sigh
Somewhere ages and ages hence:
Two roads diverged in a wood, and I —
I took the one less traveled by,
And that has made all the difference.   20

The Onset

Always the same, when on a fated night
At last the gathered snow lets down as white
As may be in dark woods, and with a song
It shall not make again all winter long
Of hissing on the yet uncovered ground,   5
I almost stumble looking up and round,
As one who overtaken by the end
Gives up his errand, and lets death descend
Upon him where he is, with nothing done
To evil, no important triumph won,   10
More than if life had never been begun.

Yet all the precedent is on my side:
I know that winter death has never tried
The earth but it has failed: the snow may heap
In long storms an undrifted four feet deep   15
As measured against maple, birch, and oak,
It cannot check the peeper's silver croak;
And I shall see the snow all go down hill
In water of a slender April rill
That flashes tail through last year's withered brake   20
And dead weeds, like a disappearing snake.
Nothing will be left white but here a birch,
And there a clump of houses with a church.

The Most of It

He thought he kept the universe alone;
For all the voice in answer he could wake
Was but the mocking echo of his own
From some tree-hidden cliff across the lake.
Some morning from the boulder-broken beach   5
He would cry out on life, that what it wants
Is not its own love back in copy speech,
But counter-love, original response.
And nothing ever came of what he cried
Unless it was the embodiment that crashed   10
In the cliff's talus on the other side,
And then in the far distant water splashed,
But after a time allowed for it to swim,
Instead of proving human when it neared
And someone else additional to him,   15
As a great buck it powerfully appeared,
Pushing the crumpled water up ahead,

And landed pouring like a waterfall,
And stumbled through the rocks with horny tread,
And forced the underbrush—and that was all.   *20*

WALLACE STEVENS

Disillusionment of Ten O'Clock

The houses are haunted
By white night-gowns.
None are green,
Or purple with green rings,
Or green with yellow rings,   *5*
Or yellow with blue rings.
None of them are strange,
With socks of lace
And beaded ceintures.
People are not going   *10*
To dream of baboons and periwinkles.
Only, here and there, an old sailor,
Drunk and asleep in his boots,
Catches tigers
In red weather.   *15*

Peter Quince at the Clavier

I

Just as my fingers on these keys
Make music, so the self-same sounds
On my spirit make a music, too.

Music is feeling, then, not sound;
And thus it is that what I feel,   *5*
Here in this room, desiring you,

Thinking of your blue-shadowed silk,
Is music. It is like the strain
Waked in the elders by Susanna:

Of a green evening, clear and warm,   *10*
She bathed in her still garden, while
The red-eyed elders, watching, felt

The basses of their beings throb
In witching chords, and their thin blood
Pulse pizzicati of Hosanna.   *15*

II

In the green water, clear and warm,
Susanna lay.
She searched
The touch of springs,
And found   *20*
Concealed imaginings.
She sighed
For so much melody.

Upon the bank, she stood
In the cool   *25*
Of spent emotions.
She felt, among the leaves,
The dew
Of old devotions.

She walked upon the grass,   *30*
Still quavering.
The winds were like her maids,
On timid feet,
Fetching her woven scarves,
Yet wavering.   *35*

A breath upon her hand
Muted the night.
She turned—
A cymbal crashed,
And roaring horns.   *40*

III

Soon, with a noise like tambourines,
Came her attendant Byzantines.

They wondered why Susanna cried
Against the elders by her side:

And as they whispered, the refrain   *45*
Was like a willow swept by rain.

Anon, their lamps' uplifted flame
Revealed Susanna and her shame.

And then, the simpering Byzantines
Fled, with a noise like tambourines.   *50*

IV

Beauty is momentary in the mind—
The fitful tracing of a portal;
But in the flesh it is immortal.
The body dies; the body's beauty lives.
So evenings die, in their green going,   *55*
A wave, interminably flowing.
So gardens die, their meek breath scenting
The cowl of Winter, done repenting.
So maidens die to the auroral
Celebration of a maiden's choral.   *60*
Susanna's music touched the bawdy strings
Of those white elders; but, escaping,
Left only Death's ironic scraping.
Now, in its immortality, it plays
On the clear viol of her memory,   *65*
And makes a constant sacrament of praise.

The Idea of Order at Key West

She sang beyond the genius of the sea.
The water never formed to mind or voice,
Like a body wholly body, fluttering
Its empty sleeves; and yet its mimic motion
Made constant cry, caused constantly a cry,   *5*
That was not ours although we understood,
Inhuman, of the veritable ocean.

The sea was not a mask. No more was she.
The song and water were not medleyed sound
Even if what she sang was what she heard,   *10*
Since what she sang was uttered word by word.
It may be that in all her phrases stirred
The grinding water and the gasping wind;
But it was she and not the sea we heard.

For she was the maker of the song she sang.   *15*
The ever-hooded, tragic-gestured sea
Was merely a place by which she walked to sing.
Whose spirit is this? we said, because we knew
It was the spirit that we sought and knew
That we should ask this often as she sang.   *20*

If it was only the dark voice of the sea
That rose, or even colored by many waves;

If it was only the outer voice of sky
And cloud, of the sunken coral water-walled,
However clear, it would have been deep air,   25
The heaving speech of air, a summer sound
Repeated in a summer without end
And sound alone. But it was more than that,
More even than her voice, and ours, among
The meaningless plungings of water and the wind,   30
Theatrical distances, bronze shadows heaped
On high horizons, mountainous atmospheres
Of sky and sea.
           It was her voice that made
The sky acutest at its vanishing.
She measured to the hour its solitude.   35
She was the single artificer of the world
In which she sang. And when she sang, the sea,
Whatever self it had, became the self
That was her song, for she was the maker. Then we,
As we beheld her striding there alone,   40
Knew that there never was a world for her
Except the one she sang and, singing, made.

Ramon Fernandez, tell me, if you know,
Why, when the singing ended and we turned
Toward the town, tell why the glassy lights,   45
The lights in the fishing boats at anchor there,
As the night descended, tilting in the air,
Mastered the night and portioned out the sea,
Fixing emblazoned zones and fiery poles,
Arranging, deepening, enchanting night.   50

Oh! Blessed rage for order, pale Ramon,
The maker's rage to order words of the sea,
Words of the fragrant portals, dimly-starred,
And of ourselves and of our origins,
In ghostlier demarcations, keener sounds.   55

EZRA POUND

Horae Beatae Inscriptio

How will this beauty, when I am far hence,
Sweep back upon me and engulf my mind!

How will these hours, when we twain are gray,
Turned in their sapphire tide, come flooding o'er us!

The Plunge

I would bathe myself in strangeness:
These comforts heaped upon me, smother me!
I burn, I scald so for the new,
New friends, new faces,
Places!   5
Oh to be out of this,
This that is all I wanted
            — save the new.

And you,
Love, you the much, the more desired!   10
Do I not loathe all walls, streets, stones,
All mire, mist, all fog,
All ways of traffic?
You, I would have flow over me like water,
Oh, but far out of this!   15
Grass, and low fields, and hills,
And sun,
Oh, sun enough!
Out, and alone, among some
Alien people!   20

ROBINSON JEFFERS

Gale in April

Intense and terrible beauty, how has our race with the frail naked
     nerves,
So little a craft swum down from its far launching?
Why now, only because the northwest blows and the headed grass
     billows,
Great seas jagging the west and on the granite
Blanching, the vessel is brimmed, this dancing play of the world is
     too much passion.   5
A gale in April so overfilling the spirit,
Though his ribs were thick as the earth's, arches of mountain, how
     shall one dare to live,
Though his blood were like the earth's rivers and his flesh iron,
How shall one dare to live? One is born strong, how do the weak
     endure it?
The strong lean upon death as on a rock,   10
After eighty years there is shelter and the naked nerves shall be

covered with deep quietness,
O beauty of things, go on, go on, O torture
Of intense joy, I have lasted out my time, I have thanked God and
    finished,
Roots of millennial trees fold me in the darkness,
Northwest wind shake their tops, not to the root, not to the root, I have
    passed   15
From beauty to the other beauty, peace, the night splendor.

The Bloody Sire

It is not bad. Let them play.
Let the guns bark and the bombing-plane
Speak his prodigious blasphemies.
It is not bad, it is high time,
Stark violence is still the sire of all the world's values.   5

What but the wolf's tooth whittled so fine
The fleet limbs of the antelope?
What but fear winged the birds, and hunger
Jeweled with such eyes the great goshawk's head?
Violence has been the sire of all the world's values.   *10*

Who would remember Helen's face
Lacking the terrible halo of spears?
Who formed Christ but Herod and Caesar,
The cruel and bloody victories of Caesar?
Violence, the bloody sire of all the world's values.   *15*

Never weep, let them play,
Old violence is not too old to beget new values.

MARIANNE MOORE

The Mind Is an Enchanting Thing

is an enchanted thing
    like the glaze on a
katydid-wing
        subdivided by sun
        till the nettings are legion.   5
Like Gieseking playing Scarlatti;

like the apteryx-awl

as a beak, or the
kiwi's rain-shawl
  of haired feathers, the mind   *10*
  feeling its way as though blind,
walks along with its eyes on the ground.

It has memory's ear
  that can hear without
having to hear.   *15*
  Like the gyroscope's fall,
  truly unequivocal
because trued by regnant certainty,

it is a power of
  strong enchantment. It   *20*
is like the dove-
  neck animated by
  sun; it is memory's eye;
it's conscientious inconsistency.

It tears off the veil; tears   *25*
  the temptation, the
mist the heart wears,
  from its eyes, — if the heart
  has a face; it takes apart
dejection. It's fire in the dove-neck's   *30*

iridescence; in the
  inconsistencies
of Scarlatti.
  Unconfusion submits
  its confusion to proof; it's   *35*
not a Herod's oath that cannot change.

T. S. ELIOT

Preludes

I

The winter evening settles down
With smell of steaks in passageways.
Six o'clock.
The burnt-out ends of smoky days.

And now a gusty shower wraps 5
The grimy scraps
Of withered leaves about your feet
And newspapers from vacant lots;
The showers beat
On broken blinds and chimney-pots, 10
And at the corner of the street
A lonely cab-horse steams and stamps.
And then the lighting of the lamps.

II

The morning comes to consciousness
Of faint stale smells of beer 15
From the sawdust-trampled street
With all its muddy feet that press
To early coffee-stands.
With the other masquerades
That time resumes, 20
One thinks of all the hands
That are raising dingy shades
In a thousand furnished rooms.

III

You tossed a blanket from the bed,
You lay upon your back, and waited; 25
You dozed, and watched the night revealing
The thousand sordid images
Of which your soul was constituted;
They flickered against the ceiling.
And when all the world came back 30
And the light crept up between the shutters
And you heard the sparrows in the gutters,
You had such a vision of the street
As the street hardly understands;
Sitting along the bed's edge, where 35
You curled the papers from your hair,
Or clasped the yellow soles of feet
In the palms of both soiled hands.

IV

His soul stretched tight across the skies
That fade behind a city block, 40
Or trampled by insistent feet
At four and five and six o'clock;
And short square fingers stuffing pipes,
And evening newspapers, and eyes

Assured of certain certainties,   *45*
The conscience of a blackened street
Impatient to assume the world.

I am moved by fancies that are curled
Around these images, and cling:
The notion of some infinitely gentle   *50*
Infinitely suffering thing.

Wipe your hand across your mouth, and laugh;
The worlds revolve like ancient women
Gathering fuel in vacant lots.

The Love Song of J. Alfred Prufrock

> *S'io credesse che mia risposta fosse*
> *A persona che mai tornasse al mondo,*
> *Questa fiamma staria senza piu scosse.*
> *Ma perciocche giammai di questo fondo*
> *Non torno vivo alcun, s'i'odo il vero,*
> *Senza tema d'infamia ti rispondo.*

Let us go then, you and I,
When the evening is spread out against the sky
Like a patient etherized upon a table;
Let us go, through certain half-deserted streets,
The muttering retreats   *5*
Of restless nights in one-night cheap hotels
And sawdust restaurants with oyster-shells:
Streets that follow like a tedious argument
Of insidious intent
To lead you to an overwhelming question. . . .   *10*
Oh, do not ask, "What is it?"
Let us go and make our visit.

In the room the women come and go
Talking of Michelangelo.

The yellow fog that rubs its back upon the window-panes,
The yellow smoke that rubs its muzzle on the window-panes
Licked its tongue into the corners of the evening,
Lingered upon the pools that stand in drains,
Let fall upon its back the soot that falls from chimneys,
Slipped by the terrace, made a sudden leap,   *20*
And seeing that it was a soft October night,
Curled once about the house, and fell asleep.

And indeed there will be time
For the yellow smoke that slides along the street,
Rubbing its back upon the window-panes;   *25*
There will be time, there will be time
To prepare a face to meet the faces that you meet;
There will be time to murder and create,
And time for all the works and days of hands
That lift and drop a question on your plate;   *30*
Time for you and time for me,
And time yet for a hundred indecisions,
And for a hundred visions and revisions,
Before the taking of a toast and tea.

In the room the women come and go   *35*
Talking of Michelangelo.

And indeed there will be time
To wonder, "Do I dare?" and, "Do I dare?"
Time to turn back and descend the stair,
With a bald spot in the middle of my hair —   *40*
(They will say: "How his hair is growing thin!")
My morning coat, my collar mounting firmly to the chin,
My necktie rich and modest, but asserted by a simple pin —
(They will say: "But how his arms and legs are thin!")
Do I dare   *45*
Disturb the universe?
In a minute there is time
For decisions and revisions which a minute will reverse.

For I have known them all already, known them all:
Have known the evenings, mornings, afternoons,   *50*
I have measured out my life with coffee spoons;
I know the voices dying with a dying fall
Beneath the music from a farther room.
    So how should I presume?

And I have known the eyes already, known them all —   *55*
The eyes that fix you in a formulated phrase,
And when I am formulated, sprawling on a pin,
When I am pinned and wriggling on the wall,
Then how should I begin
To spit out all the butt-ends of my days and ways?   *60*
    And how should I presume?

And I have known the arms already, known them all —
Arms that are braceleted and white and bare

(But in the lamplight, downed with light brown hair!)
Is it perfume from a dress   *65*
That makes me so digress?
Arms that lie along a table, or wrap about a shawl,
   And should I then presume?
   And how should I begin?

Shall I say, I have gone at dusk through narrow streets   *70*
And watched the smoke that rises from the pipes
Of lonely men in shirt-sleeves, leaning out of windows? . . .

I should have been a pair of ragged claws
Scuttling across the floors of silent seas.

And the afternoon, the evening, sleeps so peacefully!   *75*
Smoothed by long fingers,
Asleep . . . tired . . . or it malingers,
Stretched on the floor, here beside you and me.
Should I, after tea and cakes and ices,
Have the strength to force the moment to its crisis?   *80*
But though I have wept and fasted, wept and prayed,
Though I have seen my head (grown slightly bald) brought in upon
      a platter,
I am no prophet—and here's no great matter;
I have seen the moment of my greatness flicker,
And I have seen the eternal Footman hold my coat, and snicker,
And in short, I was afraid.

And would it have been worth it, after all,
After the cups, the marmalade, the tea,
Among the porcelain, among some talk of you and me,
Would it have been worth while,   *90*
To have bitten off the matter with a smile,
To have squeezed the universe into a ball
To roll it toward some overwhelming question,
To say: "I am Lazarus, come from the dead,
Come back to tell you all, I shall tell you all"—   *95*
If one, settling a pillow by her head,
   Should say: "That is not what I meant at all,
   That is not it, at all."

And would it have been worth it, after all,
Would it have been worth while,   *100*
After the sunsets and the dooryards and the sprinkled streets,

After the novels, after the teacups, after the skirts that trail along
    the floor—
And this, and so much more?—
It is impossible to say just what I mean!
But as if a magic lantern threw the nerves in patterns on a screen:
Would it have been worth while
If one, settling a pillow or throwing off a shawl,
And turning toward the window, should say:
    "That is not it at all,
    That is not what I meant, at all."   *110*

No! I am not Prince Hamlet, nor was meant to be;
Am an attendant lord, one that will do
To swell a progress, start a scene or two,
Advise the prince; no doubt, an easy tool,
Deferential, glad to be of use,   *115*
Politic, cautious, and meticulous;
Full of high sentence, but a bit obtuse;
At times, indeed, almost ridiculous—
Almost, at times, the Fool.

I grow old. . . . I grow old. . . .   *120*
I shall wear the bottoms of my trousers rolled.

Shall I part my hair behind? Do I dare to eat a peach?
I shall wear white flannel trousers, and walk upon the beach.
I have heard the mermaids singing, each to each.

I do not think that they will sing to me.   *125*

I have seen them riding seaward on the waves
Combing the white hair of the waves blown back
When the wind blows the water white and black.

We have lingered in the chambers of the sea
By sea-girls wreathed with seaweed red and brown   *130*
Till human voices wake us, and we drown.

Gerontion

> *Thou hast nor youth nor age*
> *But as it were an after dinner sleep*
> *Dreaming of both.*

Here I am, an old man in a dry month,
Being read to by a boy, waiting for rain.

I was neither at the hot gates
Nor fought in the warm rain
Nor knee deep in the salt marsh, heaving a cutlass,   *5*
Bitten by flies, fought.
My house is a decayed house,
And the jew squats on the window sill, the owner,
Spawned in some estaminet of Antwerp,
Blistered in Brussels, patched and peeled in London.   *10*
The goat coughs at night in the field overhead;
Rocks, moss, stonecrop, iron, merds.
The woman keeps the kitchen, makes tea,
Sneezes at evening, poking the peevish gutter.
                     I an old man,   *15*
A dull head among windy spaces.

    Signs are taken for wonders. "We would see a sign!"
The word within a word, unable to speak a word,
Swaddled with darkness. In the juvescence of the year
Came Christ the tiger   *20*

In depraved May, dogwood and chestnut, flowering judas,
To be eaten, to be divided, to be drunk
Among whispers; by Mr. Silvero
With caressing hands, at Limoges
Who walked all night in the next room;   *25*
By Hakagawa, bowing among the Titians;
By Madame de Tornquist, in the dark room
Shifting the candles; Fräulein von Kulp
Who turned in the hall, one hand on the door.
    Vacant shuttles   *30*
Weave the wind. I have no ghosts,
An old man in a draughty house
Under a windy knob.

After such knowledge, what forgiveness? Think now
History has many cunning passages, contrived corridors   *35*
And issues, deceives with whispering ambitions,
Guides us by vanities. Think now
She gives when our attention is distracted
And what she gives, gives with such supple confusions
That the giving famishes the craving. Gives too late   *40*
What's not believed in, or if still believed,
In memory only, reconsidered passion. Gives too soon
Into weak hands, what's thought can be dispensed with
Till the refusal propagates a fear. Think
Neither fear nor courage saves us. Unnatural vices   *45*
Are fathered by our heroism. Virtues

Are forced upon us by our impudent crimes.
These tears are shaken from the wrath-bearing tree.

The tiger springs in the new year. Us he devours.
  Think at last
We have not reached conclusion, when I   *50*
Stiffen in a rented house. Think at last
I have not made this show purposelessly
And it is not by any concitation
Of the backward devils.
I would meet you upon this honestly.   *55*
I that was near your heart was removed therefrom
To lose beauty in terror, terror in inquisition.
I have lost my passion: why should I need to keep it
Since what is kept must be adulterated?
I have lost my sight, smell, hearing, taste, and touch: *60*
How should I use them for your closer contact?

These with a thousand small deliberations
Protract the profit of their chilled delirium,
Excite the membrane, when the sense has cooled,
With pungent sauces, multiply variety   *65*
In a wilderness of mirrors. What will the spider do,
Suspend its operations, will the weevil
Delay? De Bailhache, Fresca, Mrs. Cammel, whirled
Beyond the circuit of the shuddering Bear
In fractured atoms. Gull against the wind, in the windy straits
Of Belle Isle, or running on the Horn,
White feathers in the snow, the Gulf claims,
And an old man driven by the Trades
To a sleepy corner.

                       Tenants of the house,   *75*
Thoughts of a dry brain in a dry season.

ARCHIBALD MACLEISH

Epistle to Be Left in the Earth

  . . . It is colder now
               there are many stars
                        we are drifting

North by the Great Bear
                    the leaves are falling   *5*
The water is stone in the scooped rocks
                              to southward
Red sun grey air
              the crows are
Slow on their crooked wings   *10*
                        the jays have left us
Long since we passed the flares of Orion
Each man believes in his heart he will die
Many have written last thoughts and last letters
None know if our deaths are now or forever   *15*
None know if this wandering earth will be found

We lie down and the snow covers our garments
I pray you
              you (if any open this writing)
Make in your mouths the words that were our names   *20*
I will tell you all we have learned
                              I will tell you everything
The earth is round
                    there are springs under the orchards
The loam cuts with a blunt knife   *25*
                              beware of
Elms in thunder
                    the lights in the sky are stars
We think they do not see
                              we think also   *30*
The trees do not know nor the leaves of the grasses
                                        hear us
The birds too are ignorant
                        Do not listen
Do not stand at dark in the open windows   *35*
We before you have heard this
                              they are voices
They are not words at all but the wind rising
Also none among us has seen God
(. . . We have thought often   *40*
The flaws of sun in the late and driving weather
Pointed to one tree but it was not so.)
As for the nights I warn you the nights are dangerous
The wind changes at night and the dreams come

It is very cold   *45*
                    there are strange stars near Arcturus

Voices are crying an unknown name in the sky

E. E. CUMMINGS

In Just

in Just-
spring   when the world is mud-
luscious the little
lame balloonman

whistles   far   and wee   *5*

and eddieandbill come
running from marbles and
piracies and it's
spring

when the world is puddle-wonderful   *10*

the queer
old balloonman whistles
far   and   wee
and bettyandisbel come dancing

from hop-scotch and jump-rope and   *15*

it's
spring
and
    the

      goat-footed   *20*

balloonMan   whistles
far
and
wee

Poem, or Beauty Hurts Mr. Vinal

take it from me kiddo
believe me
my country, 'tis of

you, land of the Cluett
Shirt Boston Garter and Spearmint   *5*
Girl With The Wrigley Eyes (of you

land of the Arrow Ide
and Earl &
Wilson
Collars) of you i   *10*
sing:land of Abraham Lincoln and Lydia E. Pinkham,
land above all of Just Add Hot Water And Serve —
from every B. V. D.

let freedom ring

amen. i do however protest, anent the un   *15*
-spontaneous and otherwise scented merde which
greets one (Everywhere Why) as divine poesy per
that and this radically defunct periodical. i would

suggest that certain ideas gestures
rhymes, like Gillette Razor Blades   *20*
having been used and reused
to the mystical moment of dullness emphatically are
Not To Be Resharpened. (Case in point

if we are to believe these gently O sweetly
melancholy trillers amid the thrillers   *25*
these crepuscular violinists among my and your
skyscrapers — Helen & Cleopatra were Just Too Lovely,
The Snail's On The Thorn enter Morn and God's
In His andsoforth

do you get me?) according   *30*
to such supposedly indigenous
throstles Art is O World O Life
a formula: example, Turn Your Shirttails Into
Drawers and If It Isn't An Eastman It Isn't A
Kodak therefore my friends let   *35*
us now sing each and all fortissimo A-
mer
i

ca, I
love,   *40*
You. And there're a
hun-dred-mil-lion-oth-ers, like
all of you successfully if
delicately gelded (or spaded)
gentlemen (and ladies) — pretty   *45*

littleliverpill-
hearted-Nujolneeding-There's-A-Reason
americans (who tensetendoned and with
upward vacant eyes, painfully
perpetually crouched, quivering, upon the   *50*
sternly allotted sandpile
—how silently
emit a tiny violetflavoured nuisance: Odor?

ono.
comes out like a ribbon lies flat on the brush   *55*

LOUISE BOGAN

Women

Women have no wilderness in them,
They are provident instead,
Content in the tight hot cell of their hearts
To eat dusty bread.

They do not see cattle cropping red winter grass,   *5*
They do not hear
Snow water going down under culverts
Shallow and clear.

They wait, when they should turn to journeys,
They stiffen, when they should bend.   *10*
They use against themselves that benevolence
To which no man is friend.

They cannot think of so many crops to a field
Or of clean wood cleft by an ax.
Their love is an eager meaninglessness   *15*
Too tense, or too lax.

They hear in every whisper that speaks to them
A shout and a cry.
As like as not, when they take life over their door-sills
They should let it go by.   *20*

HART CRANE

Proem: To Brooklyn Bridge

How many dawns, chill from his rippling rest
The seagull's wings shall dip and pivot him,
Shedding white rings of tumult, building high
Over the chained bay waters Liberty—

Then, with inviolate curve, forsake our eyes   5
As apparitional as sails that cross
Some page of figures to be filed away;
—Till elevators drop us from our day . . .

I think of cinemas, panoramic sleights
With multitudes bent toward some flashing scene   10
Never disclosed, but hastened to again,
Foretold to other eyes on the same screen;

And Thee, across the harbor, silver-paced
As though the sun took step of thee, yet left
Some motion ever unspent in thy stride,—   15
Implicitly thy freedom staying thee!

Out of some subway scuttle, cell or loft
A bedlamite speeds to thy parapets,
Tilting there momently, shrill shirt ballooning,
A jest falls from the speechless caravan.   20

Down Wall, from girder into street noon leaks,
A rip-tooth of the sky's acetylene;
All afternoon the cloud-flown derricks turn . . .
Thy cables breathe the North Atlantic still.

And obscure as that heaven of the Jews,   25
Thy guerdon . . . Accolade thou dost bestow
Of anonymity time cannot raise:
Vibrant reprieve and pardon thou dost show.

O harp and altar, of the fury fused,
(How could mere toil align thy choiring strings!)   30
Terrific threshold of the prophet's pledge,
Prayer of pariah, and the lover's cry,—

Again the traffic lights that skim thy swift
Unfractioned idiom, immaculate sigh of stars,

Beading thy path—condense eternity: *35*
And we have seen night lifted in thine arms.

Under thy shadow by the piers I waited;
Only in darkness is thy shadow clear.
The City's fiery parcels all undone,
Already snow submerges an iron year . . .   *40*

O Sleepless as the river under thee,
Vaulting the sea, the prairies' dreaming sod,
Unto us lowliest sometime sweep, descend
And of the curveship lend a myth to God.

RICHARD EBERHART

Go to the Shine That's on a Tree

Go to the shine that's on a tree
When dawn has laved with liquid light
With luminous light the nighted tree
And take that glory without fright.

Go to the song that's in a bird   *5*
When he has seen the glistening tree,
That glorious tree the bird has heard
Give praise for its felicity.

Then go to the earth and touch it keen,
Be tree and bird, be wide aware   *10*
Be wild aware of light unseen,
And unheard song along the air.

The Horse Chestnut Tree

Boys in sporadic but tenacious droves
Come with sticks, as certainly as Autumn,
To assault the great horse chestnut tree.

There is a law governs their lawlessness.
Desire is in them for a shining amulet   *5*
And the best are those that are highest up.

They will not pick them easily from the ground.
With shrill arms they fling to the higher branches,
To hurry the work of nature for their pleasure.

I have seen them trooping down the street   *10*
Their pockets stuffed with chestnuts shucked, unshucked.
It is only evening keeps them from their wish.

Sometimes I run out in a kind of rage
To chase the boys away; I catch an arm,
Maybe, and laugh to think of being the lawgiver.   *15*

I was once such a young sprout myself
And fingered in my pocket the prize and trophy.
But still I moralize upon the day

And see that we, outlaws on God's property,
Fling out imagination beyond the skies,   *20*
Wishing a tangible good from the unknown.

And likewise death will drive us from the scene
With the great flowering world unbroken yet,
Which we held in idea, a little handful.

W. H. AUDEN

Something Is Bound to Happen

Doom is dark and deeper than any sea-dingle.
Upon what man it fall
In spring, day-wishing flowers appearing,
Avalanche sliding, white snow from rock-face,
That he should leave his house,   *5*
No cloud-soft hand can hold him, restraint by women;
But ever that man goes
Through place-keepers, through forest trees,
A stranger to strangers over undried sea,
Houses for fishes, suffocating water,   *10*
Or lonely on fell as chat,
By pot-holed becks
A bird stone-haunting, an unquiet bird.

There head falls forward, fatigued at evening,
And dreams of home,   *15*
Waving from window, spread of welcome,

Kissing of wife under single sheet;
But waking sees
Bird-flocks nameless to him, through doorway voices
Of new men making another love.   *20*

Save him from hostile capture,
From sudden tiger's spring at corner;
Protect his house,
His anxious house where days are counted
From thunderbolt protect,   *25*
From gradual ruin spreading like a stain;
Converting number from vague to certain,
Bring joy, bring day of his returning,
Lucky with day approaching, with leaning dawn.

Paysage Moralisé

Hearing of harvests rotting in the valleys,
Seeing at end of street the barren mountains,
Round corners coming suddenly on water,
Knowing them shipwrecked who were launched for islands,
We honour founders of these starving cities   *5*
Whose honour is the image of our sorrow,

Which cannot see its likeness in their sorrow
That brought them desperate to the brink of valleys;
Dreaming of evening walks through learned cities
They reined their violent horses on the mountains,   *10*
Those fields like ships to castaways on islands,
Visions of green to them who craved for water.

They built by rivers and at night the water
Running past windows comforted their sorrow;
Each in his little bed conceived of islands   *15*
Where every day was dancing in the valleys
And all the green trees blossomed on the mountains
Where love was innocent, being far from cities.

But dawn came back and they were still in cities;
No marvellous creature rose up from the water;   *20*
There was still gold and silver in the mountains
But hunger was a more immediate sorrow,
Although to moping villagers in valleys
Some waving pilgrims were describing islands . . .

'The gods,' they promise, 'visit us from islands,   *25*
Are stalking, head-up, lovely, through our cities;

Now is the time to leave your wretched valleys
And sail with them across the lime-green water,
Sitting at their white sides, forget your sorrow,
The shadow cast across your lives by mountains.'   *30*

So many, doubtful, perished in the mountains,
Climbing up crags to get a view of islands,
So many, fearful, took with them their sorrow
Which stayed them when they reached unhappy cities,
So many, careless, dived and drowned in water,   *35*
So many, wretched, would not leave their valleys.

It is our sorrow. Shall it melt? Ah, water
Would gush, flush, green these mountains and these valleys,
And we rebuild our cities, not dream of islands.

THEODORE ROETHKE

Elegy for Jane

(My student, thrown by a horse)

I remember the neckcurls, limp and damp as tendrils;
And her quick look, a sidelong pickerel smile;
And how, once startled into talk, the light syllables leaped for
    her,
And she balanced in the delight of her thought,
A wren, happy, tail into the wind,   *5*
Her song trembling the twigs and small branches.
The shade sang with her;
The leaves, their whispers turned to kissing,
And the mould sang in the bleached valleys under the rose.

Oh, when she was sad, she cast herself down into such a pure
    depth,   *10*
Even a father could not find her:
Scraping her cheek against straw,
Stirring the clearest water.

My sparrow, you are not here,
Waiting like a fern, making a spiney shadow.   *15*
The sides of wet stones cannot console me,
Nor the moss, wound with the last light.

If only I could nudge you from this sleep,
My maimed darling, my skittery pigeon.
Over this damp grave I speak the words of my love: *20*
I, with no rights in this matter,
Neither father nor lover.

ELIZABETH BISHOP

The Imaginary Iceberg

We'd rather have the iceberg than the ship,
Although it meant the end of travel.
Although it stood stock still like cloudy rock
And all the sea were moving marble.
We'd rather have the iceberg than the ship;   *5*
We'd rather own this breathing plain of snow
Though the ship's sails were laid upon the sea
As the snow lies undissolved upon the water.
O solemn, floating field,
Are you aware an iceberg takes repose   *10*
With you, and when it wakes may pasture on your snows?

This is a scene a sailor'd give his eyes for.
The ship's ignored. The iceberg rises
And sinks again; its glassy pinnacles
Correct elliptics in the sky.   *15*
This is a scene where he who treads the boards
Is artlessly rhetorical. The curtain
Is light enough to rise on finest ropes
That airy twists of snow provide.
The wits of these white peaks   *20*
Spar with the sun. Its weight the iceberg dares
Upon a shifting stage and stands and stares.

This iceberg cuts its facets from within.
Like jewelry from a grave
It saves itself perpetually and adorns   *25*
Only itself, perhaps the snows
Which so surprise us lying on the sea.
Goodbye, we say, goodbye, the ship steers off
Where waves give in to one another's waves
And clouds run in a warmer sky.   *30*
Icebergs behoove the soul
(Both being self-made from elements least visible)
To see them so: fleshed, fair, erected indivisible.

BROTHER ANTONINUS

The Stranger

Pity this girl.
At callow sixteen,
Glib in the press of rapt companions,
She bruits her smatter,
Her bed-lore brag.   5
She prattles the lip-learned, light-love list.
In the new itch and squirm of sex,
How can she foresee?

How can she foresee the thick stranger,
Over the hills from Omaha,   10
Who will break her across a hired bed,
Open the loins,
Rive the breach,
And set the foetus wailing within the womb,
To hunch toward the knowledge of its disease,   15
And shamble down time to doomsday?

The Making of the Cross

Rough fir, hauled from the hills. And the tree it had been,
Lithe-limbed, wherein the wren had nested,
Whereon the red hawk and the grey
Rested from flight, and the raw-head vulture
Shouldered to his feed — that tree went over   5
Bladed down with a double-bitted axe; was snaked with winches;
The wedge split it; hewn with the adze
It lay to season toward its use.

So too with the nails: milleniums under the earth,
Pure ore; chunked out with picks; the nail-shape   10
Struck in the pelt-lunged forge; tonged to a cask
And the wait against that work.

Even the thorn-bush flourished from afar,
As do the flourishing generations of its kind,
Filling the shallow soil no one wants;   15
Wind-sown, it cuts the cattle and the wild horse;
It tears the cloth of man, and hurts his hand.

Just as in life the good things of the earth
Are patiently assembled: some from here, some from there;

Wine from the hill and wheat from the valley;   *20*
Rain that comes blue-bellied out of the sopping sea;
Snow that keeps its drift on the gooseberry ridge,
Will melt with May, go down, take the egg of the salmon,
Serve the traffic of otters and fishes,
Be ditched to orchards . . .   *25*

So too are gathered up the possibles of evil.

And when the Cross was joined, quartered,
As is the earth; spoked, as is the Universal Wheel—
Those radials that led all unregenerate act
Inward to innocence—it met the thorn-wove Crown;   *30*
It found the Scourges and the Dice;
The Nail was given and the reed-lifted Sponge;
The Curse caught forward out of the heart corrupt;
The excoriate Foul, stoned with the thunder and the hail—
All these made up that miscellaneous wrath   *35*
And were assumed.

The evil and the wastage and the woe,
As if the earth's old cyst, back down the slough
To Adam's sin-burnt calcinated bones
Rushed out of time and clotted on the Cross.   *40*

Off there the cougar
Coughed in passion when the sun went out; the rattler
Filmed his glinty eye, and found his hole.

DELMORE SCHWARTZ

She Was the Girl Within the Picture Frame

Sometimes the girl on boyhood's silver screen
—The surface makes me nervous as a cat—
Sometimes the girl Vermeer once marveled at,
For there is in her face the famous queen
Who makes all other ladies seem unseen   *5*
—Sometimes the Countess in the minuet
By Mozart, hopelessly her laureate,
—Darkling, I hardly know just what I mean.

The expensive suburb has began to rot.
The latest boys and girls, full of the ache   *10*

Of being, are knocking at the gate,
As if a deathless day began to dawn,
Old immortality their natural lot:
—This news is meaningless. For she was born,
Look, in some other world!—and you were not!   *15*

The Self Unsatisfied Runs Everywhere

Sunday and sunlight ashen on the Square,
Hard wind, high blue, and clouded pennant sky,
Fifth Avenue empty in the autumn air,
As if a clear photograph of a dead day.
It was the Lord's day once, solemn and full   *5*
—Now I in an aftermath, desire spent,
Move with a will appeased and see a gull,
Then gulls drop from an arch—scythes of descent!—

Having, I think, no wish beyond the foam
Toppling to them at each fresh exercise,   *10*
Knowing success like fountains, perhaps more wise
Than one who hesitantly writes a poem
—But who, being human, wishes to be a gull,
Knows nothing much, though birds are beautiful.

KARL SHAPIRO

The Minute

The office building treads the marble dark,
The mother-clock with wide and golden dial
Suffers and glows. Now is the hour of birth
Of the tremulous egg. Now is the time of correction.
O midnight, zero of eternity,   *5*
Soon on a million bureaus of the city
Will lie the new-born minute.

The new-born minute on the bureau lies,
Scratching the glass with infant kick, cutting
With diamond cry the crystal and expanse   *10*
Of timelessness. This pretty tick of death
Etches its name upon the air. I turn
Titanically in distant sleep, expelling
From my lungs the bitter gas of life.

The loathsome minute grows in length and strength,   *15*
Bending its spring to forge an iron hour
That rusts from link to link, the last one bright,
The late one dead. Between the shining works
Range the clean angels, studying that tick
Like a strange dirt, but will not pick it up.   *20*
Nor move it gingerly out of harm's way.

An angel is stabbed and is carried aloft howling,
For devils have gathered on a ruby jewel
Like red mites on a berry; others arrive
To tend the points with oil and smooth the heat.   *25*
See how their vicious faces, lit with sweat,
Worship the train of wheels; see how they pull
The tape-worm Time from nothing into thing.

I with my distant heart lie wide awake
Smiling at that Swiss-perfect engine room   *30*
Driven by tiny evils. Knowing no harm
Even of gongs that loom and move in towers,
And hands as high as iron masts, I sleep,
At which sad sign the angels in a flock
Rise and sweep past me, spinning threads of fear.   *35*

DYLAN THOMAS

The Force That Through the Green
Fuse Drives the Flower

The force that through the green fuse drives the flower
Drives my green age; that blasts the roots of trees
Is my destroyer.
And I am dumb to tell the crooked rose
My youth is bent by the same wintry fever.   *5*

The force that drives the water through the rocks
Drives my red blood; that dries the mouthing streams
Turns mine to wax.
And I am dumb to mouth unto my veins
How at the mountain spring the same mouth sucks.   *10*

The hand that whirls the water in the pool
Stirs the quicksand; that ropes the blowing wind
Hauls my shroud sail.

And I am dumb to tell the hanging man
How of my clay is made the hangman's lime.   *15*

The lips of time leech to the fountain head;
Love drips and gathers, but the fallen blood
Shall calm her sores.
And I am dumb to tell a weather's wind
How time has ticked a heaven round the stars.   *20*
And I am dumb to tell the lover's tomb
How at my sheet goes the same crooked worm.

Fern Hill

Now as I was young and easy under the apple boughs
About the lilting house and happy as the grass was green,
  The night above the dingle starry,
    Time let me hail and climb
  Golden in the heydays of his eyes,   *5*
And honoured among wagons I was prince of the apple towns
And once below a time I lordly had the trees and leaves
    Trail with daisies and barley
  Down the rivers of the windfall light.

And as I was green and carefree, famous among the barns *10*
About the happy yard and singing as the farm was home,
  In the sun that is young once only,
  Time let me play and be
Golden in the mercy of his means,
And green and golden I was huntsman and herdsman, the calves
Sang to my horn, the foxes on the hills barked clear and cold,
    And the sabbath rang slowly
  In the pebbles of the holy streams.

All the sun long it was running, it was lovely, the hay-
Fields high as the house, the tunes from the chimneys, it was air
  And playing, lovely and watery
    And fire green as grass.
  And nightly under the simple stars
As I rode to sleep the owls were bearing the farm away,
All the moon long I heard, blessed among stables, the nightjars
  Flying with the ricks, and the horses
    Flashing into the dark.

And then to awake, and the farm, like a wanderer white
With the dew, come back, the cock on his shoulder: it was all
  Shining, it was Adam and maiden,   *30*

The sky gathered again
And the sun grew round that very day.
So it must have been after the birth of the simple light
In the first, spinning place, the spellbound horses walking warm
   Out of the whinnying green stable   *35*
      On to the fields of praise.

And honoured among foxes and pheasants by the gay house
Under the new made clouds and happy as the heart was long,
   In the sun born over and over,
      I ran my heedless ways,   *40*
     My wishes raced through the house-high hay
And nothing I cared, at my sky blue trades, that time allows
In all his tuneful turning so few and such morning songs
   Before the children green and golden
      Follow him out of grace,   *45*

Nothing I cared, in the lamb white days, that time would take me
Up to the swallow thronged loft by the shadow of my hand,
   In the moon that is always rising,
      Nor that riding to sleep
   I should hear him fly with the high fields   *50*
And wake to the farm forever fled from the childless land.
Oh as I was young and easy in the mercy of his means,
    Time held me green and dying
    Though I sang in my chains like the sea.

ROBERT LOWELL

Children of Light

Our fathers wrung their bread from stocks and stones
And fenced their gardens with the Redman's bones;
Embarking from the Nether Land of Holland,
Pilgrims unhoused by Geneva's night,
They planted here the Serpent's seeds of light;   *5*
And here the pivoting searchlights probe to shock
The riotous glass houses built on rock,
And candles gutter by an empty altar,
And light is where the landless blood of Cain
Is burning, burning the unburied grain.   *10*

RICHARD WILBUR

The Beautiful Changes

One wading a Fall meadow finds on all sides
The Queen Anne's Lace lying like lilies
On water; it glides
So from the walker, it turns
Dry grass to a lake, as the slightest shade of you   5
Valleys my mind in fabulous blue Lucernes.

The beautiful changes as a forest is changed
By a chameleon's tuning his skin to it;
As a mantis, arranged
On a green leaf, grows   10
Into it, makes the leaf leafier, and proves
Any greenness is deeper than anyone knows.

Your hands hold roses always in a way that says
They are not only yours; the beautiful changes
In such kind ways,   15
Wishing ever to sunder
Things and things' selves for a second finding, to lose
For a moment all that it touches back to wonder.

Juggler

A ball will bounce, but less and less. It's not
A light-hearted thing, resents its own resilience.
Falling is what it loves, and the earth falls
So in our hearts from brilliance,
Settles and is forgot.   5
It takes a skyblue juggler with five red balls

To shake our gravity up. Whee, in the air
The balls roll round, wheel on his wheeling hands,
Learning the ways of lightness, alter to spheres
Grazing his finger ends,   10
Cling to their courses there,
Swinging a small heaven about his ears.

But a heaven is easier made of nothing at all
Than the earth regained, and still and sole within
The spin of worlds, with a gesture sure and noble   15

He reels that heaven in,
Landing it ball by ball,
And trades it all for a broom, a plate, a table.

Oh, on his toe the table is turning, the broom's
Balancing up on his nose, and the plate whirls   *20*
On the tip of the broom! Damn, what a show, we cry:
The boys stamp, and the girls
Shriek, and the drum booms
And all comes down, and he bows and says goodbye.

If the juggler is tired now, if the broom stands   *25*
In the dust again, if the table starts to drop
Through the daily dark again, and though the plate
Lies flat on the table top,
For him we batter our hands
Who has won for once over the world's weight.   *30*

SIDNEY KEYES

Greenwich Observatory

This onion-dome holds all intricacies
Of intellect and star-struck wisdom; so
Like Coleridge's head with multitudinous
Passages riddled, full of strange instruments
Unbalanced by a touch, this organism   *5*
From wires and dials spins introverted life.
It never looks, squat on its concrete shoulders,
Down at the river's swarming life, nor sees
Cranes' groping insect-like activity
Nor slow procession of funnels past the docks.   *10*
Turning its inner wheels, absorbed in problems
Of space and time, it never hears
Birds singing in the park or children's laughter.
Alive, but in another way, it broods
On this its Highgate, hypnotized   *15*
In lunar reverie and calculation.
Yet night awakes it; blind lids open
Leaden to look upon the moon:
A single goggling telescopic eye
Enfolds the spheric wonder of the sky.   *20*

Plowman

Time was I was a plowman driving
Hard furrows, never resting, under the moon
Or in the frostbound bright-eyed morning
Labouring still; my team sleek-hided
As mulberry leaves, my team my best delight   5
After the sidelong blade my hero.
My iron-shod horses, my heroic walkers.
Now all that's finished. Rain's fallen now
Smudging my furrows, the comfortable
Elms are windpicked and harbour now no singer   10
Or southward homing bird; my horses grazing
Impossible mountain-sides, long-frogged and lonely.
And I'm gone on the roads, a peevish man
Contending with the landscape, arguing
With shrike and shrewmouse and my face in puddles;   15
A tiresome man not listened to nor housed
By the wise housewife, not kissed nor handled
By any but wild weeds and summer winds.
Time was I was a fine strong fellow
Followed by girls. Now I keep company   20
Only with seasons and the cold crazy moon.

LOUIS SIMPSON

To the Western World

A siren sang, and Europe turned away
From the high castle and the shepherd's crook.
Three caravels went sailing to Cathay
On the strange ocean, and the captains shook
Their banners out across the Mexique Bay.   5

And in our early days we did the same.
Remembering our fathers in their wreck
We crossed the sea from Palos where they came
And saw, enormous to the little deck,
A shore in silence waiting for a name.   10

The treasures of Cathay were never found.
In this America, this wilderness
Where the axe echoes with a lonely sound,
The generations labor to possess
And grave by grave we civilize the ground.   15

ANNE SEXTON

Ringing the Bells

And this is the way they ring
the bells in Bedlam
and this is the bell-lady
who comes each Tuesday morning
to give us a music lesson   5
and because the attendants make you go
and because we mind by instinct,
like bees caught in the wrong hive,
we are the circle of the crazy ladies
who sit in the lounge of the mental house   10
and smile at the smiling woman
who passes us each a bell,
who points at my hand
that holds my bell, E flat,
and this is the gray dress next to me   15
who grumbles as if it were special
to be old, to be old,
and this is the small hunched squirrel girl
on the other side of me
who picks at the hairs over her lip,   20
who picks at the hairs over her lip all day,
and this is how the bells really sound,
as untroubled and clean
as a workable kitchen,
and this is always my bell responding   25
to my hand that responds to the lady
who points at me, E flat;
and although we are no better for it,
they tell you to go. And you do.

Index of First Lines and Titles

(Titles are printed in italics, first lines of poems in roman. When the first line and title are the same, the entry is given as the first line only.)

A

A ball will bounce, but less and less. It's not, 412
Acquainted with the Night, 14
Adam's Fall (from *Paradise Lost*), 287
A death-blow is a life-blow to some, 364
A face devoid of love or grace, 366
Ah, are you digging on my grave? 26
A little black thing among the snow, 297
All my stars forsake me, 265
All the world's a stage (from *As You Like It*), 276
All through that summer at ease we lay, 128
Along the field as we came by, 370
Always the same, when on a fated night, 381
A man said to the universe, 212
A Man's a Man for A' That, 202
Among School Children, 376
Ample make this bed, 85
A narrow fellow in the grass, 363
And did those feet in ancient time, 299
And then I pressed the shell, 68
And this is the way they ring, 415
Annabel Lee, 338
An old, mad, blind, despised, and dying king, 324
Anthem for Doomed Youth, 21
anyone lived in a pretty how town, 222
Apparently with no surprise, 366
Arab Love Song, An, 76
Arsenal at Springfield, The, 267
As a dare-gale skylark scanted in a dull cage, 368
A siren sang, and Europe turned away, 414
As I was going up the stair, 108
A slumber did my spirit seal, 2
A square, squat room (a cellar on promotion), 210
A sudden blow: the great wings beating still, 376
As virtuous men pass mildly away, 40

At the round earth's imagined corners, blow, 283
A thing of beauty is a joy forever, 208
Avoid the reeking herd, 220
a wind has blown the rain away and blown, 176

B

Batter my heart, three person'd God; for, you, 104
Beautiful Changes, The, 412
Beautifully Janet slept, 30
Because I could not stop for Death, 91
Be Homer's works your study and delight, 194
Bent double, like old beggars under sacks, 55
Better to Reign in Hell (from *Paradise Lost*), 286
Birthday, A, 83
Black swallows swooping or gliding, 67
Bloody Sire, The, 387
Bonny Barbara Allan, 22
Boot and Saddle, 174
Boot, saddle, to horse, and away! 174
Borgia, thou once wert almost too august, 162
Both robb'd of air, we both lie in one ground, 192
Boys in sporadic but tenacious droves, 401
Break, break, break, 64
Bright Star, 329
Bright star, would I were steadfast as thou art, 329
Broken in pieces all asunder, 284
Busy old fool, unruly sun, 278

C

Caged Skylark, The, 368
Canonization, The, 279

from *Canterbury Tales, The* (Whan that Aprille), 178
Careless Love, 90
Cargoes, 20
Case, A, 108
Castle, The, 128
"*Childe Roland to the Dark Tower Came,*" 345
Children of Light, 411
Chimney Sweeper, The (from *Songs of Experience*), 297
Chimney Sweeper, The (from *Songs of Innocence*), 295
Christmas was in the air and all was well, 142
Circus Animals' Desertion, The, 378
City in the Sea, The, 334
Cliff Klingenhagen, 118
Cliff Klingenhagen had me in to dine, 118
Clod and the Pebble, The, 53
Collar, The, 284
Come, dear children, let us away, 360
Come live with me and be my love, 51
Composed upon Westminster Bridge, September 3, 1802, 303
Computation, The, 103
contend in a sea which the land partly encloses, 134
Could man be drunk forever, 370
Creep into thy narrow bed, 78
Crouched on the pavement, close by Belgrave Square, 216

D

Dark House, by which once more I stand (from *In Memoriam*), 340
Darkling Thrush, The, 123, 211
Daughters of Time, the hypocritic Days, 89
Days, 89
Description of the Morning, A, 67
Design, 43
Devon Maid, The, 329
Disillusionment of Ten O'Clock, 382
Divine Image, The, 14
Do not go gentle into that good night, 10
Do not weep, maiden, for war is kind, 106
Doom is dark and deeper than any seadingle, 402
Dover Beach, 359

Dream, The, 131
Drink to me only with thine eyes, 87
Dulce et Decorum Est, 55
Dust as we are, the immortal spirit grows, 208

E

Eagle and the Mole, The, 220
Earth has not anything to show more fair, 303
Ecstasy, The, 280
Edward, 49
Effort at Speech Between Two People, 224
Eldorado, 117
Elegy for Jane, 404
Elegy Written in a Country Churchyard, 290
Elementary School Classroom in a Slum, An, 56
Enamel Girl, The, 69
End of the World, The, 224
from *Endymion*, 208
England in 1819, 324
Epigram Engraved on the Collar of a Dog, 199
Epistle to Be Left in the Earth, 395
from *Essay on Criticism* (First Follow Nature), 242
from *Essay on Man, An* (Go, wondrous creature), 201
Eternal Spirit of the chainless Mind! 84

F

Far far from gusty waves these children's faces, 56
Fearful of beauty, I always went, 69
Felix Randal, 367
Felix Randal the farrier, O he is dead then? my duty all ended, 367
Fern Hill, 410
First follow Nature, and your judgment frame, 241
Five years have passed; five summers, with the length, 304
Fly envious Time, till thou run out thy race, 192
For Godsake hold your tongue, and let me love, 279

Forsaken Merman, The, 360

For the first twenty years since yesterday, 103

From far, from eve and morning, 370

From harmony, from heav'nly harmony, 197

Full fathom five thy father lies (*The Tempest*), 174

G

Gale in April, 386

Garden of Love, The, 207

Gather ye rose-buds while ye may, 191

Gayly bedight, 117

General and the Particular, The (from *Rasselas*), 243

Gerontion, 393

Gifts, 125

Glory, Jest, and Riddle, The, 114

Go and catch a falling star, 112

God fashioned the ship of the world carefully, 218

God of our fathers, known of old, 79

God's Grandeur, 139

Good-Morrow, The, 189

Go to the shine that's on a tree, 401

Go, wondrous creature; mount where science guides, 201

Green grow the rashes, O, 299

Greenwich Observatory, 413

Gr-r-r—there go, my heart's abhorrence! 98

H

Had he and I but met, 107

Had it pleas'd heaven (from *Othello*), 277

Had we but world enough, and time, 93

Happy Thought, 169

Hark! ah, the nightingale— 126

Harlot's House, The, 146

Haunted Palace, The, 336

Hearing of harvests rotting in the valleys, 403

Heat, 66

He is that fallen lance that lies as hurled, 81

Helen, thy beauty is to me, 125

Here I am, an old man in a dry month, 393

Here Lies Our Master, 195

Hero and Leander, 192

He thought he kept the universe alone, 381

He was found by the Bureau of Statistics to be, 101

Hickory, dickory, dock, 151

Hinted Wish, A, 199

Holy Sonnet 6 (I am a little world made cunningly), 282

Holy Sonnet 7 (At the round Earth's imagined corners), 283

Holy Thursday (from *Songs of Experience*), 296

Holy Thursday (from *Songs of Innocence*), 294

Homage, 47

Hope is the thing with feathers, 78

Horae Beatae Inscriptio, 385

Horse Chestnut Tree, The, 401

How Annandale Went Out, 39

How many dawns, chill from his rippling rest, 400

How many times do I love thee, dear? 46

How soon hath Time, the subtle thief of youth, 285

How to Criticize Poetry (from *An Essay on Criticism*), 241

How will this beauty, when I am far hence, 385

Human Abstract, The, 298

Huswifery, 138

Hymn to the Night, 266

I

I am a little world made cunningly, 282

I am his Highness' dog at Kew, 199

I arise from dreams of thee, 324

I caught this morning morning's minion, King-, 367

Idea of Order at Key West, The, 384

Identity, 226

I envy not in any moods, 12

If all the world and love were young, 52

If aught of oaten stop, or pastoral song, 200

I found a dimpled spider, fat and white, 43

I have been one acquainted with the night, 14

I heard a thousand blended notes, 212

I heard the trailing garments of the Night, 266

I know that he exists, 364

I know that I shall meet my fate, 222

I leant upon a coppice gate, 123

I like a look of agony, 363

I long to talk with some old lover's ghost, 282

Imaginary Iceberg, The, 405

I met a traveller from an antique land, 111

Imitation (from *Poetics*), 240

Impression du Matin, 218

In a Station of the Metro, 137

Indian Serenade, The, 324

In Heaven a spirit doth dwell, 214

in Just-, 397

from *In Memoriam*
    Prologue, 339
    7   (Dark House, by which once more I stand), 340
    28   (The time draws near the birth of Christ), 340
    54   (O yet we trust that somehow good), 341
    55   (The wish, that of the living whole), 209
    96   (You say, but with no touch of scorn), 341
    114   (Who loves not knowledge), 342
    131   (O living will that shalt endure), 343

Inspiration (from *Ion*), 238

Intended for Sir Isaac Newton, 193

In Tenebris, I, 216

Intense and terrible beauty, how has our race with the frail naked nerves, 386

In the greenest of our valleys, 336

In Time of "The Breaking of Nations," 45

Introduction (from *Songs of Innocence*), 293

Invictus, 269

In Xanadu did Kubla Khan, 72

I remember the neckcurls, limp and damped as tendrils, 404

Irish Airman Foresees His Death, An, 222

is an enchanted thing, 387

I saw with open eyes, 108

Is my team plowing? 28

I sought a theme and sought for it in vain, 378

Israfel, 214

I stepped from plank to plank, 366

Is there, for honest poverty, 202

Is this a holy thing to see, 296

"Is this the region, this the soil, the clime, 286

I struck the board, and cried, "No more, 284

I taste a liquor never brewed, 17

It is a beauteous evening, calm and free, 303

It is an ancient Mariner, 307

. . . It is colder now, 395

It is morning, Senlin says, and in the morning, 114

It is not bad. Let them play, 387

It little profits that an idle king, 270

I tossed my friend a wreath of roses, wet, 125

It was a lover and his lass (from *As You Like It*), 188

It was in and about the Martinmas time, 22

It was many and many a year ago, 338

I wake and feel the fell of dark, not day, 368

I walk through the long schoolroom questioning, 376

I wandered lonely as a cloud, 302

I wander through each chartered street, 297

I was a boy when I heard three red words, 144

I was angry with my friend, 298

I went out to the hazel wood, 374

I went to the Garden of Love, 207

I wonder, by my troth, what thou and I, 189

I would bathe myself in strangeness, 386

J

Jabberwocky, 145

Janet Waking, 30

Jealousy, 37

Juggler, The, 412

Just as my fingers on these keys, 382

K

Karma, 142
Kingdom of God, The, 110
Know then thyself, presume not God to scan, 114
Kubla Khan, 72

L

La Belle Dame sans Merci, 133
Lamb, The, 120
Last night, ah, yesternight, betwixt her lips and mine, 217
Last Word, A (Ernest Dowson), 211
Last Word, The (Matthew Arnold), 78
Latest Decalogue, The, 110
Leda and the Swan, 376
Let me not to the marriage of true minds, 70
Let's talk of graves, of worms and epitaphs (from *Richard II*), 276
Let us go hence—the night is now at hand, 211
Let us go then, you and I, 390
Like as the waves make towards the pebbled shore, 274
Lines (When the lamp is shattered), 177
Lines Composed a Few Miles Above Tintern Abbey, 304
Lines Written in Early Spring, 212
Little Black Boy, The, 295
Little Lamb, who made thee? 120
Lo! Death has reared himself a throne, 334
London (William Blake), 297
London, 1802 (William Wordsworth), 87
Lovely hill-torrents are, 66
Love's Deity, 282
Love's Diet, 94
Love seeketh not itself to please, 53
Love Song of J. Alfred Prufrock, The, 390
Love's Philosophy, 325

M

Magi, The, 36
Make me, O Lord, thy Spinning Wheele compleat, 138
Making of the Cross, The, 406

Man, 190
Man He Killed, The, 107
Márgarét, are you grieving, 147
Metamorphosis, 149
Methought I saw my late espousèd saint, 286
Milton! thou shouldst be living at this hour, 87
Mind Is an Enchanting Thing, The, 387
Minute, The, 408
Morning at the Window, 219
Morning Song of Senlin, 114
Most of It, The, 381
Mowers, weary and brown, and blithe, 175
Much have I travelled in the realms of gold, 265
Music, when soft voices die, 325
Mutability, 325
My first thought was, he lied in every word, 345
My galley, charged with forgetfulness, 88
My God, I heard this day, 190
My heart aches, and a drowsy numbness pains, 331
My heart is like a singing bird, 83
My heart leaps up when I behold, 302
My Last Duchess, 343
My mistress' eyes are nothing like the sun, 20
My mother bore me in the southern wild, 295

N

Nature and Nature's laws lay hid in Night, 193
Nature of Poetry, The, 229
No longer mourn for me when I am dead, 275
No, no, go not to Lethe, neither twist, 333
Non Sum Qualis Eram Bonae sub Regno Cynarae, 217
No Second Troy, 374
Not that the earth is changing, O my God! 15
Now as at all times I can see in the mind's eye, 36
Now as I was young and easy under the apple boughs, 410

Now gentle sleep hath closed up those eyes, 108

Now hardly here and there an hackney-coach, 67

Now sleeps the crimson petal, now the white, 150

Nurse's Song (from Songs of Experience), 296

Nurse's Song (from Songs of Innocence), 294

Nymph's Reply, The, 52

O

Ode on a Grecian Urn, 330

Ode on Melancholy, 333

Ode to a Nightingale, 331

Ode to Evening, 200

Ode to the West Wind, 326

Of Man's first disobedience, and the fruit, 172

O God, in the dream the terrible horse began, 131

Oh see how thick the goldcup flowers, 29

Oh yet we trust that somehow good (from *In Memoriam*), 341

Old Adam, the carrion crow, 173

O living will that shalt endure (from *In Memoriam*), 343

O my luve is like a red, red rose, 301

Once in a saintly passion, 96

One day I wrote her name upon the strand, 189

One's self I sing, a single separate person, 34

One wading a Fall meadow finds on all sides, 412

One word is too often profaned, 53

On First Looking into Chapman's Homer, 265

Only a man harrowing clods, 45

On one fix'd point all nature moves, 203

On Refusal of Aid Between Nations, 15

On Seeing a Hair of Lucretia Borgia, 162

Onset, The, 381

On the Grasshopper and the Cricket, 329

On the Uniformity and Perfection of Nature, 203

On th' other side, Adam, soon as he heard, 287

On Time, 192

On Wenlock Edge the wood's in trouble, 369

O Rose, thou art sick! 129

Others may need new life in Heaven, 39

Our fathers wrung their bread from stocks and stones, 411

Our revels now are ended. These our actors (from *The Tempest*), 278

Out of the night that covers me, 269

Over the land freckled with snow half-thawed, 61

O, wert thou in the cauld blast, 301

O, what can ail thee, knight-at-arms! 133

O, wild West Wind, thou breath of Autumn's being, 326

O, Willie brew'd a peck o' maut, 300

O wind, rend open the heat, 66

O world invisible, we view thee, 110

Ozymandias, 111

P

Pain has an element of blank, 365

Parting, Without a Sequel, 140

Passionate Shepherd to His Love, The, 51

Paysage Moralisé, 403

Peter Piper picked a peck of pickled peppers, 157

Peter Quince at the Clavier, 382

Philomela, 126

Piping down the valleys wild, 293

pity this busy monster, manunkind, 141

Pity this girl, 406

Pity would be no more, 298

Plowman, 414

Plunge, The, 386

Poem, or Beauty Hurts Mr. Vinal, 397

Poetic Imagination (from Biographia Literaria), 243

Poetry and Action (from Preface to Poems, 1853), 246

Poetry and Emotional Need (from "On Poetry in General"), 245

Poets as Legislators of the World (from A Defence of Poetry), 246

Poison Tree, A, 298

Preliminary Problems, 250

Preludes (T. S. Eliot), 388

from *Prelude, The*, 208

Proem: To Brooklyn Bridge, 400

Prologue from *In Memoriam*, 339

Prometheus, 213

from *Prometheus Unbound* (This is the day), 328

Proud Maisie, 109

Proud Maisie is in the wood, 109

Pulley, The, 90

Q

Quinquireme of Nineveh from distant Ophir, 20

Quite unexpectedly as Vasserot, 224

R

Recessional, 79

Red, Red Rose, A, 301

Requiescat, 157

Reveille, 368

Richard Roe and John Doe, 126

Richard Roe wished himself Solomon, 126

Rime of the Ancient Mariner, The, 307

Ringing the Bells, 415

Road Not Taken, The, 380

Rough fir, hauled from the hills. And the tree it had been, 406

S

Sailing to Byzantium, 375

Samson's Blindness (from *Samson Agonistes*), 288

Science! true daughter of Old Time thou art! 144

Scythe Song, 175

Seals, Terns, Time, 132

Season of mists and mellow fruitfulness, 71

Second Coming, The, 122

Self Unsatisfied Runs Everywhere, The, 408

She dwelt among the untrodden ways, 102

She has finished and sealed the letter, 140

Shell, The, 68

She sang beyond the genius of the sea, 384

She Was the Girl Within the Picture Frame, 407

Shine, Perishing Republic, 222

Sick Rose, The, 129

Since brass, nor stone, nor earth, nor boundless sea, 82

Since there's no help, come let us kiss and part, 171

Skaters, The, 67

Slow, slow, fresh fount, keep time with my salt tears, 163

Soldier, A, 81

Soliloquy of the Spanish Cloister, 98

Something Is Bound to Happen, 402

Sometimes the girl on boyhood's silver screen, 407

somewhere i have never travelled, gladly beyond, 148

Song (Go and Catch a Falling Star), 112

Song (How Many Times), 46

Song (Lovely hill-torrents are), 66

Song (Old Adam), 173

Song for St. Cecilia's Day, A, 197

Song of the Night at Daybreak, 265

Song of the Sirens, 34

Song: To Celia, 87

Song of Wandering Aengus, The, 374

Sonnet — To Science, 144

Sonnet on Chillon, 84

Sonnet Upon a Stolen Kiss, A, 108

Speak to me. Take my hand. What are you now? 224

Speculative, 39–40

Spring and Fall, 147

Steer hither, steer, your wingèd pines, 34

Stopping by Woods on a Snowy Evening, 127

Stranger, The, 406

Strew on her roses, roses, 157

Strong Son of God, immortal Love (from *In Memoriam*), 339

Stupidity Street, 108

Style (from *Poetics*), 239

Sunday and sunlight ashen on the Square, 408

Sun Rising, The, 278

Suspense, 48

Sweet and low, sweet and low, 175

Sweet day, so cool, so calm, so bright, 283

Sweet love, renew thy force; be it not said, 274

Swiftly walk o'er the western wave, 158

T

Tables Turned, The, 205

take it from me kiddo, 397

Tell me not, sweet, I am unkind, 81
Temptation, 284
"Terence, this is stupid stuff, 371
That is no country for old men. The young, 375
That's my last Duchess painted on the wall, 343
That time of year thou mayst in me behold, 18
Thaw, 61
The apparition of these faces in the crowd, 137
The brain is wider than the sky, 63
The brain within its groove, 364
The bustle in a house, 103
The chestnut casts his flambeaux, and the flowers, 373
The Curfew tolls the knell of parting day, 290
Thee for my recitative, 130
The fire was furry as a bear, 88
The flower that smiles to-day, 325
The force that through the green fuse drives the flower, 409
The fountains mingle with the river, 325
The heavens themselves, the planets, and this centre, 185
The houses are haunted, 382
The hunchèd camels of the night, 77
The myrtle bush grew shady, 37
The nightingale has a lyre of gold, 86
The night is darkening round me, 21
The office building treads the marble dark, 408
The poetry of earth is never dead, 329
There came a wind like a bugle, 365
The sea is calm tonight, 359
The seals at play off Western Isle, 132
The soul selects her own society, 366
The spacious firmament on high, 199
The splendor falls on castle walls, 153
The Thames nocturne of blue and gold, 218
The time draws near the birth of Christ (from *In Memoriam*), 340
The wind comes from the north, 48
The wind has such a rainy sound, 17
The winter evening settles down, 388
The wish, that of the living whole (from *In Memoriam*), 209
The world is charged with the grandeur of God, 139
The world is so full of a number of things, 169

The world is too much with us, 163
They are rattling breakfast plates in basement kitchens, 219
They called it Annandale—and I was there, 39
They said to him, "It is a very good thing that you have done, yes, 47
This is the Arsenal. From floor to ceiling, 267
This is the day which down the void abysm (from *Prometheus Unbound*), 328
This onion-dome holds all intricacies, 413
Those Two Boys, 97
Thou art indeed just, Lord, if I content, 54
Thou shalt have one God only; who, 110
Thou still unravish'd bride of quietness, 330
Thou wast all that to me, love, 336
Thou who has slept all night upon the storm, 351
Three Fishers, The, 46
Three fishers went sailing away to the West, 46
Threes, 144
Tiger, The, 119
Tiger! Tiger! burning bright, 119
Time was I was a plowman driving, 414
'Tis Better to Have Loved and Lost, 12
Titan! to whose immortal eyes, 213
To—(Music, when soft voices die), 325
To—(One word is too often profaned), 53
To A.D., 86
To a Locomotive in Winter, 130
To Autumn, 71
To a Waterfowl, 263
To be or not to be (*Hamlet*), 6
To Helen, 125
To His Coy Mistress, 94
To locate a person hidden in this room, 226
To Lucasta, On Going to the Wars, 81
To Marguerite—Continued, 358
To Mercy, Pity, Peace, and Love, 14
Tomorrow, and tomorrow, and tomorrow, 92
To Night, 158
To One in Paradise, 336
To see a World in a grain of sand, 299
To the Man-of-War Bird, 351
To the Virgins, to Make much of Time, 191

To the Western World, 414
To what a cumbersome unwieldiness, 94
Turning and turning in the widening gyre, 122
'Twas brillig, and the slithy toves, 145
'Twas on a Holy Thursday, their innocent faces clean, 294
Two roads diverged in a yellow wood, 380

U

Ulysses, 270
Ulysses' Speech on Degree, 185
Unknown Citizen, The, 101
Up! up! my Friend, and quit your books, 205

V

Vale, Amor! 38
Valediction: Forbidding Mourning, A, 40
Virtue, 283

W

Waiting, 210
Wake: the silver dusk returning, 368
War Is Kind, 106
We caught the tread of dancing feet, 146
We do not know this thing, 38
We'd rather have the iceberg than the ship, 405
Weep you no more, sad fountains, 176
Western Wind, 48
Western wind, when wilt thou blow? 48
West London, 216
Whan that Aprille with his shoures soote, 178
What passing-bells for these who die as cattle? 21
When all my five and country senses see, 221
When Bill was a lad he was terribly bad, 97
When God at first made man, 90
when god decided to invent, 113
When icicles hang by the wall, 61
When I consider how my light is spent, 286
When I have fears that I may cease to be, 13

When I have seen by Time's fell hand defaced, 275
When I heard the learn'd astronomer, 25
When lilacs last in the dooryard bloom'd, 351
When lovely woman stoops to folly, 76
When my love swears that she is made of truth, 275
When my mother died I was very young, 295
When the hounds of spring are on winter's traces, 178
When the lamp is shattered, 177
When the voices of children are heard on the green (from *Songs of Experience*), 296
When the voices of children are heard on the green (from *Songs of Innocence*), 294
Where be ye going, you Devon maid? 329
Where, like a pillow on a bed, 280
While this America settles in the mould of its vulgarity, 222
Whither, midst falling dew, 263
Who have been lonely once, 90
Who loves not knowledge (from *In Memoriam*), 342
Whose woods these are I think I know, 127
Whoso list to hunt, I know where is an hind, 171
Why does your brand sae drap wi' bluid, 49
Why should I blame her that she filled my days, 374
Why was my breeding ordered and prescribed, 288
Willie Brewed a Peck o' Maut, 300
Wind Has Blown, A, 176
Windhover, The, 367
Wintertime nighs, 216
With rue my heart is laden, 370
Women, 399
Women have no wilderness in them, 399

Y

Yachts, The, 134
Yes! in the sea of life enisled, 358
Yillow, yillow, yillow, 149
You say, but with no touch of scorn (from *In Memoriam*), 341
You told me, Maro, whilst you live, 199

Index of Authors with Titles

Adams, Franklin P. (1881–1960)
  Those Two Boys, 97
Addison, Joseph (1672–1719)
  *Spacious Firmament on High,
    The,* 199
Aiken, Conrad (1889–   )
  Morning Song of Senlin, 114
Anonymous
  Bonny Barbara Allan, 22
  Case, A, 108
  Edward, 49
  Hickory, Dickory, Dock, 151
  *Weep You No More, Sad Foun-
    tains,* 176
  Western Wind, 48
Aristotle (384–322 B.C.)
  Imitation (from Poetics), 240
  Style (from Poetics), 239
Arnold, Matthew (1822–88)
  Dover Beach, 359
  Forsaken Merman, The, 360
  Last Word, The, 78
  Philomela, 126
  *Poetry and Action (from Preface
    to Poems, 1853),* 246
  Requiescat, 157
  To Marguerite—Continued, 358
  West London, 216
Auden, W. H. (1907–   )
  Paysage Moralisé, 403
  Something Is Bound to Happen,
    402
  Unknown Citizen, The, 101

Beddoes, Thomas Lovell (1803–49)
  Song (How Many Times), 46
  Song (Old Adam), 173
Bishop, Elizabeth (1911–   )
  Imaginary Iceberg, The, 405
Blake, William (1757–1827)
  *And Did Those Feet in Ancient
    Time,* 299
  *Chimney Sweeper, The (from
    Songs of Innocence),* 297
  *Chimney Sweeper, The (from
    Songs of Innocence),* 295
  Clod and the Pebble, The, 53

  Divine Image, The, 14
  Garden of Love, The, 207
  *Holy Thursday (from Songs of
    Experience),* 296
  *Holy Thursday (from Songs of
    Innocence),* 294
  *Human Abstract, The (from Songs
    of Experience),* 298
  *Introduction (from Songs of In-
    nocence),* 293
  Lamb, The, 120
  *Little Black Boy, The (from Songs
    of Innocence),* 295
  *London (from Songs of Experi-
    ence),* 297
  *Nurse's Song (from Songs of Ex-
    perience),* 296
  *Nurse's Song (from Songs of In-
    nocence),* 294
  *Poison Tree, A (from Songs of
    Experience),* 298
  Sick Rose, The, 129
  Tiger, The, 119
  To See a World, 299
Bogan, Louise (1897–   )
  Dream, The, 131
  Women, 399
Brontë, Emily (1818–48)
  Night Is Darkening, The, 21
Brother Antoninus (William O. Everson)
  (1912–   )
  Making of the Cross, The, 406
  Stranger, The, 406
Browne, William (1591?–1643?)
  Song of the Sirens, 34
Browning, Robert (1812–89)
  Boot and Saddle, 174
  *"Childe Roland to the Dark
    Tower Came,"* 345
  My Last Duchess, 343
  Soliloquy of the Spanish Cloister,
    98
  Speculative, 39
Bryant, William Cullen (1794–1878)
  To a Waterfowl, 263
Burns, Robert (1759–96)
  A Man's a Man for A' That, 202
  Green Grow the Rashes, 299

O, Wert Thou in the Cauld Blast,
301
Red, Red Rose, A, 301
Willie Brewed a Peck o' Maut,
301
Byron, George Gordon, Lord (1788 – 1824)
Prometheus, 213
Sonnet on Chillon, 84

Carroll, Lewis (1832 – 98)
Jabberwocky, 145
Chaucer, Geoffrey (1340? – 1400)
*Whan That Aprille with His
Shoures Soote*, 178
Clough, Arthur Hugh (1819 – 61)
Latest Decalogue, The, 110
Coleridge, Mary Elizabeth (1861 – 1907)
Gifts, 125
Jealousy, 37
Coleridge, Samuel Taylor (1772 – 1834)
Kubla Khan, 72
*Poetic Imagination (from Bio-
graphia Literaria)*, 243
Rime of the Ancient Mariner, The,
307
Collins, William (1721 – 59)
Ode to Evening, 200
Crane, Hart (1899 – 1932)
Proem: To Brooklyn Bridge, 400
Crane, Stephen (1871 – 1900)
*God Fashioned the Ship of the
World Carefully*, 218
Man Said to the Universe, A, 212
War Is Kind, 106
Cummings, E. E. (1894 – 1962)
*Anyone Lived in a Pretty How
Town*, 223
A Wind Has Blown, 176
In Just, 397
*Pity This Busy Monster, Manun-
kind*, 141
Poem, or Beauty Hurts Mr. Vinal,
397
*Somewhere I Have Never Travel-
led*, 148
When God Decided to Invent, 113
Wind Has Blown, A, 176

Dickinson, Emily (1830 – 86)
Ample Make This Bed, 85
Apparently with No Surprise, 366

*Because I Could Not Stop for
Death*, 91
Brain Is Wider than the Sky, The,
63
Brain Within Its Groove, The, 364
Bustle in a House, The, 103
Death-Blow Is a Life-Blow, A, 364
Face Devoid of Love or Grace, A,
366
Hope Is the Thing with Feathers,
78
I Know That He Exists, 364
I Like a Look of Agony, 363
I Stepped from Plank to Plank,
366
I Taste a Liquor Never Brewed, 17
Narrow Fellow in the Grass, A,
363
Pain Has an Element of Blank,
365
*Soul Selects Her Own Society,
The*, 366
There Came a Wind Like a Bugle,
365
Donne, John (1572 – 1631)
*Batter My Heart, Three Person'd
God*, 104
Canonization, The, 279
Computation, The, 103
Ecstasy, The, 280
Good-Morrow, The, 189
Hero and Leander, 192
Holy Sonnet 6 (I am a little world
made cunningly), 282
Holy Sonnet 7 (At the round
earth's imagined corners, 283
Love's Deity, 282
Love's Diet, 94
Song (Go and catch a falling star),
112
Sun Rising, The, 278
*Valediction: Forbidding Mourn-
ing, A*, 40
Dowson, Ernest (1867 – 1900)
Last Word, A, 211
*Non Sum Qualis Eram Bonae sub
Regno Cynarae*, 217
Drayton, Michael (1563 – 1631)
Since There's No Help, 171
Dryden, John (1631 – 1700)
A Song for St. Cecilia's Day, 197

Eberhart, Richard (1904–)
  Go to the Shine That's on a Tree,
    401
  Horse Chestnut Tree, The, 401
  Seals, Terns, Time, 132
Eliot, T. S. (1888–1965)
  Gerontion, 393
  Love Song of J. Alfred Prufrock,
    The, 390
  Morning at the Window, 219
  Preludes, 388
Emerson, Ralph Waldo (1803–82)
  Days, 89

Fearing, Kenneth (1902–)
  Homage, 47
Fletcher, John Gould (1886–1950)
  Skaters, The, 67
Freneau, Philip (1752–1832)
  On the Uniformity and Perfection
    of Nature, 203
Frost, Robert (1874–1963)
  Acquainted with the Night, 14
  Design, 43
  Most of It, The, 381
  Onset, The, 381
  Road Not Taken, The, 380
  Soldier, A, 81
  Stopping by Woods on a Snowy
    Evening, 127

Goldsmith, Oliver (1728–74)
  When Lovely Woman Stoops to
    Folly, 76
Graves, Robert (1895–)
  Richard Roe and John Doe, 126
Gray, Thomas (1716–71)
  Elegy Written in a Country
    Churchyard, 290

Hardy, Thomas (1840–1928)
  Ah, Are You Digging on My
    Grave? 26
  Darkling Thrush, The, 123, 211
  In Tenebris, I, 216
  In Time of "The Breaking of
    Nations", 45
  Man He Killed, The, 107
Hazlitt, William (1778–1830)
  Poetry and Emotional Need (from
    "On Poetry in General"), 245

H. D. (Hilda Doolittle) (1886–1961)
  Heat, 66
Henley, William Ernest (1849–1903)
  Invictus, 269
  To A. D., 86
  Waiting, 210
Herbert, George (1593–1633)
  Collar, The, 284
  Man, 190
  Pulley, The, 90
  Temptation, 284
  Virtue, 283
Herrick, Robert (1591–1674)
  To the Virgins, to Make Much of
    Time, 191
Hodgson, Ralph (1871–1962)
  Stupidity Street, 108
Hopkins, Gerard Manley (1844–89)
  Caged Skylark, The, 368
  Felix Randal, 367
  God's Grandeur, 139
  I Wake and Feel the Fell of Dark,
    368
  Spring and Fall, 147
  Thou Art Indeed Just, Lord, 54
  Windhover, The, 367
Housman, A. E. (1859–1936)
  Along the Field as We Came By,
    370
  Chestnut Casts His Flambeaux,
    The, 373
  Could Man Be Drunk Forever,
    371
  From Far, from Eve and Morn-
    ing, 370
  Is My Team Plowing? 28
  Oh See How Thick the Goldcup
    Flowers, 29
  On Wenlock Edge, 369
  Reveille, 368
  Terence, This Is Stupid Stuff, 371
  With Rue My Heart Is Laden, 370

Jeffers, Robinson (1887–1962)
  Bloody Sire, The, 387
  Gale in April, 386
  Shine, Perishing Republic, 222
Johnson, Samuel (1709–84)
  General and the Particular, The
    (from *Rasselas*), 243
  Hinted Wish, A, 199
Jonson, Ben (1572–1637)

Slow, Slow, Fresh Fount, 163
Song: To Celia, 87

Keats, John (1795–1821)
  Bright Star, 329
  Devon Maid, The, 329
  from *Endymion*, 208
  La Belle Dame sans Merci, 133
  Ode on a Grecian Urn, 330
  Ode on Melancholy, 333
  Ode to a Nightingale, 331
  On First Looking Into Chapman's Homer, 265
  On the Grasshopper and the Cricket, 329
  To Autumn, 71
  When I Have Fears, 13
Keyes, Sidney (1922–43)
  Greenwich Observatory, 413
  Plowman, 414
Kingsley, Charles (1819–75)
  Three Fishers, The, 46
Kipling, Rudyard (1865–1936)
  Recessional, 79
Kunitz, Stanley (1905–   )
  Careless Love, 90

Landor, Walter Savage (1775–1864)
  On Seeing a Hair of Lucretia Borgia, 162
Lang, Andrew (1844–1912)
  Scythe Song, 175
Lawrence, D. H. (1885–1930)
  Suspense, 48
Longfellow, Henry Wadsworth (1807–82)
  Arsenal at Springfield, The, 267
  Hymn to the Night, 266
Lovelace, Richard (1618–58)
  To Lucasta, On Going to the Wars, 81
Lowell, Robert (1917–   )
  Children of Light, 411

MacLeish, Archibald (1892–   )
  End of the World, The, 224
  Epistle to Be Left in the Earth, 395
Marlowe, Christopher (1564–93)
  Passionate Shepherd to His Love, The, 51
Marvell, Andrew (1621–78)
  To His Coy Mistress, 93

Masefield, John (1878–1967)
  Cargoes, 20
Meynell, Alice (1847–1922)
  Song of the Night at Daybreak, 265
Milton, John (1608–74)
  Adam's Fall (from *Paradise Lost*), 287
  Better to Reign in Hell (from *Paradise Lost*), 286
  How Soon Hath Time, 285
  Methought I Saw, 286
  On Time, 192
  Samson's Blindness (from *Samson Agonistes*), 288
  When I Consider How My Light Is Spent, 286
Moore, Marianne (1887–   )
  Mind Is an Enchanting Thing, The, 387
Muir, Edwin (1887–1959)
  Castle, The, 128

Owen, Wilfred (1893–1918)
  Anthem for Doomed Youth, 21
  Dulce et Decorum Est, 55

Plato (427?–347 B.C.)
  Inspiration (from *Ion*), 238
Plutzik, Hyam (1911–   )
  Identity, 226
Poe, Edgar Allan (1809–49)
  Annabel Lee, 338
  City in the Sea, The, 334
  Eldorado, 117
  Haunted Palace, The, 336
  Israfel, 214
  Sonnet—To Science, 144
  To Helen, 125
  To One in Paradise, 336
Pope, Alexander (1688–1744)
  Be Homer's Works Your Study and Delight, 194
  Epigram Engraved on the Collar of a Dog, 199
  from *An Essay on Man*, 201
  Glory, Jest, and Riddle, The, 114
  How to Criticize Poetry (from *An Essay on Criticism*), 241
  Intended for Sir Isaac Newton, 193

Pound, Ezra (1885–)
  Horae Beatae Inscriptio, 385
  In a Station of the Metro, 137
  Plunge, The, 386

Ralegh, Sir Walter (1552?–1618)
  Nymph's Reply, The, 52
Ransom, John Crowe (1888–)
  Janet Waking, 30
  Parting, Without a Sequel, 140
Robinson, E. A. (1869–1935)
  Cliff Klingenhagen, 118
  How Annandale Went Out, 39
  Karma, 142
Roethke, Theodore (1908–63)
  Elegy for Jane, 404
Rossetti, Christina (1830–94)
  Birthday, A, 83
  Wind Has Such a Rainy Sound, The, 17
Rossetti, Dante Gabriel (1828–82)
  On Refusal of Aid Between Nations, 15
Rukeyser, Muriel (1913–)
  Effort at Speech Between Two People, 224

Sandburg, Carl (1878–1967)
  Threes, 144
Schwartz, Delmore (1913–66)
  Self Unsatisfied Runs Everywhere, The, 407
  She Was the Girl Within the Picture Frame, 407
Scott, Sir Walter (1771–1832)
  Proud Maisie, 109
Sexton, Anne (1928–)
  Ringing the Bells, 415
Shakespeare, William (1564–1616)
  All the World's a Stage (from *As You Like It*), 276
  Full Fathom Five (from *The Tempest*), 174
  Had It Pleas'd Heaven (from *Othello*), 277
  It Was a Lover and His Lass (from *As You Like It*), 188
  Let Me Not to the Marriage of True Minds (Sonnet 116), 70
  Let's Talk of Graves (from *Richard II*), 276

  Like as the Waves (Sonnet 60), 274
  My Mistress' Eyes (Sonnet 130), 20
  No longer Mourn for Me (Sonnet 71), 275
  Our Revels Now Are Ended (from *The Tempest*), 278
  Since Brass, Nor Stone (Sonnet 65), 82
  Sweet Love, Renew Thy Force (Sonnet 56), 274
  That Time of Year (Sonnet 73), 18
  To Be or Not to Be (from *Hamlet*), 6
  Tomorrow, and Tomorrow, and Tomorrow (from *Macbeth*), 92
  Ulysses' Speech on Degree (from *Troilus and Cressida*), 185
  When Icicles Hang, 61
  When I Have Seen by Time's Fell Hand (Sonnet 64), 275
  When My Love Swears (Sonnet 138), 275
Shapiro, Karl (1913–)
  Minute, The, 408
Sharp, William (1856?–1905)
  Vale, Amor! 38
Shelley, Percy Bysshe (1792–1822)
  England in 1819, 324
  Indian Serenade, The, 324
  Lines (When the lamp is shattered), 177
  Love's Philosophy, 325
  Mutability, 325
  Ode to the West Wind, 326
  Ozymandias, 111
  Poets as Legislators of the World (from *A Defence of Poetry*), 246
  This Is the Day (from *Prometheus Unbound*), 328
  To— (Music, when soft voices die), 325
  To— (One word is too often profaned), 53
  To Night, 158
Simpson, Louis (1923–)
  To the Western World, 414
Spender, Stephen (1909–)
  Elementary School Classroom in a Slum, An, 56
Spenser, Edmund (1552–99)
  One Day I Wrote Her Name upon the Strand, 189

Stauffer, Donald (1902–52)
    Nature of Poetry, The, 229
Stephens, James (1882–1950)
    Shell, The, 68
Stevens, Wallace (1879–1955)
    Disillusionment of Ten O'Clock, 382
    Idea of Order at Key West, The, 384
    Metamorphosis, 149
    Peter Quince at the Clavier, 382
Stevenson, Robert Louis (1850–94)
    Happy Thought, 169
Swift, Jonathan (1667–1745)
    Description of the Morning, 67
Swinburne, Algernon Charles (1837–1909)
    When the Hounds of Spring, 178

Taggard, Genevieve (1894–1948)
    Enamel Girl, The, 69
Taylor, Edward (1647?–1729)
    Huswifery, 138
Tennyson, Alfred, Lord (1809–92)
    Break, Break, Break, 64
    from *In Memoriam*
        Prologue, 339
            7 (Dark house, by which once more I stand), 340
            28 (The time draws near the birth of Christ), 340
            54 (Oh yet we trust that somehow good), 341
            55 (The wish, that of the living whole), 209
            96 (You say, but with no touch of scorn), 341
            114 (Who loves not knowledge), 342
            131 (O living will that shalt endure), 343
    Now Sleeps the Crimson Petal, 150
    Splendor Falls, The, 153
    Sweet and Low, 175
    'Tis Better to Have Loved and Lost, 12
    Ulysses, 270
Thomas, Dylan (1914–53)
    Do Not Go Gentle into That Good Night, 10
    Fern Hill, 410

    Force That Through the Green Fuse Drives the Flower, The, 409
    When All My Five and Country Senses See, 221
Thomas, Edward (1878–1917)
    Thaw, 61
Thompson, Francis (1859–1907)
    Arab Love Song, An, 77
    Kingdom of God, The, 110
Thomson, James (1834–82)
    Once in a Saintly Passion, 96
Turner, W. J. (1889–1946)
    Song (Lovely hill-torrents are), 66

Whitman, Walt (1819–92)
    One's-Self I Sing, 34
    To a Locomotive in Winter, 130
    To the Man-of-War Bird, 351
    When I Heard the Learn'd Astronomer, 25
    When Lilacs Last in the Dooryard Bloom'd, 351
Wilbur, Richard (1921–   )
    Beautiful Changes, The, 412
    Juggler, The, 412
Wilde, Oscar (1856–1900)
    Harlot's House, The, 146
    Impression du Matin, 218
Williams, William Carlos (1883–1963)
    Yachts, The, 134
Wilmont, John, Earl of Rochester (1648–80)
    Here Lies Our Master, 195
Winters, Yvor (1900–68)
    Preliminary Problems, 250
Wither, George (1588–1667)
    Sonnet Upon a Stolen Kiss, A, 108
Wordsworth, William (1770–1850)
    Composed upon Westminster Bridge, September 3, 1802, 303
    It Is a Beauteous Evening, Calm and Free, 303
    I Wandered Lonely as a Cloud, 302
    Lines Composed a Few Miles Above Tintern Abbey, 304
    Lines Written in Early Spring, 212
    London, 1802, 87
    My Heart Leaps up when I Behold, 302
    from *Prelude, The*, 208

*She Dwelt Among the Untrodden
  Ways,* 102
Slumber Did My Spirit Seal, A, 2
Tables Turned, The, 205
World Is Too Much with Us, The,
  163
Wyatt, Thomas (1503?–42)
  *My Galley, Charged with Forget-
    fulness,* 88
  Whoso List to Hunt, 171
Wylie, Elinor (1885–1928)
  Eagle and the Mole, The, 220

Yeats, William Butler (1865–1939)
  Among School Children, 376
  Circus Animals' Desertion, The,
    378
  *Irish Airman Foresees His Death,
    An,* 222
  Leda and the Swan, 376
  Magi, The, 36
  No Second Troy, 374
  Sailing to Byzantium, 375
  Second Coming, The, 122
  Song of Wandering Aengus, The,
    374